American
POLYGAMY

American
POLYGAMY

·············· • ··············

A History of Fundamentalist Mormon Faith

CRAIG L. FOSTER & MARIANNE T. WATSON

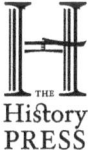

THE
History
PRESS

Published by The History Press
Charleston, SC
www.historypress.com

For Craig L. Foster
To my wife, Suzanne Long Foster; my children; and my granddaughter.

For Marianne T. Watson
To my husband, the wind beneath my wings; my children, my hope; and especially my parents, my foundation.

CONTENTS

Preface

It is important to understand that Fundamentalist Mormons are not a homogenous body; the term Fundamentalist *encompasses several diverse groups as well as several extended "independent" family groups, each quite distinct in history and practice, although they share a common heritage and most beliefs about plural marriage.*

At the beginning of the Book of Mormon, the ancient prophet Nephi introduces himself by stating, "[H]aving been born of goodly parents..." (I Nephi 1:1). Both authors feel they too could say the same, not only about their parents but also about their ancestors. Both are products of a great heritage within Mormonism. For Craig, it is six generations of membership in the Church of Jesus Christ of Latter-day Saints, while for Marianne it is six generations of a combined heritage—church members for one hundred years and then Fundamentalist Mormon ancestry for most of the last century.

Both authors were raised with stories of ancestors who sacrificed and suffered for the gospel of Jesus Christ. Part of that suffering and sacrifice was for the principle of celestial plural marriage as experienced by their ancestors at different times and in different ways. Hardships of living the Principle not only included the expected marital and familial complexities of polygynous relationships but also involved significant outside pressure in the form of judicial prosecution and imprisonment and legislative attacks upon people's freedoms—indeed, upon their very existence. Ultimately, the foes of Mormon plural marriage won the battle between freedom of religion and conformity to the dictates of mainstream society, and the LDS Church was forced to cease practicing a principle so important to its theology.

This is where the heritage of the two authors began to diverge. While Craig's grandmother was born in 1892 as a post-Manifesto baby to the fifth wife, that was the extent of his family's civil disobedience. His grandmother's generation and the following generation moved obediently, and no doubt with a bit of relief, into socially and ecclesiastically acceptable monogamy. Marianne's ancestors did not. And for their decision to continue living plural marriage against societal or ecclesiastical dictates to conform, her more recent ancestors paid heavily through suffering excommunication and ostracism, prison terms and governmental harassment.

With such backgrounds, the authors bring different perspectives to this work but a mutual desire to honestly share a fascinating, sometimes troubling, poignant, even painful history of dedication and sacrifice. One author is a respectful outsider looking in while the other is an insider reaching out to help those on the outside understand a lifestyle, belief and dedication of faith so much at odds with modern society.

This volume is offered as a brief overview of Fundamentalist Mormon history rather than an in-depth or comprehensive study and analysis. For those familiar with the topic, there are obvious gaps and probable oversimplifications of many aspects of this history due to its constrained scope and limited space provided in this kind of genre. If there have been inadvertent mistakes, inaccuracies, inadequacies or omissions, we apologize.

Acknowledgements

As with any work of this nature, we are deeply indebted to many unnamed people who kindly and generously offered advice, assistance, information and research materials. Many who did so requested that we not publish their names for fear of legal or other reprisal against themselves or family members. For this reason, some sources are cited as "anonymous." While they are anonymous to the readers, they are known to us, the authors, and we are profoundly grateful to them.

We would particularly like to thank documentarian Steven L. Mayfield and attorney Kenneth D. Driggs. Steven provided his expertise in photography and donated a number of the photographs that appear in the volume. We enjoyed his pleasant camaraderie during our several jaunts to various research destinations; we value his keen observations and thoughtful feedback. For many years, our friend Ken Driggs has freely shared his incredible wealth of knowledge, documents and writings about Fundamentalist Mormonism. Ken's continual support, encouragement and mentoring both in research and writing have been invaluable.

The authors recognize and acknowledge the many contributions of others who shared so liberally and extended to us their genuine friendship. To these we owe a huge debt of gratitude: Alvin S. Barlow, Dowayne Barlow, Newell G. Bringhurst, Kody Brown, Ross Chatwin, Harvey Dockstader, Enoch Foster and family, Brian C. Hales, Nick Hanna, William R. "Willie" Jessop, Jeffrey O. Johnson, Donna K. Mackert, John Nielsen, Evelyn J. Thompson, Don Timpson and Anne Wilde. The authors also sincerely thank the representatives of the Latter Day Church of Christ and the Righteous Branch of the Church of Jesus Christ of Latter Day Saints for their kind assistance. We give special thanks to several members of the Centennial Park group and other residents in Hildale/Colorado City for their gracious hospitality and sharing their hearts and homes during Fourth of July celebrations and on other occasions.

Finally, Craig lovingly and deeply thanks his wife, Suzanne, and his family for their lifelong patience and support while working on this and other writing projects, especially for his many hours and numerous trips away from home. Marianne extends her profound gratitude to her husband, sister wives and all our children, and to her mother, Evelyn J. Thompson, her late father and her large, extended family, all who have enriched her life.

A Matter of Faith

For most religious people, life's journey is a matter of faith. This is also true for the various peoples and factions who self-identify as "Mormon," including those known as Fundamentalist Mormons. Today's Fundamentalists who practice polygamy are better understood by reviewing their religion in context of its Mormon roots, before they became separated a century ago from the Church of Jesus Christ of Latter-day Saints.

Mormons in the broad sense believe the gospel of Christ had become corrupted over the centuries and that Mormonism's founder, Joseph Smith (1805–1844), acting under the power of God, restored the ancient gospel taught and lived by biblical patriarchs and by Jesus Christ in his day. They believe Joseph Smith's account that he saw and talked with both God the Father and his son, Jesus Christ, who then appointed him to perform a prophetic mission. That mission began in 1823, with Smith's translating *The Book of Mormon* from records engraved on gold plates compiled by ancient inhabitants of the Americas given to him by an angel. His mission included establishing in 1830 the Church of Jesus Christ of Latter-day Saints (also known as the Church of Jesus Christ or the Mormon or LDS Church). Mormons believe Smith continued to receive revelations from God as a beginning of the "restoration of all things"—yet to culminate in the fulfillment of biblical end-time prophecies with a full restoration of the Tribes of Israel, the establishment of Zion and the destruction of the wicked. Most revelations Smith received became added scripture, canonized as part of Mormon scripture in *The Doctrine and Covenants*.

Non-Mormon scholar Harold Bloom described Joseph Smith as "an authentic religious genius," unique in America's national history. He recognized what early Mormons saw—that Smith's restored gospel was "truly a biblical religion." Most observers, even many contemporary Saints themselves, do not perceive the Church of Jesus Christ faith in this light due to a lack of familiarity with archaic religion—but Bloom recognized it in Joseph Smith's proclamation: "God himself was once as we are now, and is an exalted man, and sits in yonder heavens! That is the great secret."[1] This theology is encapsulated in a well-known Mormon couplet, "As man now is, God once was. As God now is, man may be."[2] Smith's vision far exceeded urging his people to gain salvation alone through Christ—he wanted his people, those willing, to gain salvation through Christ *and* become gods *like* Christ in a covenant Zion society. For Bloom, that prophetic vision of god-making for humans, with Jesus Christ as its core, distinguished Joseph Smith's restored gospel from modern Judaism and Christianity.[3]

For Smith, this meant that there is not just a singular salvation for all. Rather, there are degrees of glory, a ladder to be climbed, with the highest exaltation reserved for those who live faithful to *all* God's commandments. This concept is key to understanding *why* Joseph Smith introduced plural marriage. Professor Bloom accurately saw in Joseph's theology that "the essentials for the attainment of godhood lead... directly to a plurality of wives" and that "[p]lural marriage was to be the secret key that unlocked the gate between the divine and human." He concluded, "If the entire quest of Joseph's life was to restore archaic religion, in which...God and man, were to differ only in degree, not in kind, then the culmination of that quest had to be plural marriage."[4] That context is the basis for the plurality of wives in Mormon scripture. Early Mormons who accepted plural marriage did so as a matter of faith, endeavoring to establish family relationships that could last for time and eternity and eventually help qualify them for the highest exaltation in heaven. This same purpose motivates contemporary Fundamentalist Mormons, who have been separated from the LDS Church for almost one hundred years, to view plural marriage as a sacred essential. For them, it is still a matter of faith.

JOSEPH SMITH AND THE
ORIGINS OF MORMON POLYGAMY

Mormon history holds that Joseph Smith himself acted on faith and obedience to live plural marriage after receiving a revelation and a personal commandment to live it as a fundamental part of the "restoration of all things." Smith originally received this revelation, included as Section 132 in *The Doctrine and Covenants*, in answer to his question about how God justified Abraham, Isaac, Jacob, David, Moses and Solomon marrying more than one wife. The revelation expounded the important Mormon doctrine of "the eternity of the marriage covenant"—instructing *how* marriages could endure beyond death under certain conditions and make them candidates as gods over a numerous posterity in the hereafter. Moreover, Joseph Smith taught that for all Saints, even the least, by repenting, sacrificing and living all God's commandments acceptably, thus proving faithful in all things, it is possible to know Jesus Christ personally both in this world and in heaven—to hear, see and even touch or feel Jesus Christ in the flesh as well as other departed kindred and prophets, as did the ancients. Smith termed this doctrine as "making one's calling and election sure." Prerequisites included forming unions in plurality that could endure beyond mortality with partners and families deeply bonded and centered on God.

Joseph received the revelation concerning the plurality of wives as early as 1831. He did not immediately begin living the Principle and reluctantly entered his first plural marriage in 1834 or 1835 in Kirtland, Ohio, when he married Fanny Alger, a secret he kept from his first wife, Emma, as well as the rest of the town's residents. This first marriage in plurality was a dismal failure. Emma discovered the marriage, and by some accounts, she at least saw them kissing in the barn or possibly even caught them *in flagrante delicto*. Alger soon left Kirtland, and it appears Joseph Smith shied away from plural marriage and did not marry his next plural wife for at least four to six years.[5]

Critics of Joseph Smith and Mormonism have portrayed Joseph Smith as a lustful philanderer because of his plural marriages. Available evidence paints a different picture. Although Smith's first attempt to marry plurally was fitful and problematic, his vision of eternity pushed him to continue plural marriages, which he did after settling in Nauvoo, Illinois, in 1839. He then quietly married several women between the ages of fourteen and fifty-eight, including both single women and women already married. These latter polyandrous marriages were for eternity only and did not

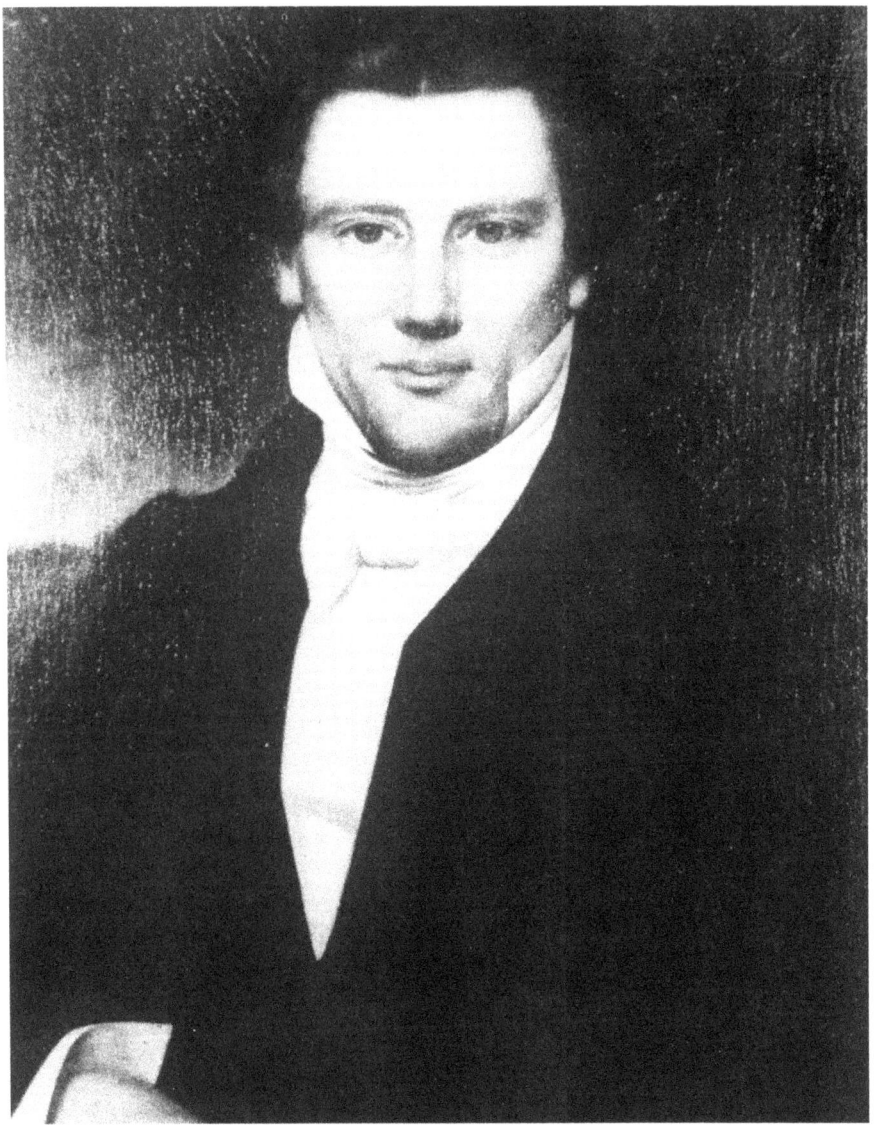

Joseph Smith Jr. (1805–1844), founder of the Church of Jesus Christ of Latter-day Saints. *Wikimedia Commons, U.S. PD-1923.*

involve sexual relations. By then, the membership of the LDS Church had grown to tens of thousands. A small number of Joseph's inner circle of believers also embraced and began living "the Principle" under his teaching and guidance. Marriages were performed in secret, and church leaders publicly denied plural marriages. Nevertheless, rumors abounded, and Smith's martyrdom in 1844 resulted in part from the negative publicity these marriages engendered.[6]

Note that most non-Mormons refer to plural marriage as polygamy, which technically means to have "more than one spouse—wife or husband." The more precise word is *polygyny*, which specifically means for a man to have "more than one wife at the same time." However, in this book, we will use *polygamy* as well as terms traditionally used by Mormons and Fundamentalists: *plural marriage, the Principle, patriarchal marriage* and *celestial marriage*.

MORMONS MOVE WEST
AND CONTINUE POLYGAMY

Despite Joseph Smith's murder in 1844, members of the LDS Church had faith that Smith's teachings truly were of God and continued to quietly practice plural marriage on a limited basis, partly due to significant persecution Mormons already faced. The Saints, as they called themselves, had suffered persecution, including violent acts of murder, plunder and rape in New York, Ohio and Missouri and other places where they settled. The persecution intensified when they moved to Illinois, finally culminating in the death of Joseph Smith. It did not abate until the Mormons relocated west, outside the 1847 boundaries of the United States. From Nauvoo, they migrated in pioneer companies to the Rocky Mountains, lands then considered in Mexico's territory. While crossing the plains, the next leader, Brigham Young, testified that the departed Joseph Smith appeared to him from time to time and gave guidance and said to tell the Saints to "get the Spirit of God." In 1847, the Mormons began settling in the Salt Lake valley near the Great Salt Lake, where they were able to practice their religion unmolested for a time, including openly living plural marriages.

The Mormons embraced the barren desert wasteland and immediately began developing farms and communities. For them, their task was to build the kingdom of God in what became Utah Territory. As they were able to openly practice plural marriage, living in plural households became routinized to a degree, and certain practices were established along with it. Of the estimated 20 to 30 percent of Latter-day Saints who practiced plural marriage, most men had only two wives, with some having three to four wives. The percentage having five wives or more was quite low, less than 10 percent, and only Heber C. Kimball had wives close to the number in Brigham Young's family. Both Kimball and Young married several wives

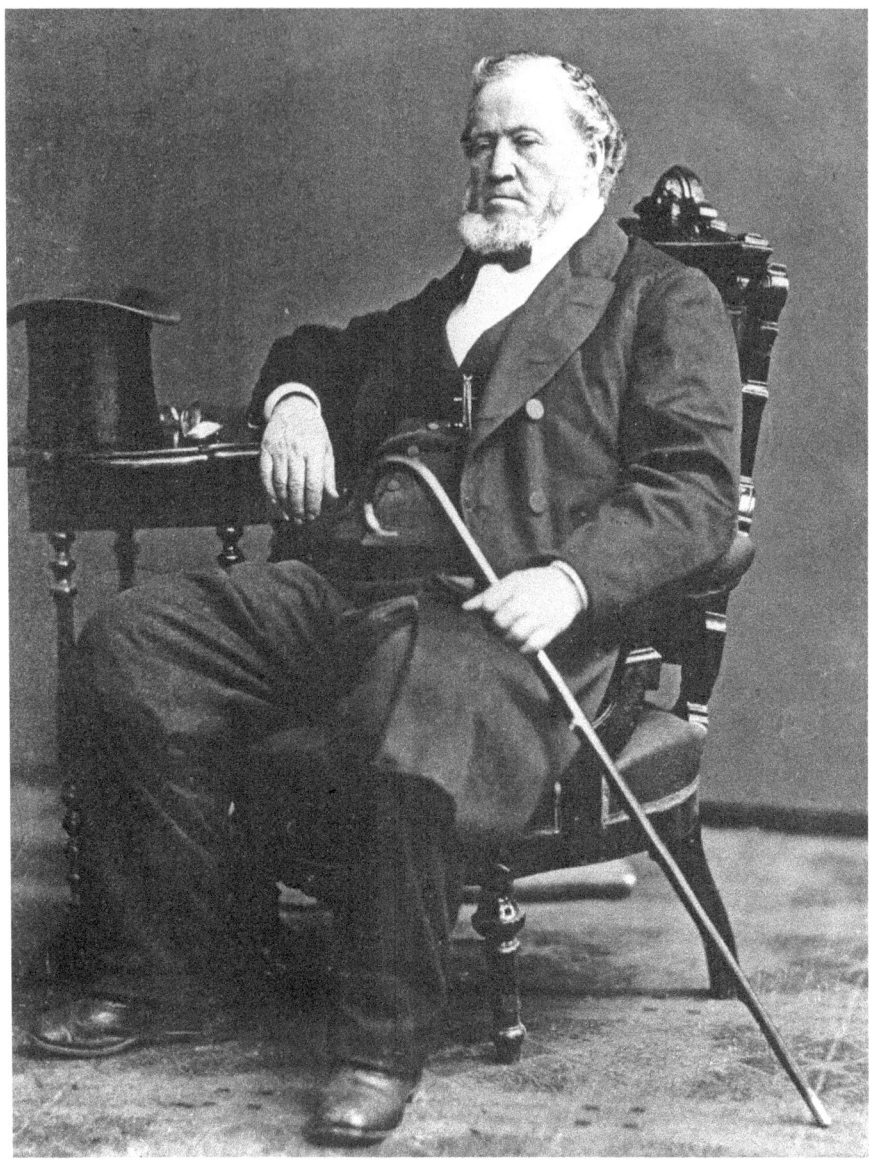

Second LDS Church president Brigham Young (1801–1877). *Wikimedia Commons, U.S. PD-1923.*

in name only, such as older widows, in order to care for them financially and lead them spiritually. Despite having fifty-five wives, Young fathered children with only sixteen of his wives. This, of course, still seems almost incomprehensible to most monogamists.[7] The five succeeding LDS Church presidents who were polygamists married far fewer wives—between three and sixteen.[8]

In Utah and other places where Mormons settled between 1850 and 1890, the practice of plural marriage became accepted as a divine doctrine necessary for fulfilling all of God's laws. Church members were taught that when a man and his wives lived righteously, the children born from such unions would eventually help build Zion on the earth in fulfilment of all biblical end-of-days prophecies and produce a generation worthy to meet the Savior at his Second Coming. It should be noted that living plural marriage righteously demanded high moral conduct and respect for each individual union—intimate relationships between a husband and each wife were considered private and sacred and not shared or discussed with other wives.

In the nineteenth century, some writers and cartoonists portrayed polygamist Mormons living in harem-like houses where life seemed to be a sexual free-for-all, such as a cartoon portraying Brigham Young sleeping in the same bed with several wives. Such situations never took place and would have been considered sinful, resulting in excommunication, and viewed with horror and disgust by early Mormons, who maintained a very prim and proper lifestyle.

For these early members, as with Joseph Smith, it truly was a matter of faith—difficult in the best of times—to practice something so foreign to their Victorian sensibilities. Almost all individuals who participated in plural marriage struggled with the many sacrifices it demanded. Yet many early Mormon plural families became genuinely converted, seeing beauty and divinity in the doctrine and practice. Indeed, numbers of women and men recorded personal spiritual experiences affirming the divinity of this practice. Those who faithfully lived the Principle emerged as pillars of early Mormon communities and passed their deeply held religious views and convictions on for posterity.

PROSECUTION AND PERSECUTION
OVER POLYGAMY

Although the early Mormons left the boundaries of the United States in 1847, their refuge in the West ended up being included within the United States almost immediately as a result of the Mexican-American War. Despite relative isolation at first, they did not escape the influence of non-Mormons.

Every year, a seasonal flow of people traveled the Overland Trail by way of Salt Lake City, with some choosing to stay in the new, bustling community. The Mormons' isolation and renewed interaction with non-Mormons produced mixed effects for both Latter-day Saints and their practice of plural marriage. Soon enough, rumors of Mormon polygamy in the West spread back to the eastern states; national disgust and revulsion resulted. After 1852, when church leaders decided to publicly announce plural marriage as an official Mormon doctrine and practice, the nation revived its resistance against Mormons and their practice of plural marriage.

In 1862, the U.S. Congress passed the Morrill Anti-Bigamy Act, the first of several bills directly aimed at the LDS Church and polygamy. That act made little impact in stopping Mormon polygamy. However, by the 1880s, all Latter-day Saints in the Rocky Mountain region began to suffer the effects of what became known as the "Polygamy Raid," or more commonly as "the Raid," due to a relatively quick succession of anti-polygamy laws passed that were destructive for the LDS Church and its members. The first, the Edmunds Anti-Polygamy Act of 1882, made judicial prosecution easier because federal appointees could prosecute "unlawful cohabitation" without requiring proof of actual polygamous marriages. Under this act, even people who appeared to be cohabiting, such as a man carrying groceries into a woman's home, could be arrested and prosecuted. The law also took away voting rights from polygamists, made them ineligible for jury duty and forbade them from holding public office. The effects of the act on many Latter-day Saints were powerful but still did not dissuade them collectively from continuing to practice a commandment they believed to be from God.

The Edmunds-Tucker Act of 1887 was much more draconian and spiteful in nature. The act disincorporated the LDS Church and allowed the federal government to escheat or confiscate all church properties over $50,000 in value. It didn't stop there; the act required an anti-polygamy oath for prospective voters, jurors and public officials. It also required plural wives to testify against their husbands. Further attacking plural families, the act declared all children born from polygamous unions to be illegitimate and annulled Utah territorial laws that had allowed such children to inherit. The act also disenfranchised women, who had been able to vote in Utah Territory since 1870.

The federal government did all it could to crush into submission the LDS Church and its adherents. The effects were devastating. Federally-sponsored marshals began hunting for polygamists and their plural wives to make arrests. Many church members went into hiding. Men wanted for

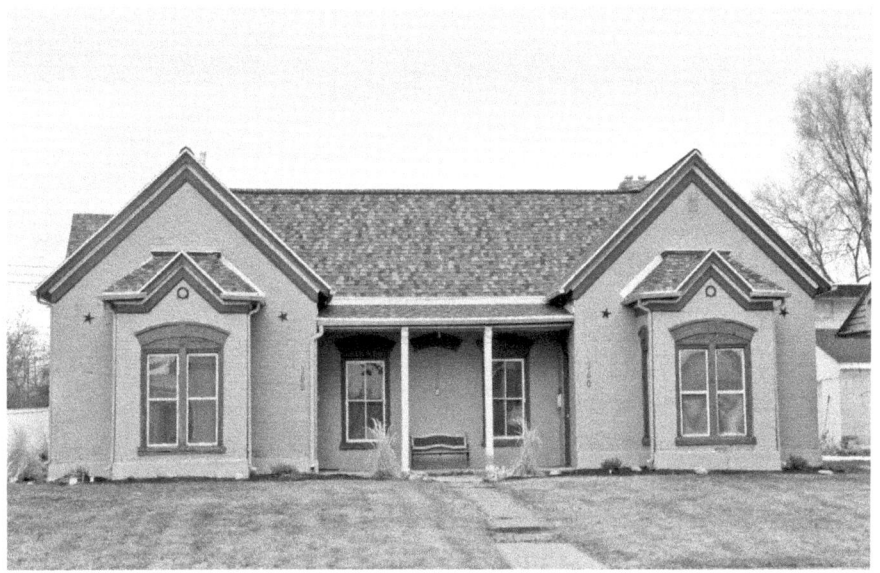

Two-wife polygamist home built in the 1880s in Provo, Utah. Its identical side-by-side apartments suggest the equality of wives. *Steven L. Mayfield Collection.*

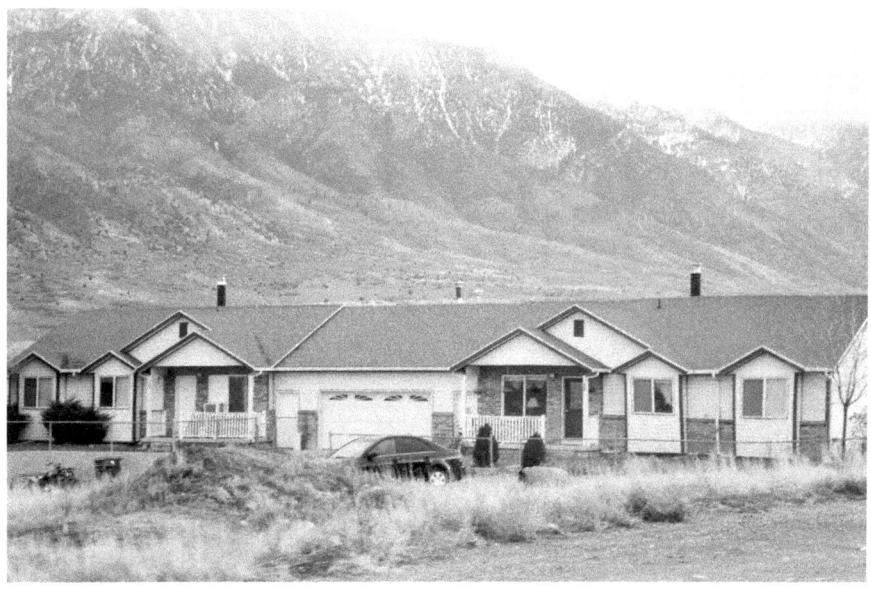

Contemporary two-wife polygamist home located in a polygamist community; this duplex represents a common pattern of home building among Fundamentalist Mormons. *Steven L. Mayfield Collection.*

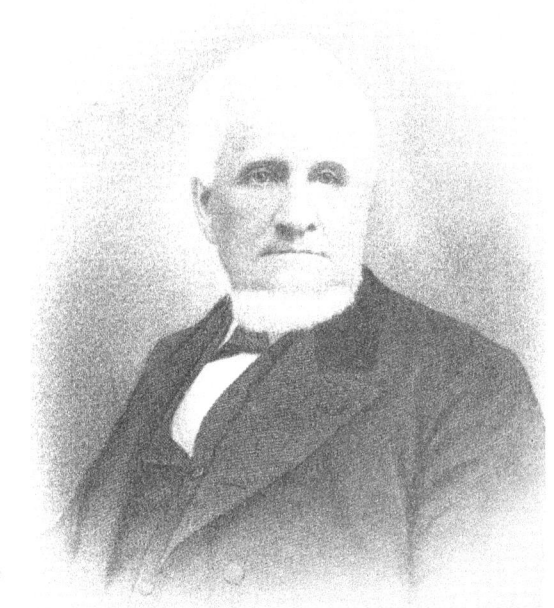

Third LDS Church president John Taylor (1808–1887). Fundamentalist Mormons believe he gave authority in 1886 for continuing plural marriage outside the LDS Church. *Author's collection.*

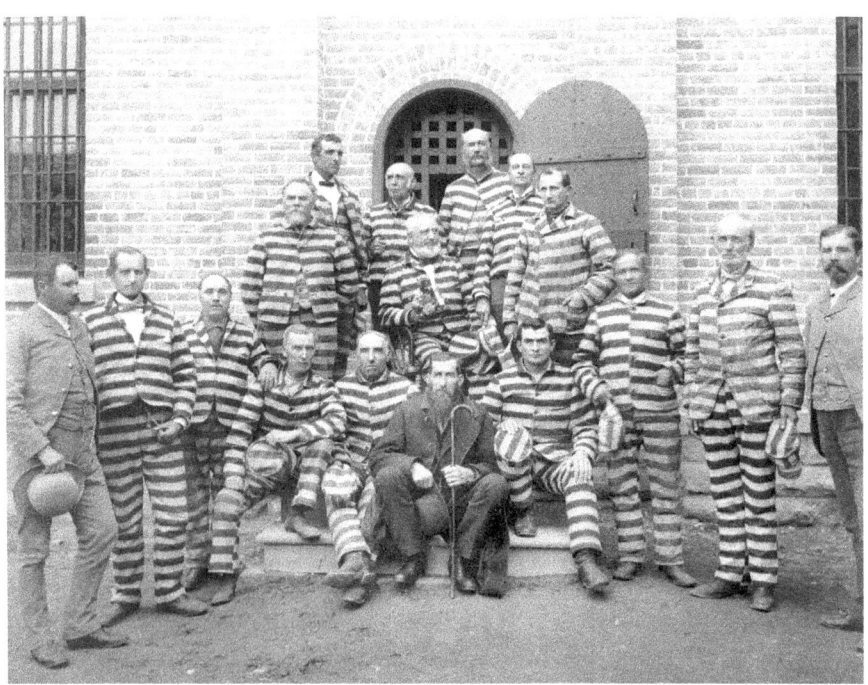

Mormon prisoners at the Utah Penitentiary, including George Q. Cannon (*center, middle row*), circa 1889. *Wikimedia Commons, U.S. PD-1923.*

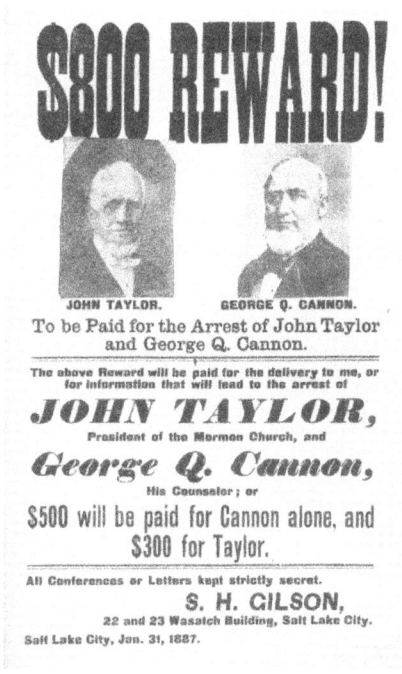

$800 REWARD!

JOHN TAYLOR.   GEORGE Q. CANNON.

To be Paid for the Arrest of John Taylor
and George Q. Cannon.

The above Reward will be paid for the delivery to me, or
for information that will lead to the arrest of

JOHN TAYLOR,

President of the Mormon Church, and

George Q. Cannon,

His Counselor; or

**$500 will be paid for Cannon alone, and
$300 for Taylor.**

All Conferences or Letters kept strictly secret.

S. H. GILSON,

22 and 23 Wasatch Building, Salt Lake City.

Salt Lake City, Jan. 31, 1887.

An 1880s "Polygamy Raid" wanted poster
for John Taylor and George Q. Cannon.
Authors' collection.

unlawful cohabitation fled to different parts of Utah and into neighboring states. Church leaders sent some polygamists on missions to Hawaii or foreign lands to evade arrest. Plural wives, wanting to avoid capture and being forced to testify against their husbands, fled with their children and went into hiding. While some Latter-day Saints buckled under the pressure and agreed to neither live nor teach plural marriage, the majority held strong to their faith, firmly believing they had been divinely inspired and that their plural marriages were of eternal importance.

Hundreds of Mormon men ended up serving time in the territorial prison, usually on the more nebulous charges of unlawful cohabitation. Even women were arrested and placed in jail if they refused to testify against their husbands.[9] Worse yet, men could be repeatedly arrested for the same offense, even after serving a sentence. LDS apostle Lorenzo Snow, while in the state penitentiary, appealed this action and won a court decision affirming guilty parties could not be prosecuted twice for the same crime. After this, many men turned themselves in or allowed themselves to be caught in order to serve the maximum sentence of six months and then finally be free to return to their families.[10]

John Taylor, president of the church following Brigham Young's death, served as leader for most of the 1880s and remained adamant in his determination to maintain God's commandments in the face of federal prosecution. He openly practiced and encouraged civil disobedience for Mormon-targeting laws that he considered unconstitutional. For example, President John Taylor stated in 1880:

> *The United States says we cannot marry more than one wife. God says different…and his laws must be obeyed. If the United States says different the Saints cannot obey it.…Rebellion is not on the program but we will*

> *worship God according to the dictates of our own conscience....Polygamy*
> *is a divine institution....The United States cannot abolish it. No nation*
> *on earth can prevent it, nor all the nations of the earth combined. I defy the*
> *United States. I will obey God.*[11]

The federal government responded by printing wanted posters offering a reward for Taylor's arrest as well as for his first counselor, George Q. Cannon. Thus, church leadership was forced into hiding, sometimes called "living on the Underground," and trusted Saints developed secret codes with a network of safe houses, some with hidden rooms or escape tunnels, throughout Mormon country.

JOHN TAYLOR AND THE 1886 REVELATION

John Taylor spent most of his ten years as LDS Church president on the Underground. The farm home of John Wickersham Woolley, known in secret code as the halfway house, was one of Taylor's favorite hiding places during the Raid period. Located on the outskirts of Centerville, only fourteen miles north of Salt Lake City, the Woolley home was conveniently close to church headquarters but just enough out of the way to afford seclusion.

Important to this story, the Woolley home also was the site where Fundamentalists believe President Taylor spent most of one night conversing with both Jesus Christ and the Prophet Joseph Smith some forty-two years after Smith's martyrdom.[12] Previously, it had been reported that Joseph Smith had visited Taylor while in another safe house, but according to one of Taylor's sons, the Woolley farm was the only place where he met the Savior.

From that experience in 1886, Taylor produced a revelation that said, in part:

> *Thus saith the Lord: All commandments that I give must be obeyed by*
> *those calling themselves by my name unless they are revoked by me or by my*
> *authority, and how can I revoke an everlasting covenant, for I the Lord am*
> *everlasting and my everlasting covenants cannot be abrogated nor done away*
> *with, but they stand forever.*[13]

For John Taylor, this revelatory experience was transformative. Before this event, Taylor had tried to find ways to comply with anti-Mormon laws.

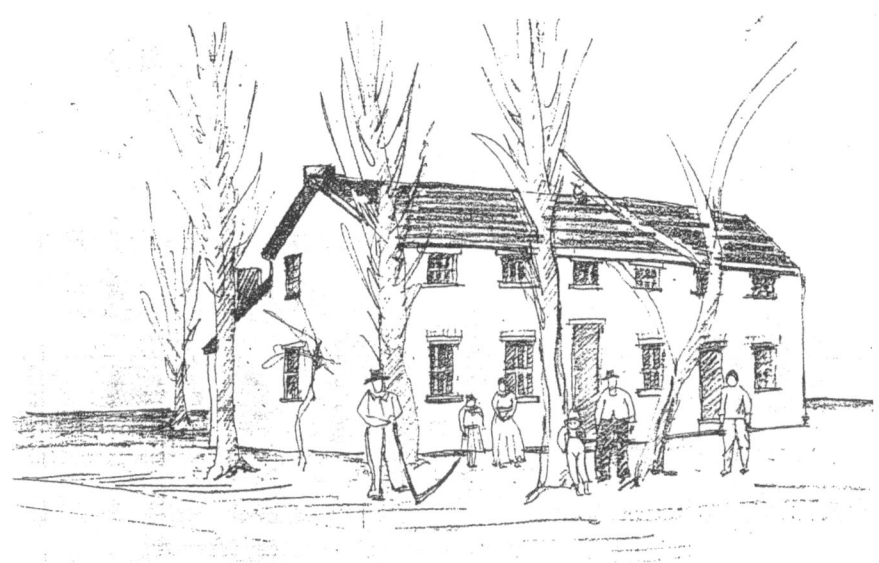

Sketch drawn from an old poor-quality photo of the John W. Woolley home that shows clearly the full length of the house before section at right removed. *Figures from left to right*: son John E. Woolley, granddaughter Julia Cherry, married daughter Amy Woolley Cherry, grandson Thomas Cherry, John W. Woolley and Marcus Eakle Woolley, adopted son of John E. Woolley. *Donna K. Mackert Collection.*

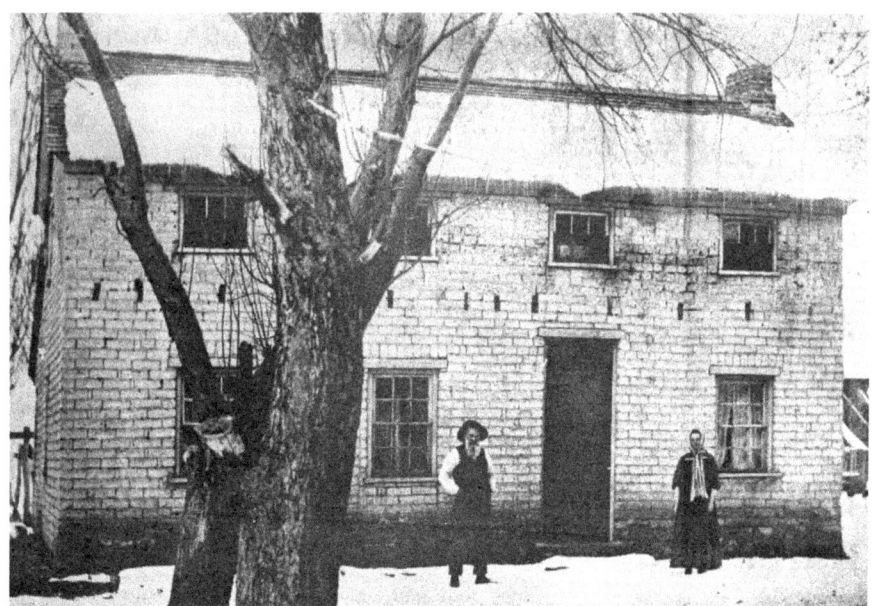

John W. Woolley and his daughter Amy Woolley Cherry in front of John's home after section removed at right, circa 1913. *Donna K. Mackert Collection.*

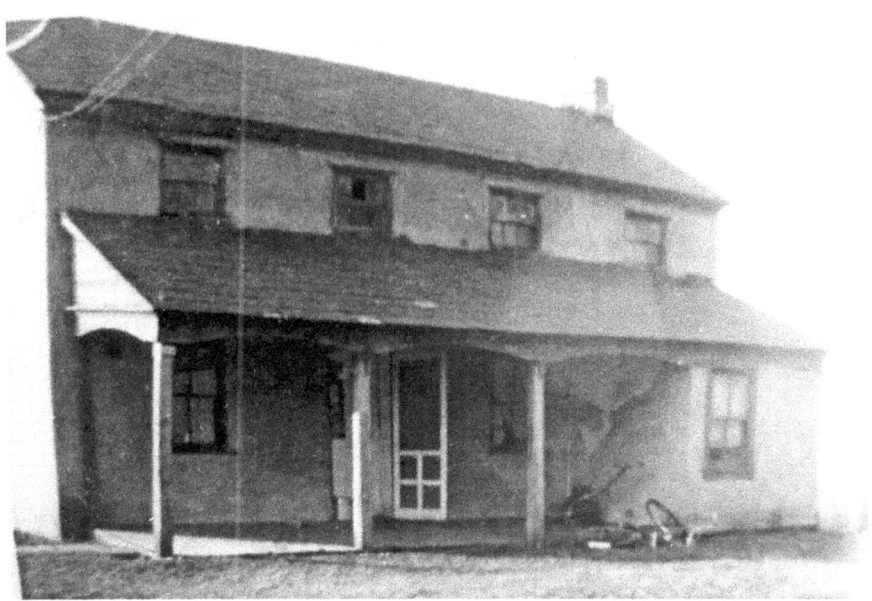

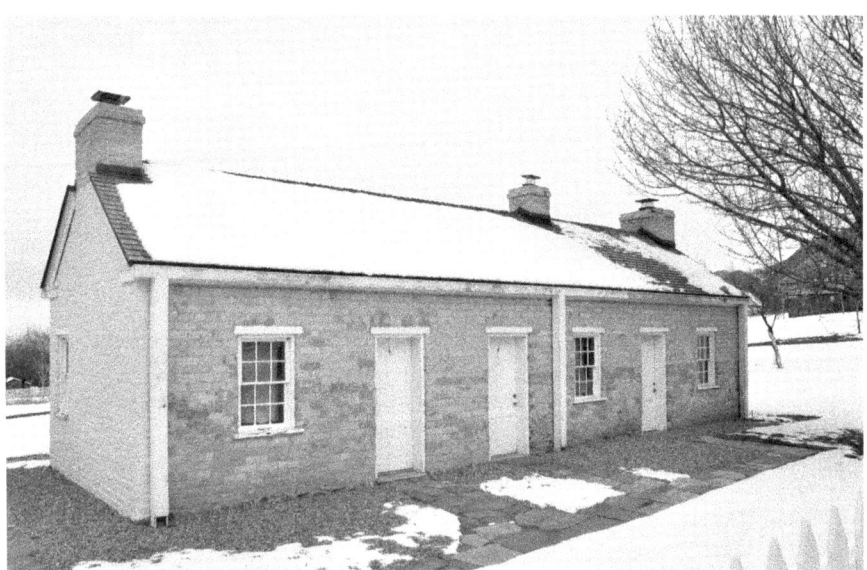

Top: John W. Woolley Home about 1930s after porch reinstalled and a room added at front on the first floor. *Donna K. Mackert Collection.*

Bottom: John W. Woolley home, 2018. Originally built in the 1850s as a two-wife Mormon pioneer house, it was relocated in 1979 and replicated in 1983 at This is the Place Heritage Park in Salt Lake City. It is now known as the Charles C. Rich Home after its original owner. *Steven L. Mayfield Collection.*

Copy of John Taylor's 1886 revelation in his original handwriting. *Authors' collection.*

After the revelation, he took a different stance. Taylor had married fifteen women by the time the Morrill Anti-Bigamy Act—which made polygamy illegal on a national level—passed in 1862, and for the next thirty years, he did not marry any new wives, thus technically not violating the act. With the passage of the 1882 Edmunds Act, which outlawed cohabitation, he attempted to comply by living separately from his plural wives, as they were all past child-bearing age. Yet on December 19, 1886, less than three months after receiving the 1886 revelation, seventy-eight-year-old John Taylor married twenty-six-year-old Josephine Elizabeth Roueche. Thus, "President Taylor had chosen for the first time in his life to specifically violate federal laws on polygamy and unlawful cohabitation."[14]

Taylor's 1886 revelation, described by one LDS historian as "a genuine personal revelation to John Taylor," is now practically unknown among most members of the mainstream LDS Church.[15] The church never published or canonized it in LDS scripture, which would have given it status like other revelations contained in *The Doctrine and Covenants.* As with other revelations received during the 1880s, one by Taylor and two by Wilford Woodruff, it appears Taylor never submitted the 1886 revelation for consideration to be canonized.[16] In the years following Taylor's death, and especially after 1904, church leaders either denied the existence of the revelation or downplayed and ignored it. These factors all resulted in the revelation being partially lost to history, except among Fundamentalist circles where it is still freely circulated.

THE LORIN C. WOOLLEY STATEMENT

John Wickersham Woolley and his son Lorin Calvin Woolley were well known for their civic roles in the pioneer development of Utah but especially for their dedication to the LDS Church. They were among those who ardently believed in the continued practice of plural marriage. Both said they promised to ensure its perpetuation at the time John Taylor received the 1886 revelation in the Woolleys' Centerville home.

John served decades on the Davis Stake High Council and as an ordinance worker in the Salt Lake Temple, serving first under Apostle Lorenzo Snow, who afterward became the fifth LDS Church president, and then under sixth LDS Church president Joseph F. Smith.[17] In 1913, John was called to be a church patriarch, a position of honor and spiritual importance reserved for mature brethren known for faithfulness and wisdom.

Much of Lorin C. Woolley's life was also taken up in church service. During the time of the Polygamy Raids, he spent a lot of time "in defense of the General Authorities of the Church," making numerous trips on horseback, carrying mail or messages between the hiding places of church leaders and church headquarters in Salt Lake City.[18]

During the Polygamy Raid period, President John Taylor received a heavenly visitation and a revelation in answer to prayer. Lorin stood guard in his father's home that night of September 26–27, 1886, when this occurred and later wrote three accounts of what happened. The last account, written in 1929, provides the most detail and became known as "The Lorin Woolley Statement." Part of it tells what Lorin witnessed during the night:

> *The brethren retired to bed soon after nine o'clock. The sleeping rooms were inspected by the guard as was the custom. President Taylor's room had no outside door. The windows were heavily screened.*
>
> *Sometime after the brethren retired…I was suddenly attracted to a light appearing under the door leading to President Taylor's room, and was at once startled to hear the voices of men talking there. There were three distinct voices. I was bewildered because it was my duty to keep people*

out of that room and evidently someone had entered without my knowing it. I made a hasty examination and found the door leading to the room bolted as usual. I then examined the outside of the house and found all the window screens intact. While examining the last window, and feeling greatly agitated, a voice spoke to me, saying, "Can't you feel the Spirit? Why should you worry?"

At this I returned to my post and continued to hear the voices in the room. They were so audible that although I did not see the parties I could place their positions in the room from the sound of their voices. The three voices continued until about midnight, when one of them left, and the other two continued. One of them I recognized as President John Taylor's voice. I called Charles Birrell [the other guard, who had been sleeping] *and we both sat up until eight o'clock the next morning.*

When President Taylor came out of his room about eight o'clock of the morning of September 27, 1886, we could scarcely look at him on account of the brightness of his personage.

He stated, "Brethren, I have had a very pleasant conversation all night with Brother Joseph." (Joseph Smith) I said, "Boss, who is the man that was there until midnight?" He asked, "What do you know about it, Lorin?" I told him all about my experience. He said, "Brother Lorin, that was your Lord."[19]

For believers, these details, and the words of Taylor's revelation, were evidence of divine intervention, which they needed to accept the rest of Lorin Woolley's accounts. This revelation, along with Lorin's report, convinced them that a "priesthood-authorized" way had been prepared for those willing to continue the sacred practice of plural marriage.

According to Lorin, John Taylor held a meeting at the John Woolley farm with a few other church leaders, who encouraged Taylor to sign "some kind of edict to be used in Congress, concerning the surrendering of Plural Marriage," which might give Latter-day Saints relief from the federal prosecutions. When the meeting ended without consensus, Taylor's counselor George Q. Cannon suggested that he ask the Lord for direction. That night, in answer to his prayers, Taylor received the heavenly visitors, who gave him the 1886 revelation as well as instructive counsel regarding plural marriage. The next morning, everyone in the household, about thirteen people, including the guards and John Woolley's wife and his eighteen-year-old daughter, Amy, gathered, anxious to hear what President Taylor had to say. For eight hours, they listened while he told some of his experiences the previous night, personally wrote the revelation he had received and emphatically declared that he would never sign a proposed manifesto to concede plural marriage in order to appease the government's demands. He talked about the importance of plural marriage, and everyone present covenanted that they would defend the Principle for the

The 1886–1887 Quorum of Seven according to Fundamentalists included LDS Church president John Taylor with his two first presidency counselors (*below*) and four other men he called in 1886 (*shown on next page*). According to Lorin Woolley, Taylor and Cannon informed and gave the same appointment to Joseph F. Smith in 1887 upon Smith's return from Hawaii.

This page, clockwise from top right: LDS Church president John Taylor, age seventy-seven. *Authors' collection*; First Counselor George Q. Cannon, age fifty-nine. *Wikimedia Commons, U.S. PD-1923*; Second Counselor Joseph F. Smith, age forty-seven. *Wikimedia Commons, U.S. PD-1923. Opposite, clockwise from top left*: John W. Woolley, age fifty-four. *Authors' collection*; Lorin C. Wolley, age twenty-nine. *Authors' collection*; Samuel Bateman, age fifty-four. *FamilySearch.org FamilyTree*; Charles H. Wilcken, age fifty-five. *Wikimedia Commons, U.S. PD_1923*.

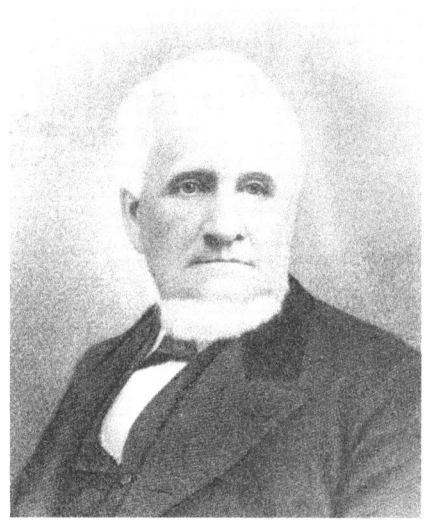

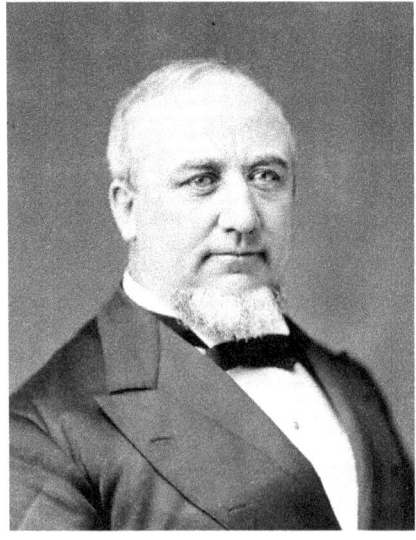

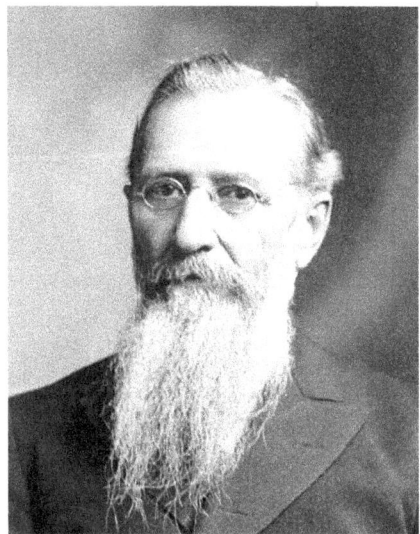

rest of their lives. One of the guards in attendance, Daniel R. Bateman, later related that President Taylor "counseled us not to begin our work until told to do so by proper authority" and that "much of the instruction he was giving we would forget, but that at the proper time it would come back to us."[20]

After the meeting, Taylor had his secretary, L. John Nuttall, make five copies of the revelation. Then he privately called into his room five

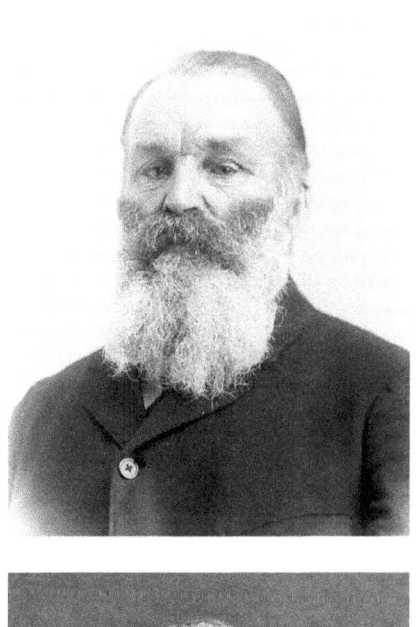
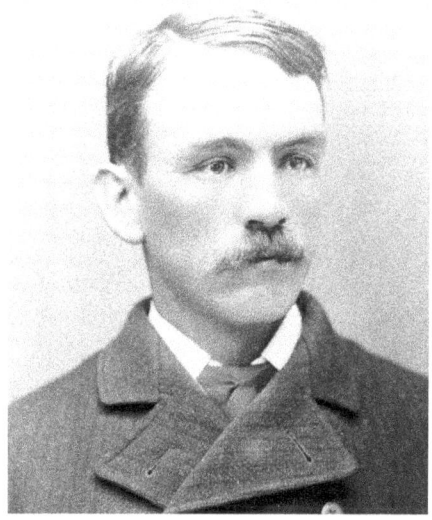
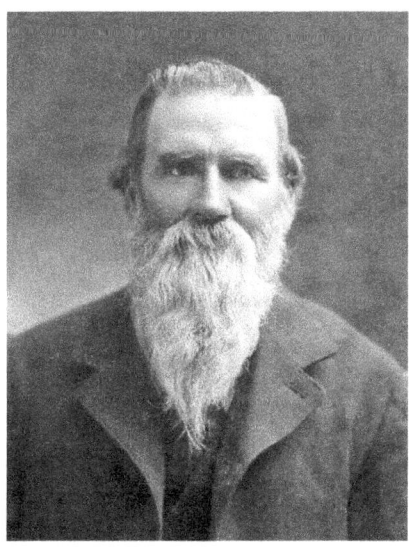
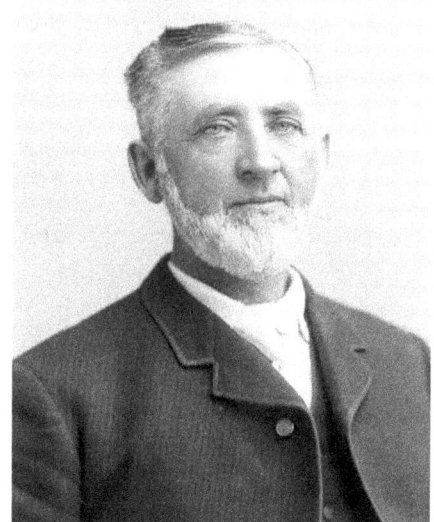

men: John W. Woolley, Lorin C. Woolley, Charles H. Wilcken, Samuel Bateman and Apostle George Q. Cannon, Taylor's first counselor in the church presidency. Lorin Woolley, at age twenty-nine, was the youngest of five; the others were all in their forties or fifties. Taylor gave each a copy of the revelation and then laid hands on every man, one by one, ordaining them apostles and patriarchs, and specifically giving them authority to perform marriages and to call others when needed to ensure the work would continue. Lorin said the resurrected Prophet Joseph Smith directed the proceedings and "laid his hand upon the heads while John Taylor set them apart or acted as mouth."[21] Two of the five, Lorin included, who had not known the Prophet while he lived, were introduced and privileged to shake his hand. President Taylor also put the five men under covenant to ensure that no year passed without children being born in the covenant of plural marriage and said they were to accomplish their missions apart from the LDS Church, if necessary, as it appeared the church would "go monogamous."

John Woolley was the first to marry a new plural wife after these events. One week later, on October 4, 1886, he married an English convert, Ann Reed Everington, age fifty-nine, who had been divorced twice and widowed once.[22] Ann's son Brigham Henry "B.H." Roberts, now a stepson of John W. Woolley, would later become known nationally in a clash of state versus federal government because of his polygamous family.[23]

Not quite three months after the 1886 revelation, as previously discussed, President Taylor married his last plural wife in December. He then moved with his new bride a few miles from John Woolley's place to the safe house of Thomas Reusche in Kaysville, the home of his bride's parents, where he lived the remaining seven months of his life.

In July 1887, dying from kidney and heart trouble, President Taylor sent a trusted emissary to bring Joseph F. Smith quietly back from Hawaii, where he had been serving a mission while avoiding federal marshals. When Smith arrived in Utah, John Woolley was sent to bring him to the Reusche residence. There, on July 18, 1887, one week before his death, President Taylor, who could barely whisper by then, held his last First Presidency meeting. For three hours, he consulted alone with his counselors, Smith and George Q. Cannon.[24] According to John and Lorin Woolley, Cannon and Taylor told Smith about the 1886 revelation on that occasion, and Taylor gave Smith the same appointment he had given the five. Counting both Taylor and Smith, this completed a quorum of seven apostles, which Lorin called a "Council of Friends," a reference to Mormon scripture citing Jesus's words to his apostles, "you are mine apostles…ye are my friends."[25]

In the years that followed, Cannon and Smith diligently participated in ensuring new plural marriages continued, especially among the leaders of the church. They did this during the subsequent church presidencies of Wilford Woodruff (1887–98) and Lorenzo Snow (1898–1901). It is also certain that Joseph F. Smith, after becoming sixth church president, privately encouraged and permitted some new plural marriages, accomplished indirectly through men he trusted.

2

A Changing Mormon World

W hen Wilford Woodruff succeeded John Taylor as LDS Church president in 1887, he inherited a desperate situation, with leaders and members alike suffering the effects of federal prosecution and the church on the brink of bankruptcy and ruin. While most members insisted they were willing to continue their version of civil disobedience, church leaders desperately sought to find a way to preserve their ability to continue plural marriage and at the same time appease both the federal government and popular public opinion.

However, by May 1890, when the U.S. Supreme Court upheld the constitutionality of the Edmunds-Tucker Act, allowing the confiscation of LDS Church property, it was apparent the church's court appeals had failed. Woodruff realized the court decision meant not only the loss by escheatment (government confiscation) of general church property but also the loss of the holy temples, where members perform sacred ordinances believed necessary for eternal salvation.

THE MANIFESTOES OF 1890 AND 1904

President Woodruff spent much time in meditation and prayer and later stated he received a vision in answer. "The Lord showed me by vision and revelation exactly what would take place if we did not stop this practice [of plural marriage]. All the temples [would] go out of our

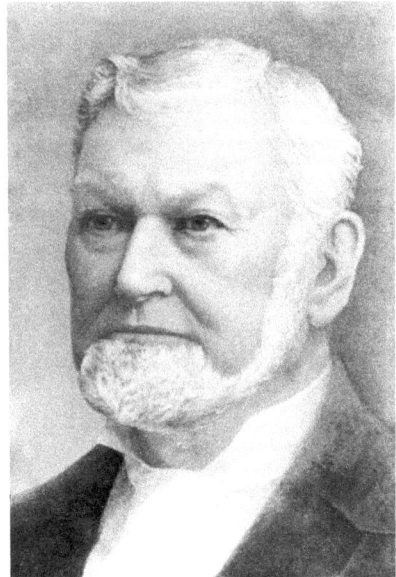
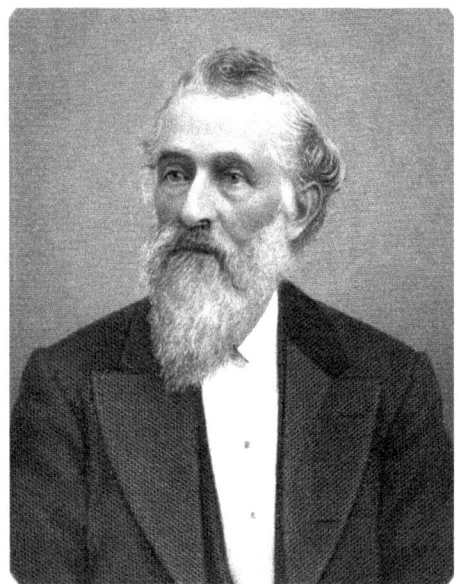
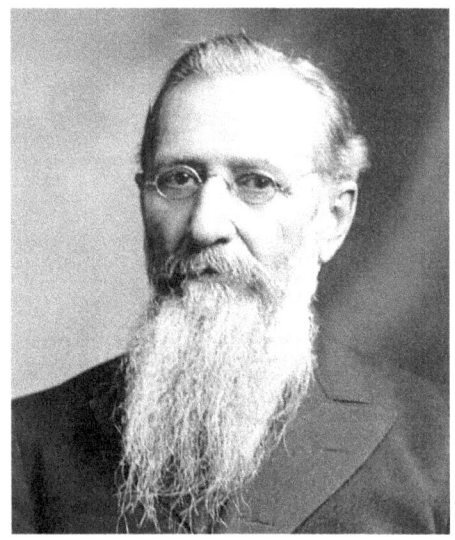

Clockwise from top left: Fourth LDS Church president Wilford Woodruff (1807–1898). Fifth LDS Church president Lorenzo Snow (1814–1901). Sixth LDS Church president Joseph F. Smith (1838–1918). *Wikimedia Commons, U.S. PD-1923.*

hands." God "has told me exactly what to do, and what the result would be if we did not do it."[26]

Woodruff recorded in his own journal that he was "under the necessity of acting for the Temporal Salvation of the Church."[27] With that in mind, he issued the 1890 Manifesto, which he publicly stated he felt inspired to write because of the precarious position of the church. This manifesto was reluctantly accepted by church members in October of that same year.

The 1890 Manifesto opened the way for achieving Utah statehood six years later. Two scholars noted about this period:

> [A]*fter the achievement of statehood in 1896 something of an era of good feeling emerged. Mormons interpreted this as an "understanding" with Gentiles, as permission by implied consent that continued cohabitation would be tolerated so long as new polygamous marriages came to an end.*[28]

But for most polygamists and their wives, this was a difficult transition, as one historian described:

> *With the exception of Joseph Smith's death, it seems that no change within the Church of Jesus Christ of Latter-day Saints produced as great a reaction as the discontinuance of the practice of plural marriage. Earlier, when Joseph Smith introduced that principle, a great deal of resistance and opposition was encountered from those to whom this revolutionary doctrine was taught. Most, if not all who first entered this system did so reluctantly and after a great deal of soul searching. Ironically, when the practice of the principle was officially discontinued in 1890, many who had taken plural wives found that for them discontinuance was as bitter as commencement had been for their forerunners....There were some who never accepted the change.*[29]

For the next decade, church leaders openly disavowed plural marriage while privately promoting the practice among selected individuals, especially among higher-ranking priesthood leaders. The church also began establishing settlements in northern Mexico and southern Alberta, Canada, where approved families willing to live plural marriage could be sent far away from the scrutiny and critics of the church. By not entering into plural marriages within the jurisdiction of the United States, they felt they were living up to the agreement of the 1890 Manifesto while still obedient to a divine law.

About the time Lorenzo Snow succeeded Woodruff as the next church president in 1898, Utah's criminal code was revised to include a statute specifically outlawing unlawful cohabitation. More worrisome, a new media onslaught began, accusing church leaders of duplicity, bad faith and breaking their word. A case in 1900 exacerbated tensions when John W. Woolley's stepson B.H. Roberts won election as a Utah representative to the U.S. Congress but was denied his seat on grounds of continued

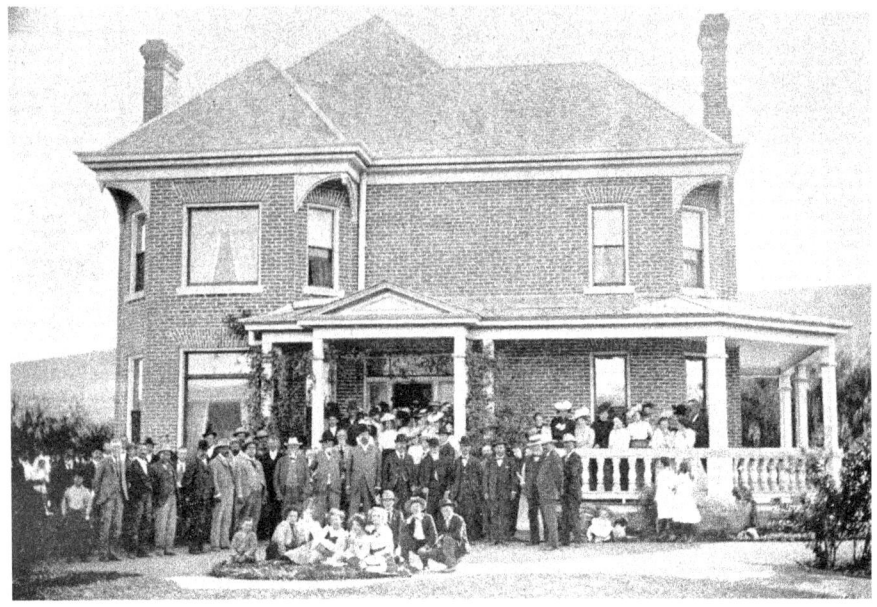

Anthony W. Ivins Home in Colonia Juarez, Chihuahua, Mexico, where Ivins performed numerous church-sanctioned plural marriages between 1886 and 1904, both before and after the 1890 Manifesto. The church established several communities in the area known as the "Mormon Colonies." *Donna K. Mackert Collection.*

cohabitation with his plural wives. For these reasons, President Snow "took a more conservative stand regarding polygamy. During his presidency, the number of plural marriages performed sharply declined."[30] Snow's three-year presidency ended with his death in 1901 amid increasing strain with the nation.

Joseph F. Smith then became church president. In 1904, the church's unofficial policy of winking at post-Manifesto plural marriages was exposed in front of the entire nation when Utahans elected Reed Smoot to the U.S. Senate. Other congressmen challenged his election because Smoot, a monogamist, had been called as one the Twelve Apostles, the second-highest quorum in the LDS Church. Critics considered the church to be at least insincere if not traitorous in its commitment to end plural marriage. They saw Smoot's election to the Senate as an opportunity to publicly disgrace the church and its practices.

The Smoot hearings before Congress became a public relations disaster for Joseph F. Smith when he and other church leaders were forced to testify before Congress. The hearings revealed that new plural marriages had taken place and polygamy continued to be practiced by some church members, especially ones in leadership positions. Due to negative publicity and pressure both from within and without for a second manifesto, Smith issued the 1904 Second Manifesto, which stated, in part:

> *I, Joseph F. Smith,* President of the Church *of Jesus Christ of Latter-day, hereby affirm and declare that no such marriages have been solemnized with the sanction, consent, or knowledge* of the Church....*And I hereby announce that all such marriages are prohibited, and if any officer or members...shall assume to solemnize or enter into any such marriage, he will be* deemed in transgression against the Church.[31]

This manifesto began to end church-sanctioned plural marriage and ensured an ever-increasing shift toward the church becoming dedicated to monogamy. However, Fundamentalist Mormons perceive the 1904 Second Manifesto as a carefully worded statement by Smith in his role as church president and not in his presiding position over the priesthood. Thus,

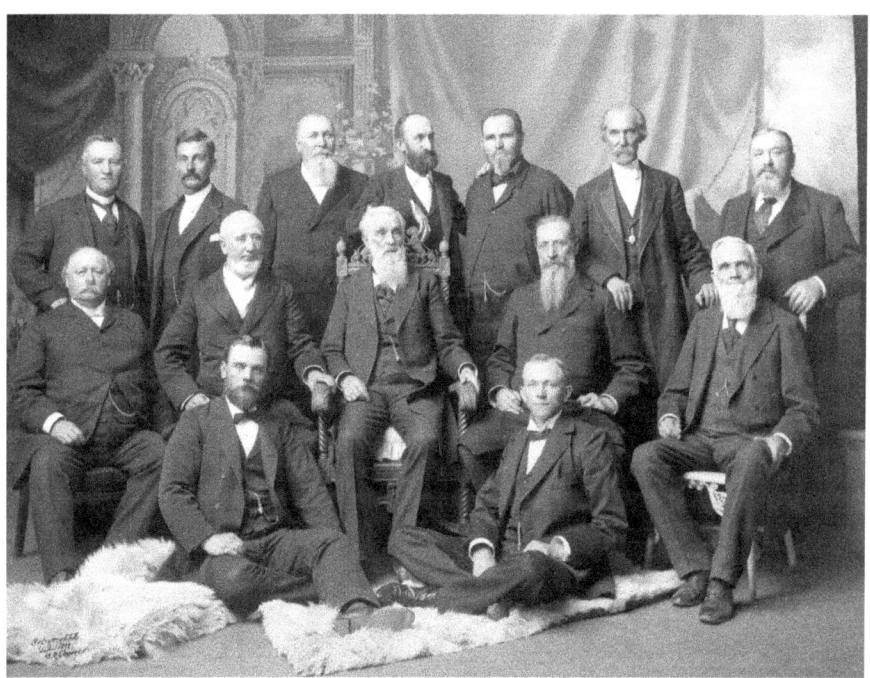

Lorenzo Snow's LDS Church First Presidency and Quorum of Twelve Apostles, September 1898, just after the death of Wilford Woodruff. All these leaders practiced plural marriage. Within a decade, two were asked to resign and seven died. Their replacements were all monogamists, either never having lived plural marriage or who by then had only one living wife. *Wikimedia Commons, U.S. PD-1923.*

believers in continued plural marriage deemed any who entered plural marriage under the circumstances were *not in transgression against God*, only against the church, a position they felt they could justify before God.

Evidence suggests Smith still privately encouraged plural marriages among some brethren he trusted, stipulating that men with priesthood authority who performed such ceremonies do so *without* his specific knowledge so that *as church president* he had no personal knowledge of new plural marriages being performed. He warned men they had to take responsibility for living or performing plural marriage—that if their involvement in plural marriages was exposed, the LDS Church would be compelled to excommunicate them. Unfortunately, public denunciations but private encouragement of continued plural marriages proved to be problematic and placed many Latter-day Saints in a state of uncertainty over whether plural marriage was a principle that must be lived.

One historian summarized the tumultuous post–Second Manifesto era under President Smith and the president's dual stance on plural marriage:

> *President Smith had two conflicting goals: he hoped to preserve plural marriage and save the Church from legal action and disincorporation. In order to accomplish both of these goals, he gave divergent instructions. He instructed most church leaders to maintain the Church's honor by disciplining any members who violate church policy and the law of the land respecting polygamy, but he authorized others to enter and perform plural marriages. The Twelve were carrying out President Smith's instructions when they excommunicated new polygamists, and the new polygamists were carrying out President Smith's instructions (accomplished via specific individuals) when they put themselves in jeopardy of excommunication. Joseph F. Smith divided the Church against itself: he had laid down two paths a good Mormon might travel, paths which led in opposite directions.*[32]

The historian added:

> *Of the two camps faithful Saints could join—one monogamous, the other polygamous, John W. Woolley* [and his son Lorin C. Woolley were]...*clearly destined to work in the latter.*[33]

John and Lorin Woolley became largely responsible, directly or indirectly, for most of the polygamous marriages among Fundamentalist Mormons in the last century. They did this by presenting to willing Mormons their case

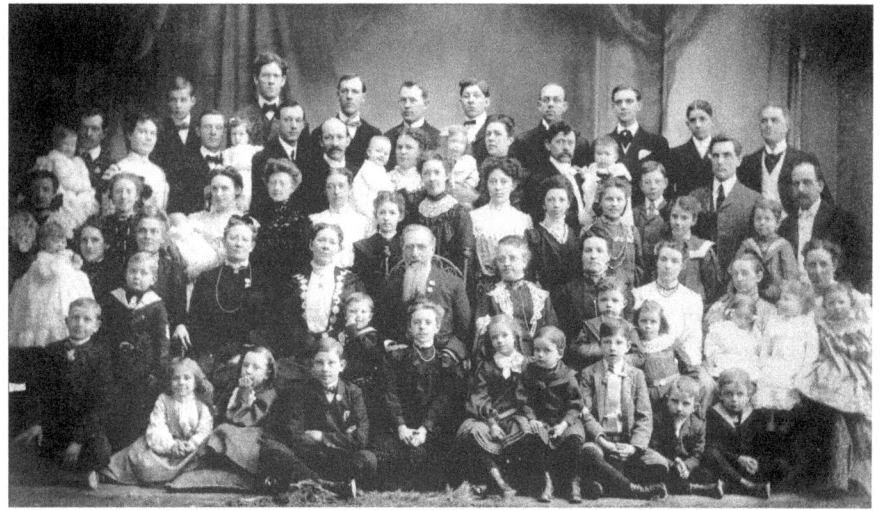

President Joseph F. Smith's large plural family in 1904. *Wikimedia Commons, U.S. PD-1923.*

for "priesthood-authorized" marriages apart from the LDS Church. That legacy has been passed to current generations. For such people, the 1890 and 1904 Manifestoes were never applicable.

JOHN W. TAYLOR'S EXCOMMUNICATION TRIAL

Word of the 1886 revelation spread quietly among a few church members despite its practically unknown status. Of note, Apostle John W. Taylor, a son of the late church president John Taylor, learned about the revelation from his father not long before he died and said he found the original in his father's papers after his death. At the time of the 1890 Manifesto, he mentioned his father's revelation to his fellow apostles and emphasized that plural marriages should never be discontinued. Nevertheless, he acquiesced and publicly supported the Manifesto partly because he recognized it would physically and temporally save the Church and its holy temples. He and others in high leadership encouraged and clandestinely participated in new post-Manifesto plural marriages, allowing marriages to be performed outside the United States boundaries, thus following the letter of the official declaration but certainly not the spirit.[34] Taylor felt his father's revelation was still being followed, and in the next two years, he also married two plural wives, including Janet Maria Woolley, the niece of John W. Woolley.

For most Mormons, the Second Manifesto sharply curtailed new plural marriages both inside and beyond U.S. borders, and LDS Church leaders began disciplining any members found to have entered new plural marriages. However, after the Second Manifesto, Taylor found himself at odds with his brethren and secretly married another wife. In 1905, Taylor and his co-Apostle Matthias F. Cowley were both pressured to resign from the Quorum of the Twelve to help save face for the church because of their continuing involvement in plural marriage. Still, in the years that followed, both men continued to enter and perform plural marriages.

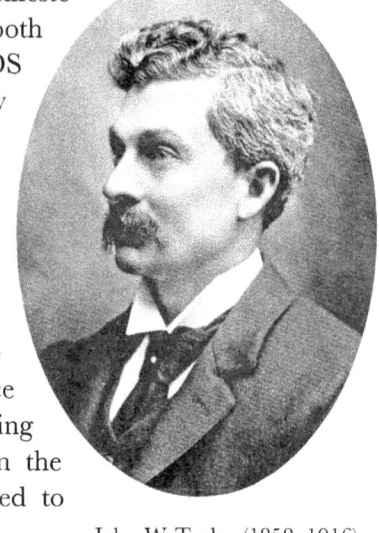

John W. Taylor (1858–1916), son of President John Taylor. *Authors' collection.*

By 1910, the *Salt Lake Tribune* had begun publishing names of suspected "new" polygamists to again expose church duplicity over plural marriage. In response, President Joseph F. Smith sent a letter to all presidents of stakes instructing them to excommunicate any members found advocating or practicing plural marriage.[35] Many were excommunicated in the following months and years, with some later becoming associated with Fundamentalism.[36]

In 1911, John W. Taylor was excommunicated for his outspoken objections over the Second Manifesto and his continued participation in new plural marriages. A month later, Matthias F. Cowley was disfellowshipped. At Taylor's trial for his membership, he presented his father's 1886 revelation, which was read aloud and discussed in depth, and Taylor admitted he had given copies of the revelation to several individuals.[37] Through him and others, the revelation had been circulated among selected church members. For example, in 1915, Utah inventor and businessman Nathaniel Baldwin tracked down a copy from an unnamed stranger and quoted from it in a pamphlet he published.[38] Although John W. Taylor died an early death in 1916, the word of the revelation continued to spread quietly but surely. In little more than a decade, living the Principle in Mormon country had fallen from the former respect and high social esteem once held for faithful adherents.

PERSONAL HISTORIES OF JOHN W. WOOLLEY
AND LORIN C. WOOLLEY

John Wickersham Woolley and his son Lorin Calvin Woolley hailed from a prestigious early Mormon family with close connections to LDS Church leadership. With that foundation, they played vital roles in the emergence of a people dedicated to perpetuating old-fashioned Mormonism, including plural marriage. A review of their personal histories is important for understanding why their message to continue plural marriage was accepted by believers in the 1920s.

John was the son of Edwin D. Woolley, who was born and raised in Chester County, Pennsylvania, where he worked as a farmer. He married Mary Wickersham in 1831, and John was born nine months later at their home in Chester County. Shortly after, Edwin moved his family to Ohio, where he again took up farming, less than one hundred miles from Kirtland, Ohio, then the LDS Church headquarters. Hearing of the Mormons, Edwin walked the distance to Kirtland to meet the Prophet Joseph Smith. Finding him absent, he was welcomed instead by the Prophet's father, Joseph Smith Sr., who returned with Edwin to stay for a few weeks and teach his family about the restored gospel. Edwin and Mary were soon baptized and joined the church. By then, John was almost six years old; he recalled being dandled on the knee of Father Smith.

The Woolley family eventually moved with the Mormons to Illinois and helped establish the city of Nauvoo. There, Edwin worked as a merchant and became close friends with Joseph Smith and his brother Hyrum. John grew from a boy to a young man in Nauvoo, where he joined with other young boys in a "whittling and whistling brigade" that kept a lookout for questionable characters in town up to no good. At age eight, Woolley received a patriarchal blessing from Joseph Smith Sr., the presiding patriarch of the "Church of the Latter Day Saints," as the LDS Church was then called. In this blessing, Woolley was promised he would "be called to responsible stations" that would involve receiving "keys" and that he would one day be called "the Lord's anointed."

In Nauvoo, Joseph Smith introduced the doctrine of plural marriage, first officially presenting it to a trusted few in October 1843 at Edwin D. Woolley's home. Edwin was among the first Mormons to enter plural marriage.[39] He married a total of six women and had twenty-seven children.[40] He earned a reputation as a staunch defender of the restored gospel and the church.

After the Latter-day Saints were forced to leave Nauvoo, Edwin Woolley and his family, including sixteen-year-old John, crossed the plains to Utah with Brigham Young's pioneer company in 1848. In Utah, Edwin became a close confidant and business partner of Brigham Young. He also served for years as the bishop of the Salt Lake City Thirteenth Ward and in various public offices. John grew up associating with the Youngs and other prominent Mormon families in the city.

As a grown man, large in physical stature, John also worked in important church and community positions. At age twenty-five, he participated in the rescue of the ill-fated Martin and Willie handcart companies stranded in the 1856 fall snowstorms on the Wyoming plains. He helped guide two wagon trains and one freight train across the plains. John served in the Nauvoo Legion, Utah Territory's extensive militia organization, attaining the rank of major. He worked as a deputy sheriff and deputy territorial marshal in Salt Lake City, where he also served as a second counselor to his father in the Thirteenth Ward bishopric.[41] After moving to Centerville in 1864, his church callings included serving for fifty years on the Davis Stake high council and nearly twenty years as an ordinance worker in the Salt Lake Temple under both Lorenzo Snow and Joseph F. Smith.[42] John involved himself in county government, functioning as an elected director of the Centerville Co-op Store and also filling the office of justice of the peace for many years.[43]

During the years when John W. Woolley worked in the Salt Lake Temple, following both the First and Second Manifestoes, he secretly performed

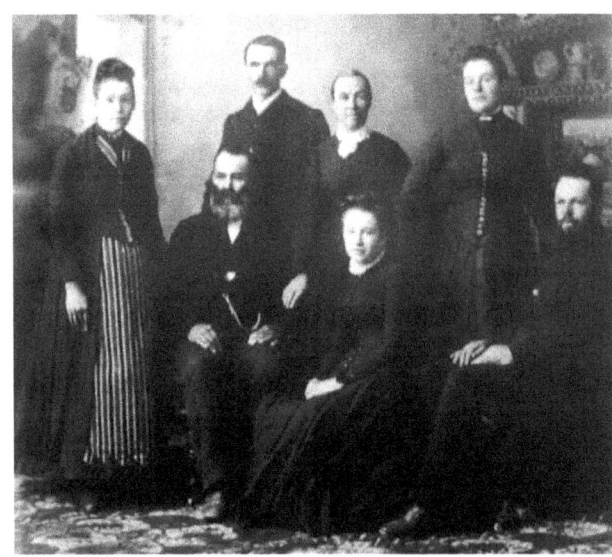

John W. and Julia Ensign Woolley family in the 1880s. Lorin C. Woolley is standing behind his father. *FamilySearch.org Family Tree.*

sanctioned plural marriages for couples sent to him by certain church brethren. For example, in 1909, when Warren Longhurst wanted to marry a second plural wife, he asked Anthony W. Ivins, who had performed his first plural marriage sealing in Mexico in 1903, "anticipating a repetition of that favor." President Ivins said, "My position in the Church prevents me from doing this for you at the present time. However, I can send you to some one who can." Ivins sent Warren to Woolley to perform the marriage.[44]

John Woolley married his first wife, Julia Ensign, in 1851. They had six children together. Of these, at least three, John, Lorin and Emma, became involved in plural marriage. Two children, Lorin and Amy, were present in the 1886 events.

John is credited by one family historian as having married seven wives, though only four are certain, with two other possibilities identified.[45] After his first wife, Julia, John's earliest possible plural wife was Sophia Ester (unknown maiden name), who was listed in the 1860 census in his household as age eighteen from Denmark. No further information has been found for Sophia.

As mentioned before, John married Ann Reed Everington one week after the 1886 events. A biographer wrote that Ann "was one of John's eventual seven wives" and that "this marriage was viewed by both parties as a marriage of fortune."[46] This union brought five adult stepchildren to John's family, including Brigham Henry "B.H." Roberts, who frequently visited John's home, often bringing his mother and taking a special interest in his stepsister

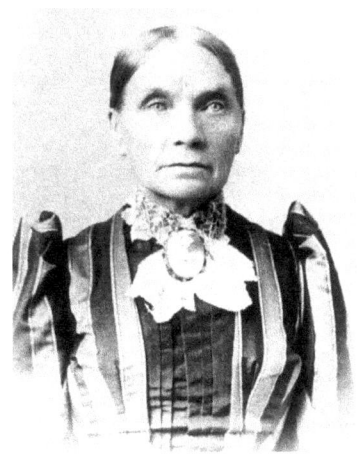

Anne Reed Everington Woolley (1828–1910), a plural wife of John W. Woolley. *FamilySearch.org Family Tree.*

Amy Woolley. Amy's diaries reveal a plural family relationship with Ann and some of her children.[47]

Mary Jane Ensign, a half sister of John's first wife, Julia, may have not married John while she lived but possibly arranged for her posthumous temple sealing as a wife to him before she died at age thirty-one, shortly after giving birth to her last child, a baby girl, who died a year later. Mary Jane had separated from or divorced her husband before her death, and her burial monument includes only her maiden surname. John raised her three sons, Henry, Horace and Samuel Rugg, with the help of Mary Jane's widowed mother,

Ruth Kelson Ensign, who brought the boys to live at John's home after his first wife, Julia, died in 1892. Ruth legally adopted her grandsons to protect against possible claims of their birth father, who had left the church and gone to California.

It is possible though uncertain that John married Ruth plurally, as a caretaker husband for the sake of the boys. The 1900 census shows Ruth, Horace and Samuel in John's household; Henry was listed in the household of John's wife Ann. John included the Rugg boys among his heirs in his will and clearly considered them his adopted sons. Horace, the second son, recalled fond memories of living with John on his farm, saying those "were the best years of his childhood."

Olive, Lorin Woolley's daughter, related that she knew her grandfather John well, as she lived next door to him until she married, just three months before he passed away. She remembered that "he had a keen mind and a very keen sense of humor...yet [was] very stern and straight-laced" but "extremely gentle and kind with everyone."

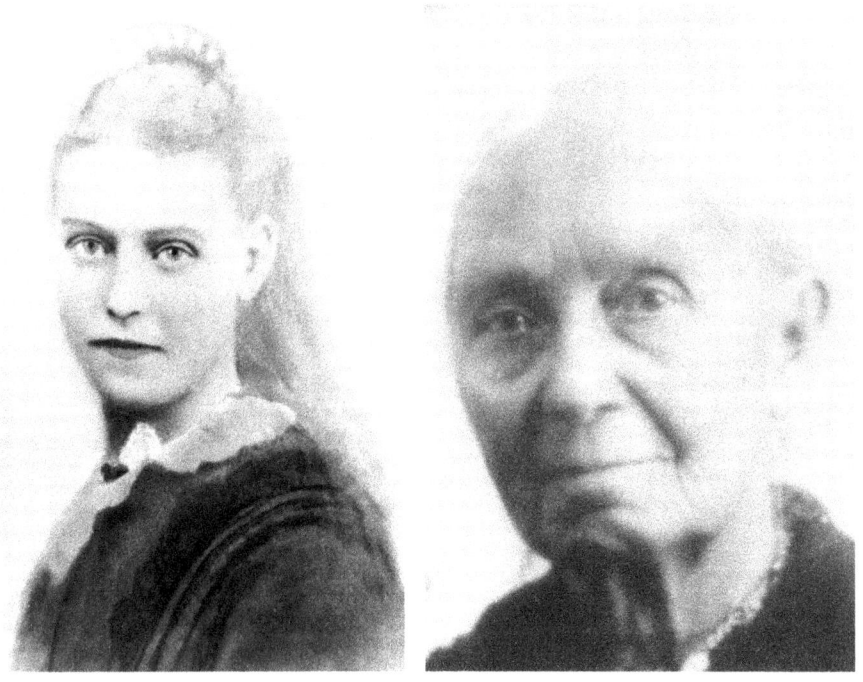

Left: Mary Jane Ensign (1859–1890). She was sealed posthumously to John W. Woolley, who raised her three sons. *FamilySearch.org Family Tree*.

Right: Ruth Kelson Ensign (1820–1915). *FamilySearch.org Family Tree*.

She said her grandfather "had a lot of friends, more than [some] people gave him credit for," and remembered some came to visit and talk way into the night in "deep" conversation. Olive reported, "Quite a few [LDS Church] general authorities used to come to visit, and it wasn't unusual for them to pull the blinds down while visiting, and they always came when everyone else was away." The 1890 to 1893 diaries of Amy Woolley, John's youngest daughter, also show that John received many visitors, including prominent church leaders—among them Joseph F. Smith, Wilford Woodruff and George Q. Cannon. Some also came who had been there with President Taylor in 1886—Samuel Bateman, Charles H. Wilcken and George Earl. Olive said her grandfather John "bore strong testimony of the [1886] eight-hour meeting and…the truthfulness of the revelation of John Taylor which was received in his home."[48]

Lorin C. Woolley was the third-eldest child of John and Julia. He was born in Salt Lake City in 1856 and moved to Centerville when almost eight. In his youth, he got the nickname "Noisy" from his peers due to his tendency to rattle off answers in priesthood classes. When just a young teen, he earned the confidence of church leaders, who sent him to care for church cattle. At the tender age of sixteen, Lorin received the temple ordinance called the endowment, usually reserved for those leaving on church missions or first getting married.[49] During the time of the polygamy raids, he spent a lot of time "in defense of the General Authorities of the Church," making numerous trips on horseback between the hiding places of church leaders and church headquarters in Salt Lake City.[50] It was in this last capacity that Lorin Woolley said he was present, acting as a bodyguard, when John Taylor received his revelation in 1886.

Just three years before, in 1883, Lorin had married his first wife, Sarah Ann Roberts. They had the privilege of hosting President Taylor for his last birthday in November 1886 along with several of his Underground companions and guards.

After Taylor's death, Lorin served his first mission and was sent to Indian Territory from 1887 to 1889. Seven years later, he was sent again to the same mission, this time for only six months. Two brethren recorded that Lorin testified in 1897 while in Indian Territory that he had seen Joseph Smith since his death.[51]

Raised as a farmer, Lorin spent much time farming his own land next to his father's farm, as well as helping his father plant and harvest crops. Lorin, like John, engaged in building businesses and developing their local community. When in his late fifties and early sixties, he served as officer, director or board member for various businesses and banks.[52]

Lorin and his wife Sarah Ann had nine children. According to their youngest daughter, Olive, Sarah Ann told Lorin if he ever took another wife, she didn't want to know about it. Lorin honored her request, but when she suspected he had married plurally, "she was quite brokenhearted."[53] Lorin Woolley once stated, "A man has no right to preach what he doesn't practice, so...I practice what I preach."[54] Evidence indicates he married at least four wives late in life, including two aged spinster cousins, Alice May Woolley and Sarah Viola Woolley, who never had children. He also married forty-eight-year-old widow and schoolteacher Edith Blackhurst McClelland Gamble in 1923 after her post-Manifesto polygamist husband died earlier that year. In 1932, two years before his death, Lorin married his last known plural wife, Goulda Nellie Kmetzsch, a recent German immigrant, when she was twenty-eight and he was seventy-five. They had only two years together before his passing, and she never remarried. Lorin had no known children from his plural wives.[55] Olive said her father introduced Goulda as his wife to her but not to his other children.

Olive described Lorin as about five feet, eight inches tall, with a slight build. He walked with a limp due to an accident in his youth and used a cane later in life. Olive noted that he loved books and brought library books home to read to his family and "brought the stories to life." She said that when he asked for an opinion, he gave it, and "you always knew where [he] stood and you didn't have to 'beat around the bush' with him." She also believed "he never betrayed a confidence." After Olive learned to drive in the early 1920s, every Monday, she took him to Idaho, which provided hours to talk with him alone. She "did not know of anyone who had a deeper understanding of human life and nature" and felt she could go to her father for anything. Olive said her father was not judgmental or reactionary, even though he was justice of the peace, and would take time to help others with their problems.[56]

THE WOOLLEYS' STRANGE TALKS

Even before their later excommunications from the LDS Church, both John and Lorin Woolley seem to have deliberately drawn attention to plural marriage in a church meeting at a time when it was not acceptable to do so—*after* the 1890 and 1904 Manifestoes. The *Salt Lake Telegram* reported a Kaysville congregation was left "puzzled and perplexed" after both Woolleys gave talks in a church meeting.[57] According to the news article, John Woolley's speech was particularly bewildering. He said he came to announce an upcoming stake conference but then spoke for over an hour on an array of topics, the most controversial being polygamy. Some in attendance insisted the elder Woolley's "sermon was a strong plea in favor of polygamy and a covert encouragement to the good Mormons to practice it." They said that while Woolley acknowledged that "of course, it is forbidden," he promised the time would come "when it would be practiced openly by Mormons" and alluded to the idea that the higher kingdom of heaven was reserved for those who practiced plural marriage on earth.[58]

The Woolleys' church talks drew enough attention that a newspaper reporter contacted Kaysville bishop (and future Utah governor) Henry H. Blood for comment. Blood downplayed the two Woolleys' remarks. He said, "I am sure that Mr. Woolley did not say that polygamy is being practiced now. I certainly would have noticed if he said anything like that." Blood continued, "As to polygamy being practiced in the future, I recall that he intimated that polygamy would not, he thought, be practiced in his lifetime" but "would come in some future generation."[59]

In his shorter talk, Lorin Woolley mentioned a prophecy that up to one half of the church membership would eventually apostatize and suggested there were presently many in the fold who were apostate. He then said something curious—that "he had been summoned to Salt Lake City by the authorities of the church to attend a meeting Sunday night and that a crisis was at hand and probably would occur that night."[60]

Circumstantial evidence suggests the Woolleys' Sunday talks in Kaysville were somehow connected with John W. Taylor's first day of trial before the Quorum of Twelve Apostles held earlier that week. Notably, Taylor brought a copy of the 1886 revelation to his trial, which was read and discussed.[61] Since Taylor was their in-law, having married John Woolley's niece, and had homes in Kaysville, the Woolleys likely knew of his trial and its outcome and considered it a crisis. In the trial, members of the Twelve rejected the 1886 revelation as being irrelevant or nonbinding—one even referred to it as "purported"—and they clearly would not consider *any* new plural marriages as authorized. Their opposition seemed to threaten the continuation of plural marriage anywhere within the Church of Christ.

In 1912, in the wake of John W. Taylor's 1911 trial, Lorin Woolley filed a signed affidavit with the LDS Historian's Office giving a brief account of what happened in 1886 with President John Taylor at his father's home.

President Smith possibly knew about the affidavit and may have even encouraged it. Lorin's affidavit was the first of three statements he wrote about the events. It contains the least information of the three. Accounts he wrote in 1921 and 1929 contain more detail. Some mainstream LDS Church members point to differences in the three statements, written years after the events, to suggest Lorin embellished his testimony over time,[62] but Fundamentalists see no meaningful contradictions and compare any differences to variations in statements made by Joseph Smith when describing his first vision of God the Father and the Son.

Despite any controversy over John W. Woolley's remarks in Kaysville, President Smith and other church leaders called him in 1913 as a church patriarch, a trusted position of honor and spiritual importance. After serving as a patriarch for less than a year, John received a visit in January 1914 from two Quorum of the Twelve members. At their behest, he signed an affidavit naming four men for whom he had performed plural marriages, saying he had done it believing he had authority from President Joseph F. Smith given through Matthias F. Cowley.[63] John was excommunicated the same month for "insubordination and disobedience to the regulations of the Church" and for continuing to perform plural marriages "contrary to the orders of LDS Church leaders."[64] Although no longer officially a member, John remained faithful to the LDS Church.

John's excommunication caused him to lose prominence in the tight-knit Mormon community. He lost his ecclesiastical positions as a temple worker, a patriarch and a member of the Davis Stake High Council and was soon replaced in his civic office as a justice of the peace by his son Lorin, who held that office until his own excommunication ten years later. Nevertheless, John still attended some church meetings and conferences.

After John lost his membership, Lorin, with his daughter Olive, took him to a Davis Stake conference in Bountiful. Afterward, she remembered standing with her father, waiting outside for her grandfather. As John came out the north door, President Joseph F. Smith emerged from the south door and made a "perfect bee-line" for the elder Woolley. Putting his arms around John's shoulders, President Smith said, "I want you to know, John, they outvoted me…[and] I want to bring you back into the Church…but because the Twelve are so hepped up about this thing, we have got to do it secretly."

John replied, "Well, Joseph, I was cut off with such a ballyhoo, the only way I'll go back is with a ballyhoo." Olive said her grandfather refused to come back secretly, although he never really felt he was cut off.[65]

By 1916, of the five men said to be commissioned in 1886, only John and Lorin Woolley, plus Joseph F. Smith, still lived. Daniel Bateman, a guard who had attended the eight-hour meeting, testified that "before President Joseph F. Smith died" in 1918, "he had counseled him [Bateman] and Lorin C. Woolley that the time had now come to teach the principles of Patriarchal Marriage to the Latter-day Saints."[66]

EARLY DEVELOPMENT OF
FUNDAMENTALIST MORMONISM

Three developments in the early 1920s gave rise to the importance for the Woolleys to share their "good news" that a path had been prepared by President Taylor for those willing to believe, take the risks and make the inevitable sacrifices to continue plural marriage. First, seventh LDS Church president Heber J. Grant took action in 1921 to stop new plural marriages by excommunicating several church patriarchs who had performed such marriages during Smith's administration. Suddenly, this made the mission and appointments given in 1886 more urgent to John and Lorin Woolley, who were the last living of those appointed. Second, as a result of that urgency, in 1921, Lorin Woolley penned his second account of the 1886 event, this one meant for sharing with church members who were open to learning about it. Third, beginning in 1921, rags-to-riches Utah inventor Nathaniel Baldwin provided a virtual stage for Lorin Woolley and Daniel Bateman to tell about the 1886 events to a receptive audience that quickly embraced their message of a priesthood-sanctioned way to continue plural marriage despite any or all objections by church or country. Bateman confirmed and supported what the Woolleys claimed, losing his church membership in consequence. Bateman became pivotal in his role of supporting the Woolleys, testifying about what he witnessed and corroborating their statements

Lorin Woolley's explanations to small but accepting audiences were remarkable for those who believed. However, his account stunned most LDS Church members who heard of or read it. Most could not consider

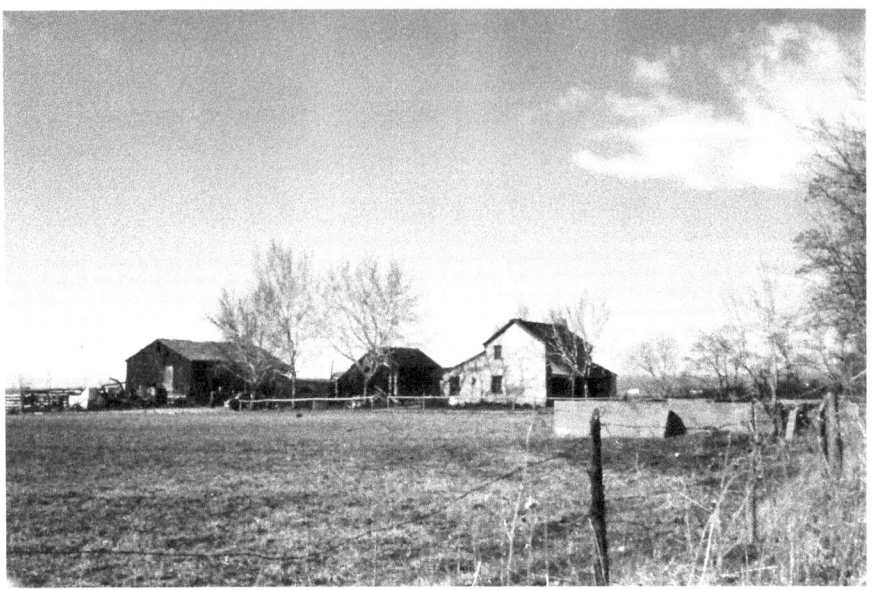

John W. Woolley farm in Centerville, Utah, a favored "safe house" during the 1880s raid period and where President John Taylor received the 1886 revelation. *Donna K. Mackert Collection.*

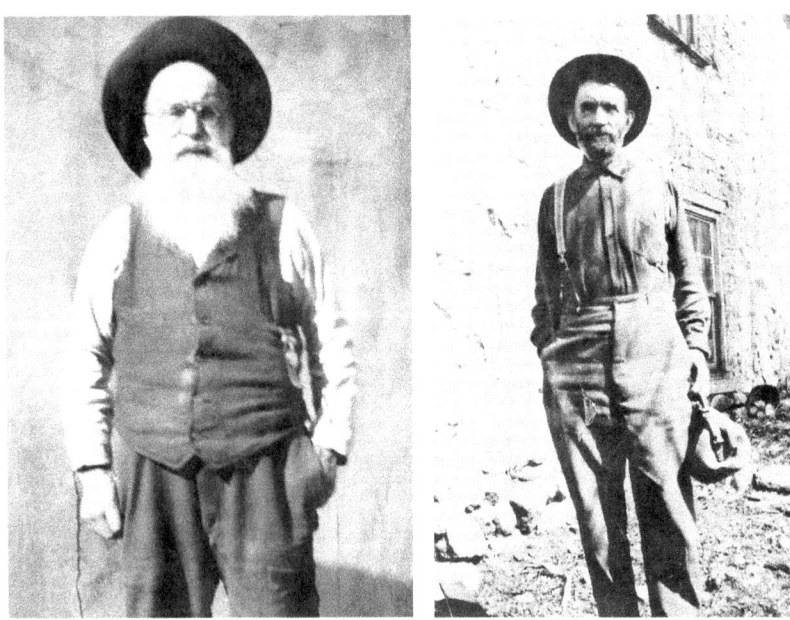

Left: John W. Woolley (1831–1928); *Right*: Lorin C. Woolley (1856–1934). *Both, authors' collection.*

the Woolleys, who held no high positions in church leadership, could be privileged with such experiences as claimed, nor could they believe they would receive apostolic authority or callings outside of the traditions they had known. Although there had been a few examples of men beyond the traditional Quorum of the Twelve Apostles to receive an apostleship by Brigham Young, including some of his own sons and Joseph F. Smith, the nephew of *the* Joseph Smith, they saw no precedent for allowing an apostolic calling outside the presiding quorums of the church. Thus, Lorin's account was generally mocked and disbelieved. Both church leaders and members tended to view it as spurious and untrue.

Lorin Woolley was excommunicated in January 1924 for "conduct violative of the order and discipline of the church." Interestingly enough, involvement in polygamy was *not* the cause of his excommunication. Instead, he was called to a church court for "pernicious falsehoods," including assertions attributed to Lorin but reported by others that President Grant and Apostle James E. Talmage had taken plural wives in the "recent past." Talmage, who wrote about Woolley's excommunication, believed Lorin had also told a lie about being a government officer.[67]

While it is documented that Lorin told certain people about being involved in some way with the government, the charges that led to his excommunication did not affect those who believed him, his father and Dan Bateman. For these believers, like earlier generations who had heard and believed the message of Joseph Smith, it simply became a matter of faith to believe.

NATHANIEL BALDWIN

Inventor and philanthropist Nathaniel Baldwin played a pivotal role in enabling a growing awareness of the 1886 events among potential believers from about 1921 to 1925, when a nucleus of such families formed through association and employment at Baldwin's radio factory in East Mill Creek, Utah. If the early days of what became known in the 1940s as Fundamentalist Mormonism can be compared to the spread of a wildfire, then the initial sparks that truly caught flame began at Baldwin's factory.[68] Without Baldwin's patronage, the community might have developed differently. The descendants of that nucleus remain at the core of most Fundamentalist Mormon communities today.

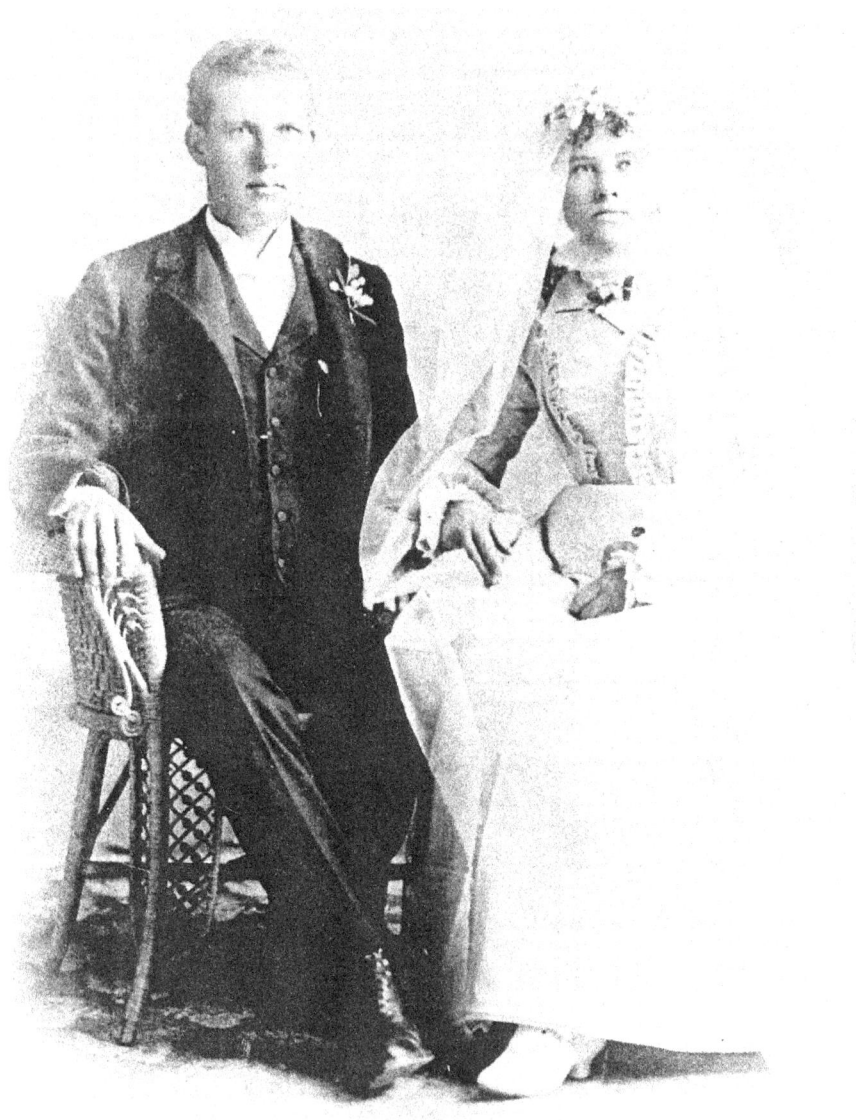

Nathaniel Baldwin and his first wife, Elizabeth Butler, who married in 1899. *Authors' collection.*

After getting married and graduating from Stanford University, Nathaniel Baldwin began his career in 1901, teaching physics as an assistant professor at church-owned Brigham Young Academy (BYA), which was later renamed Brigham Young University, under Professor Josiah Hickman, who soon became an intimate friend. They shared the belief taught by Joseph Smith that "the doctrine of plural and celestial marriage is the most holy and important doctrine ever revealed to man on the earth and that without obedience to that principle, no man can ever attain to the fulness of exaltation in celestial glory."[69]

Through Hickman, Baldwin became aware of the dual stance of President Joseph F. Smith to publicly deny but privately encourage plural marriage. Hickman confided that he had been called to a private meeting where President Joseph F. Smith "emphasized the great importance of this principle [of plural marriage] and gave encouragement to this select group [to live plural marriage], and gave them to understand that if they were willing to face the danger attendant upon this step, they had his benediction."[70] In 1905, the university fired Baldwin, partly "because he would not accept the manifesto regarding plural marriage [as being of divine origin]."[71]

Baldwin's search for employment took him into the Utah mountains to record scientific data at a power plant. For nearly a decade, his mountain jobs allowed him time alone in nature, where he simultaneously experimented with sound. His work resulted in the development of a highly effective loudspeaker and other related inventions, including telephone receivers and radio headsets (headphones) that revolutionized the radio industry. In 1914, on the verge of entering World War I, the U.S. Navy tested Baldwin's radio headsets, then began ordering more. Baldwin soon moved production from his wife's kitchen and built his first factory, a small log cabin, in East Millcreek, a suburb of Salt Lake City. This began his rapid rise to financial success.

When Baldwin first started production in East Millcreek, he began actively attending the LDS Church again. Being in a new place with a bishop "who was somewhat steeped in old fashioned Mormonism," Baldwin felt he had a degree of freedom to teach "Mormonism as it was given through the Prophet Joseph Smith and in the Scriptures." Baldwin considered the gospel his most important business and began publishing pamphlets expounding scripture, prophecy and doctrine. Baldwin's bishopric advised that he might believe as he pleased but that he "should not talk so loud." Baldwin made no promises except "to learn and do the will of the Lord." However, certain doctrinal issues, especially his public expressions in support of plural marriage, kept him at odds with church authorities.[72] Word quietly spread of Baldwin's penchant for hiring members from plural families, although such employees were always a minority of his workers.

In August 1921, Baldwin met Lorin C. Woolley. Three weeks later, Baldwin and several friends visited John and Lorin Woolley in Centerville, where they "heard many remarkable testimonies particularly regarding the teaching and practice of polygamy by…church leaders." He had earlier, in 1915, obtained a copy of the 1886 revelation and quoted from it in a pamphlet he published in 1917. When he learned the Woolleys' story, he immediately accepted it. For the next four years, Baldwin clearly sought the Woolleys' friendship and counsel in both religion and business, and he traveled numerous times to their Centerville homes for that purpose.

In November 1921, Baldwin was excommunicated for insubordination. In retrospect, he wrote:

> *I feel to say with sincerity that if I were wrong in my beliefs about old fashioned Mormonism, and particularly about the doctrine of the plurality of wives, and anybody could show me my error and prove it to me by the Scriptures….I would never cease to sing his praises….Then I could easily repent and be in harmony with my people. Of course I would lose few friends, but how many more I would gain, and prominent ones too!*[73]

Only weeks later, in January 1922, demand for his radio products suddenly skyrocketed. Baldwin moved his production into his newly built eighteen-thousand-square-foot brick factory and hired more employees. During this

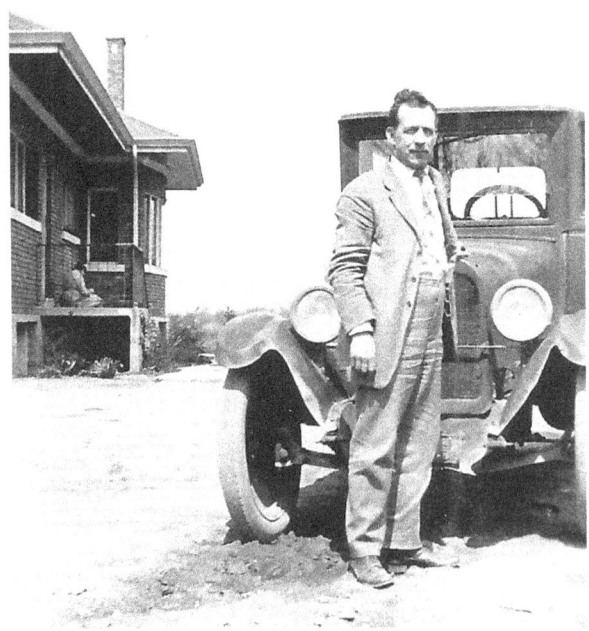

Nathaniel Baldwin in 1922, at apex of his business success and the year he married his plural wife Josie. *Authors' collection.*

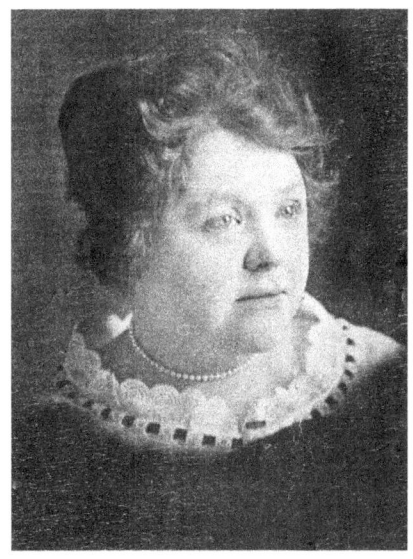

Left: Josephine "Josie" Sandberg Steed (1892–1953), a widow of polygamist Thomas J. Steed. She married Nathaniel Baldwin as a plural wife in 1922. *FamilySearch.org Family Tree*.

Below: Baldwin Radio factory built in 1922. *Authors' collection*.

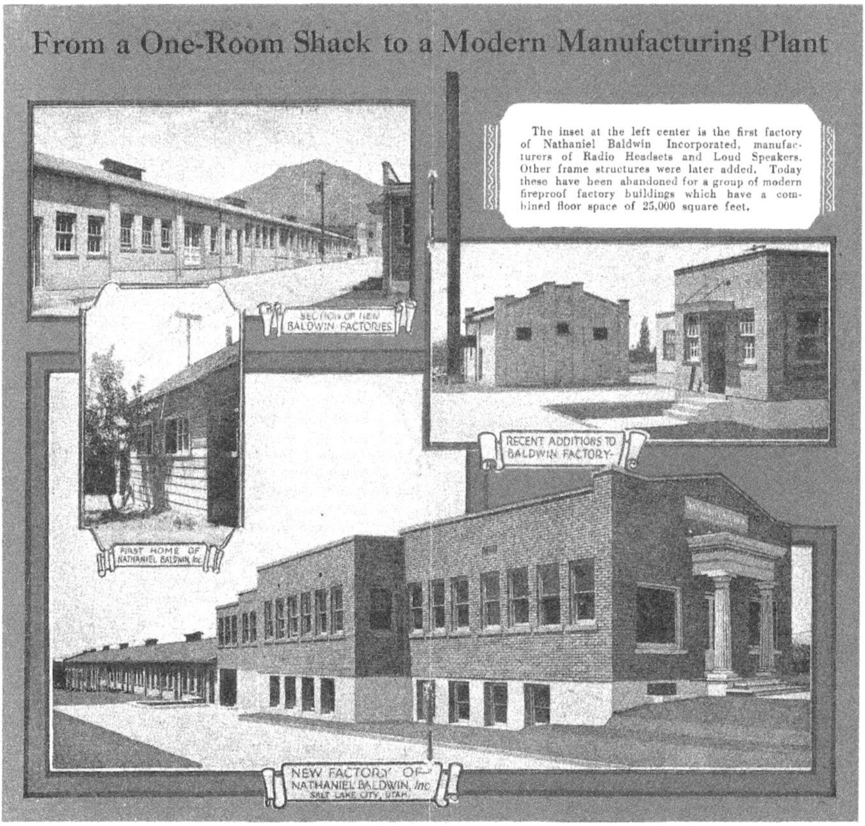

From a One-Room Shack to a Modern Manufacturing Plant

The inset at the left center is the first factory of Nathaniel Baldwin Incorporated, manufacturers of Radio Headsets and Loud Speakers. Other frame structures were later added. Today these have been abandoned for a group of modern fireproof factory buildings which have a combined floor space of 25,000 square feet.

SECTION OF NEW BALDWIN FACTORIES

RECENT ADDITIONS TO BALDWIN FACTORY

FIRST HOME OF NATHANIEL BALDWIN Inc.

NEW FACTORY OF NATHANIEL BALDWIN, Inc. SALT LAKE CITY, UTAH.

phenomenal burst in business growth, Baldwin took a significant step in his personal life. In March 1922, at age forty-three, he married a plural wife, thirty-year-old Josephine "Josie" Sandberg Steed, a widow.[74]

By June that year, 150 employees worked in three shifts producing 150 radio headsets a day.[75] But with orders rushing in ten times that number, production could not meet demand.[76] The year 1922 proved to be the apex of Baldwin's career. With his name printed on every unit sold, he became known around the world.

When several other manufacturers came with offers to buy him out or seeking contracts to produce his products, he consulted Lorin C. Woolley, who recommended not selling but "letting a home company have the [production] work on royalty."[77] Baldwin liked the idea and simultaneously decided to incorporate his factory as Nathaniel Baldwin Inc., with Lorin Woolley as one of seven original incorporators.[78] Importantly, he also organized Omega Investment Company, an entity designed to receive profits generated from Baldwin's several businesses and spend them for religious and philanthropic purposes—publishing books, buying land, assisting people in need and so forth. Omega's board of directors consisted of Baldwin, his first wife and his son, plus nine trusted friends—including six men connected with continuing polygamy: Matthias F. Cowley, John T. Clark, Clyde Nielsen, Daniel R. Bateman, Margarito Bautista and Israel Barlow Jr.[79] Within a few months, Lorin C. Woolley was added to the board.

Across the street from his factory, Baldwin built a new office building for Omega that doubled as a meeting place for small religious gatherings. Frequently, some of his employees gathered in the Omega offices for informal after-work gospel discussions. One, Moroni Jessop, recalled:

> *A few selected men would be called into a private office, the door would be shut, and we would hold meetings with uncle Lorin* [Woolley] *and Dan Bateman. Part of the time Baldwin would be there too….Such meetings would happen, once, twice and sometimes three times a week.*[80]

Baldwin sponsored a biweekly Wednesday scripture study class at the Omega headquarters. Eighty-year-old Israel Barlow, a church patriarch who had been excommunicated for performing plural marriages, led the lessons. Baldwin occasionally used his factory lunchroom for private, after-hours meetings for his special friends. In these ways, Baldwin provided a ready audience to hear Lorin Woolley and Daniel Bateman speak. John Woolley, by then in his nineties, verified their words when asked and, through most

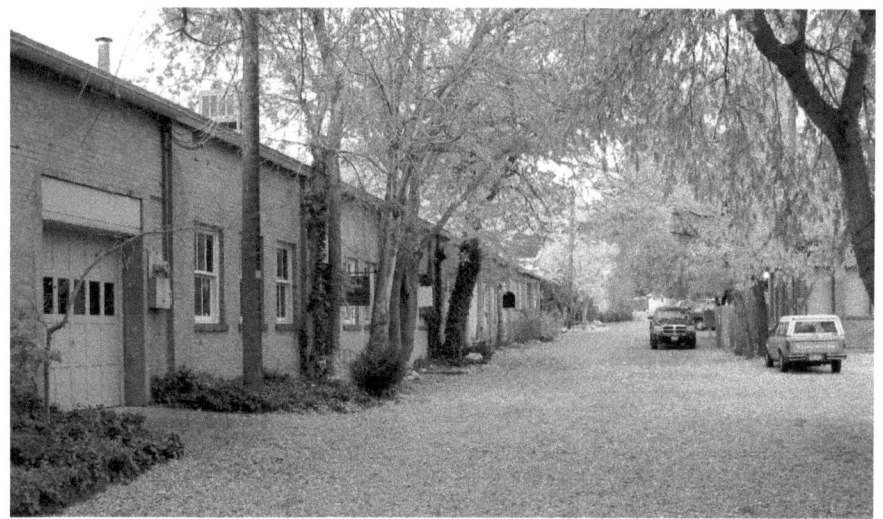

Baldwin Radio factory in 2017 as renovated rental spaces for art studios, businesses and a restaurant. *Author's collection.*

of the 1920s, performed several plural marriages at his home in Centerville for those involved.

To increase production, Baldwin granted a manufacturing license to a group of seven Utah businessmen, including David A. Smith, a son of the late Joseph F. Smith, who was by then a member of the Presiding Bishopric of the LDS Church.[81] Baldwin counted on the royalties from this contract to increase production and build other businesses. Unfortunately, the contract failed, and Baldwin never received the promised royalties. Without these funds and with his expenses for expanding, Baldwin's cash flow dramatically suffered.

Ernest R. Woolley, a cousin of Lorin's, promised to help. Baldwin's dealings with Ernest at first inspired hope but ended in frustration and panic when it became obvious Ernest could not obtain the needed financing. By autumn 1925, Baldwin was unable to pay employee wages or suppliers. After employees filed complaints, Baldwin's company was court-ordered into receivership. The receivers immediately fired any employees or company directors with new polygamy connections. By early 1926, Baldwin had become convinced that Ernest, along with Lorin and others, had tried to steal his company, and he made a startling decision to cooperate with the receivership. Further, with the legal support of Matthias F. Cowley, he filed a lawsuit against Ernest, Lorin and others. The parting was rancorous, as Baldwin no longer trusted Lorin.[82] In the end, the court ruled in favor of Baldwin.

In 1927, Baldwin received his company back in good shape, but his fortune did not last. New partners, unaffiliated with the Woolleys or former religious friends, got him into legal trouble. He got full blame as president of the company and was sentenced to five years in a federal prison; he served only two, released early for good behavior. Meanwhile, Baldwin lost his company and everything he owned, never again to succeed in business. He died years later, a pauper living in a son's home, still bitter against Lorin Woolley. Ironically, his youngest daughter converted with her husband to the Woolley tradition, and from her, a large posterity continues among today's Fundamentalists.

Nathaniel Baldwin's impact cannot be underestimated for helping spread early Fundamentalist beliefs via his radio factory where, for only a few years, a small core of believers in continued plural marriage grew, developed and flourished. The results of this short watershed period in the early 1920s practically guaranteed the movement would last.

PROMINENT FAMILIES

Several pro-polygamy families known for their stalwart Mormon pioneer ancestry coalesced around the Baldwin factory and the Woolleys in the early 1920s. These converts forged bonds and made permanent ties through shared religious convictions and new marriages between families. The LDS Church excommunicated such believers when their involvement with new plural marriages was discovered. Most of the family surnames of that era are still prominent among Fundamentalists today. Families who became believers in the 1920s include the surnames of Alder, Anderson, Bateman, Bautista, Bistline, Broadbent, Cox, Hull, Jenson, Johnson, Kelsch, Kilgrow, Kingston, Kimball, LeBaron, Nielsen, Olson, Spencer and Thompson. Five specific families—Barlow, Jessop, Musser, Steed and Allred—discussed next became especially prominent in the early movement.

Barlow

Israel Barlow Jr. and some members of his family, including John Y. Barlow, Edmund F. Barlow and Ianthius W. Barlow, became early believers in the

Woolleys' accounts. The Barlows hailed from an eminent early Latter-day Saint family. Israel Barlow Jr., like his father before him, was actively involved in both church and community in West Bountiful, where the family had lived since 1848, except for a few years spent running a church ranch on Antelope Island in the middle of the Great Salt Lake.[83]

The Barlows operated a sugar mill and made molasses, and Israel Jr. served as the Davis County assessor. Annie Yeates Barlow, wife of Israel Jr., served as president of the West Bountiful Relief Society, the local women's organization of the church, for over thirty years. Israel Jr., a church patriarch, was nearly seventy years old in 1910 when the *Salt Lake Tribune* listed him among "Some New Polygamists" and was subsequently tried before the Davis Stake High Council and excommunicated, "for marrying illegally and in violation of the rules and regulations of the Church...for lying and for treating the council with contempt in neither appearing in person nor responding in any way to the summons of the council served upon him to appear...and answer the charges made against him."[84]

Some of Israel Jr.'s sons and grandsons worked for Baldwin in the early 1920s. In his eighties, Israel Jr. led scripture study at Baldwin's Omega building until his death in November 1923. The Barlows, who intermarried with the Jessop and Kelsch families in particular, claim a collective posterity among Fundamentalist groups and independents numbering in the thousands.

Jessop

The Joseph Smith Jessop family of Millville in Utah's northern Cache Valley made a significant impact on the spread of Fundamentalist Mormonism. The Jessops were well respected and a part of the cultural fabric of Millville. When the town was incorporated in 1902, Joseph Smith Jessop became one of the four town trustees, serving a few more times over the following decades. Joseph, his son Joseph Lyman and his brother Moroni "Rone" played in the Millville Brass Band and joined a traveling dramatic company that performed in towns in northern Utah and southern Idaho.[85] Lyman served a term as the town marshal in 1920.

Joseph S. Jessop, his brother Rone and his sister Frances became actively involved with the polygamy movement after working at the Baldwin radio factory and meeting the Woolleys, although Frances's husband, Martin Olson, never married a plural wife. Within a short time, these Jessop siblings and their families went from being pillars of the Millville community to

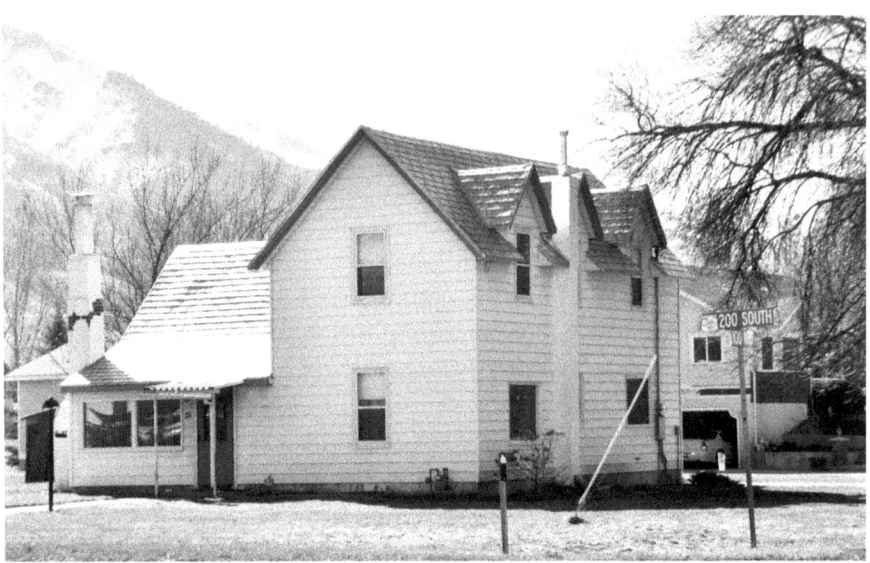

Joseph Smith Jessop home in Millville, Utah. *Steven L. Mayfield Collection.*

being outcasts. A daughter of Joseph S. Jessop, Fawnetta "Fawn," later remembered, "We were blacklisted" after the family heard and accepted the news of the Woolleys' message, which had been brought by relatives Israel Barlow Jr. and John Y. Barlow.[86]

In the latter half of 1923, a series of events solidified the Joseph S. Jessop family's commitment to the belief that plural marriage was as necessary and valid as it had ever been. On September 1, Lyman noted that family members were fasting and praying for his sister Martha "Mattie" Jessop, who wanted "to know the Lord's will concerning her...marrying in plural marriage." Mattie soon after became a plural wife of John Y. Barlow. When news of her marriage leaked to members of the community, she was excommunicated, which "made a great big splash" in the town. Her brother Richard recounted being subsequently questioned by church authorities and then refused entrance into the LDS Logan Temple.[87] About the same time, when another sister, Genevieve Jessop Anderson, died from a prolonged illness, the Jessop family asked Lorin C. Woolley to speak at her funeral in the Millville church house. He shocked and angered some in attendance by testifying of the reality of the resurrection but more specifically by stating, "I know there is a resurrection for I have seen and shook hands with resurrected men who have died since I was a grown man." Fawn Jessop Broadbent remembered, "The people didn't receive it

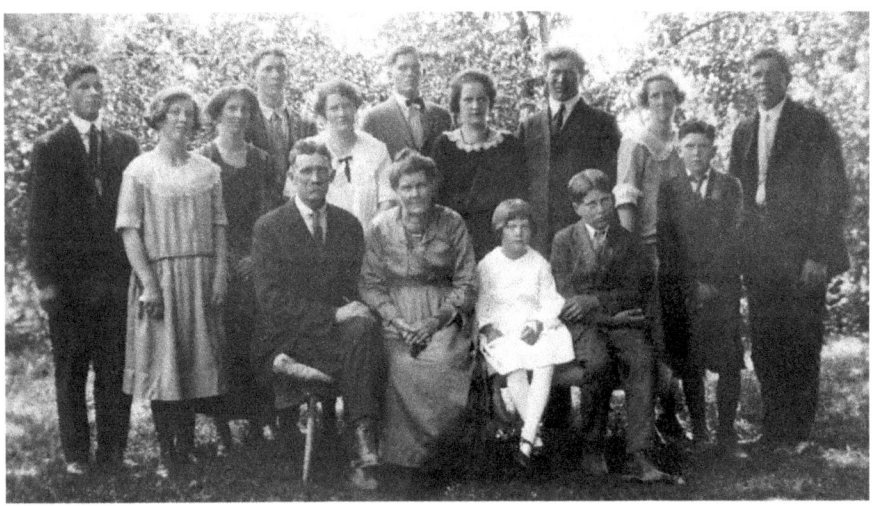

Joseph Smith Jessop family in 1923. *Authors' collection.*

at all," and some of her unbelieving family members referred to Woolley as "a little black devil."[88] In 1930, Joseph S. and his wife Martha's youngest son, John Millward Jessop, died. They again asked Lorin Woolley to speak at the funeral, this time held in the family's backyard because they were not allowed to have it in the Millville church.

Before this last funeral, Joseph S. had married Gertrude Annie Marriott as a plural wife, which added to the family's estrangement in the small community. At the time of the 1930 census, a Millville census taker wrote "illegal wife" above Annie's name when enumerating the Jessop household, obviously reflecting his own attitude toward plural marriage and the family.[89]

Some Millville relatives of the Jessops, the Jensons and Olsons, also became converts. In the 1930s, the Jenson family hosted in their home at various times Lorin C. Woolley and Joseph White Musser, another early Fundamentalist leader. The Jensons had been respected church and community leaders but experienced ostracism after accepting the Woolleys' message in the early 1920s. All three families eventually left Millville, some settling in the Salt Lake Valley and others farther south.

The Jessop name remains prominent among Fundamentalists. Family historians report that Joseph Smith Jessop's posterity numbers over ten thousand because nearly all his children became involved in plural marriages and had large families.

Musser

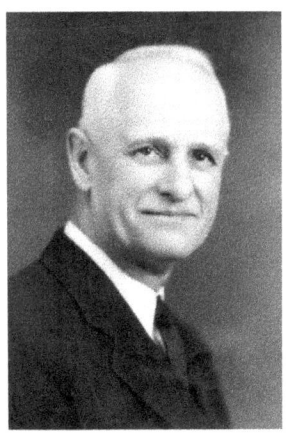

Joseph W. Musser, age sixty.
Authors' collection.

Some have called Joseph White Musser the "father of the Mormon Fundamentalist movement" because of his prolific writings that articulate doctrine and the Fundamentalist position in relation to the LDS Church. Like the Barlow and Jessop families, he too came from early Mormon stalwarts. Joseph's father, Amos Milton Musser, became an assistant church historian and a special bishop of the church. Joseph's mother, Mary Elizabeth White, was the second of four wives. Musser served two LDS missions, was involved in local church leadership and married two church-sanctioned post-Manifesto plural wives.[90] One among many trusted brethren during Joseph F. Smith's administration, he received delegated authority in 1915 to perform post–Second Manifesto plural marriages.

Musser was excommunicated in 1921 for pursuing additional plural marriages. He first met Lorin C. Woolley in 1922 after he and his wife Ellis were invited to an evening fireside at the Baldwin radio factory. Afterward, he brought Lorin home to stay the night, and they talked until late. Joseph noted in his journal, "The testimony of Lorin C. Woolley always rings true" and that he "love[d] to hear" him "talk and rehearse the things that happened while he was guarding the brethren."[91] He too believed that plural marriage should not, indeed could not, be given up for acceptance by the rest of society, and he became a firm believer in the Woolleys' message. Nevertheless, even after he published numerous books and pamphlets expounding priesthood doctrines and criticizing the LDS Church for apostasy in its rejection of earlier tenets, he believed it was still God's church and foresaw its ultimate victory: "I have faith in the ultimate success of the Mormon Church. It alone of all institutions in the world, is built on principles of truth, justice and mercy….And tho [*sic*] the Church has changed many of its tenets in order to comply with the convenience of men, it will not fall."[92]

Musser's children grew up actively engaged with the LDS Church. After Lorin Woolley called him as a member of the Priesthood Council, only his son Guy believed and joined him. Through Guy, some of Musser's descendants are still involved as Fundamentalists.

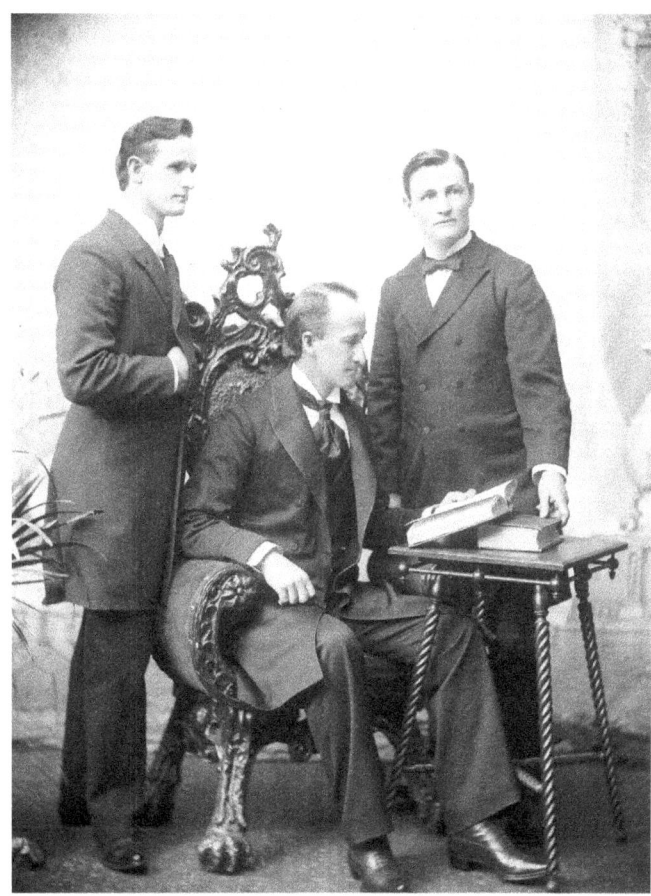

Left: Joseph W. Musser (*left*) with Indian Territory missionary companions Elias Kimball (*seated*) and W.W. Chipman in April 1897. *Authors' collection*.

Below: Joseph W. Musser with two of his plural wives, a daughter and four grandchildren. *Authors' collection*.

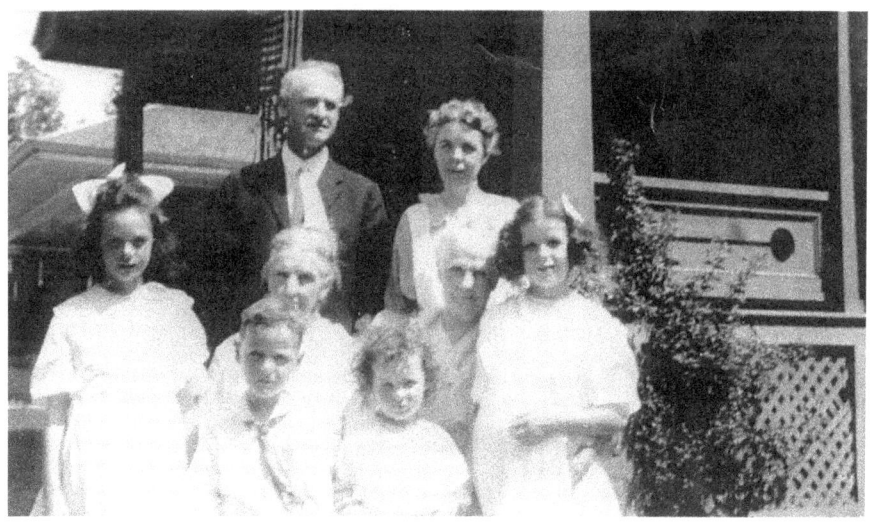

Steed

Descendants of the Steed family of Davis County, Utah, have played a major role in the world of Fundamentalist Mormons. In 1851, Thomas Steed and a cousin settled in Farmington with their families. Thomas married a total of four wives and farmed their homestead on Steed Creek at the mouth of Steed Canyon in the south part of Farmington. He owned a gristmill that burned down while he was away on one of his several missions for the LDS Church. He later helped build the historic Farmington Rock Chapel and served on the Davis Stake High Council at the same time as John W. Woolley.[93]

Thomas's son Walter William Steed grew up in Farmington, where he became prominent in the community and church. He farmed and raised stock, became a director for both the Davis Weber County Canal company and Davis County Bank and helped found Clearfield State Bank. He also served as a school trustee and a Davis County commissioner. Walter actively served in the church, filling several positions. Like his father, he was a member of the Davis Stake High Council.[94]

In 1897, Walter married Alice Belle Clark as a sanctioned post-Manifesto plural wife. She was the daughter of Ezra T. Clark, who had served on the

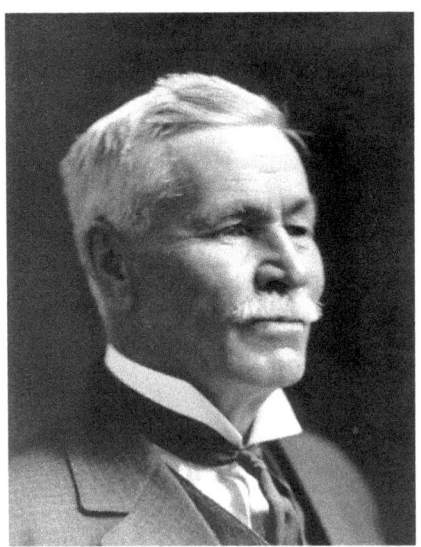 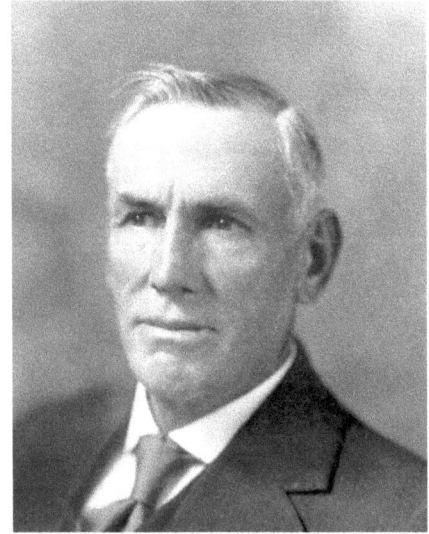

Left: Thomas J. Steed (1852–1921). *Right*: Walter W. Steed (1858–1940). *Both, FamilySearch.org Family Tree.*

high council with Thomas Steed and John W. Woolley and was the father-in-law of John's daughter Emma. After this marriage, Walter moved both wives to Syracuse, where he farmed and became involved in a local co-op that was known as Steed's Post Office.[95]

According to a family biographer who opposed polygamy, Walter began associating with John W. Taylor, Matthias Cowley, "and other prominent Mormons who challenged the LDS Church manifesto abandoning polygamy," and "defiantly" married his third wife, Lillie Sandberg, in 1918. Within a few years, "Walter was 'outed' by a neighbor, excommunicated from the LDS Church, and forced to 'go underground' to avoid prosecution by the law." His life as a Fundamentalist took a toll on the Steed family, and according to the same biographer, "Walter spent little time with his first two wives after marrying Lillie."[96]

Walter's plural wife Lillie was a younger sister of Ellen Sandberg Taylor and an older sister of Josephine Sandberg Steed Baldwin. Ellen had been a plural wife of John W. Taylor. Josephine first married as a plural wife to Walter Steed's older brother, Thomas J. Steed. After Thomas's death, she again married plurally, this time to Nathaniel Baldwin, as mentioned.

Walter's Fundamentalist posterity, numbering many thousands, has been mostly involved in the southern Utah/northern Arizona communities of Hildale and Colorado City.

Allred

Byron Harvey Allred Jr., a prominent Mormon in Idaho, became involved with continued plural marriage in the late 1920s, after the Baldwin radio era. A post-Manifesto polygamist, Harvey had known both John W. Taylor and Matthias F. Cowley due to his 1903 sanctioned plural marriage in Mexico. He had been sent by President Joseph F. Smith to Cowley, who recommended moving to the Mormon colonies in Mexico so he could live "the fulness of the gospel." After marrying a plural wife and living five years in Mexico, he returned to the United States and moved both his families to Idaho, where his first wife soon died in childbirth.

Later, Harvey was elected as an Idaho state legislator and also served one session as Idaho's Speaker of the House in 1917. Harvey first learned of continued plural marriage in 1925. In 1927, he became reacquainted with Lorin Woolley and remembered Lorin's testimony during his mission to Indian Territory that he had seen the Prophet Joseph Smith since his

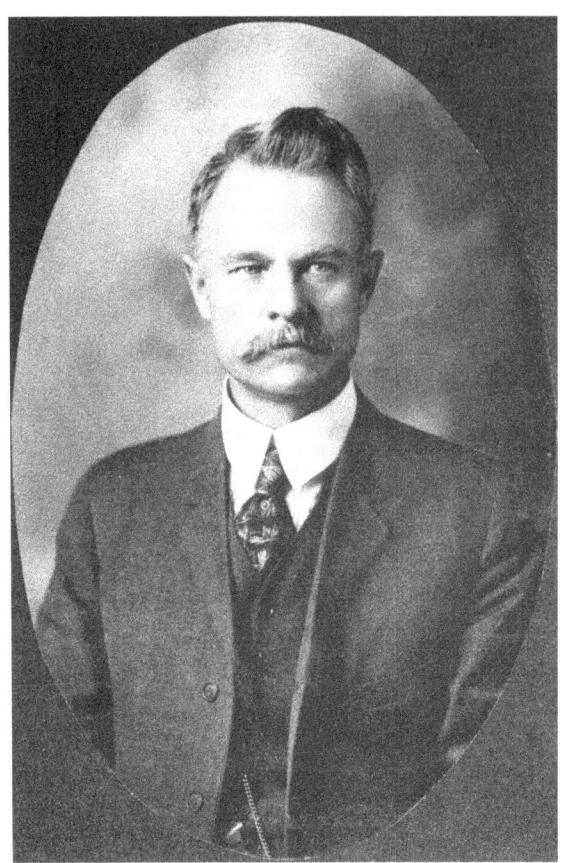

Left: B. Harvey Allred (1870–1937). *Authors' collection.*

Below: B. Harvey Allred home (1917–19) at 1504 Warm Springs Avenue in Boise, Idaho, 2018. *Author's collection.*

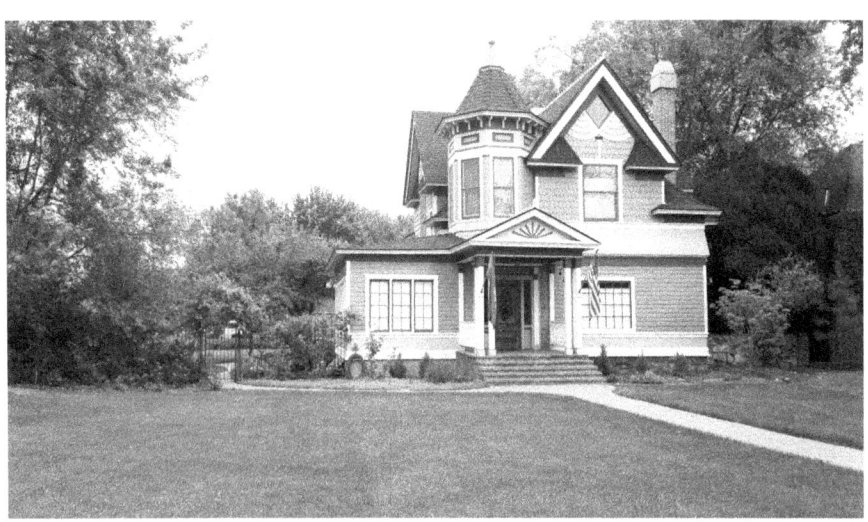

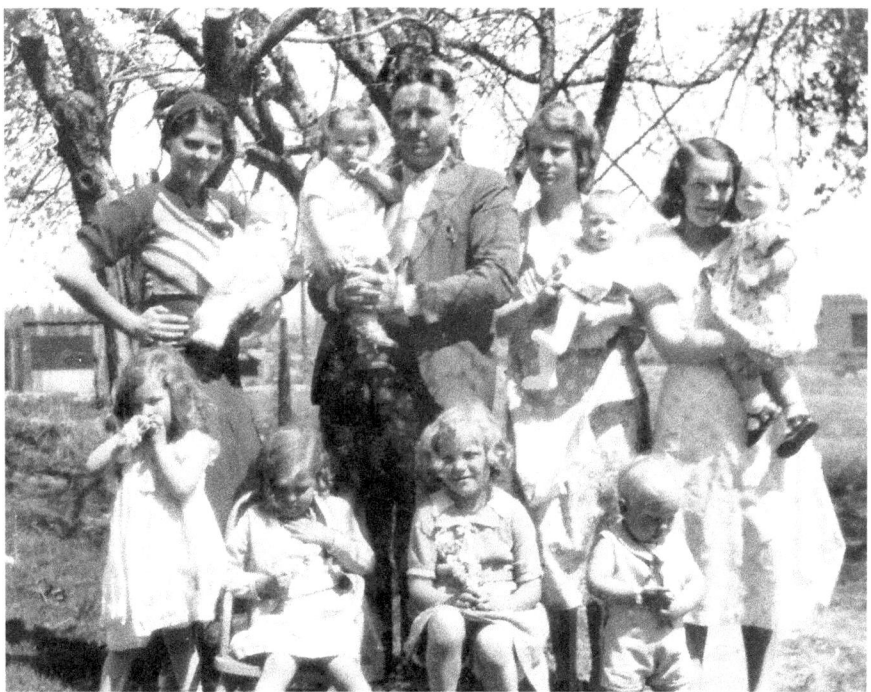

Morris Q. Kunz with three of his wives and eight children, circa 1935. Morris's first two wives, Rhea and Olive, were daughters of B. Harvey Allred. Ellen Halliday was his third wife. *Donna K. Mackert Collection.*

death.[97] After learning Lorin's full account, he believed. He soon began a manuscript chiding Mormons and their leaders for their abandonment of certain doctrines, especially plural marriage. He included an account of the 1886 events. He published his book, *A Leaf in Review*, in 1933.

Harvey married his last plural wife in 1935. Charged with "teaching and/or encouraging the practice of so-called polygamous or plural marriage contrary to the adopted rule and the express instructions of the Church," he was excommunicated in January 1936. He died a year later, on January 18, 1937.[98]

Harvey's niece Sylvia Allred was probably the first Allred to marry plurally. In June 1928, John W. Woolley performed her marriage to her husband, Isaac Carling Spencer, who had earlier come from southern Utah to work at the Baldwin radio factory. Several of Sylvia's and Harvey's children also became involved, and three of Harvey's sons, Rulon, Marvin and Owen, later emerged as leaders. Among contemporary Fundamentalists, Allreds number in the thousands and Spencers in the hundreds. Many of them married Kunzes, Barlows, Jessops and other early Fundamentalists.

THE WOOLLEYS IN THE LATE 1920s

After Nathaniel Baldwin's break from Lorin Woolley, Lorin hired Baldwin's former employees Moroni Jessop and Jessop's nephew Lyman to work on the Woolley farms in Centerville. These two men worked seasonally for Lorin and John for the next few years. Lyman made a special effort to bring his older children, one or two at a time, to meet John Woolley, whom they affectionately called "Grandpa." John took the opportunity to have them sit in a specific rocking chair and tell them that was where the Savior sat on a September night in 1886 talking with President Taylor. That chair, still owned by a Fundamentalist family, continues to provide a tangible link to accounts retold of the 1886 events in the Woolley home. At least two plural wives, Sylvia Allred and Mary Viola Anderson, who were married to their respective husbands by John Woolley just before his death, each told of how he invited them to sit in that chair and explained why it was important.[99] Mary recalled her marriage on November 11, 1928, weeks before John Woolley died:

> *When we* [my second husband and I] *went there it was afternoon, and I had taken time off work long enough to get the sealing done....On*

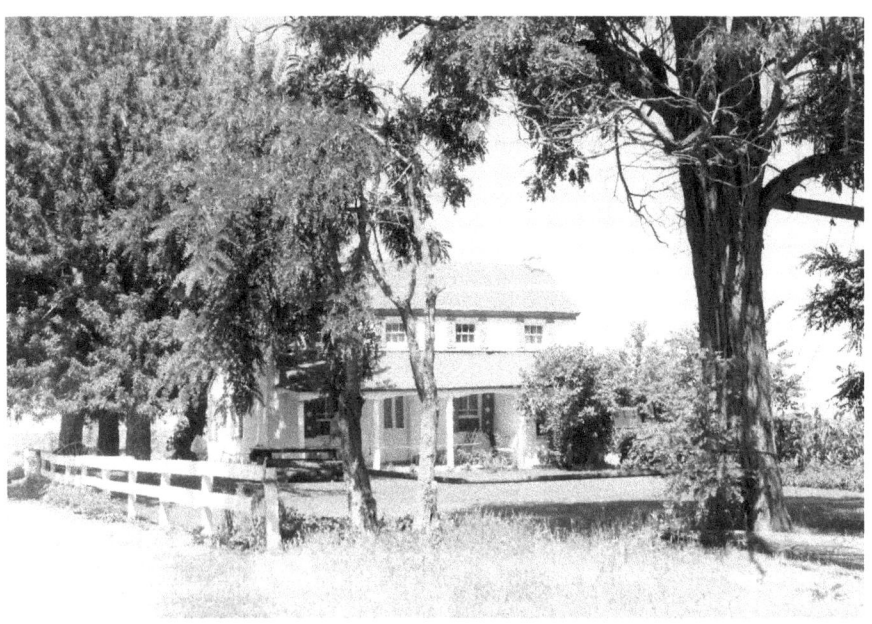

John W. Woolley Circleville home, circa 1960s. *Donna K. Mackert Collection.*

that day he invited us to come into the front room and invited me to sit down in the rocking chair. He said, "You see this rocking chair you are sitting in." I said, "Yes." He said, "The Saviour has sat in that chair." So I felt honored and privileged to sit in the same chair. We got married in the same room that the Saviour and the Prophet Joseph Smith were in at the time of the 8-hour meeting [in 1886]. *There was a good spirit there. You couldn't help but feel it. It seemed like the atmosphere, and the influence, was still there after all those years.*[100]

Some who kept diaries, including Lyman Jessop and Joseph Musser, recorded things John and Lorin Woolley told them. Musser recorded many of Lorin's sayings, dreams, predictions and spiritual experiences. In July 1926, Lorin C. Woolley prophesied of "perilous times to come in which… those who would live the law [of plural marriage] would be at the point of annihilation because the persecution would be so great."[101] With such apocalyptic expectations in mind, Woolley sent Lyman Jessop and two of his brothers, Richard and Vergel, to northern Arizona to meet with polygamists Carling Spencer, Jerry Johnson and Elmer Johnson at Lee's Ferry, Arizona, and with Isaac Carling in Short Creek, Arizona. Their purpose, in anticipation of persecution, was to see if either place might work for a potential "gathering place for the saints."[102]

THE 1928 VISITATION AND THE COUNCIL OF FRIENDS

On December 4, 1928, nine days before John Woolley's death, John and Lorin sought God for specific direction because they were the last of the men called in 1886. Lorin told a few how he and his father received the direction they needed. He said they were visited by six beings from heaven in answer to prayer.[103] He said they were instructed to call others to the same calling they had been given—in other words, call men to the apostleship of Christ with the same appointment to keep plural marriage alive.

Moroni Jessop, who worked on the Woolley farms, related, "Lorin told me all about it. John W. told me a little about it." He later reported what he had learned from them about the 1928 visitation:

In the year 1928, Grandpa Woolley died.…A message then came that grandpa Woolley was wanted on the other side, too, to give a report of what was wanted. Some nine days previous to the death of grandpa, a meeting was held in his home at Centerville. In that meeting he was given just nine days to live and make preparations before he was to pass over.... That special priesthood meeting was held on the 4th of December.... There were just eight men at that priesthood meeting. Six of them were from the other side, two from this side. John W. Woolley and his son Lorin were the only two from this side. The other six were resurrected beings. They were: Jesus Christ, Joseph Smith, the prophet, his father Joseph Smith senior, Hyrum Smith, John Taylor and Joseph F. Smith....Lorin told me the Savior produced the bread and wine at that supper right before us. He said, "Lordie, what wonderful wine that was!"[104]

John W. Woolley died on December 13, 1928. His granddaughter Olive remembered his funeral, held at the Centerville church house, was "very big."[105] David A. Smith, son of the late president Joseph F. Smith (whose company had failed its contract with Nathaniel Baldwin), spoke at the funeral, remarking, "How my father loved that man [John Woolley]."[106]

After his father's death, Lorin Woolley acted according to the divine instructions he said he and his father had received. Over the next two and a half years, he called six men to the apostleship of Christ to again fill a council of seven. This council became known as the "Council of Seven" or "Council of Friends," or more commonly the "Priesthood Council." Woolley gave to these men the responsibility for the continuation of plural marriage after his death.[107] Lorin explained this council was not a church quorum or in lieu of the presiding LDS Church leadership quorum, but it was a priesthood quorum acting outside and apart from the church to accomplish a certain "Priesthood Work." From Lorin's words, the various groups of believers came to call their purpose by the term "the Work," or "the Priesthood Work."

The six men called by Lorin Woolley to serve in this council were Joseph Leslie Broadbent, John Yeates Barlow, Joseph White Musser, Charles Frederick Zitting, LeGrand Woolley and Louis Alma Kelsch. Woolley ordained these men the same way he said he had been ordained by John Taylor—bestowing upon them "every key, power, and authority"

Clockwise from top left: Lorin C. Woolley (1856–1934). *Authors' collection*; J. Leslie Broadbent (1891–1935). *Authors' collection*; John Y. Barlow (1874–1949). *FamilySearch.org Family Tree*; Joseph W. Musser (1872–1954). *Authors' collection*; Charles F. Zitting (1894–1954). *FamilySearch.org Family Tree*; Louis A. Kelsch (1895–1974). *FamilySearch.org Family Tree*. Photo of LeGrand Woolley (1887–1932) unavailable.

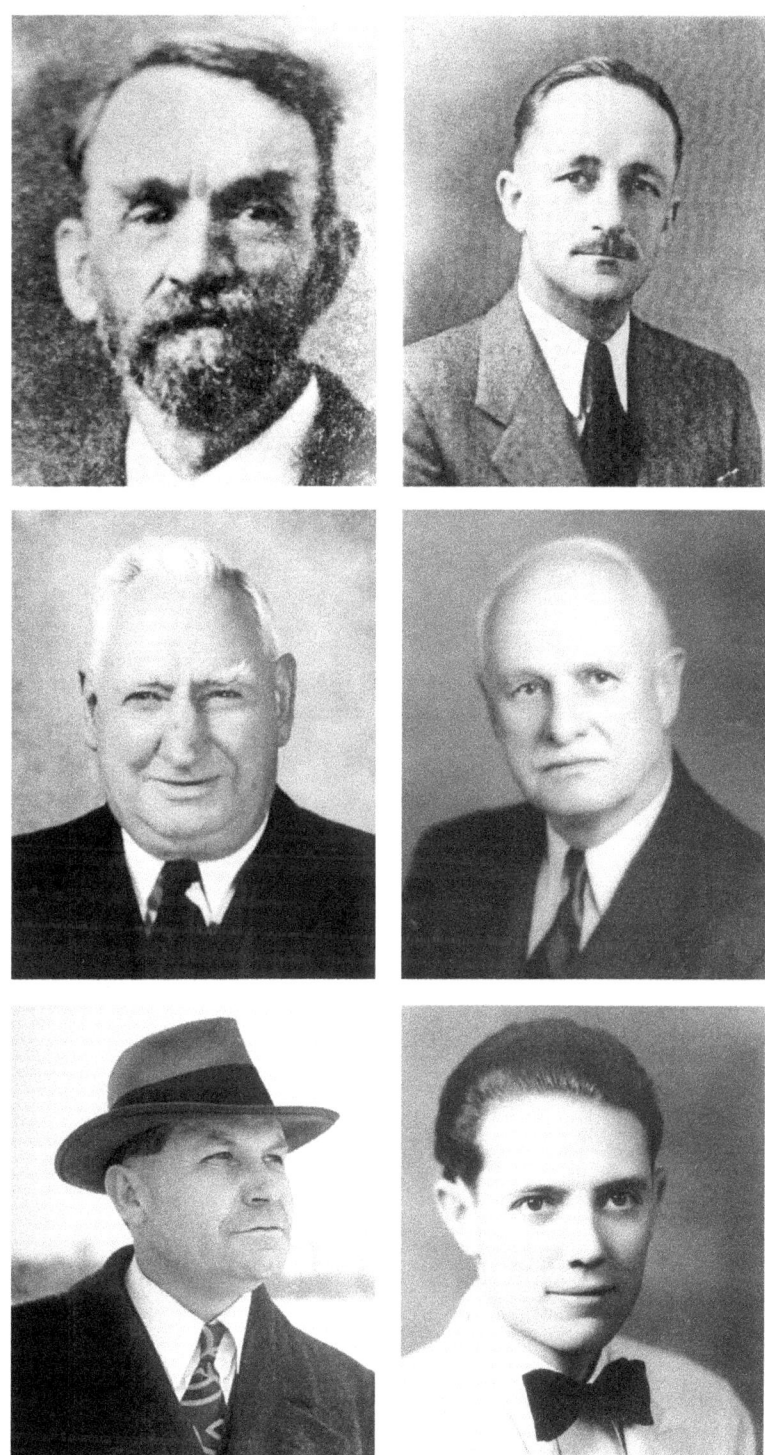

that he himself held and giving them a specific charge to ordain others as necessary to ensure that no year passed without children born from polygamous unions. These men were told by Woolley their mission was to testify of truth and perpetuate every gospel law and ordinance restored and established by Joseph Smith that the LDS Church could not or would not preserve.

One of the first orders of business conducted by the Priesthood Council in 1929 was to compile and publish a full account of Lorin Woolley's statement about the 1886 events. With it, the council included a short affidavit by Daniel Bateman supporting Lorin's account. Publications containing Lorin Woolley's statement continued to vex the LDS Church as the church committed to monogamy, expanded its worldwide missionary program and distanced itself from its polygamous past. President Grant repeatedly repudiated continued plural marriage, denied the existence of the 1886 revelation and denounced Lorin Woolley and others by name in church meetings. This led to a turbulent time in the 1930s for both the Church of Jesus Christ and Fundamentalists.

THE TURBULENT 1930S

I n the early 1930s, the Priesthood Council began compiling additional materials to publicly address the LDS Church's departure, as the council saw it, from fundamental teachings of Joseph Smith. For this, the members published pamphlets citing the 1886 revelations and other revelations unknown to most LDS church members and included with them Lorin Woolley and Daniel Bateman's statements about the 1886 events. They also published correspondence between polygamists and church leaders debating plural marriage and other abandoned doctrines.[108] The Priesthood Council boldly mailed thousands of its publications to local bishops, other church leaders and members.

In efforts to permanently end plural marriage in the church, President Heber J. Grant initiated surveillance of suspected polygamists, instituted a loyalty oath for members under suspicion and increasingly cooperated with local, state and federal governments for the prosecution of polygamists. Ultimately, these efforts resulted in two polygamy raids during his administration. Grant's adamant opposition seemed to generate even greater fervency among believers who clung to the original teachings of Joseph Smith as they understood them.

THE 1933 FINAL MANIFESTO

The spread of Fundamentalist literature became intolerable for LDS Church leaders because the church by then had been struggling for forty years to persuade a doubtful nation that its efforts to end polygamy were

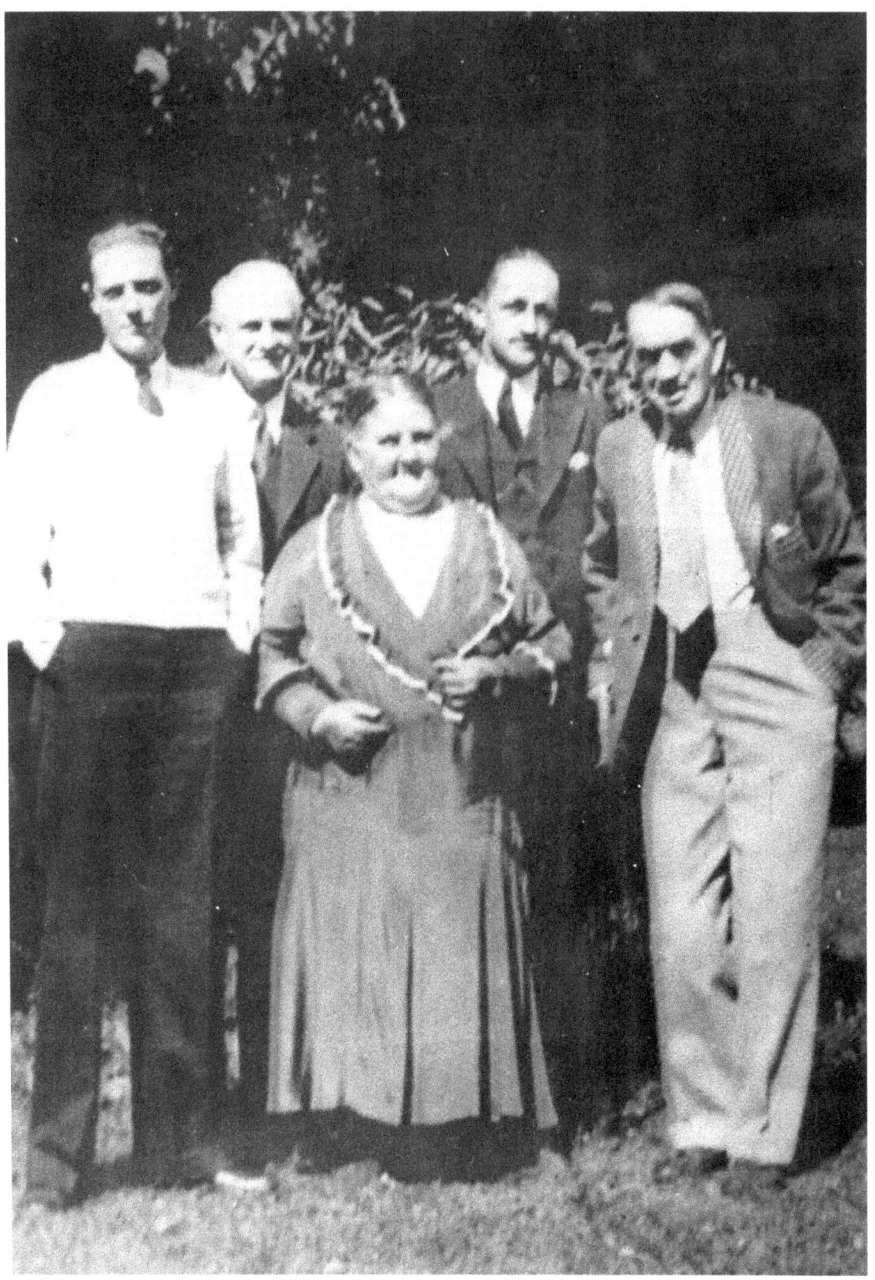

Anna Kmetsch with four sons-in-law, 1933. *Left to right*: Louis Kelsch, Joseph Musser, Leslie Broadbent and Lorin Woolley. *Authors' collection*.

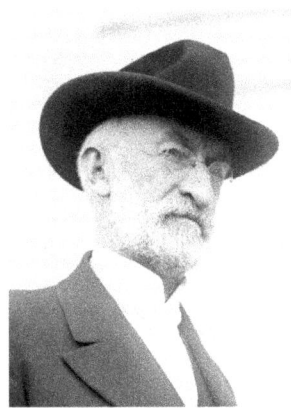

Seventh LDS Church president Heber J. Grant (1856–1945). *Wikimedia Commons, U.S. PD-1923.*

genuine. President Grant rigorously directed the excommunication of any members involved in new plural marriages. In the April 1931 General Conference of the church, President Grant also promised to "give such legal assistance as we legitimately can in the criminal prosecution of such [plural marriage] cases." Two years later, Grant presented an "Official Statement," a sixteen-page statement, sometimes called the "Third" or "Final Manifesto," that went far beyond previous church statements to deny the legitimacy of plural marriages after 1890 or the existence of the 1886 revelation.[109] Simultaneously, the church initiated cooperation with the government for the surveillance and prosecution of polygamists and also introduced a compulsory loyalty oath for any church members whose actions or sympathies might be suspect. Further, the church gave behind-the-scenes encouragement to the mostly Mormon Utah State Legislature to pass anti-polygamy legislation.[110]

For the Fundamentalists, a place of refuge became increasingly important in 1934, when it was rumored that "[t]he officers of the law are looking seriously into the family life of several of us, and it looks like persecution is nearing."[111] Only a few days later, Lyman Jessop recorded:

> *We have news from reliable sources that Officers of the Federal Government of the U.S. are here from Washington at the solicitation of Heber J. Grant and his helpers to persecute and imprison and penalize those who are trying to obey the fulness of the gospel. Heber J. Grant says to them, "Give them the limit and the Church will furnish the money to fight the case."*[112]

The threats appeared to be real—a few days later, one man and his wife, Abe and Rosa Teerlink, were arrested and briefly jailed on charges relating to polygamy. Some polygamists immediately went into hiding. For the next few months, in response to threats of legal prosecution, the Priesthood Council directed energies toward holding prayer circles and encouraging personal and communal fasting. The council published yet another book in defense of Fundamentalist beliefs, wrote an open letter of warning to President Grant and "all those who are persecuting the saints" and began searching for a place of refuge, even considering a proposition for Mexico.[113]

DEATH OF LORIN C. WOOLLEY

In the growing crisis, Lorin C. Woolley died on September 20, 1934, after a lingering illness of almost a year.

Before his death, he had told some of his closest associates, "When I die, I want men like Leslie Broadbent and John Barlow to speak at my funeral, and I don't want to be taken to the church house where they won't let me preach the gospel in it while I live."[114] Nevertheless, his funeral was held in the Centerville church house, and Governor Henry H. Blood, who also was the North Davis Stake president, and two brethren of the Centerville bishopric spoke, expressing the following:

> *John W. Woolley, father of the deceased would go on as a Patriarch of his family throughout the eternities, and that Lorin would do likewise, each of them having lived the Patriarchal order* [plural marriage] *in the New and Everlasting covenant of Marriage, as well as having lived all other principles of the Gospel, as revealed, to the best of their knowledge.*[115]

The speakers lauded Lorin, one stating, "No request was ever made of him for help that he did not respond to liberally." Noting that Lorin had served two missions, one said, "[A]nd don't tell me he will lose any of his reward. He did not go out for dollars and cents, but for the glory of God."[116]

At the funeral, Governor Blood also "announced the death of Pres. Anthony W. Ivins." A large extra of the *Deseret News* announced Ivins's death but only published a few lines about Woolley's passing. That same evening, a small crowd of believers held a private meeting to honor Lorin's life. They sang his favorite hymn, "Come Come Ye Saints," as well as a song, "The Seven," composed by Lorin's plural wife Goulda in honor of Lorin and the six men he had called to the Priesthood Council. Those gathered heard each of the six men speak and pay "beautiful tribute [to Lorin] as best they could by preaching the gospel to us."[117]

Lorin left behind a small but flourishing group of believers under the direction of the Priesthood Council, led by J. Leslie Broadbent. The legacy of John W. and Lorin C. Woolley continues to this day, and the major polygamous groups all trace their origins to these two men.

The small nucleus determined to hold firmly by faith to the "fullness of the restored gospel" as they understood Joseph Smith's Mormonism. At the time of Lorin's death, they did not know of secret plans in progress by the Utah legislature to significantly increase the penalty for unlawful cohabitation as preparation for more intense prosecution of polygamists.

DAVIS COUNTY COOPERATIVE SOCIETY

Fundamentalists, like other segments of American society, were hit hard during the Great Depression. It was especially difficult to provide for their large families. One Fundamentalist group that had its birth in the midst of the depression was the Davis County Cooperative Society (DCCS).

The DCCS or the Latter Day Church of Christ is more commonly known by outsiders as the Kingston group and by insiders as "The Order" or "The Co-Op."[118] The group has its origins with Charles William Kingston, his son Charles Elden Kingston, other family members and a small group of like-minded people.

Like other early Fundamentalists, many early Co-Op members belonged to the LDS Church. According to representatives, Elden Kingston desired to live the Law of Consecration in which a person or family consecrates all their property and time to God for the building up of His Kingdom on earth. Kingston attempted to do so by consecrating everything to the LDS Church. However, the LDS Church was not living the Law of Consecration by that time (which is still the case, as it only accepts tithes of 10 percent as well as other specified donations). After his attempt to consecrate everything and being turned down, Elden approached J. Leslie Broadbent, then successor of the Council of Friends. According to Elden,

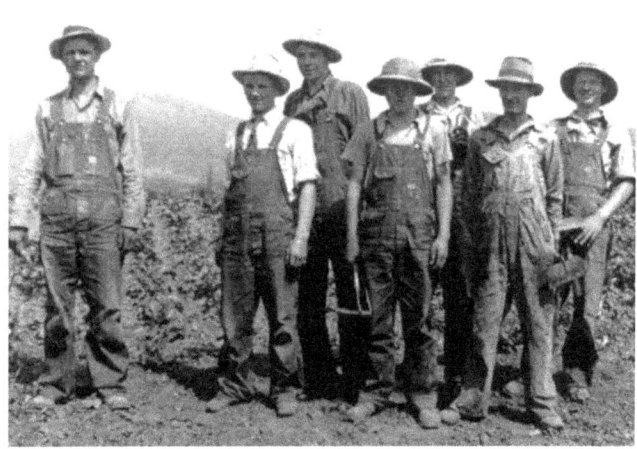

Kingston brethren in 1940. *Courtesy of Latter Day Church of Christ.*

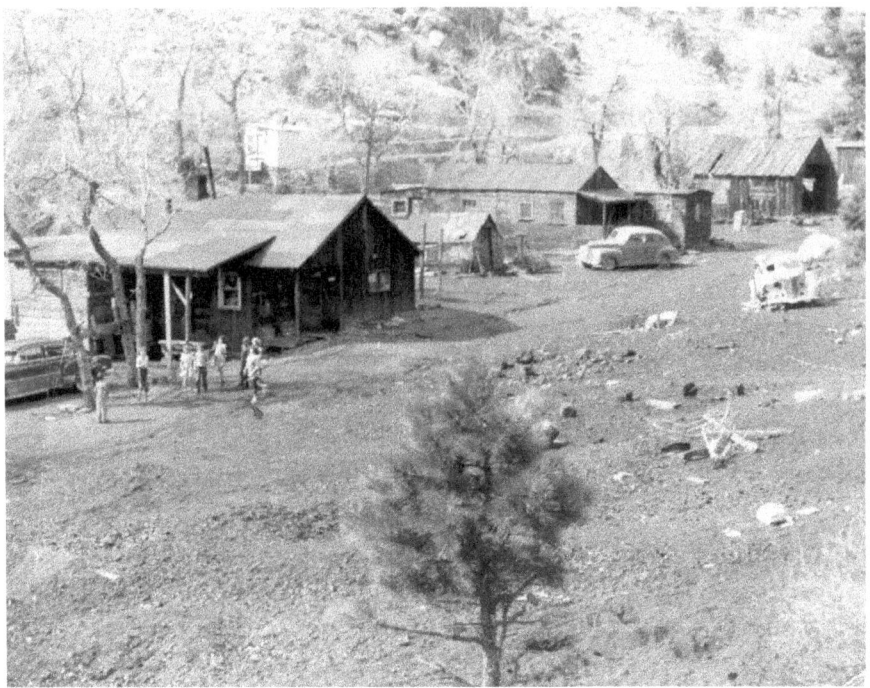

Kingstons' Trail Canyon coal mine. *Photo courtesy of Latter Day Church of Christ.*

Broadbent said the council was also unable to accept his consecration. After this final refusal, Co-Op members believe Elden Kingston was visited by a heavenly messenger who commanded him to establish a United Order that could accept consecrated time and properties from people desiring to live the Law of Consecration.[119]

In 1935, Elden and other associates created the DCCS. They incorporated in 1941 with the purpose of abolishing war and bloodshed and establishing "peace, good-will and brotherly love between ALL men." The goal was that all members "should have the opportunity to engage in productive enterprises suitable to their capacity and training" and "to bring about a condition so that…all members are self-sustaining by means of their own labors." In the early years of the DCCS, there were attempts to promote gospel egalitarianism as a better way of ridding themselves of worldly things in order to bring themselves closer to God. At one point, this included all men wearing denim coveralls and the women blue dresses.[120] This custom lasted only a few years, and Kingston members' attire now blends in with mainstream society.

THE 1935 UNLAWFUL COHABITATION LAW
AND *TRUTH* MAGAZINE

Just six months after Lorin Woolley died, his successor J. Leslie Broadbent died suddenly on March 16, 1935, after a short bout with flu. Broadbent's unexpected death at age forty-three was a shock to those who looked to him for leadership.[121]

When it had become apparent he was dying, Leslie told Joseph Musser, with only his plural wife Rula Kelsch Broadbent as a witness, that Musser was to succeed him in presiding over the Priesthood Council. However, because Musser's appointment had not been established as a fact in the Priesthood Council or among the people, Joseph Musser said nothing when John Y. Barlow asserted leadership based on his seniority in the council, having been ordained two months before Musser. Musser sustained Barlow as presiding member of the Priesthood Council on that basis. Barlow often leaned on Musser for getting divine answers when needed. Many knew by experience that Musser could get the word of the Lord for them when petitioned. Unfortunately, over the years that followed, John Barlow sowed seeds that would eventually result in a major split among followers after his death.

There was little opportunity for polygamy adherents to mourn Broadbent's passing. The same week of his death, the Utah State Legislature passed House Bill No. 124, which elevated the punishment for unlawful cohabitation from a misdemeanor to a felony, scheduled to go into effect two months later, May 15, 1935. The law was signed by Governor Henry H. Blood, who had spoken at Lorin Woolley's funeral six months before.[122]

When the brethren of the Priesthood Council learned about the new anti-polygamy law, they studied it over with an attorney and determined it was intended "to make trouble." The next day, the "largest assembly ever" gathered at Broadbent's home for a fast meeting. Later, several brethren met with the Priesthood Council, each affirming his resolve and "covenanted to keep all the commandments of the Lord."[123]

On May 10, 1935, just days before the law went into effect, Lyman Jessop and others met with brethren of the Priesthood Council and discussed a proposal from Price Johnson of Short Creek, Arizona, suggesting that place be made a place of refuge.[124] The last-minute plan was accepted.

At the same time, the Priesthood Council accepted Joseph W. Musser's proposal to publish a monthly magazine they named *TRUTH* to recirculate nineteenth-century sermons about plural marriage and

TRUTH

VOL. 1.	JUNE 1, 1935	NO. 1

ANNOUNCEMENT

WITH this issue TRUTH begins its life journey. There is need for the message its columns will bear. The world is sick. It gropes in darkness. Complete dissolution threatens the established governments. The situation can be saved only by quick and heroic action. God is the great Physician. Man must turn unto him. It will be our aim to help blaze the way leading through the maze of perplexity, prejudice, hatred and ignorance, up toward the "great white throne". We approach this delicate but all-important task with a deep sense of dependence on the Lord. We shall work hard to discharge our duty.

As we view it, the fundamentals governing man's existence on earth and his efforts to achieve salvation in the life to come, may be grouped under four general headings: POLITICAL, SOCIAL, ECONOMIC and SPIRITUAL. These four must be fully co-ordinated in the lives and actions of mankind before a complete success is possible. To the extent that this co-ordination is perfect, just to that extent may man hope to achieve. Growing out of these four governing principles are, of course, countless shoots and branches, all designed to strengthen and beautify the parent tree. But it is to the four principles mentioned that special attention is now directed.

The POILTICAL part of the world mechanism is sadly out of order. All governments are feverishly restless, continuously engaged in talking peace while preparing for war, and the whole earth is in commotion, and men's hearts are failing them. This situation can be corrected only when Jesus Christ shall set up his reign under the form of government known as the Kingdom of God, which is destined to subvert all other kingdoms and governments and sweep them from the earth.

TRUTH will endeavor to teach "this gospel of the Kingdom" as Christ has outlined it, to the end that mankind may receive full protection in civil and religious rights, finally arriving at a state of righteousness and universal peace.

The SOCIAL structure of modern Christendom is toppling to ruin. A complete breakdown threatens. The monogamic order of marriage, the boast of modern civilization, has failed. Gnawing at its very vitals, to which the glorious principle of marriage is slowly but surely succumbing, are the death-dealing agencies of infidelity, birth control and divorce. The remedy is comprehended in God's order of marriage known today as Celestial or Patriarchal marriage. It was revealed to Abraham by the Lord, and in the present dispensation was restored through the "Mormon" Prophet, Joseph Smith.

TRUTH will champion the cause of this great social law and will endeavor to lead men to a clearer light.

The world has fallen into an ECONOMIC maelstrom, which threatens commercial destruction. It struggles seemingly to no purpose, each effort taking it deeper into the quagmire of failure. God, through his Prophet, has said: "The wisdom of their wise men shall perish and the understanding of their prudent men shall be hid." This prophetic edict is fulfilled in the pres-

Truth magazine first edition cover. *Authors' collection.*

other gospel topics. The magazine also served as a medium to publicly address objections to LDS Church surveillance and the church's treatment of polygamists.

A REFUGE IN SHORT CREEK

To avoid possible arrest, Lyman Jessop, Carl Jentzch and Ianthius W. Barlow journeyed 350 miles south to Short Creek. They met with seven men from the area in a private priesthood meeting to make a plan of action. Each man "consecrated [his] all to the building of the Kingdom of God" and preparing Short Creek "for the coming of the saints...to build a city of Zion and feed eventually millions of people."[125] John Y. Barlow soon moved there with part of his family. Before the end of the summer, the small flock comprised sixty to one hundred souls.[126]

Building "the Kingdom" in the Short Creek desert during the Great Depression was no easy task.[127] They expended much energy just to obtain the basic needs of water, food and shelter along with gardening, hauling wood for cooking and baking, grinding wheat for bread and maintaining the few automobiles. They drew plans for a windmill, began ploughing land and planting crops, started gathering machine parts to construct a power plant and laid out streets for the city-to-be. Assignments were given to log trees or work at the local sawmill.

About two weeks after arriving, despondency set in among the men; then, contentions arose and grew until outright strife emerged. "The source of the deepest division," according to Lyman Jessop, "was John Y. Barlow's plan to form a trust or holding company as the beginning of a united order" with controversy centering on trust clauses that appeared "harsh and unfair." Also, the men differed over issues of authority regarding the presiding brethren, and one priesthood meeting erupted in verbal arguments. After Barlow provided an opportunity for every brother to express his views and ask forgiveness of one another, tensions eased somewhat.[128]

A few polygamists had been living in Short Creek before the decision was made to make it a place of refuge in 1935. The previous year, four LDS Short Creek branch members had been excommunicated for preaching or practicing polygamy.[129] The new residents who arrived in 1935 did not attend the LDS Short Creek branch meetings until they received personal invitations to do so. When some began attending, disagreements over doctrine soon surfaced. One Sunday meeting became especially strained

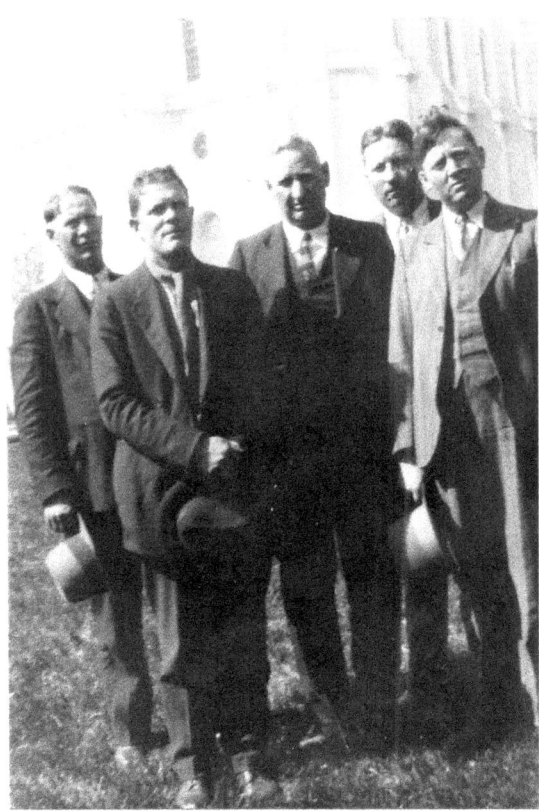

Left to right: Richard Jessop, Joseph Lyman Jessop, John Y. Barlow, Morris Kunz and Arnold Boss at LDS St. George Temple, 1930s. *Authors' collection.*

when some "[t]ook issue in favor of the laws of the Lord in preference to those of the land." The following Sunday, church leaders from the LDS Zions Park Stake came to set matters straight. They defended "the law of the land against polygamy, quoted scripture, and spent much time belittling anyone who should oppose the Manifesto, calling them silly people." After the meeting, some of the polygamists asked a local church leader to allow further discussion, which led to a "hot" scene of debate.[130] Instead of further reproof from the Stake leaders, complaints were made within a week to initiate prosecution against several on polygamy charges.[131]

Soon, a photographer showed up in Short Creek on a much-exaggerated tip wanting to see "the 400 people and 40 new homes under construction." He snapped a photo of the only house under construction and took a few shots of the little village. By that time, however, articles about the polygamists in Short Creek had already been published in the *Salt Lake Tribune*, and rumors circulated that leaders of the LDS Church were "urging the officers of Mohave County, Arizona, to arrest and embarrass" the polygamists.[132]

Two days later, the Mohave County sheriff and the county attorney came to Short Creek, looking to find someone to sign complaints so they could make arrests. After getting a local homesteader to do the deed, a media circus began. Six were arrested, four men and two women, on charges related to polygamy. The arrests drew media personnel "from the Atlantic to the Pacific coasts and north and south from Canada to the Mexican border." Short Creek justice of the peace J.M. Lauritzen held trial in the small schoolhouse, which "filled to overflowing with visitors from all across the state." Paramount News "set up a movie camera in the schoolhouse and [filmed] the entire proceedings." Reporters from a half-dozen newspapers noted every moment, with flashbulbs "exploding across the makeshift courtroom," and described the trial as "a comedy of errors." In the end, Lauritzen dismissed all charges because they were based on hearsay, "information and belief" amounting to rumor.[133]

The very next day, LDS Church authorities presented a loyalty oath to suspected members of the Short Creek branch, requiring them, on threat of excommunication, to declare their support of the First Presidency of the Church "without any mental reservation" and to "denounce the practice and advocacy of plural marriage."[134] This same loyalty was required for the Jessop, Jenson and Olson families in Millville, Utah; eight refused to sign and were excommunicated.

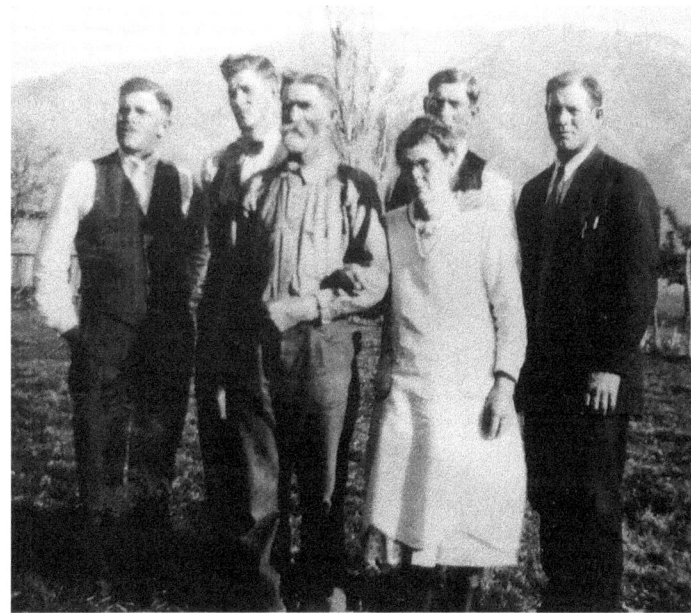

Joseph S. and Martha M. Yeates Jessop with sons. *Authors' collection.*

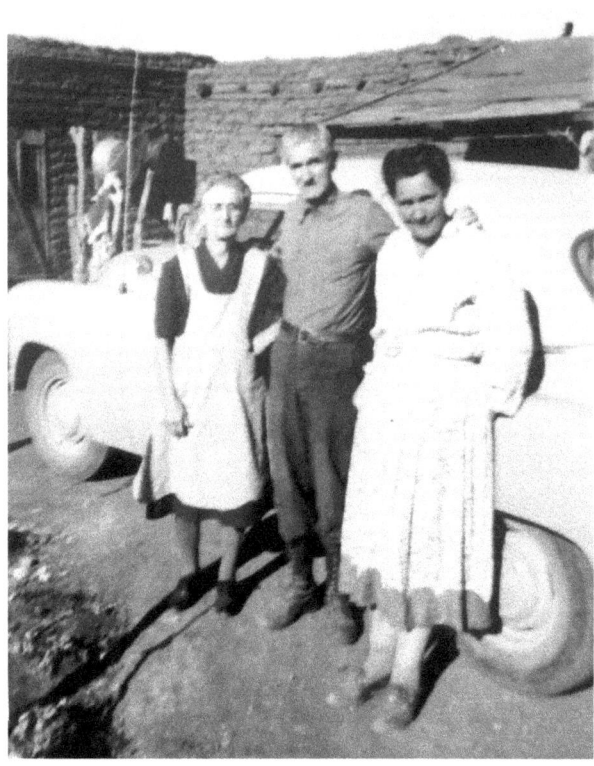

Isaac Carling Spencer and wives Lydia Johnson (*left*) and Sylvia Allred in Mexico. *Authors' collection.*

Meanwhile, new complaints against the polygamists were made and warrants again issued. Eventually, only two men and one woman were convicted: Price W. Johnson, Isaac Carling Spencer and Spencer's plural wife Sylvia Allred, who was pregnant with her fifth child. The *Kansas City Times* quoted Apostle Melvin J. Ballard as "admitting to the [church's] partial responsibility for the prosecution of Spencer, Allred and Johnson when it shared information with the government that had been gathered for Church trials."[135] The two aging men spent a difficult year in prison and were let out early for good behavior. Sylvia received a suspended sentence after the birth of her baby.[136] When it was all over, the Spencer family moved to Mexico to live their religion more freely.

Following the passage of Utah's 1935 Unlawful Cohabitation Law, it was no small irony that the very first prosecutions took place *not in Utah* but in Short Creek, Arizona, the very place where the polygamists sought refuge. It had been a last-minute decision, born of desperation, to go underground to avoid legal prosecution over plural marriage. Although wanting refuge, the polygamists drew attention to themselves rather than avoiding scrutiny.

Nevertheless, the polygamists persevered in their efforts to build a community at Short Creek. Eventually, the LDS Church withdrew its branch from the town. The Short Creek community later survived other government raids that again were supported by the LDS Church.

DIFFERENCES OVER AUTHORITY

After the drama of the 1935 arrests and after those convicted were released, disagreement over the United Trust plan persisted. In 1936, the Priesthood Council reversed several decisions of the previous year. It unanimously decided John Y. Barlow should discontinue his active management of affairs at Short Creek, except in spiritual matters. Instead, the council wanted local brethren to organize and manage their own affairs, free from domination of the Priesthood Council. This decision, however, was not accepted by a majority vote of the brethren at Short Creek. What happened next exposed a controversy over priesthood authority that has lived on among Fundamentalist Mormon communities in various ways ever since.

Joseph W. Musser and Louis A. Kelsch made a special trip to Short Creek to talk personally with John Y. Barlow after it became clear the Priesthood Council decision had been rejected. Musser expressed the council's position to Barlow "that under the present set-up the group could not prosper; that there seemed a disposition toward a one-man rule; that many of the Saints were complaining; that the present arrangement was not in accordance with the spirit of the action of the Priesthood Council taken recently." They again advised Barlow to resign from management of the affairs of the Short Creek trust group and confine his labors more particularly to the spiritual realm. They reminded him that the work of the Priesthood Council members was "especially along the line of keeping faith in patriarchal marriage alive, and not in the direction of colonizing." Further, they asked Barlow pointedly if he claimed to hold "the keys of Priesthood," an expression then understood by many as the Mormon doctrine of making one's calling and election sure by having the Savior lay on hands and declaring, "Well done, thou good and faithful servant." Barlow answered in the negative.[137]

In a priesthood meeting the next morning, full discussion of the matter was encouraged. Musser and Kelsch learned firsthand that a main reason for rejecting the Council's decision to remove Barlow as the head of Short Creek's temporal affairs was "on account of supposing it [the idea] to have been the submission of Bro. Musser and not the action of the Priesthood

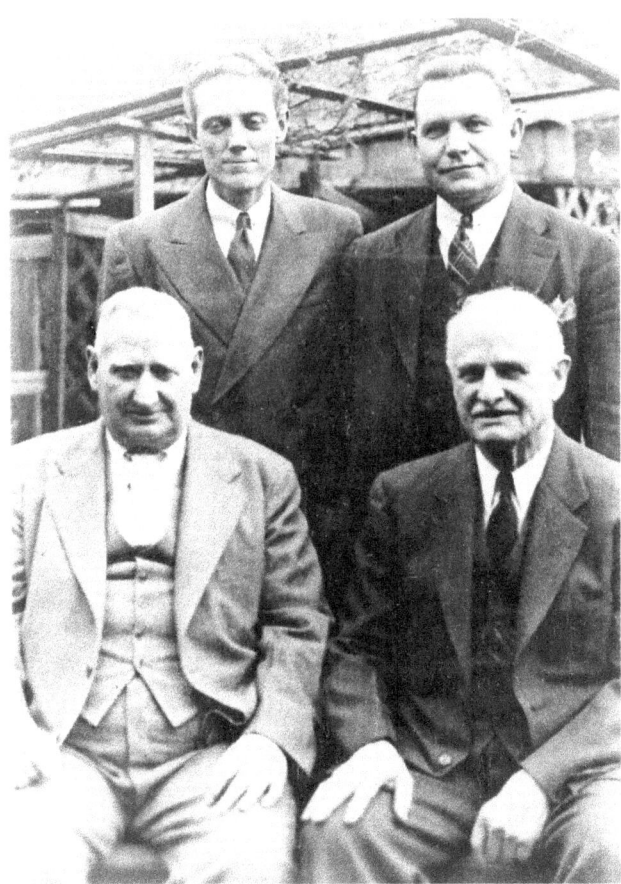

Left: Four Priesthood Council members, circa 1940. *Clockwise from bottom left*: John Y. Barlow, Louis A. Kelsch, Charles F. Zitting and Joseph W. Musser. *Authors' collection.*

Below: Joseph W. Musser, 1930s. *Authors' collection.*

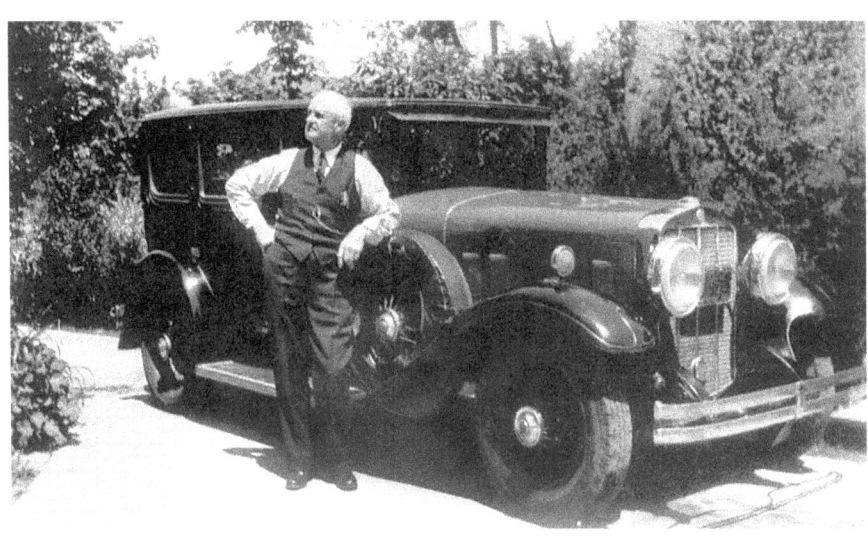

[Council]." Instead, the residents had organized, using the former United Trust plan first presented by Barlow, which once again placed him at the head, and they had begun operating under that agreement. Despite this action, controversy still existed.

Musser described four basic responses among the thirteen men present. Several expressed their feeling that the group was prospering more since voting to keep Barlow as head of the United Trust and expressed a desire to continue under it. The majority expressed the belief that Barlow held the keys to Priesthood and was the mouthpiece of God on earth. For some, this last idea was the *only* reason for accepting Barlow's management of temporal affairs. Two men expressed emphatic dissent, stating that "they did not believe Bro. Barlow held the keys to Priesthood, but that he did have authority to seal [marriages] and [that he] was the senior member in the Priesthood group, and as such presided at the meetings of the group, etc."[138]

Musser then explained his view that the special mission and labors of the Priesthood group was to keep plural marriage alive, that "we were not called upon to colonize only as the Lord might dictate such a move." He stated, "[I]t was the feeling of the Priesthood [Council] that the affairs of the Saints should be conducted by them in their local communities and not by the Priesthood [Council,]" who hold themselves "in readiness to give counsel and advice from time to time as may be required and proper."[139]

Musser, it seemed, made a complete reversal of his position the year before by declaring that "the time had *not* come for the establishing of the United Order."[140] Instead, he urged the brethren to unite themselves in spirit in serving the Lord and to live the spirit of the United Order *in their families*, extending that spirit out among the Saints in preparation for future blessings. In the meantime, "they should display charity and love toward all men who are striving to serve the Lord" and not consider those who did not wish to join in their temporal communal experiment out of harmony with the gospel. He counseled that "no man should refuse his neighbor help when it was needed, even though the neighbor may not be a member of a Trust group."[141] Musser apparently did not consider the trust format under which they were operating equivalent to the law of united order and only as a man-made organization so that local brethren could work together—at best, he saw it was only a preparation for living true united order when God would direct it.

In answer to the question over "who held the Keys of the Priesthood," Musser wisely sidestepped the issue, promising that when the Lord wanted any man to know, and that man was prepared to receive the fact, the Lord would reveal it in a clear way. He urged, however, that "John Y. Barlow, by reason of his seniority in ordination presided over the group." Musser emphasized there must be no autocratic rule, that the agency of every individual must be respected. This was a direct reference to the tendency toward a "one-man rule," which he and Louis Kelsch had discussed earlier with Barlow.[142]

From the expressions made at this priesthood meeting, it is apparent that Musser and Barlow operated, at least in some measure, from very different paradigms. These differences over the applications of free agency and priesthood authority eventually led to a split in the community of believers after Barlow's death.

LDS CHURCH SURVEILLANCE OF FUNDAMENTALISTS AND LOYALTY OATHS

To coordinate legal prosecution, the LDS Church instituted surveillance of suspected polygamists in addition to requiring a church loyalty oath for ferreting out suspected members. These actions were implemented at the urging of the First Presidency counselor J. Reuben Clark, who had overseen the U.S. Justice Department's activities against suspected subversives during World War I, which "predisposed him" to an oath of allegiance for suspected Fundamentalists.[143] During the next several decades, the church provided its surveillance records to law enforcement for legal prosecution of polygamists. In 1938, under the direct supervision of Clark, the surveillance program began in the Salt Lake City Hawthorne Ward, where several suspected polygamists lived and held small gatherings.

Clark descended from early Mormon polygamists, and his mother, Mary, was John W. Woolley's sister. Despite or because of this heritage, he had long opposed post-Manifesto polygamy. Clark, who "had risen early in his career to become one of the nation's highest legal advisors," could not "look upon polygamy after the 1890 Manifesto with the least degree of allowance." His opposition to plural marriage increased after the church's 1904 Second Manifesto. Clark felt it was almost impossible for a church member to be loyal after becoming involved in what he called the "web of renegade polygamy." Clark had been called as a member of the First Presidency by President Grant in 1933. His first assignment was to draft Grant's "Official Statement" denouncing plural marriage and to suppress the practice of polygamy. Clark "went at it with a vengeance."[144]

Clark selected Hawthorne Ward bishop Fred E. Curtis for this special assignment and instructed him to observe and report activities of suspected members. Curtis then provided his evidence to Clark and to Presiding Bishop Joseph Anderson, who then contacted local church leaders about members under suspicion. Curtis also coordinated with the Salt Lake City Police Department.

Meanwhile, Clark used his influence to encourage the Salt Lake City Public Library to exclude Fundamentalist literature from library holdings, and he asked the city's postmaster to prohibit the mailing of such publications. Once suspected members were identified, church officers dealt with them in one of three ways: 1) disfellowshipping; 2) excommunication; or 3) a demand for a signed loyalty oath for anyone wanting to clear his or her name. As the frequency of excommunications escalated, *Truth* magazine declared the entire situation as contrary to LDS scripture, comparing it to early Mormon persecutions.

Curtis found that not all bishops or stake presidents were anxious to excommunicate sympathizers or believers in continued plural marriage and complained to President Clark, especially when it became clear that the polygamists' movement was growing rather than shrinking. In August 1941, Curtis expressed apprehension: "This group is growing by leaps and bounds and the attendance of young people is astounding....[O]ver 100 people attend and meetings are being held in all parts of the city and county. New members are being introduced each week." He pleaded with Clark that "something must be done."[145]

Something was being done. The LDS First Presidency met with area stake presidents, telling them that the district attorney "was a good Latter-day Saint and would persecute [*sic*] the 'new polyg's criminally if it were deemed wise.'" President Clark announced criminal prosecution should begin as soon as possible.[146] Bishop Curtis's surveillance files were turned over to law enforcement; legal prosecution of polygamists resulted four years later, in 1944, in a joint local, state and federal polygamy raid.

THE 1944 RAID AND
THE PRIESTHOOD SPLIT

I n the early morning hours of Tuesday, March 7, 1944, combined federal, state and local law enforcement officers simultaneously pounded on the doors of polygamists' homes throughout the Salt Lake City area and in Short Creek. Officers had already cut the electricity to each home according to their well-prepared raid plan.

One polygamist, Joseph Lyman Jessop, recalled the loud knocking and rude awakening of his family in darkness and the five officers who pushed their way in without invitation, making their way through the house, shining flashlights everywhere. Without producing a search warrant, they pushed open the doors of bedrooms, throwing "things right and left to see what was there and who they might find" and "threatening to slap mothers and children alike if they made any noise." Within a few seconds, leading officer George Beckstead, chief deputy sheriff of Salt Lake County, pushed Lyman's first wife, Winnie, out of the way and entered his bedroom with an arrest warrant. Two officers ransacked his room, rummaging for evidence, while Beckstead announced an arrest warrant for Lyman that charged him with conspiracy and unlawful cohabitation and ordered him to "get dressed now."[147] Lyman recalled:

> By the time I was dressed, they were counting the children and questioning all they could. Beckstead was questioning [my third wife] Beth in the hall....I immediately...[put] my finger over my mouth [motioning] to not answer their questions. The officers said [to her], "Go ahead and

*answer and don't pay any attention to him" as the questioning continued.
I said, "Don't talk. You don't have to answer their questions." The officer
guarding me said, "You shush." The questioning continued, and I said
again, "Don't talk" and then the officer poked me and said "You shush!"
Beckstead said, "Take him back!" and the other men pushed me back into
my room and closed the door while Beckstead tried to question farther.*[148]

An officer stayed next to Lyman when they came out of his room again.
Another officer stood in the bedroom doorway of Lyman's second wife,
Maleta, questioning her, trying to get answers. Lyman again called out,
"Don't talk."

Striking Lyman with his flashlight, the officer ordered, "You shush! We'll
do with you what we please! You're under arrest!"

Lyman pleaded, "You men get out of here. I'll go with you, but get out!"[149]

As they pushed Lyman outside, he managed to tell his frightened, wide-
eyed little boys goodbye. He counted at least seven more men emerging from
doorways around the house, where they had been stationed. Lyman made no
resistance. With him, the dozen men loaded into two cars and sped furiously
with sirens blazing to the Salt Lake City jail. More police cars arrived with
their captives, all people he knew.[150] Their stories were much like his.[151]

That day, law officials arrested thirty-four men and twelve women,
including all members of the Priesthood Council, for involvement in plural
marriage, with federal charges against twenty. A lead prosecutor, Assistant
U.S. Attorney John S. Boyden, predicted that the arrests "would halt the
practice of polygamy in this area" and that the church had given its complete
cooperation.[152] LDS Church president Heber J. Grant and his counselors,
J. Reuben Clark and David O. McKay, announced: "We commend and
uphold the federal and state prosecutions," stating church-sanctioned
plural marriage had ended in 1890 and the church had "repeatedly issued
warnings against any apostate group that persisted in the practice" and
excommunicated any who did not heed the warning.[153]

Time magazine announced, "It was the biggest raid on polygamists
since the orthodox Mormon church officially outlawed plural marriage in
1890."[154] Several media outlets, including *Time*, *Newsweek* and the *Salt Lake
Tribune*, published photos of young, attractive polygamous wives who had
been arrested. *Time* quoted one, Rhea Allred Kunz, a mother of eight, as
saying, "Plural marriage cannot be stamped out. Regardless of wars and
pestilence, there has always been a surplus of worthy women." *Newsweek*
estimated there were 2,500 Fundamentalists at the time.[155]

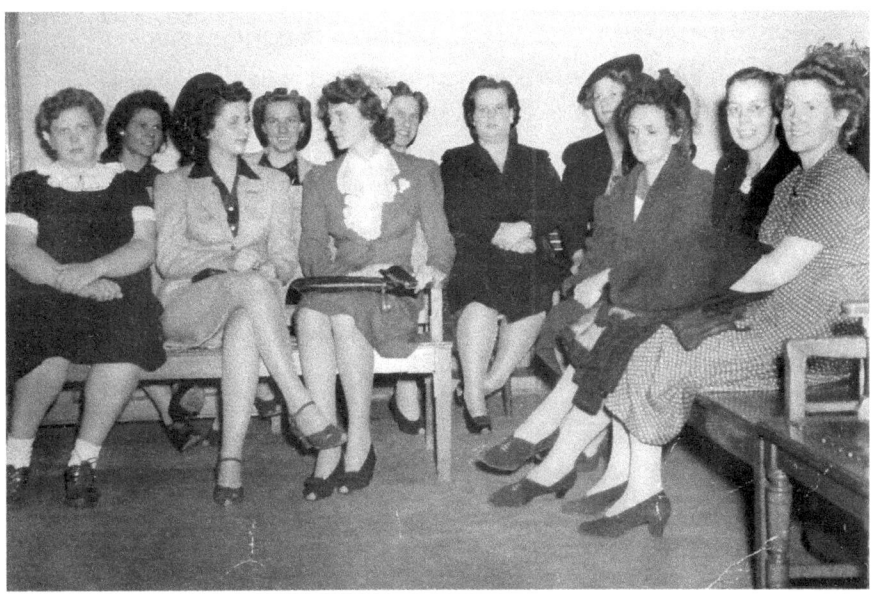

Women arrested in 1944 Polygamy Raid. *Donna K. Mackert Collection.*

The captives who could not arrange bail the first day were jailed. Fourteen shared a dormitory cell. Late that night, from ten o'clock until midnight, they quietly held a prayer and testimony meeting:

> [E]*very man spoke his feelings and expressed thankfulness for the privilege of being incarcerated for the Gospel's sake, yet our situation was pleasant in comparison with that which the Prophet Joseph and Hyrum and others and our Lord Jesus Christ suffered for the same cause. We know that our suffering up to now has been practically nothing compared to theirs.*[156]

The next day, police marched them across the street to the courthouse for arraignment. Lyman remembered feeling they were a spectacle: "[P]eople peered from everywhere to see this bunch of notorious polygamists. Four stories of windows full of faces and hallways lined to see us. We were front-line news in the papers."[157]

The judge set bonds at about $2,500 each, and relatives, friends and attorneys scrambled to raise the funds. Joseph W. Musser later recalled they were able, with the help of the Lord, to arrange some $200,000 for bonds within a week.[158] John McLaughlan later testified in court that he was excommunicated by the LDS Church "after I went bond for these people."[159]

The polygamists had long sensed and predicted trouble coming. Just a month earlier, John Y. Barlow had warned his people: "[I]t looks like we're going to get persecution. Now is the time to button up your coat and prepare yourselves."[160]

Joseph W. Musser apparently knew a federal grand jury was "investigating our group activities and particularly the *TRUTH* magazine and its sponsors." Days before the raid, he wrote in his journal that government prosecutors hoped "to stamp out plural marriage…to stop TRUTH publication, and to make us like the rest of the people."[161] He felt "confident this new crusade would fail because of the faith of his followers."[162] He wrote:

> *No principle of life and salvation will be destroyed or taken from the earth in this dispensation of the fulness* [sic] *of times. Men trying to do it will come to naught. Some of us may have to go to prison, but what of that. We should be willing to bear such a testimony to the nation if that course is the will of the Lord.*[163]

Walking the streets of the city after posting bail, Lyman Jessop noted:

> *People everywhere are beginning to take sides for or against us, realizing that the issue is not us as individuals, but the law of religious freedom. We can hear as we pass people, some saying, "They should pay with their lives," while others say, "The issue is absurd! Those people should be let alone! As long as they are not harming anyone else, it is their business!"*

Four years earlier, in November 1940, Reed E. Vetterli, a former FBI agent, was appointed Salt Lake City chief of police. Polygamists, keenly aware of church surveillance activities that involved local police, noted correctly that surveillance stopped immediately after Vetterli's appointment. In December 1940, *TRUTH* editorialized:

> *It is a noteworthy fact that the "peeping Tom" operations carried on for the past several months, in which nosey busy-bodies, agents of the Church, who were nightly protruding their insolence into the affairs of certain of the Saints, have stopped. This is a step in the right direction. Let there be no "peeping," no "spying," no "sneaking" about people's windows after dark.*[164]

In fact, Bishop Fred E. Curtis became frustrated when he lost police coordination and support after Vetterli's appointment. When Curtis

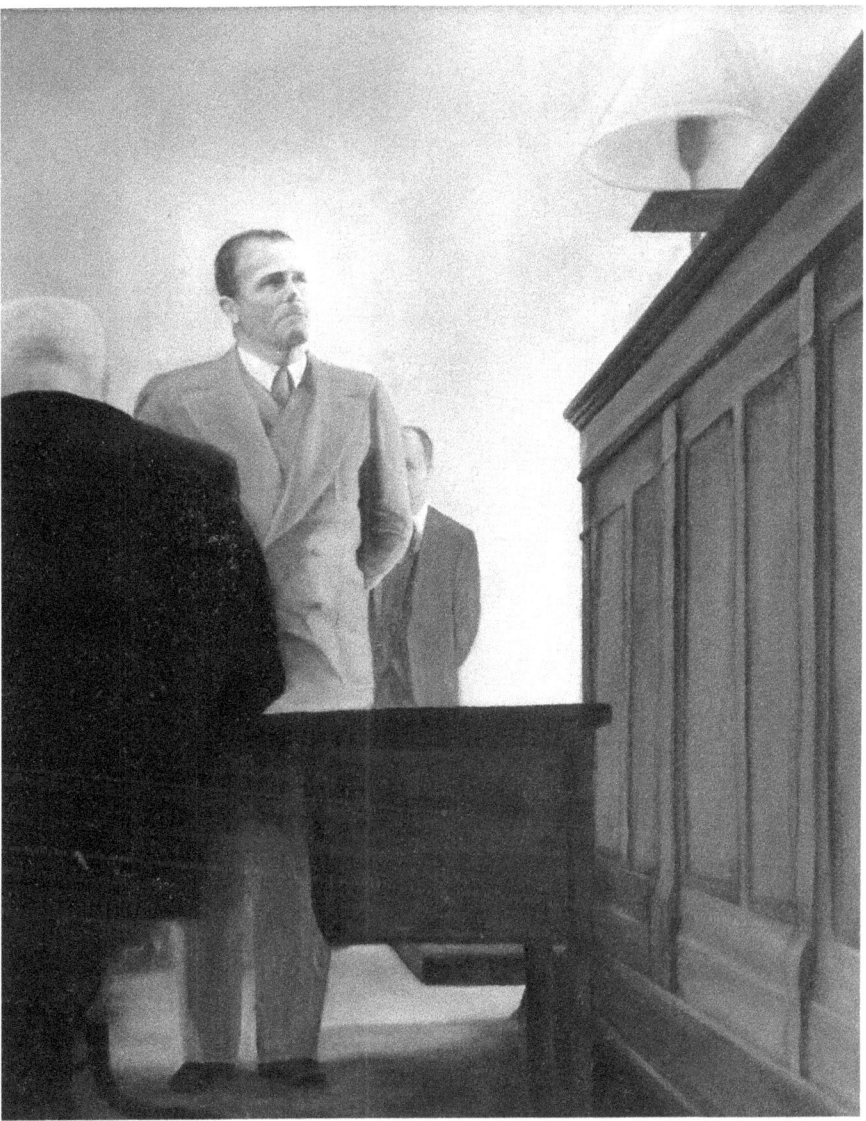

Photo of painting of Joseph Lyman Jessop in court, May 1945, telling the judge: "Justice has not been served." *Authors' collection.*

interviewed Vetterli, also a church member, early in 1941, he learned that the two officers previously tasked with investigating polygamists had been assigned to other work because Vetterli did not know that the former chief had been investigating. Vetterli assured him "he wanted to cooperate in every way possible," but Curtis felt worried. He wrote to President J. Reuben

Clark that "possibly...a word to Chief Vetterli from a member of the First Presidency would help materially in having this investigation continued, as it would be a shame for this investigation to be dropped at this time when so much valuable information has already been secured." Nevertheless, Vetterli did not renew the department's participation as Curtis hoped. In August 1941, Curtis wrote to Clark, "[W]e have had no cooperation whatsoever from...Chief Vetterli....[He] promised full cooperation...however has given us none whatsoever."[165]

In 1944, it became obvious that Vetterli had cooperated with the church's plan when the Salt Lake Police Department coordinated with state law enforcement and the FBI for the polygamy raid.

Thirty-two of the men were charged with state crimes, including unlawful cohabitation and conspiracy.[166] Twenty defendants had federal indictments.[167]

On May 20, 1944, fifteen of the forty-six originally arrested were convicted and sentenced to serve one to five years in the Utah State Penitentiary. They immediately filed appeals and remained free on bond.[168] The state trials for conspiracy were another matter. Some charges of conspiracy involved activities such as leading music or playing the piano in religious meetings. All seven of the Priesthood Council members were charged with conspiracy for mailing *Truth* magazine because it published articles about plural marriage, which prosecutors claimed were "lewd" and "obscene," thus violating federal law prohibiting obscene literature being sent through the mail. Eventually, after almost three years, all conspiracy charges were dismissed when an appellate court judge concluded that he saw "no obscene or filthy word or expression of lewd suggestion...nothing more than an argument in favor of a practice that for many years was a tenet of the Mormon Church."[169]

After researching the cases, historian and constitutional attorney Ken Driggs stated: "Today the allegation [of conspiracy] is beyond ridiculous, but the fact prosecutors made the argument in 1944 probably is indicative of how much hostility was directed at Fundamentalists."[170]

In the wake of the raid, polygamous families tried to present their lives in a positive light to sympathetic reporters. *Life* photographer Johnny Florea arranged to take pictures of several families and featured Rulon Allred's family in a March 1944 issue and Joseph Lyman Jessops's in a June 1944 issue. This last issue also contained Florea's photos of 55 women and 283 children, the families of the 15 convicted men, who had gathered at a park where Florea snapped over one hundred photographs.[171] About the same time, Joseph Musser published another book about plural marriage that

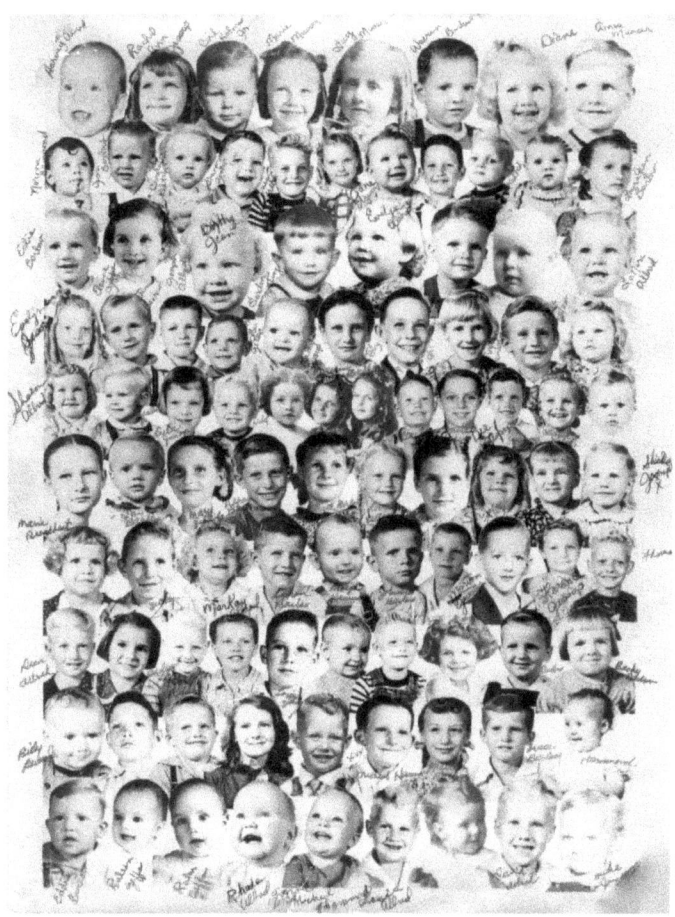

Children of polygamists arrested in 1944 raid. Composite published in Fundamentalist book *Celestial Marriage* after the raid. *Authors' collection.*

featured a composite photograph of many of the children whose parents were arrested in the raid.[172]

In May 1945, after losing appeals, the fifteen convicted men began their one- to five-year sentences in the Utah State Penitentiary. As religious men, they conducted themselves as model prisoners and labored admirably in their prison work assignments. Perhaps the most difficult test for each man individually came after a few months when a document "Declaration of Policy" was prepared, offering the men early release if they agreed to sign the document to no longer live plural marriage. The men believed LDS Church leaders were behind the state's efforts to have them sign the policy because of the negative publicity resulting from the fifteen going to prison and subsequently appearing as martyrs. Although emotions were intense among the men because of how they had been treated, Joseph Musser convinced

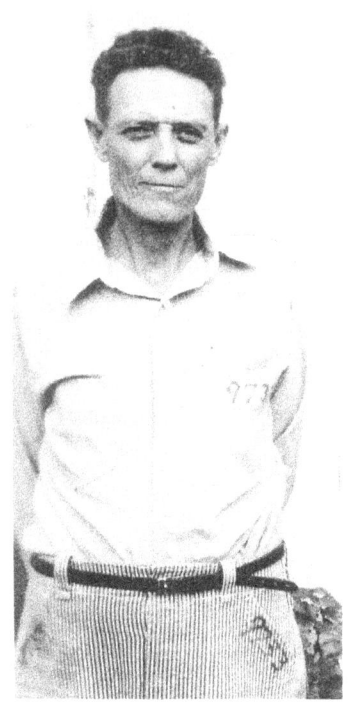

Louis A. Kelsch in prison clothes, 1940s. *Authors' collection.*

nine others to sign, explaining that God desired for them to do their duty to protect the church from negative publicity and urging them to go home and earn a living to support their wives and children. Ultimately, four men refused to sign, choosing instead to remain in prison for conscience's sake.

Joseph Musser had first used the term *Fundamentalists* to describe polygamists excommunicated from the LDS Church. In the early 1940s, he wrote, " [T]his group may be called the 'Priesthood Group' or the 'Fundamentalists'…because of their refusal to accede to certain changes in the fundamentals of the Gospel."[173] However, polygamists themselves did not use or recognize this term until after the 1944 raids, when contemporary newspaper articles started using the term.[174] Joseph Lyman Jessop's diaries, which span from 1910 to 1954, did not include the word until 1945, when he became a prisoner and objected to being called by that term.[175] The LDS Church referred to the polygamists as "cultists" in 1944, and Apostle Mark E. Petersen said the church regarded the term *Fundamentalists* as a misnomer because it "gave the impression (which is what the cultists sought) that they are old line Mormons, which they are not."[176] Polygamists adopted the term and have self-identified as Fundamentalist Mormons ever since.

Several important developments came from the raid and its aftermath: 1) the community of polygamists gradually became known as Fundamentalists or Fundamentalist Mormons after their arrests; 2) the 1944 raid did not end plural marriage as predicted, and none of the men who served time ever gave up their belief in or practice of plural marriage; 3) the community grew and adherents became more staunch in their beliefs; 4) those sentenced to prison were considered religious martyrs; 5) the community became more reclusive, going underground for at least two generations; and 6) internal division over authority, doctrine and ideology emerged among the men while in prison, with some separating over disagreement with Priesthood Council leadership.[177]

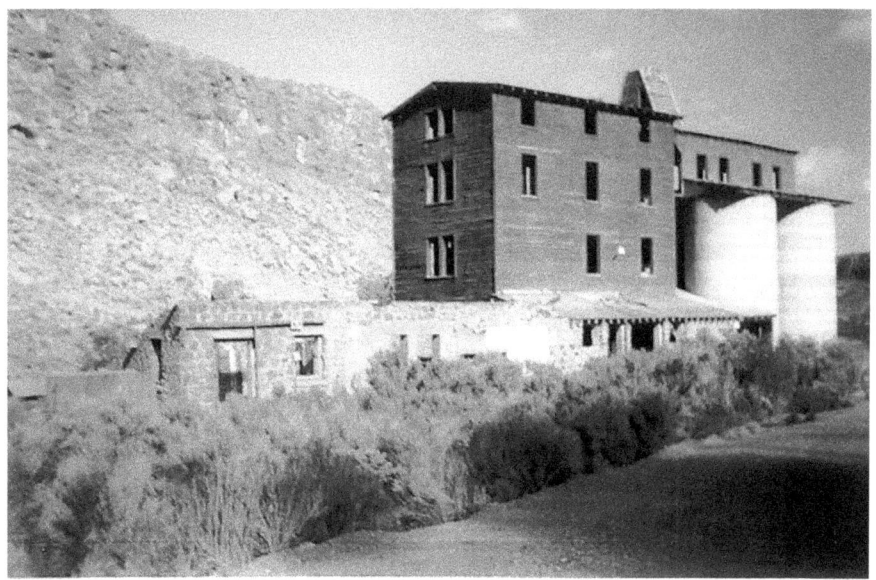

Osiris Mill built by polygamists, including Joseph Lyman Jessop, in late 1940s near Antimony, Utah. *Authors' collection.*

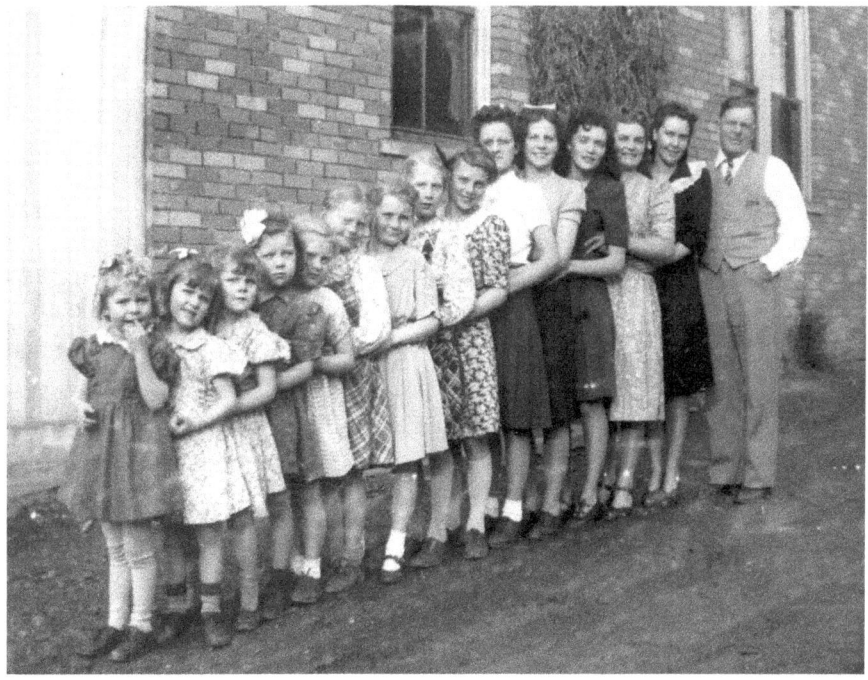

Joseph Lyman Jessop with daughters and a granddaughter about 1946. *Authors' collection.*

THE PRIESTHOOD SPLIT

Differences among members of the Priesthood Council that had slowly grown over several years erupted in 1950 with bitterness and rancor and culminated in separating the community permanently in 1952. The "Priesthood Split" divided the larger Fundamentalist community into two distinct groups, the Musser group and the Johnson or Short Creek group, with a third division comprising a few families who remained aloof from either side, later becoming known and self-identifying as "Independent" Fundamentalists.

The split was probably inevitable after John Y. Barlow died because of differences between Barlow and Joseph W. Musser, which had surfaced early. When J. Leslie Broadbent died in 1935, even before his burial, Barlow told others that "from now on things will be run different."[178] After the death of Barlow on December 29, 1949, the Priesthood Council consisted of Musser and Charles F. Zitting, who had been called by Lorin C. Woolley, and seven men called by John Y. Barlow in the 1940s: Leroy S. Johnson, J. Marion Hammon, Guy H. Musser, Rulon T. Jeffs, Richard S. Jessop, Carl N. Holm and Alma A. Timpson. Two members, Louis A. Kelsch and LeGrand Woolley, were still living but had withdrawn and did not participate in any council matters after about 1945.

Barlow's tendency toward an autocratic leadership style was apparent from the outset. It showed when Barlow first moved to Short Creek in 1935 and initiated his United Trust plan, which fomented much disunity among brethren because of its "harsh and unfair" clauses.[179] A year later, he allowed the same type of plan to be reinstituted, even though the Priesthood Council had unanimously agreed for him to withdraw from its management.[180]

Musser disagreed with some of Barlow's policies and certain practices of the newer members of the Priesthood Council. He "spoke out against these practices, including marriages of very young girls, taking wives without the knowledge or consent of the bride's parents, and the expectation that each wife should give birth to a child every year." However, because "John Y. Barlow himself advocated these ideas, Joseph Musser's admonitions [against them] had little effect."[181]

A major point of contention erupted over Musser's calling of Dr. Rulon C. Allred. In 1950, Joseph Musser privately ordained Allred an apostle and patriarch, called him as a member of the council and appointed him as his Second Elder.[182] When Musser informed the other council members about it, they initially sustained this action, but at the same meeting some

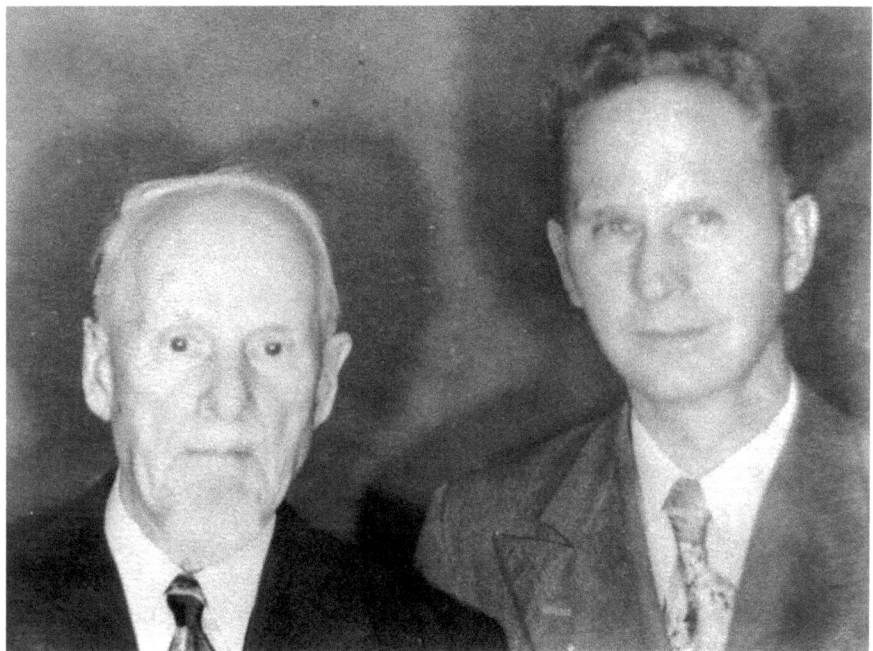

Joseph W. Musser (*left*) and Dr. Rulon C. Allred about 1952. *Authors' collection.*

began having second thoughts, saying that Allred was only Musser's counselor, not a member of the council. They felt that Musser was trying to place Allred ahead of them in seniority. Musser allowed them their differences of opinion without argument. However, when he announced Allred's calling to a Salt Lake congregation of Fundamentalists, opposing council members became openly defiant. One charged Allred of having "impugned this Priesthood [Council] by going to Bro. Musser and asking for a blessing." Musser denied this and said, "Any man that claims Allred asked for that blessing is a damned liar!"[183] Later, in private, he stated, "[T]he Council will not sustain me, and I refused to be over-ridden in the matter....I did what the Lord told me to do, and if these brethren will not uphold me, they will be broken to smithereens."[184]

The council members began citing various other reasons for their lack of support, even accusing Musser, who was quite incapacitated from an earlier stroke in June 1949, of being a demented old man who didn't know what he was doing.[185] Leroy Johnson told Musser and Lyman Jessop, "If the Lord wants to use an incapacitated leader [referring to Joseph Musser] to lead some people astray, that is the Lord's business."[186]

Ultimately, it became an issue of authority—whether Musser could authoritatively act without getting the entire council's explicit approval. Some claimed that it was improper for Musser to have called Allred privately, even though three of them had been privately called by Barlow the same way before it was made known to the others.

In a priesthood meeting on December 3, 1950, the council members told Allred "that they were empowered to accept or reject Joseph [Musser]'s actions, and that they had decided Rulon [Allred] was not a member of the Council, nor an Apostle as Joseph had told him. The Council informed Allred that he was an assistant to Joseph, holding only a commissioned authority during Joseph's life."[187]

Friction between Musser and the other council members culminated on May 6, 1951, when the council members openly refused to sustain Musser's calling of Allred.[188] Between May 1951 and the summer of 1952, the Priesthood Council, consisting of Charles F. Zitting and the seven men called by Barlow, entirely rejected Musser. Most Fundamentalists, whether they lived in Salt Lake or in Short Creek, sided with them. A much smaller number stayed with Musser.

On January 12, 1952, Joseph W. Musser filled his vacated quorum with new members whose names he said were received by revelation. They were Rulon C. Allred, Margarito Bautista, John Butchereit, Eslie D. Jenson, Owen A. Allred, Marvin L. Jessop, Joseph B. Thompson and Joseph Lyman Jessop. Musser told them, "Brethren, I have spent the night with the Lord. He has disappropriated them [the other council members] and has instructed me to call you in their place."[189] Later, speaking of the council members he dismissed, he said, "They have been rejected because they would not accept the word of The Lord."[190]

Musser's new Priesthood Council emphasized free choice in marriage matters, still holding to old-fashioned Mormon practices of courtship and marriage in which parents and priesthood leaders were consulted. Joseph Musser died in 1954, leaving Rulon C. Allred as his successor. The group was known at first as the Musser group, then the Allred group. The group organized as a 501c3 corporation for legal and tax purposes under the IRS code, calling it the "Corporation of the Presiding Elder of the Apostolic United Brethren" (AUB), but continues to teach that the LDS Church is God's church, though out of order, and theirs is a priesthood work outside of it.[191]

The council members who in Musser's view had "disappropriated" themselves continued to function together. Charles F. Zitting, who lived in the Salt Lake area, was recognized by some as presiding until he died in

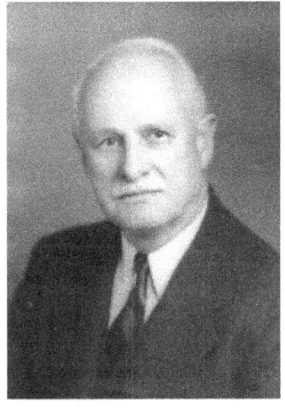
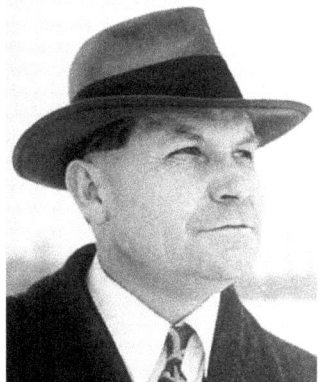
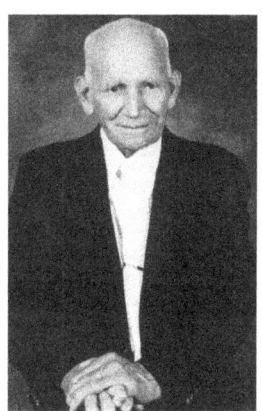
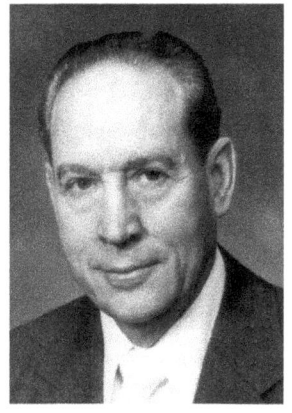
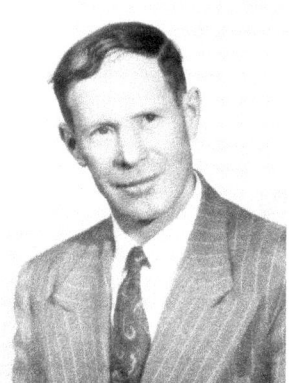

Clockwise from top left: Joseph W. Musser (1872–1954). *Authors' collection*; Charles F. Zitting (1894–1954). *FamilySearch.org Family Tree*; LeRoy S. Johnson (1888–1886). *Authors' collection*; J. Marion Hammon (1905–1988). *FamilySearch.org Family Tree*; Richard S. Jessop (1894–1978). *Authors' collection*.

1954, six months after Musser.[192] Sixty-six-year-old Leroy S. Johnson, who lived in Short Creek, and had acted as de facto leader while Zitting lived, then assumed full leadership after his death.[193]

The practice of leaders deciding marriage partners began with council members in Short Creek earlier in the 1940s and was rather well established by the time Barlow died. For example, in 1948, one of Lyman Jessop's daughters was married secretly, being persuaded at the moment, after a dance, to marry one of John Barlow's sons without her parent's knowledge or consent. Returning home afterward, she told no one for two weeks, then finally confided in her father, who took the matter to Joseph Musser. Because Barlow supported those involved, the situation could not be resolved until after his death.

After the split, some young women were urged by Short Creek priesthood leaders "to leave their father's homes and marry according to their direction…because the father is out of harmony with them…[and] that he

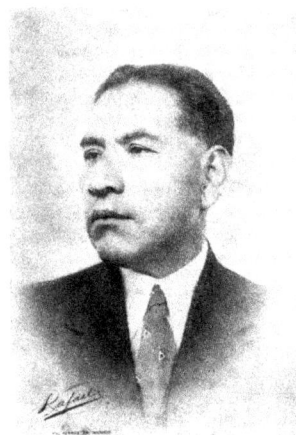

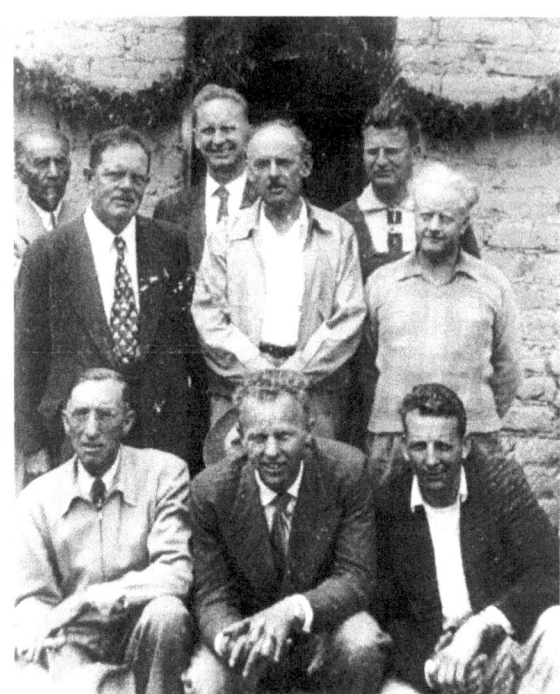

Above: Margarito Bautista
(1879–1961). *Authors' collection.*

Right: Musser's New Priesthood
Council visiting Mexico about
1955. *Authors' collection.*

has lost his rights to the family, therefore the children of that father should listen and obey they who call themselves the Priesthood."[194]

In August 1952, another of Lyman Jessop's daughters, a thirteen-year-old, was taken from Salt Lake to Short Creek after he refused to grant his permission for her to marry. When the note she left was discovered, he immediately went after her and brought her back before any marriage could be performed.[195] The following month, another young girl was spirited away to Short Creek to become a plural wife. Lyman wrote:

> *It seems certain that somebody's teaching and practicing some damnable doctrines of just taking away at will some of our daughters against the consent of parents until the attitude and practice is disgusting, to say the least, and we (some of us) feel it must not be tolerated when it involves members of our own families. How far will this priestcraft go?*[196]

But in early 1953, Musser's council learned of "brethren [in Short Creek] assuming the right to go into another man's house and advise the wives there to leave their husband because the husband was not in harmony with the brethren who claimed leadership."[197]

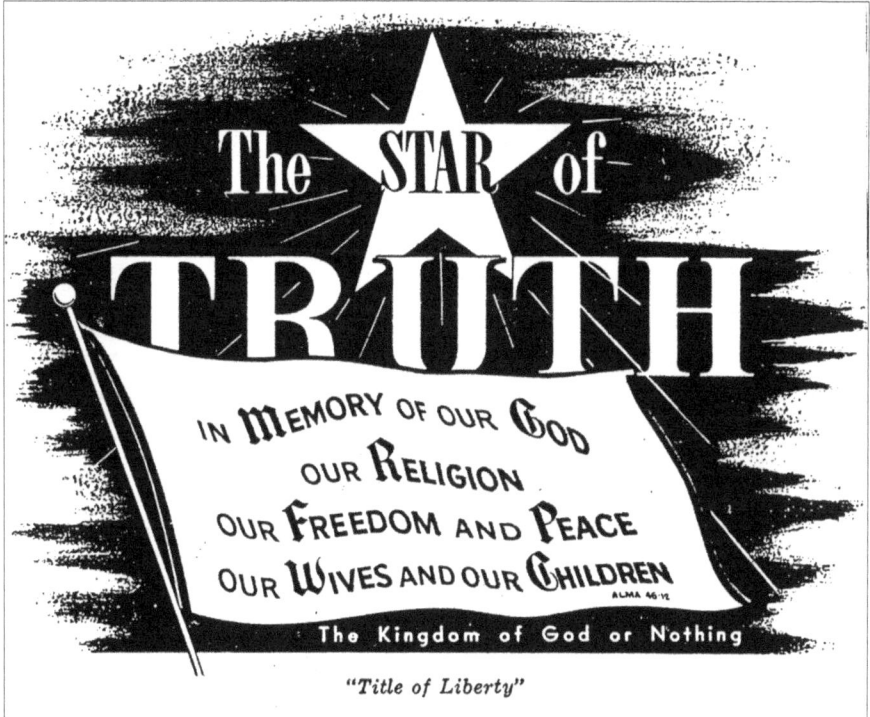

The STAR of TRUTH

IN MEMORY OF OUR GOD
OUR RELIGION
OUR FREEDOM AND PEACE
OUR WIVES AND OUR CHILDREN
ALMA 46-12

The Kingdom of God or Nothing

"Title of Liberty"

VOLUME I   JANUARY, 1953   NUMBER 1

A STATEMENT

In the time of our Lord 1949, I suffered from what I was told was a paralytic stroke. I was told by my Doctor to give up the publication of Truth, and I prepared my son to take it over. He has assiduously done so, and has done a noble job of it. At a later time, when I was much better, I asked my son for the privilege of taking the Truth off his hands and engineering it myself. He refused to turn it over to me. On a number of occasions I repeated my request and I went to the Printer about it, but with no success. Later I had the matter legally investigated and found that those publishing Truth claimed that Truth had gone out of business. On this premise they submitted claim of ownership, without my knowledge or consent. My lawyer told me I could go to Court to recover my rights, but I did not want

Dedicated to God's service and the glory of His Name; to the building up of His Kingdom and the establishment of His Priesthood upon the earth

First issue of *Star of Truth* magazine, January 1953. *Authors' collection.*

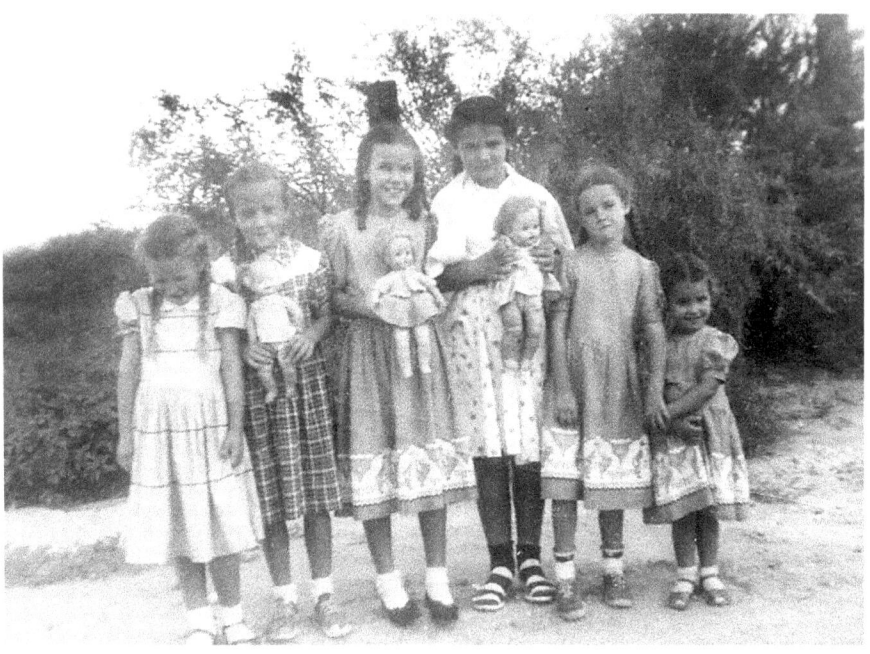

Leroy Johnson daughters, 1950s. *Authors' collection.*

Time and distance between the groups allowed some softening over the next few decades, especially important for families with relatives on both sides of the fence. However, arranged, appointed or "placement" marriages directed by council members became the norm during Leroy Johnson's administration from the 1950s to the 1980s, although his leadership style was mostly gentle and persuasive. The people wholly embraced the concept, believing this to be a more godly pattern than when individuals, even with parental and priesthood guidance, chose their own mates.

Council practices of involving themselves in families, arbitrarily and unilaterally declaring a man unworthy of governing his own family and pitting family members against one another became ingrained in Short Creek in the period surrounding the split. It played out again later under Rulon Jeffs when he did the same thing against families involved with Centennial Park. And it happened again, even more radically, with Warren Jeffs, who pitted his own people against one another and tore families apart.

6

THE 1953 SHORT CREEK RAID

The dark, quiet desert morning was broken at four o'clock by flashing lights and police sirens as the caravan of lawmen and others came pouring into the small community of Short Creek. There were about one hundred lawmen, including Arizona highway patrolmen, the Mohave County sheriff and his deputies, Arizona National Guardsmen, ATF agents, superior and juvenile court judges, the Arizona state attorney general and his associates, policewomen, nurses, doctors and others. There also were twenty-five carloads of numerous journalists.[198]

The raid had been in the planning for some time, and the date had not been chosen by happenstance. It was set for Sunday morning, the twenty-sixth of July, a holiday weekend when Arizona officials expected there to be a larger than normal gathering of polygamists. Like other communities throughout Mormon country, Short Creekers celebrated July 24, commemorating the date of the early pioneers' arrival in the Salt Lake Valley, with a large picnic, music and other demonstrations in honor of their ancestors' sacrifices and accomplishments in settling this rugged country. Thus, Arizona officials expected their raid to make an even greater impact.

The dramatic arrival before sunrise was also intended for effect. "The officers had hoped they could surprise the polygamists, break into their homes, and catch them in bed with their unlawful wives to gather evidence to convict them."[199] That was not to be, as the Short Creek residents had been forewarned of the planned raid, and all but the youngest children were gathered in the small schoolyard, well groomed, dressed and peacefully singing patriotic songs as the lawmen arrived, guns ready for a fight.

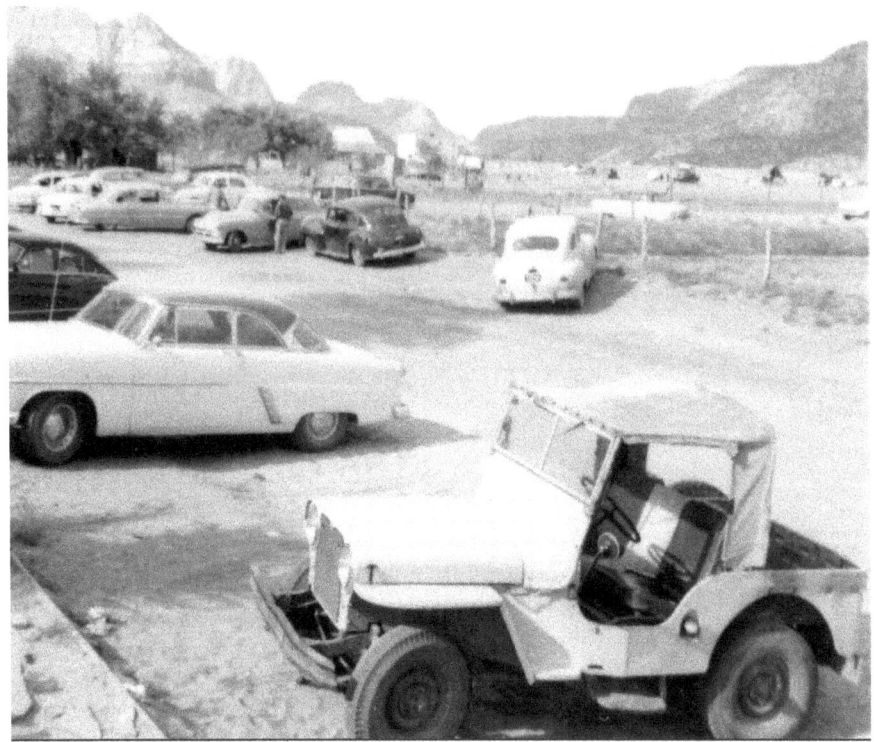

Above: Main Street during Polygamy Raid on July 24, 1953. *Authors' collection.*

Opposite, top: Another view of Main Street during Polygamy Raid on July 24, 1953. *Authors' collection.*

Opposite, middle: Behind the schoolhouse. *Authors' collection.*

Opposite, bottom: School courtyard. *Authors' collection.*

Little did the lawmen realize they had almost had a fight on their hands. Alvin S. Barlow, a fifteen-year-old at the time, years later remembered how the adults in the small community had been incensed when they heard they were to yet again be hounded by outsiders for practicing their religious beliefs.

There were veterans of World War II and the Korean War among them. Indeed, two of the Short Creek men were in military uniform the morning of the raid. Tom Jessop, one of the two, had literally just returned the night before from a tour of duty in Korea. Barlow remembered that some of these veterans were willing to fight for their beliefs, and he commented that they

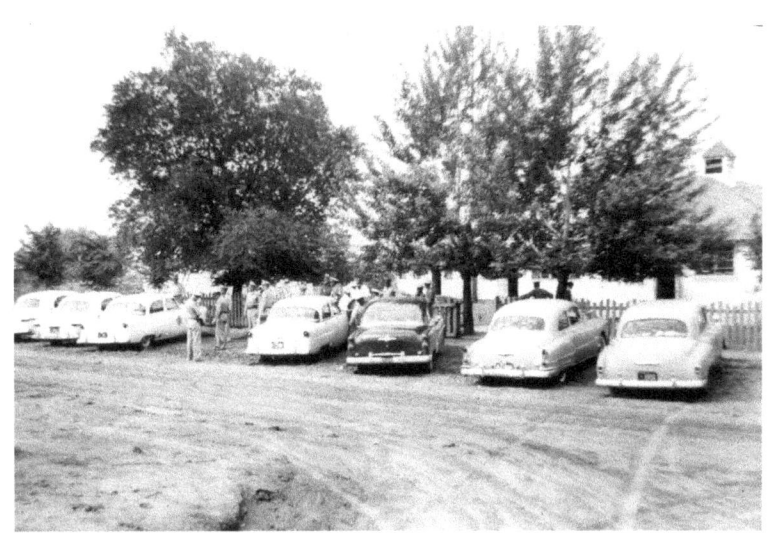

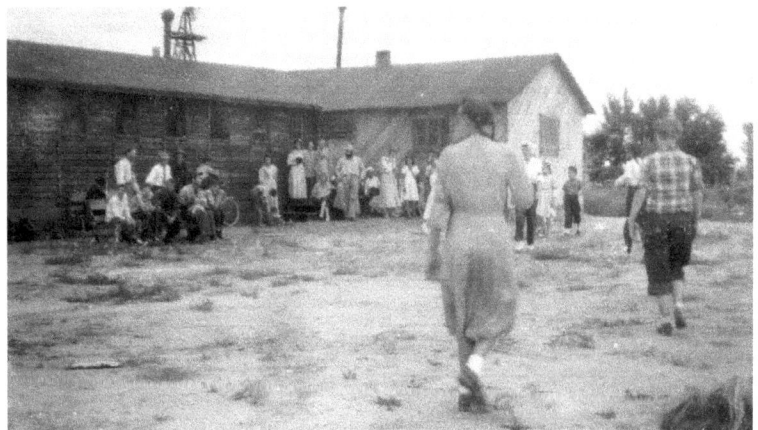

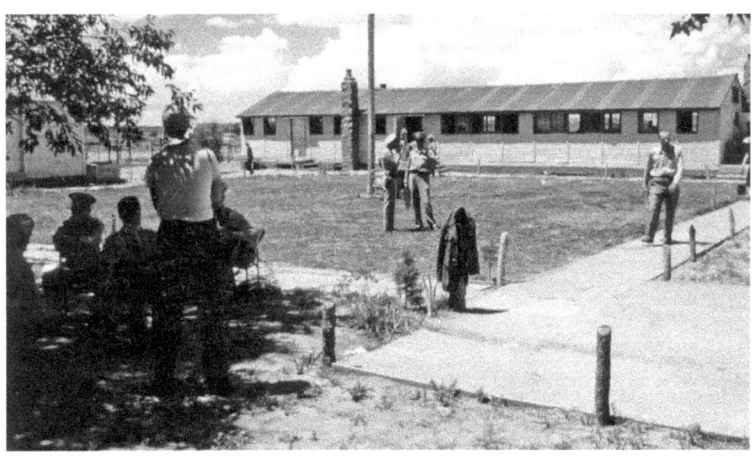

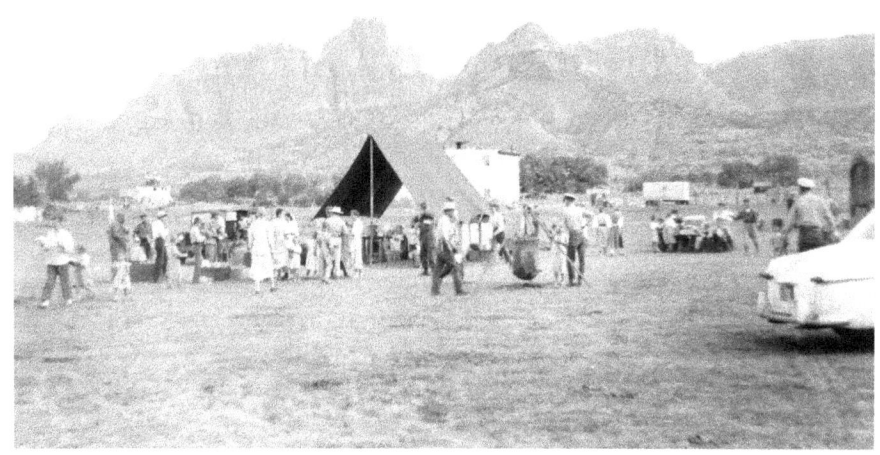

Camp kitchen. *Authors' collection.*

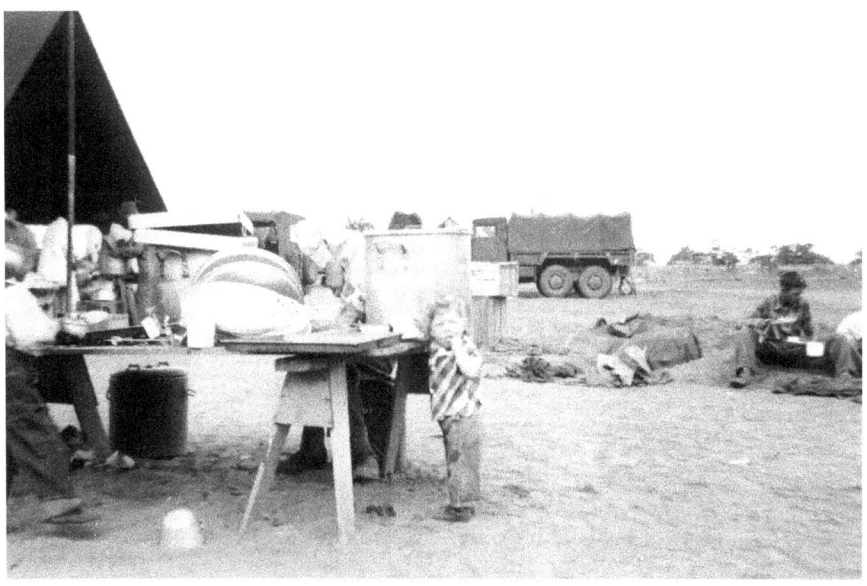

Lucy Mackert at camp kitchen. *Donna K. Mackert Collection.*

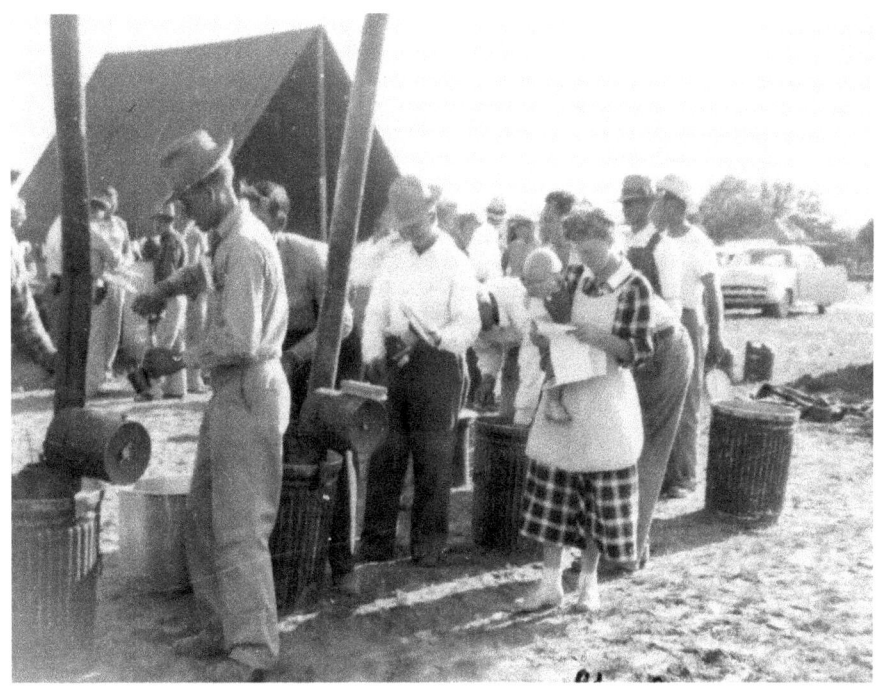

Short Creek residents at mealtime. *Authors' collection.*

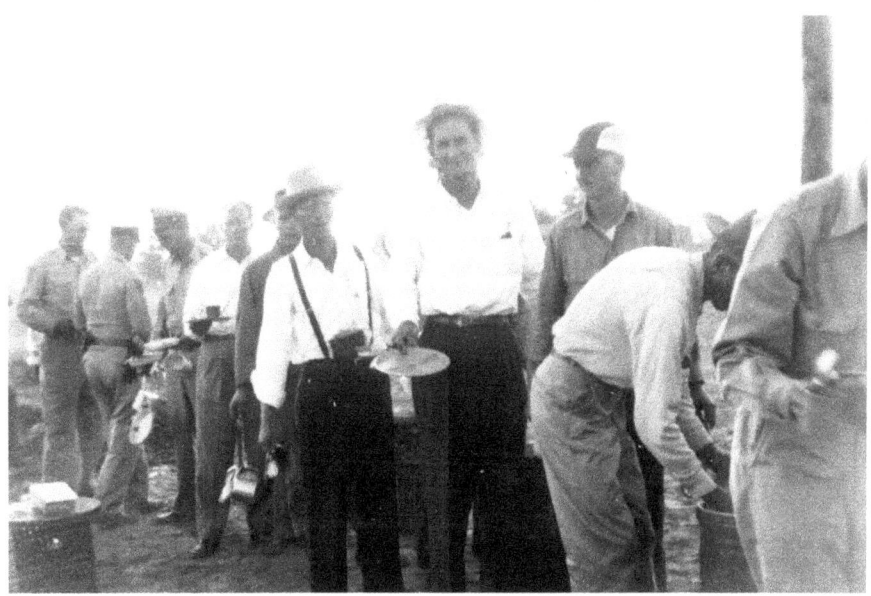

Short Creek men and police officers waiting in line at camp kitchen. *Authors' collection.*

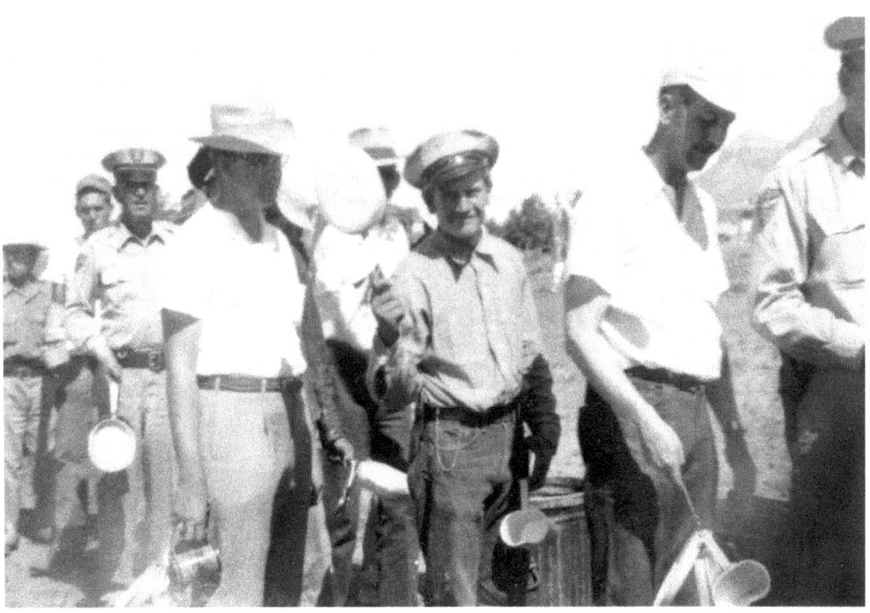

Another view of Short Creek men and police officers waiting in line to be fed. *Authors' collection.*

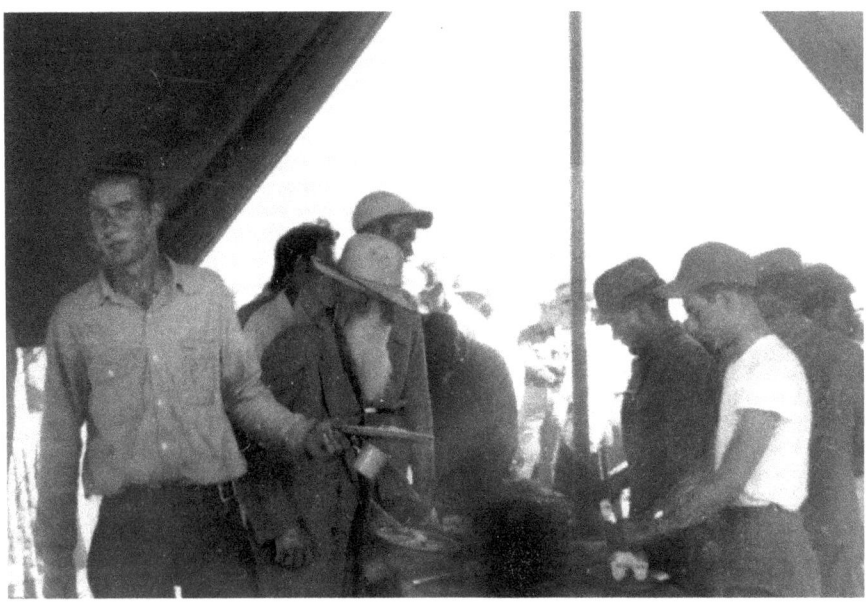

Food line and servers under a kitchen tent. *Authors' collection.*

could have done a pretty good job given their experience as sharpshooters and with handling explosives. Cooler heads, however, prevailed. Leroy S. Johnson, the community's leader, told them there would be no fighting, nor would there be any running. He was tired of running and hiding and urged a peaceful resolution to the forthcoming confrontation. Thus, Johnson decided to gather the community to sing and peacefully await the inevitable invasion of their small enclave.[200]

Mohave County sheriff Fred Porter climbed out of a vehicle and announced that they had a job to perform. Lawmen then secured the small settlement, and prepared warrants were issued to all but a few of the adults. "The charges against the Fundamentalists included rape, statutory rape, carnal knowledge, polygamous living, cohabitation, bigamy, adultery, and misappropriation of school funds."[201] There were 263 children in the community, and "[t]he principle objective [was] to rescue these children from a life-time of immoral practices without their ever having had an opportunity to learn of or observe the outside world and its concepts of decent living."[202]

Within a short time, tents were set up at the command center, and a breakfast of bacon and eggs was prepared for the captives and their captors. Edson Jessop later recalled that meal as a humiliating, degrading experience. They "had to hunker down on the ground, in the sun and flies, eating tasteless food brought from Phoenix—within sight of our own homes, stocked with fresh garden vegetables, milk, eggs, home-baked bread and the civilized comfort of chairs and white tablecloths."[203]

A DEHUMANIZING EXPERIENCE

This was just the beginning of what many of the polygamists felt was a dehumanizing experience that disregarded their constitutional rights and turned their quiet lives upside down. The children had been awakened and ordered to dress and come out of their homes, and the people were forced to wait together in the heat of the day in the center of the community while officials processed the adults and performed other duties. During that time, reporters roamed the streets taking photos and writing notes about the "[d]irty, ramshackle buildings, starkly etched against the faded red backdrop of the vermillion cliffs, cluster[ed] along [a] dusty road.... The stamp of poverty, deep and warping, is everywhere."[204]

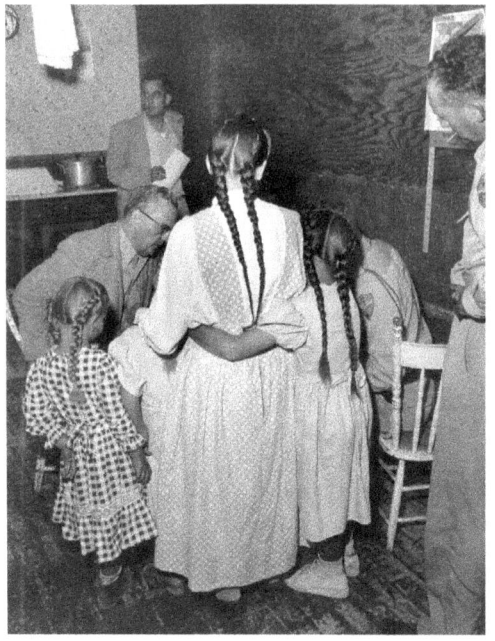 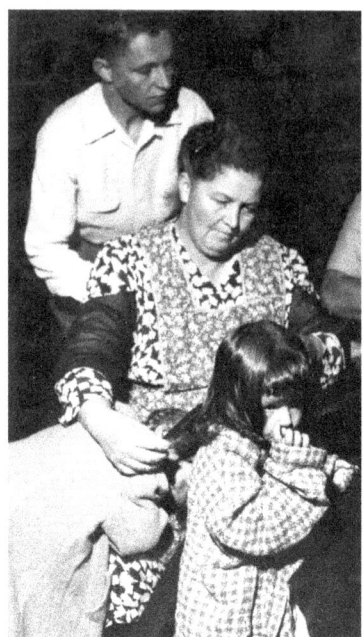

Left: Ester Holm being questioned by officers. *Authors' collection.*

Right: Fawn Broadbent with officers. *Authors' collection.*

In the late afternoon, they were finally allowed to return to their homes. A little later, thirty-six men and eight women who were either childless or had grown children were loaded into cars to be driven to Kingman. They arrived late that same night to what they described as a filthy and poorly kept jailhouse. The humiliation continued for those left behind in Short Creek, as "a court photographer and a deputy sheriff photographed each home and each wife with her children. They also photographed outbuildings and junked, rusting cars the children played in, incorrectly labeling such cars as 'dwellings' for some of the polygamous families. Later the Fundamentalists would mention among their resentments the added indignity of being linked with this image of slovenly indigence."[205] Furthermore, all the homes were carefully searched for any documentation of plural marriages, particularly with underage brides.

On Monday, July 29, in a scene reminiscent of the Roosevelt administration's rounding up of Japanese Americans at the beginning of World War II, the women were forced to hurriedly pack for themselves and their children. They and their children were then marched down to the

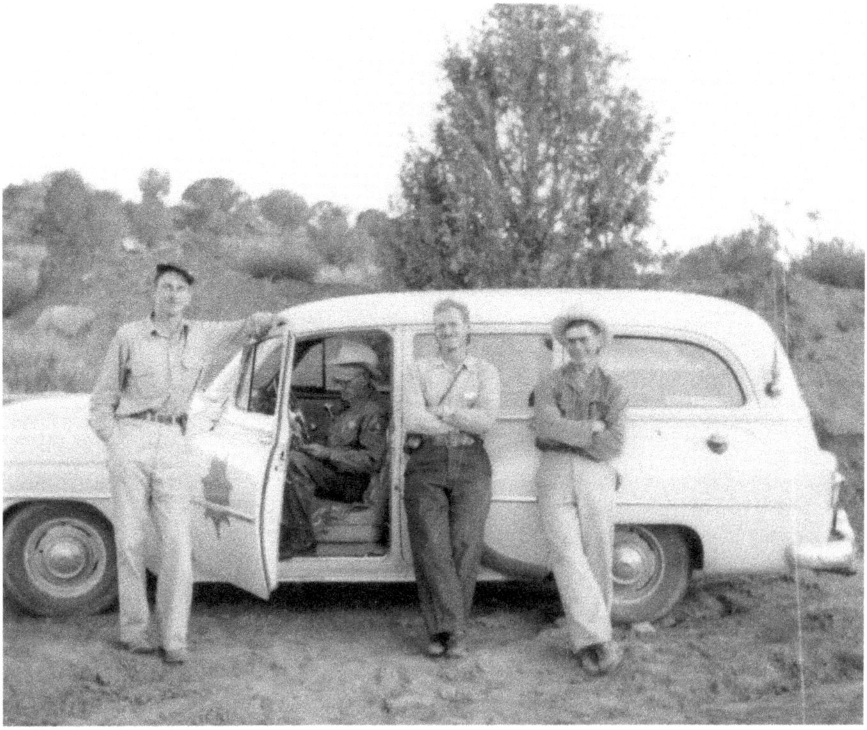

Short Creek youth caught by cops posing by a police car. *Authors' collection*.

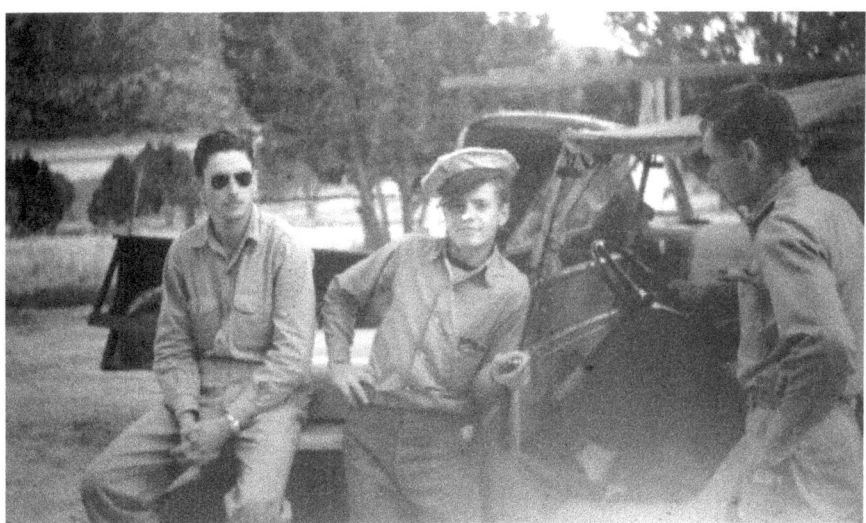

Short Creek youth David Broadbent (*left*), Merrill Jessop (*center*) and Jerry Jessop. *Authors' collection*.

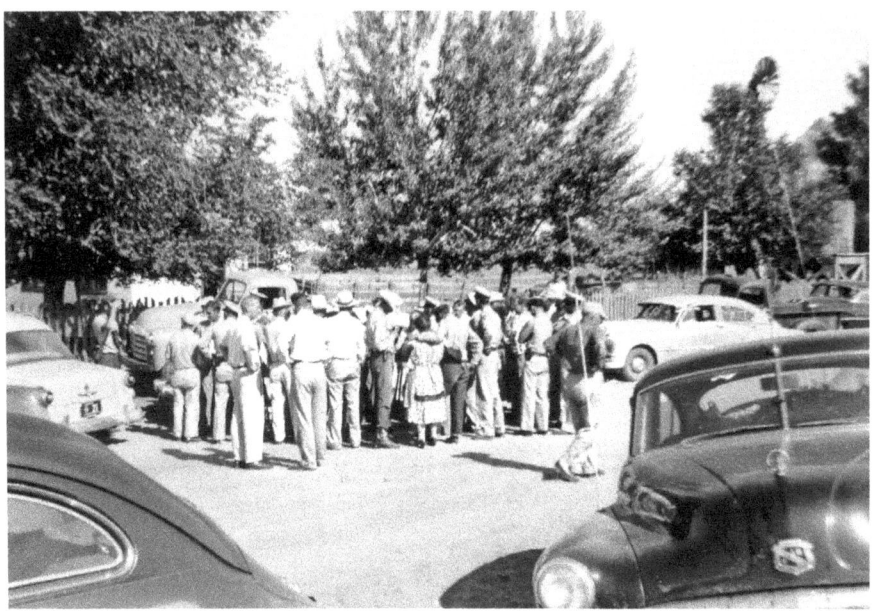

Gathering in street in preparation for transporting women and children to Phoenix. *Authors' collection.*

schoolyard and once again forced to wait, corralled together in the fenced-in portion of the schoolyard until they were loaded onto five buses brought in to transport them.

State welfare officials explained to the 56 women that the government was taking custody of 153 out of the 263 children—99 children of plural wives resided in Utah, so the Arizona authorities did not take them. There also were 10 children of monogamous parents so they were not taken either.[206] These and a few of the teenage boys were left behind to try to care for the farm animals and perform other chores for the community. Alvin Barlow, then fifteen years old, remembered standing in the middle of the road watching the buses leave.

Because of so many children and the chaos of the whole situation, it took three hours to get the buses loaded, and people were tired and restless before the trip even began. The trip to Phoenix ended up being seventeen agonizing hours of discomfort. For example, the bus drivers had been told to not stop for any reason, including restroom stops. The buses did not have built-in toilets, and the only way for relief was a single child's "potty" chair in the aisle of each bus with no hope of privacy or comfort.[207]

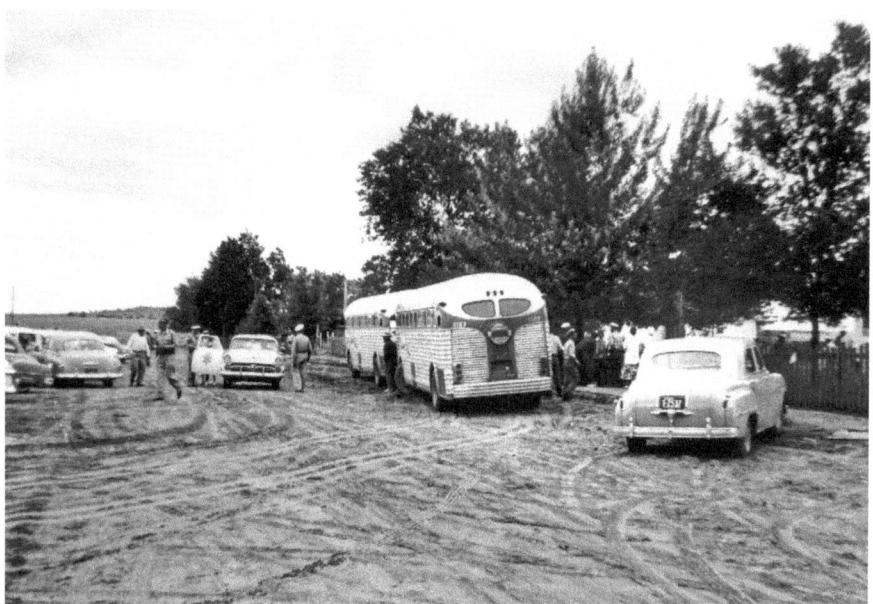

Main Street and one of the buses that took the women and children to Phoenix. *Authors' collection.*

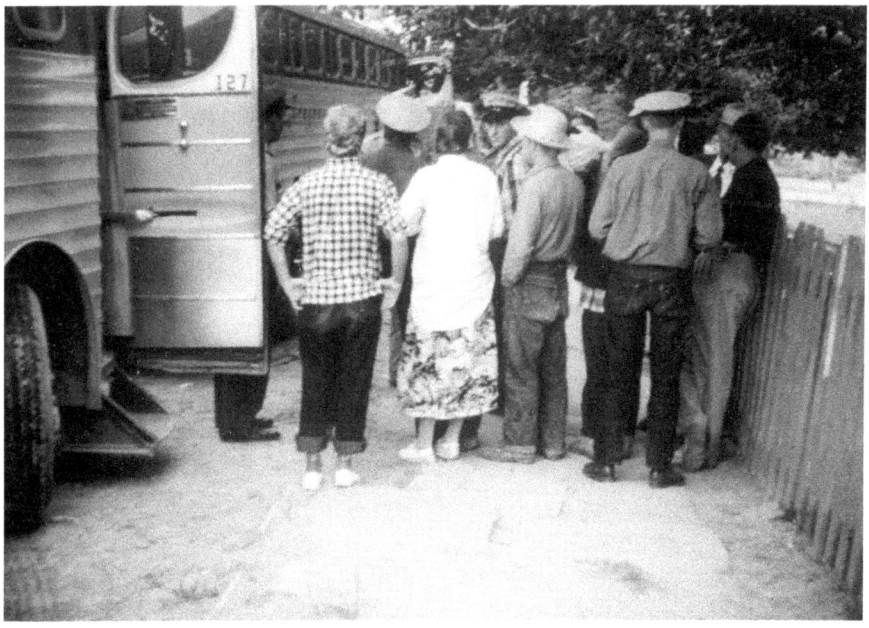

Mothers and children being loaded on buses. Karen Truman is in jeans at left. *Authors' collection.*

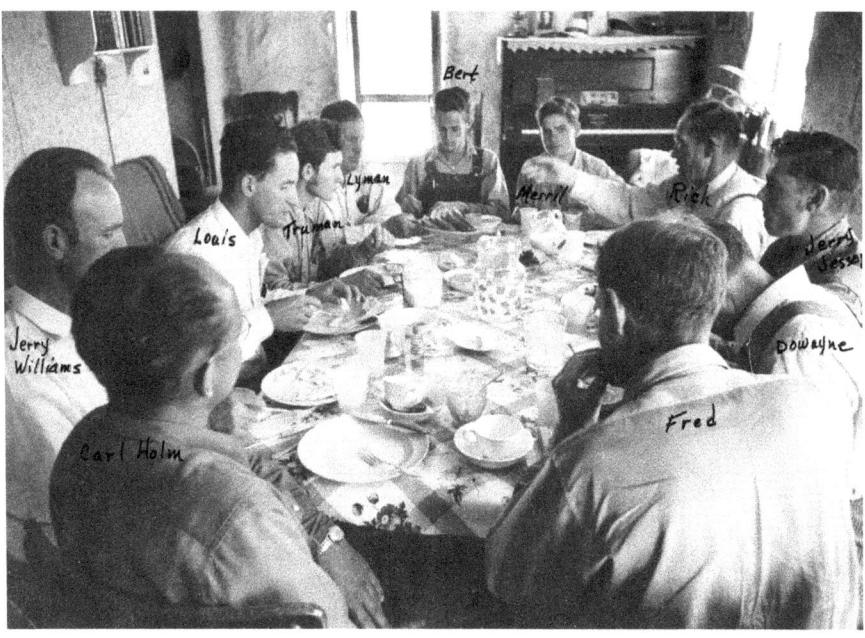

Right: Joseph Smith Jessop, age eighty-four, by flagpole ready for arrest: "If its blood you want, take mine!" *Authors' collection.*

Below: Men at breakfast the morning of Joseph Smith Jessop's funeral. *Authors' collection.*

When the buses arrived in Phoenix and nearby Mesa, the women and children were taken first to the National Guard Armory and the YMCA but shortly thereafter parceled out to foster homes in the Phoenix-Mesa area and as far away as Snowflake, St. Johns and St. Davids, the latter three being Mormon settlements. The state had arranged for the Fundamentalist women and children to be housed in LDS homes.[208]

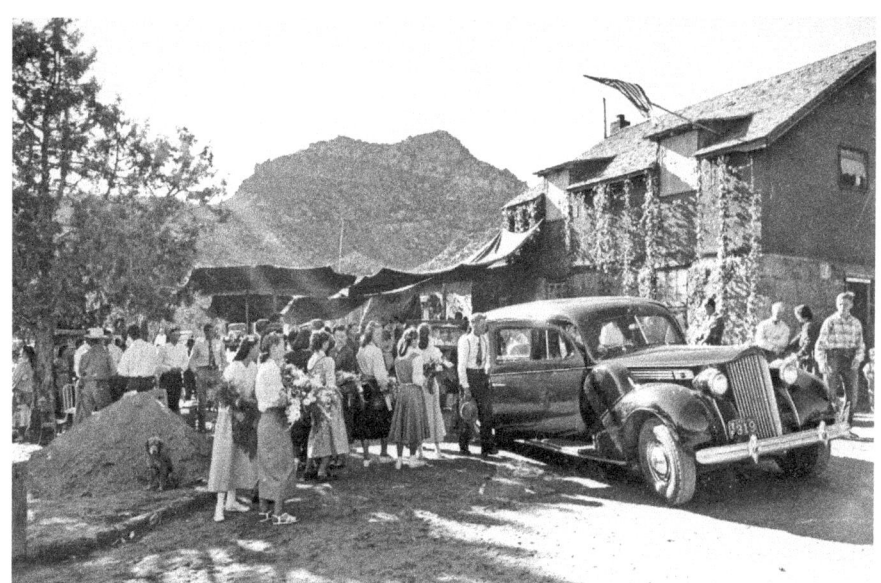

Gathering of relatives for Joseph Smith Jessop's funeral. *Authors' collection.*

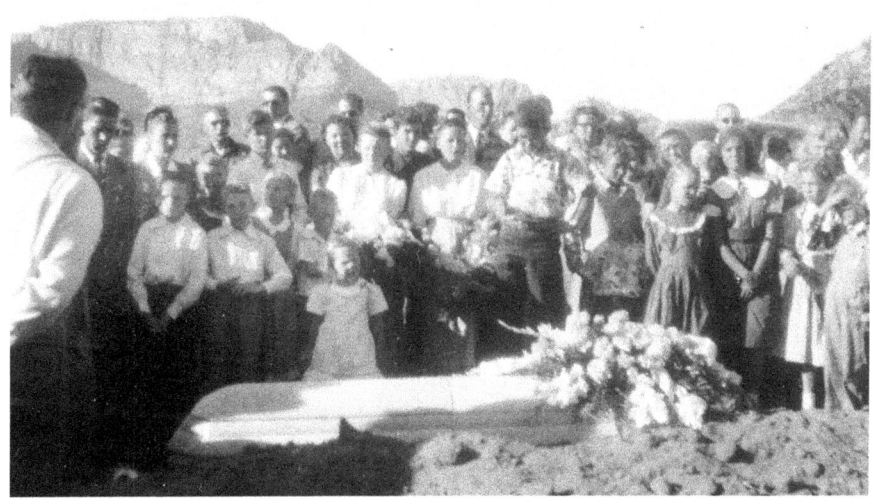

Joseph Smith Jessop's burial. *Authors' collection.*

One of the early casualties of the Short Creek Raid was eighty-three-year-old Joseph Smith Jessop, an early follower of Lorin C. Woolley who had sacrificed much for the continuation of plural marriage and the doctrines in which he firmly believed. In his old age, he had moved to Short Creek with the hope of freely practicing his religion. He, like the other polygamous adults, was arrested and taken to Kingman. Although released almost immediately and allowed to return to Short Creek, he grieved over what had befallen his small community. About five weeks later, Jessop died from the trauma of the raid, especially from the excruciating bus ride to Kingman without restroom stops. A few days before his death, he commented, "The old fire burns in me strong, but it is going out."[209]

A week after the raid, Leroy Johnson was able to raise enough money to get all the men and the eight women released on bail. They slowly made their way back to Short Creek. The first phase of the raid was over, but the battle had just begun. While it was a long, traumatic experience for the Fundamentalists, the battle did not unfold triumphantly the way the state officials had originally predicted.

HOWARD PYLE'S FOLLY

The Sunday morning of the initial raid, Governor Howard Pyle of Arizona explained and justified his actions to the press. He accused the Fundamentalists of "the foulest conspiracy you could possibly imagine," described the community as "dedicated to the production of white slaves" and asserted girls were being forced into a "shameful mockery of marriage." He explained that girls under age fifteen were forced to marry men of all ages, and authorities told news media that four of the plural wives were thirteen years old, two were fourteen and two others were fifteen.[210]

While the term "white slavery" could certainly be debated, Governor Pyle's accusations were not without basis. Martha Sonntag Bradley, in her book *Kidnapped from that Land*, identifies at least nine wives aged fifteen and below with at least two being thirteen at the time of the raid and several older wives who had married at age fifteen or younger.[211]

In spite of the government's best efforts at positive spin, public sentiment quickly shifted in favor of the Fundamentalists, particularly the women and children. Editorials began to appear in newspapers questioning not only the constitutionality of the government's actions but also both the sagacity and intentions of such a move. For example, under a title of "Reprehensible Raid," one editorial asked, "Was it law enforcement or a publicity stunt?"[212]

The media dubbed the raid "Pyle's Folly," and the *Arizona Republic* wrote that the law enforcement's actions would have made the Keystone Kops "green with envy." Criticism came from practically all sides as religious and community leaders condemned the raid and its aftermath. Democrats accused the Republican governor's actions as "odious and un-American."[213]

Ultimately, charges of rape and contributing to the delinquency of a minor were dropped and the men pleaded guilty to conspiracy to violate laws against bigamy and open and notorious cohabitation. They were given one-year suspensions and allowed to return to Short Creek.

The return of the women and particularly the children, however, was not as straightforward or as easy to achieve. Upon their arrival in Phoenix, the children were made wards of the state and placed on welfare for their subsistence. Mothers were allowed to stay with their children, but since they were permitted to come and go as they wished, they had to pay for their own food and lodging. Despite freedom to come and go, they were informed that should they return home for even a short visit, their children would be placed in foster homes with intent to adopt them permanently. Basically, the women and their children were captives of an uncaring and indifferent state government.[214]

THE VERA BLACK CASE

It took two to four years for all of the children to be returned to their homes and families, and ultimately all went home. But the legal maze the Fundamentalists were forced to negotiate in both Arizona and Utah was incredible. On the Utah side, the test case concerning the children of Leonard and Vera Black drew the most attention. Vera was Leonard Black's second wife, and they had been married since about 1935 and were the parents of eight children, one of them handicapped. Their children were taken away from them, and there followed a kind of judicial tug-of-war as the children were taken, returned, then taken again. Washington County, Utah juvenile judge David F. Anderson had made it clear in correspondence with the chief Arizona prosecutor that he would "take all possible steps to protect the children from growing up to be polygamists."[215]

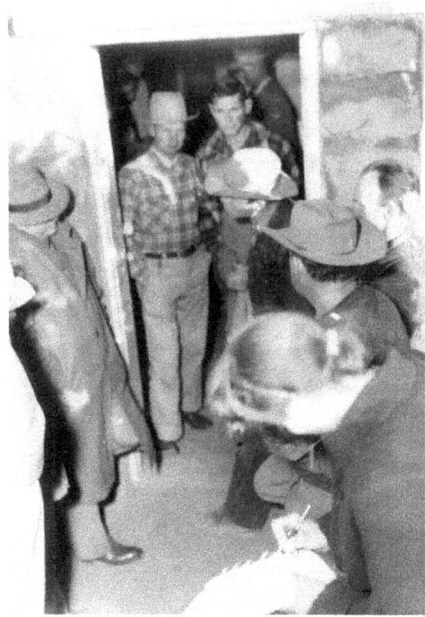 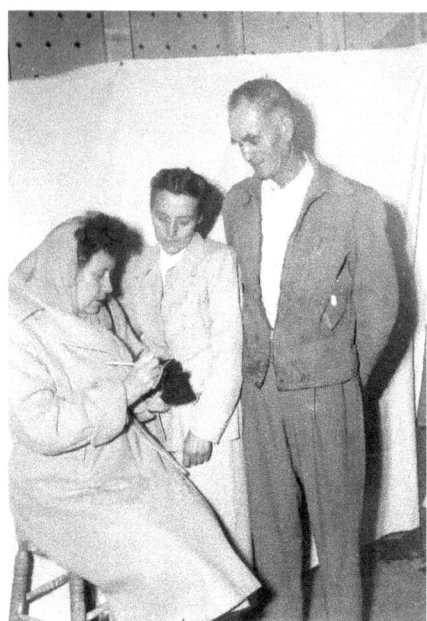

Left: Friends and reporters await news of Vera Black's trial. *Authors' collection.*

Right: Vera *(center)* and Leonard Black with a social worker. *Authors' collection.*

The children were taken away again when Vera refused to sign a statement promising they would not practice or teach plural marriage. Ultimately, the case was taken to the Utah Supreme Court:

> *In one of the harshest opinions in the court's history Justice George M. Worthen laid down a per se rule of law that polygamous parents had virtually no rights to their children. State child welfare authorities could strip polygamists of their children and adopt them out to more traditional homes in order "that children should not be subjected to its evil influence and environment."*[216]

When it became apparent the state was not going to rule in their favor, Vera ultimately signed the demanded statement to get her children back. In June 1956, Vera Black testified, "I still believe in the law of polygamy. It is my religious belief, but I will teach the children to obey the laws of the state and will discourage my children from entering into polygamous marriages as long as the state has laws against it." A few days after the hearing, Vera

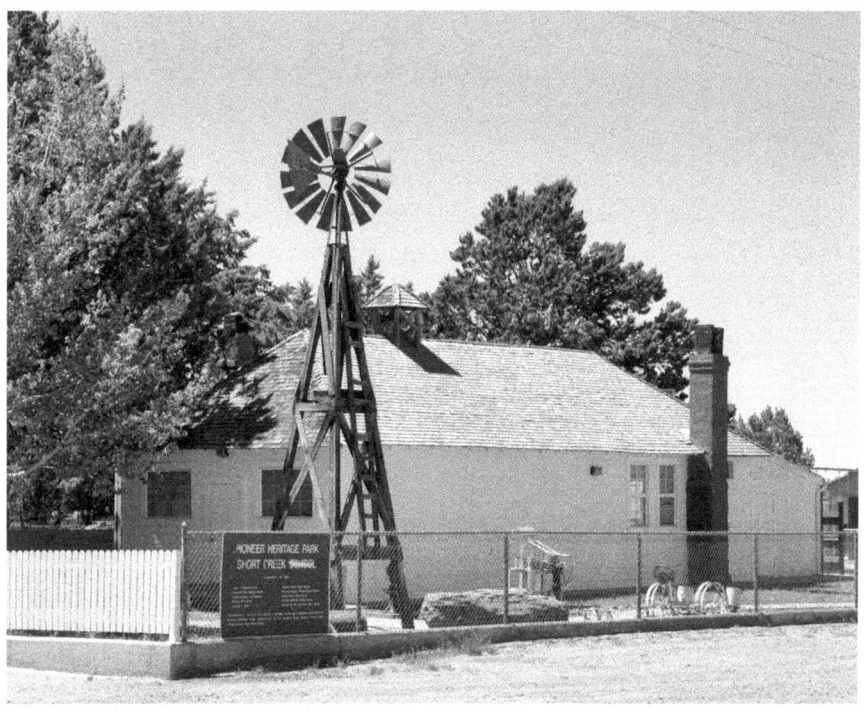

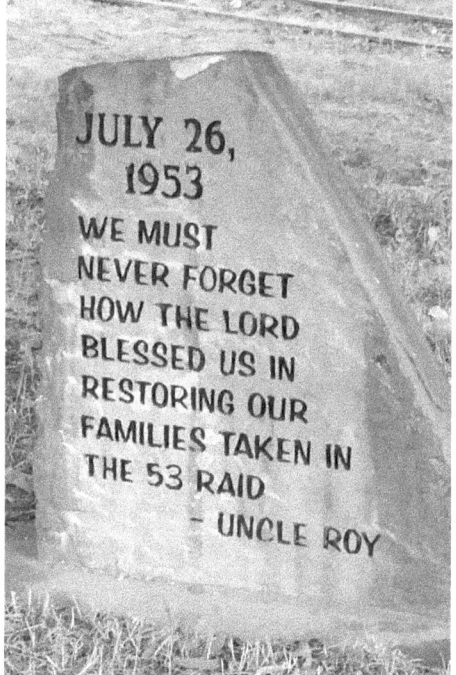

Above: School House Park Memorial, circa 2017. *Steven L. Mayfield Collection.*

Left: 1953 Short Creek Raid Memorial in the Isaac Carling Park in Colorado City. *Steven L. Mayfield Collection.*

was reunited with her children and returned to Short Creek, where she and Leonard continued in their faith as before but were no longer harassed by state officials.[217] This case also generated deep backlash and public outrage against the state when media stories, photos and editorial cartoons portrayed officers taking her children.

For Fundamentalists, the raid and its aftermath conflicted with their view of constitutional rights and freedom to practice their religion as they wished. Like their forefathers, they too suffered varying degrees of judicial prosecution and, some would say, persecution. And also like their forefathers, they too sought both divine and legal relief with mixed success. The effects of the raid and its aftermath reinforced for Fundamentalists a sense of alienation from the mainstream American populace and for most of them an intense distrust of the outside that continues to affect Fundamentalist Mormons.

A Time of Change, Conflict and Growth

T hroughout the 1950s and into the early years of the 1960s, Fundamentalist Mormons felt as if they were continually under attack. Many were still feeling the effects of the 1953 Short Creek raid and the seemingly endless legal jousting in its aftermath, including the fact that a number of women and children were still in Arizona's custody, when the federal government also got involved.

THE END OF THE 1950s AND THE 1960s

In 1955, the Congressional Judiciary Committee's Subcommittee to Investigate Juvenile Delinquency held hearings investigating Short Creek and its residents. These series of hearings were held in Phoenix and even in Short Creek, where Utah and Arizona deputy sheriffs worked together to cordon off the community. Officials "heard testimony about family relationships, religious doctrine, and the marriages of juveniles." Short Creek women were brought in to answer questions "about their beliefs, the environment in which they had been raised, their family relationships, and what they had observed about the marital relationships in other families." These women's answers were intentionally vague and not totally forthcoming given they had little reason to trust government representatives.[218]

That same year, 1953, two Fundamentalist men were sentenced to up to five years in the Utah State Penitentiary for unlawful cohabitation.[219] There

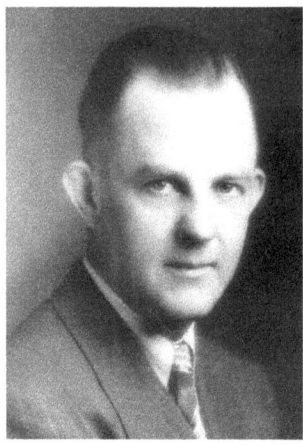

Independent Fundamentalist David B. Darger (1902–1981). *FamilySearch.org Family Tree.*

were other men who were arrested in 1955 and 1956 for unlawful cohabitation. One of the men, David Brigham Darger, grandfather of Joe Darger of TLC's *My Three Wives* fame, was arrested in Los Angeles, California, and returned to Utah to face charges. Ultimately, between 1955 and 1957, five men were sentenced to prison for unlawful cohabitation.

While these various arrests and convictions were announced in the news, they were not done so with the media fanfare of the 1953 Short Creek raid. Law officials recognized what a public relations fiasco their attempts had been garnering big media attention and encouraged a more muted media coverage of their ongoing "raid" against the polygamists. Because of this approach, despite occasional sensationalistic newspaper articles discussing "harems" in America, the specter of modern American polygamists slipped from the daily attention of most Americans.

That was not the case, however, for law officials of the Intermountain West and certainly was not the case for Fundamentalist Mormons. Throughout the 1950s and into the 1960s, law officials of Utah and surrounding states made a concerted effort to, if not actually stamp out polygamy, at least harass, punish and make life difficult for those practicing plural marriage. In spite of their continued efforts, by this point, even law officials probably recognized they were fighting a losing war given the fact that in 1956 the Utah State Welfare Board had reported an estimated two thousand people in Utah living in polygamous households.[220] Those numbers were bound to significantly increase.

Nevertheless, law officials carried on their campaigns against polygamists. In March 1960, polygamist leaders received news that law officials and, frustratingly to Fundamentalists, LDS Church officials, were planning "another all-out effort against the polygamists that summer." A friendly Salt Lake City police officer warned Rulon Allred that Nevada authorities were preparing to move against suspected polygamists in Elko and Wells. Allred immediately moved his families from those two places.

In April 1961, Walter L. Budge, Utah attorney general, announced "an all-out war against polygamists."[221] The State of Utah had pledged cooperation with all the western states. A large amount of money had

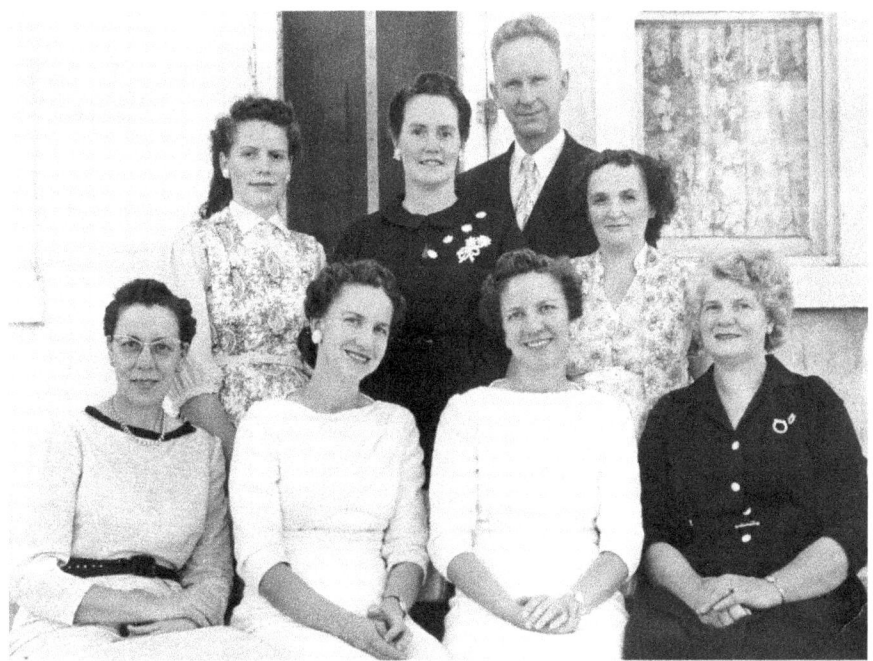

Rulon C. Allred and seven wives, 1959. *Authors' collection.*

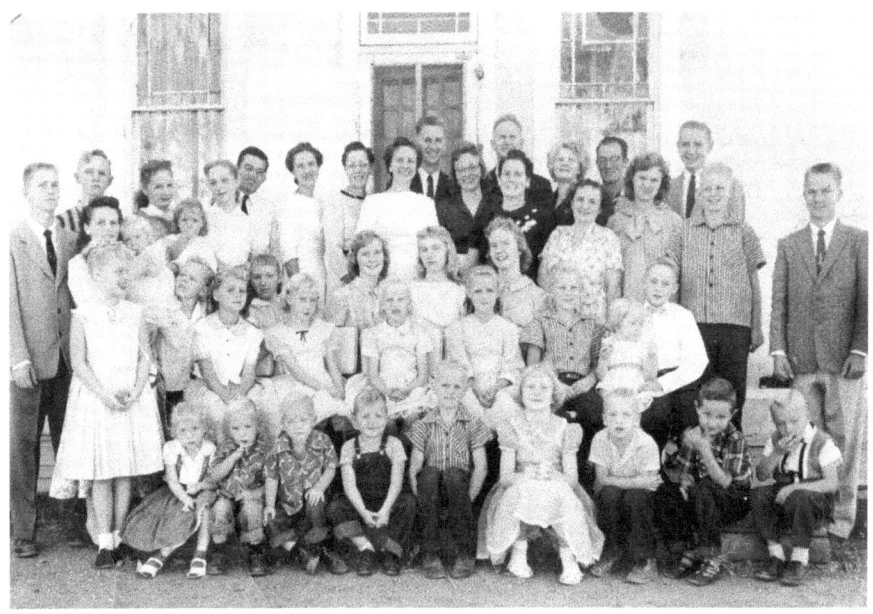

Rulon C. Allred family, 1959. *Authors' collection.*

been "appropriated for prosecution and for agents to work on a full-time investigation." That same year, Utah considered legislation that would "punish women who lived plural marriage with five years of jail time in the state penitentiary, same as men." Furthermore, polygamous parents would be considered felons and would lose all rights as citizens, including their children, who would "become wards of the state, adopted out to foster homes, and their parents would forever lose custody." The bill did not make it through the legislature.[222]

It is little wonder that Fundamentalist families exhibited a combination of a persecution complex and fortress mentality, as they rightfully believed they were under assault from practically all directions. Wives and children were compelled to use aliases in public, to constantly be on the move in order to avoid the authorities; they lived in fear of the outside world. Polygamous men were forced to be on the run and to travel great miles to visit far-flung wives and children.

For example, upon getting word in July 1955 of an imminent raid against his household, Rulon C. Allred moved his seven wives and their children from Salt Lake City to Pocatello and Blackfoot, Idaho, as well as Mountain City, Nevada. A month later, he moved two of his wives to Elko and another wife to Albuquerque, New Mexico. By February 1956, he had moved that same wife from New Mexico to Central Point, Oregon, and by summer to Finley Point, Montana, while a couple of his other wives lived in other parts of Montana and Idaho. Each of these early moves had been in response to authorities' efforts to apprehend Allred's plural wives. In this game of cat-and-mouse between the lawmen and polygamists, the moves and efforts to avoid arrest took on an almost comical version of cloak and dagger that even included disguises and decoys. By 1961, Rulon Allred had resettled wives in different parts of Salt Lake City and in Pinesdale, Montana.[223]

Because of this extended period of judicial prosecution and, as the Fundamentalists saw it, persecution, forms and places of refuge were sought out. Each Fundamentalist group reacted differently and took a different approach. Some decided the best approach was to hunker down and try to be as inconspicuous as possible, while others sought a refuge outside of Utah.

In 1961, Rulon Allred purchased 640 acres of ranch land at the base of the Bitterroot Mountains in western Montana. He hoped to create not only a place of refuge but also a United Order community. Ultimately Pinesdale, Montana, was established as a community for the Allred group that allowed polygamist husbands to have one or two wives there and others in Utah.

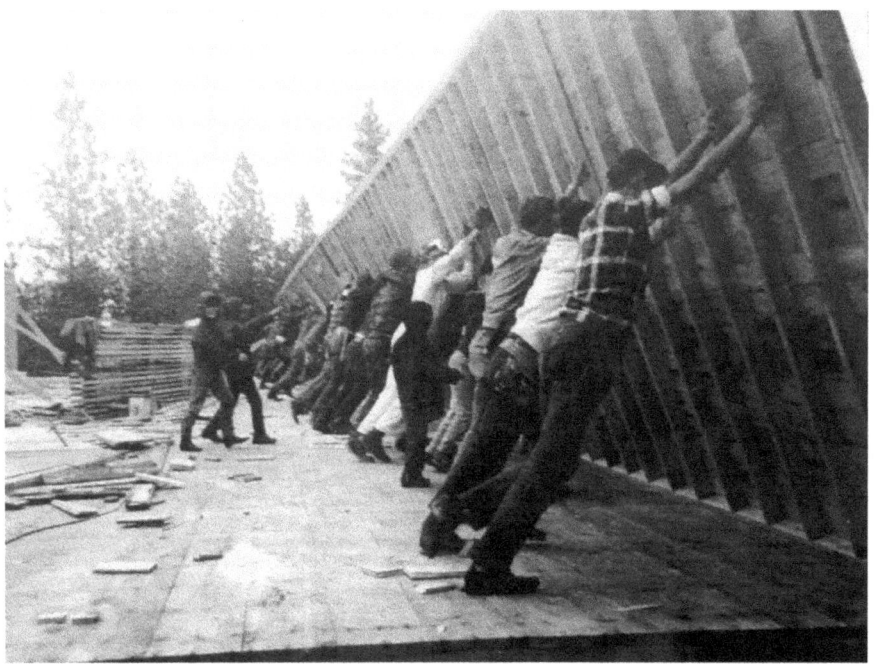

Construction of first community school in Pinesdale, Montana. *Authors' collection.*

The small woodland hamlet had its ups and downs, including ostracism and prejudice from surrounding communities that looked down on the fledgling community as a hotbed of sin. Pinesdale residents were "plagued" by the "dirty jokes and righteous indignation" of outsiders. One resident recalled that when he would tell outsiders where he lived, he would hear offensive comments like "I've half a mind to move up there myself. I'm a great stud." Problems continued off and on between Pinesdale residents and surrounding communities. As late as 1972, outsiders gathered in Hamilton to discuss how to force the polygamists out of the Bitterroot Valley. Community representatives "were able to convince some of the top citizens that driving out the polygamists would do more harm than good."[224] Nevertheless, over the years, relations between "Pineys," as residents are commonly known, and outside communities have warmed, and Pinesdale, which was incorporated in 1983, is now a bustling community.

Located in Davis County and Salt Lake City, members of the Kingstons, or Davis County Cooperative Society, an extremely secretive group, seemed to be able to keep their heads down and, for the most part, fly under the radar during this difficult time. Staying mostly to themselves, marrying one

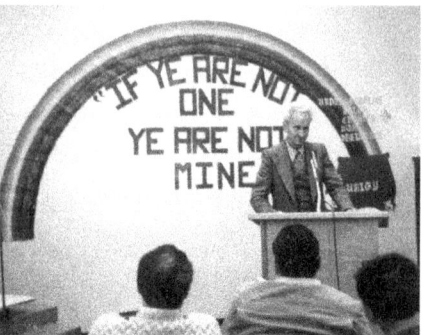

Above: Rulon C. Allred speaking in Pinesdale. *Authors' collection.*

Left: Allred Group council member Marvin L. Allred playing baseball at Pinesdale conference. *Authors' collection.*

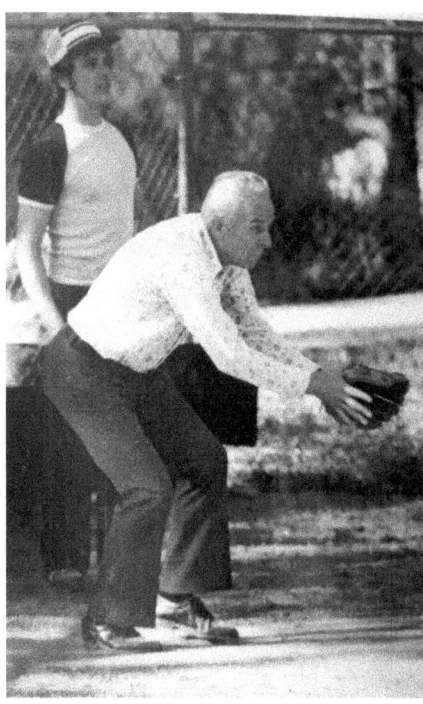

another, including a number of intra-familial marriages, the group quietly built an extensive business empire, only rarely coming to public notice during this time. One of the few moments of unwanted publicity was when the Kingstons expanded their business operations in the community of Bountiful just a few miles north of Salt Lake City. The city manager asked the state attorney general's office to investigate the "polygamous cult" because of his fear of their greater presence in his city.[225]

For the Short Creek group, most of their legal battles were behind them by the beginning of the 1960s. Their experiences had left them battle-worn and distrustful of the outside world. Ironically, in the first half of the 1960s, there were several changes that, in spite of being distrustful of the outside world, made their community more accessible for outsiders. In 1961, the Arizona side of Short Creek was renamed Colorado City. The Utah side wasn't renamed until 1968, when it was organized under the name of Hildale.[226]

An event that brought the most amount of change and outside scrutiny in a time when Short Creek residents would have preferred more anonymity was the completion of an oiled highway from Hurricane, Utah, to Short Creek in 1962 followed by a paved highway in 1965 that stretched from

Hurricane to Fredonia, Arizona, with Short Creek approximately halfway in between.[227] From that point forward, the way was literally paved for a curious outside world to visit the small community hoping to catch a view of some polygamists. In 1962, Short Creek had an estimated population of about four hundred but was steadily growing.

Before the 1960s, Fundamentalist Mormons tended to blend with the general population because dress styles were similar. While there began to be a slight shift in the later 1950s, it was during the social turmoil of the so-called Sexual Revolution in the 1960s that a significant dividing point occurred between Fundamentalists and mainstream America. This similarly affected some members of the LDS Church.

Most Fundamentalists continued to wear long-sleeved shirts and long dresses or skirts, although styles differed somewhat by group. For example, many Independents and other Fundamentalist Mormons to this day blend with most Americans in styles of dress. Members of the Allred group (AUB) generally wear the popular styles of the day but "still preserve the tradition of long sleeves, and long pants and dresses." Thus, while they follow the popular clothing trends, most AUB women wear clothing that goes to the ankles and wrists. Some time ago, an AUB woman said that for this reason she was able to pick out another AUB woman at a bus stop where several mothers had gathered to wait for their children. The AUB woman wore long pants, a long-sleeved shirt and long hair in a ponytail, while the other mothers wore knee-length shorts, short-sleeved shirts and bobbed hair.[228]

Women of the Kingstons, on the other hand, while usually having long hair and conservative dress styles, like most Fundamentalists, appear to vary in the length of their blouses and shirt sleeves. Some wear tops with long sleeves, while others have short sleeves.

Fundamentalist Mormons in the two Short Creek groups, the FLDS and Centennial Park, have the most conservative dress codes. The men of the Centennial Park group usually wear jeans and long-sleeved shirts or business attire, while women and girls wear dresses, skirts and long-sleeved blouses and sweaters. Like other Fundamentalist counterparts, FLDS and Centennial Park women also wear their hair long.[229]

Certainly, most distinctive in both hair and dress style are the FLDS. FLDS women of all ages are known for their prairie dresses in a rainbow of pastels or muted autumn colors and their long, poofed hair and fancy braiding. According to some, "Modern FLDS women believe the intricacies of the braiding and the height of their hair is reflective of their womanhood and spirituality." Different from the past, FLDS women are not allowed to let their long hair hang loose down their backs because they consider it immoral.[230]

Ironically, the well-known image of the FLDS women with pastel dresses and poofed hair is a relatively new development. At the time of the 1953 Short Creek raid, the men wore jeans or overalls with long-sleeved shirts; women mostly wore work dresses or occasionally jeans, while girls in pigtails wore jeans and short-sleeved plaid shirts or skirts and blouses. They would have fit in well in any rural American community of that

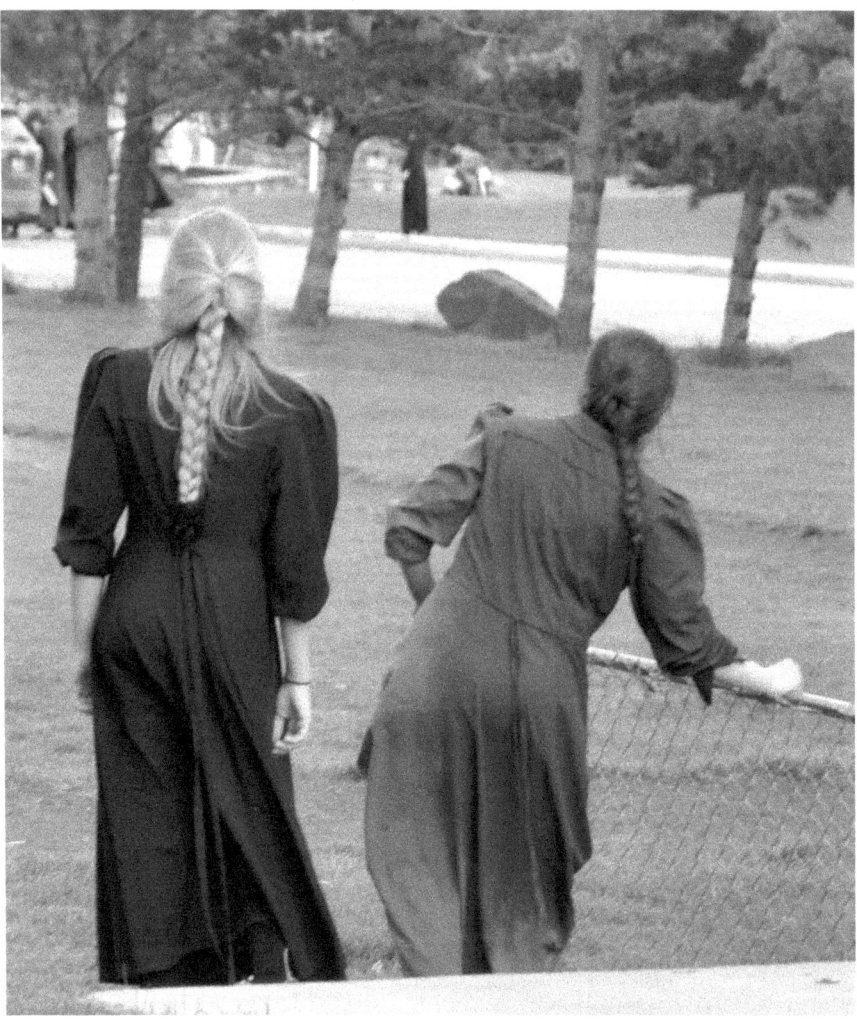

FLDS young women's braided hairstyles. *Anne Wilde Collection.*

period. After returning to Short Creek from their sojourn in non-Mormon communities, Leroy Johnson, the group's leader, began a retrenchment in which females of any age were discouraged from wearing jeans and instead encouraged to wear only dresses. The only dress requirements then were modesty and that the dress was at least below the knees. There were no restrictions on pattern or color. In fact, most women preferred bright colors and floral patterns, as Leroy Johnson was, himself, partial to floral patterns, opining that they brought out the women's femininity.[231]

Both dress and hairstyles changed with the death of Leroy Johnson and new leadership of Rulon Jeffs in 1986. Rulon first forbid the wearing of red because of the belief that red was sacred to Jesus Christ, who will be dressed in red when he returns in glory at His Second Coming, and anyone wearing red was exhibiting pride. Jeffs then banned wearing floral and other patterned clothing because this too reflected sinful pride. He then dictated a specific design of dress that should be worn and encouraged plain, non-patterned, light pastels or muted fall colors. In his opinion, such fabrics were more conducive to the spirit of God. While women could wear darker dresses (greens, blues and browns) for outdoor work, pastels were considered more appropriate for indoor activities since "pastel colors evoke femininity and don't come across as bold or strong."[232]

THE 1970s: A TIME OF CHANGE AND GROWTH

The 1970s included times of change and growth as well as sorrow for members of the Allred group. In 1970, the Allred group numbered approximately 2,500 and showed rapid growth both from children being born as well as from converts. New converts from different locations as well as purchases of new properties allowed the group to branch out farther than just the Salt Lake Valley and Pinesdale, Montana. By this time, Pinesdale alone had almost 400 people and continued to grow throughout the 1970s despite off-and-on squabbles and other problems within the small community.

In 1971, Marvin Allred, Rulon Allred's younger brother, with his sons bought 225 acres of land between Santaquin and Mona in the north part of Juab County, Utah. This property was just west of the highway that would later become the I-15 freeway. The ridge separating Juab County from Utah County was called Rocky Ridge for the rocky terrain. This name was adopted for the new community.[233]

Work on the first home started in October 1971, and that winter, men, women and even children spent many hours slowly building the house. Although the first residents were basically the extended family of Marvin Allred, numerous members of the AUB donated time and labor to the construction of the first homes. The first families were able to take up residence in June 1972.[234]

The first years at Rocky Ridge demanded roughing it compared to surrounding communities. There was a problem with rattlesnakes dislodged from their traditional habitat. Also, at first they didn't even have running water. They were without telephones, and it was quite awhile before they had TV reception. But that didn't affect the children, as all ages played together roaming the hills behind them, riding bikes, playing games of flag football and baseball. Each Monday evening, the whole community would gather together for Family Home Evening. And everyone worked together, helping one another with building projects, farming and chores.[235]

Rocky Ridge was originally envisioned as a United Order community where the property on which houses were built, as well as business and agricultural ventures, would be community owned. People would be encouraged to work and serve according to the skills they felt they had to

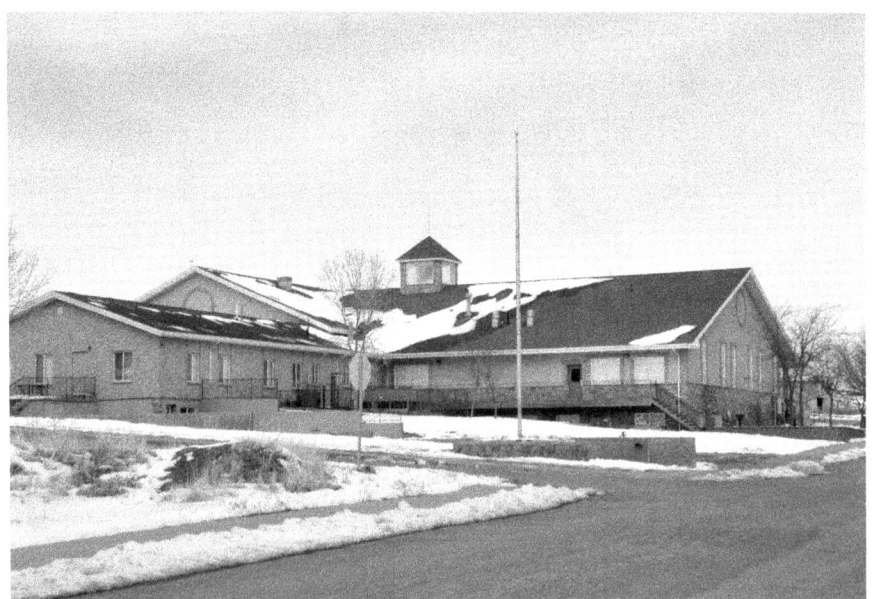

Rocky Ridge chapel. *Steven L. Mayfield Collection.*

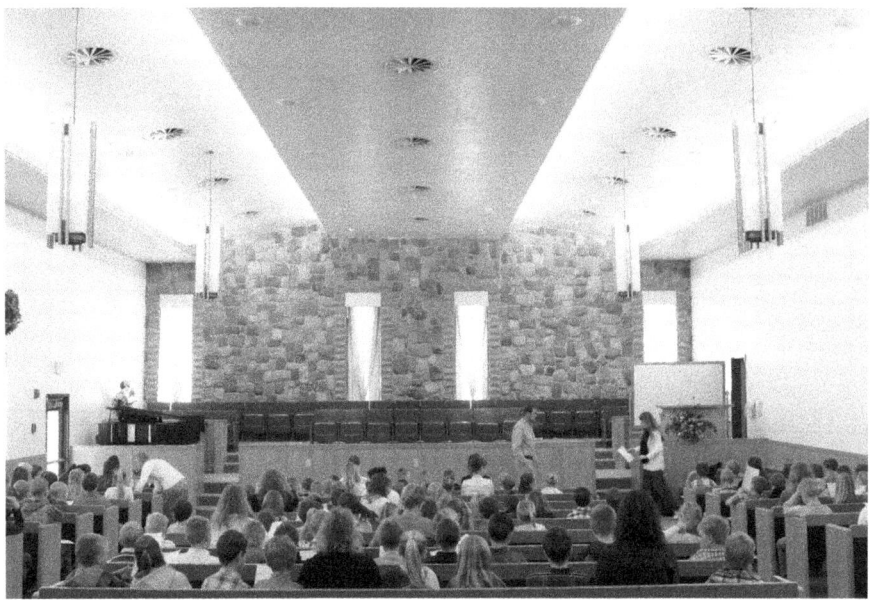

Children's Primary meeting inside Rocky Ridge chapel. *Authors' collection.*

offer for the betterment of the community. However, it was less formal in the early years and did not become more organized until enough people moved in to really have a large United Order community. They did not have permission to create a subdivision until the 1990s and did not incorporate as a community until 1996.[236]

Like the community of Pinesdale in Montana, those at Rocky Ridge had a cordial relationship with their surrounding neighbors. At first, their neighbors did not realize they were polygamists, but word soon spread. Nevertheless, local folks were still friendly to the newcomers. The children attended local schools and, like their friends and relatives in Pinesdale, while at school they always referred to their siblings as their cousins, figuring it was better that way. In fact, some families went by different surnames in order to hide the fact their fathers were polygamists. In 1973, another AUB community was started outside of Cedar City in southern Utah at the direction of Rulon Allred.

In about 1972, Owen Allred's garage was moved from Murray to Bluffdale to make way for Fashion Place Mall being built. Allred's garage had been used for years as the place for their meetings, with Sunday school classes spilling over into the neighboring homes of Lyman Jessop and Marvin Allred. Some of the meetings were practically wall-to-wall people with about

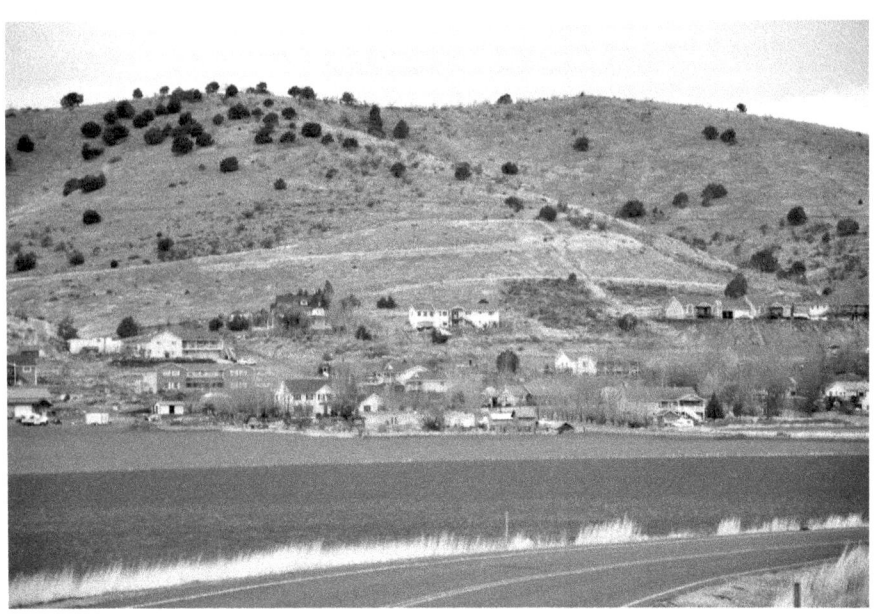

View of Rocky Ridge community, 2016. *Steven L. Mayfield Collection.*

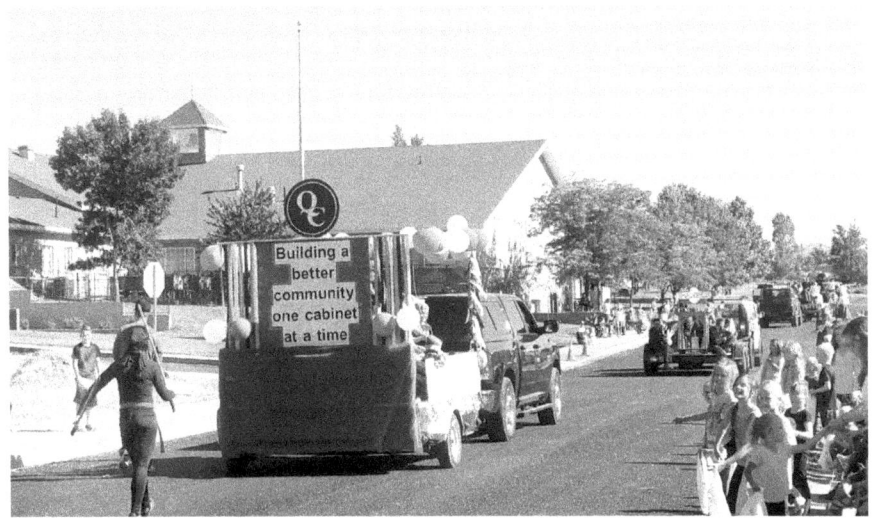

Parade during Rocky Ridge Days, July 2018. *Authors' collection.*

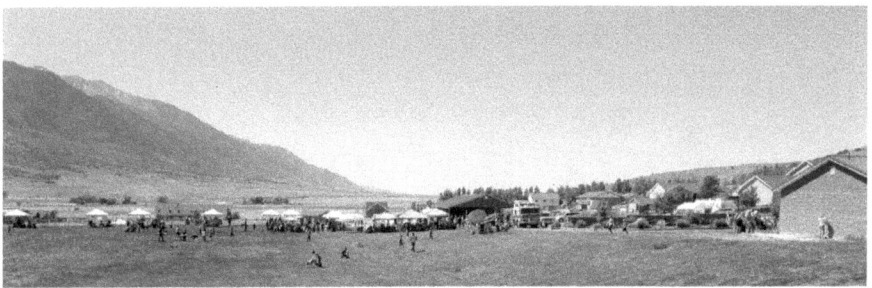

Park activities during Rocky Ridge Days, July 2018. *Authors' collection.*

four hundred trying to squeeze into the garage and other places outside of the garage. With the move to Bluffdale, the group's headquarters was now ostensibly in that small farming community at the south end of the Salt Lake Valley. At the time of the move, Bluffdale had fewer than one thousand residents and was still unincorporated.

In 1975, the Allred group officially incorporated as the Presiding Elder of the Apostolic United Brethren and became known as the Apostolic United Brethren or AUB. While incorporating for tax and legal purposes, the group's leaders and most members considered themselves members of the Church of Jesus Christ of Latter-day Saints, knowing the church could not and did not recognize them as members and many had never been official members of the LDS Church.

It was only a few years later that members of the AUB faced their greatest crisis and trial of faith. On the cold, cloudy afternoon of May 10, 1977, seventy-one-year-old Rulon C. Allred, a naturopathic doctor and leader of the AUB, was working in his medical office in the Salt Lake City suburb of Murray when two women entered the crowded office. One sat down in the waiting room next to a waiting patient, Dick Bunker, while the other slipped back to a treatment room next to the medical lab. She found Rulon Allred and fired several shots with a handgun, almost instantly killing him. Melba Allred, Rulon's secretary (one of his wives), rushed to the sound of the shots and saw the woman walk swiftly to the waiting room and bolted outside with her accomplice. Bunker rushed to the door and was shocked to see the two trying to reenter the office. As they again charged in, he grabbed the girl who had sat briefly next to him while the shooter pointed her gun at his temple and pulled the trigger. The gun was empty. She then grabbed her partner's gun and pointed it at Bunker, ordering him to "Let her go!" He did so but then pushed both women out the office door, trying unsuccessfully to lock it

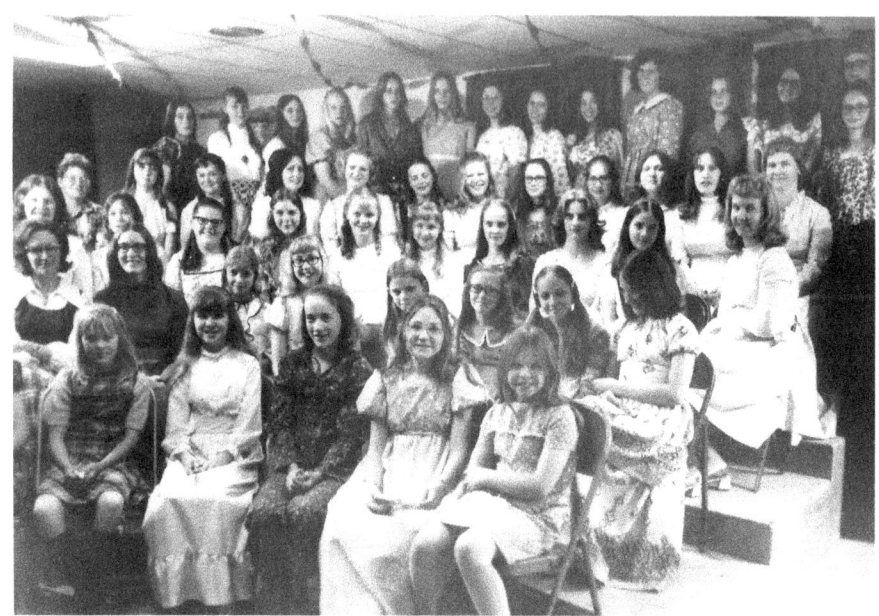

Allred Group Young Women's Organization, 1974. *Authors' collection.*

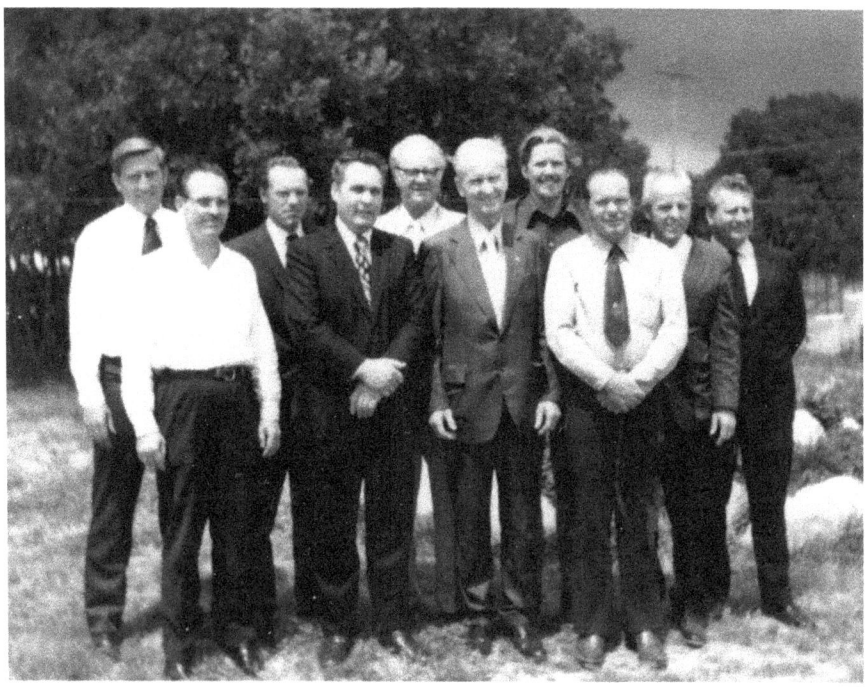

Allred Group Council members, 1974. *Authors' collection.*

then running for cover as they pushed back in, the gun firing but missing him. The shooter ran to make sure Rulon Allred was dead. She stood over the body and fired at his head, missing the target. Realizing he was dead, the two again made their escape. The entire tragic episode occurred in less than five minutes.[237]

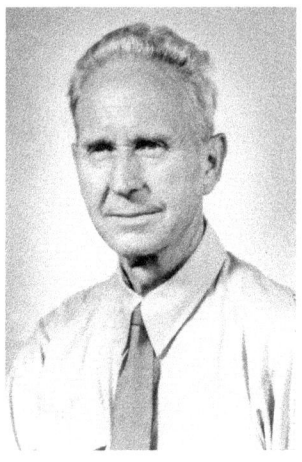

Rulon C. Allred (1906–1977). *Authors' collection.*

Word quickly spread through the Salt Lake Valley among the Allred group, and the media announced the news to the world that polygamist leader Rulon C. Allred had been murdered in his office. A crowd of followers quickly gathered to numbly watch as police combed the crime scene. News media also gathered, with at least a dozen reporters present. TV cameras were rolling when the police finally brought Allred's body out of his office. He lay on a stretcher, all covered by a sheet, except for his shoes. Dismayed followers who had gathered at the scene broke down in tears, and Allred's youngest daughter, barely nine years old, later remembered how the television news played that macabre scene over and over. That scene was painful especially for family members; they were haunted by the image of their beloved brother, father or husband's murdered body covered by a sheet, except for his familiar shoes.[238]

The two women eluded police, and at first, people were unsure of the motive. While it was immediately suggested it might have to do with polygamy, the police thought it did not, and Owen A. Allred, Rulon's brother and next in line to head the AUB, adamantly declared that the killing "had nothing to do with religious rivalry." He continued, "I have heard reports of a power struggle among polygamist groups in the press. There was no struggle with anyone. He was not trying to compete with anyone."[239] Nevertheless, the police finally concluded that they could think of no other reason why Allred would have been so viciously gunned down. After considering a few suspects, the police focused on Ervil LeBaron, who had been making threats.[240]

Rulon Clark Allred's funeral was held on May 14, 1977, in the newly constructed Bingham High School in South Jordan, that being one of the few convenient places large enough to hold all family, friends and followers who wanted to attend. At least 2,600 people were in attendance. Also present were numerous uniformed police, with a long line of police cars in front of the building, as well as plainclothes officers spread out among the mourners

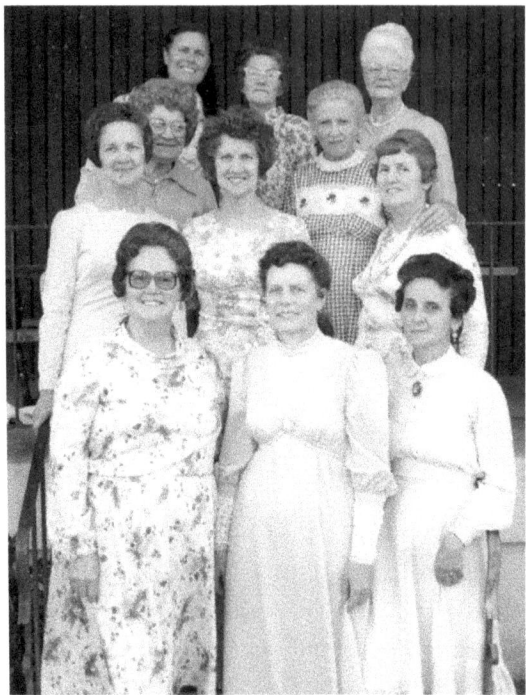

Rulon C. Allred's eleven wives, photo taken shortly after his murder. *Authors' collection.*

to prevent any more possible violence. It was only later the family learned that Ervil LeBaron, knowing his brother Verlan was attending the funeral, had ordered his death. Ervil had given orders that Verlan should die, no matter who else might be in the way. His henchmen had arrived armed with two automatic rifles and a pistol but had seen the strong police presence and had driven on rather than attempt the slaughter.[241]

THE LEBARONS AND "LEBARONISM"

The surname LeBaron, in connection with Fundamentalist Mormons and polygamy, began to draw unsavory attention as early as the 1930s. In 1955, two LeBaron brothers, Joel and Ross, at odds over which held greater authority, started two different churches and began developing unique theologies. LeBaron family dynamics ultimately led to Joel excommunicating another brother, Ervil, who in turn formed his own church and then began his murderous revenge upon Joel and others in the 1970s. Ervil LeBaron left a legacy of murder and violence that has tainted other undeserving Fundamentalists' reputations ever since by mere association.

In April 1952, Allred group Fundamentalists held a conference in Colonia Industrial in Ozumba, Mexico, after the "Priesthood Split" had become definitive. Although LeBaron family members had given their allegiance to Joseph Musser and later Rulon Allred, they courted an on-off relationship with the Priesthood Council, sometimes supporting them but ultimately going their own way, claiming their own prophetic authority.[242]

On September 21, 1955, in Salt Lake City, brothers Joel, Floren and Ross LeBaron formed their own church, making Joel president and patriarch. They claimed to hold the "same keys" they decided had been passed from Joseph Smith to their great-grandfather Benjamin F. Johnson, then to their father, Alma Dayer LeBaron, who, they claimed, conferred them "on his sons." Afterward, they filed papers incorporating the Church of the Firstborn of the Fullness of Times. In the following days, they tried unsuccessfully to convert the Priesthood Council and other Fundamentalists.[243]

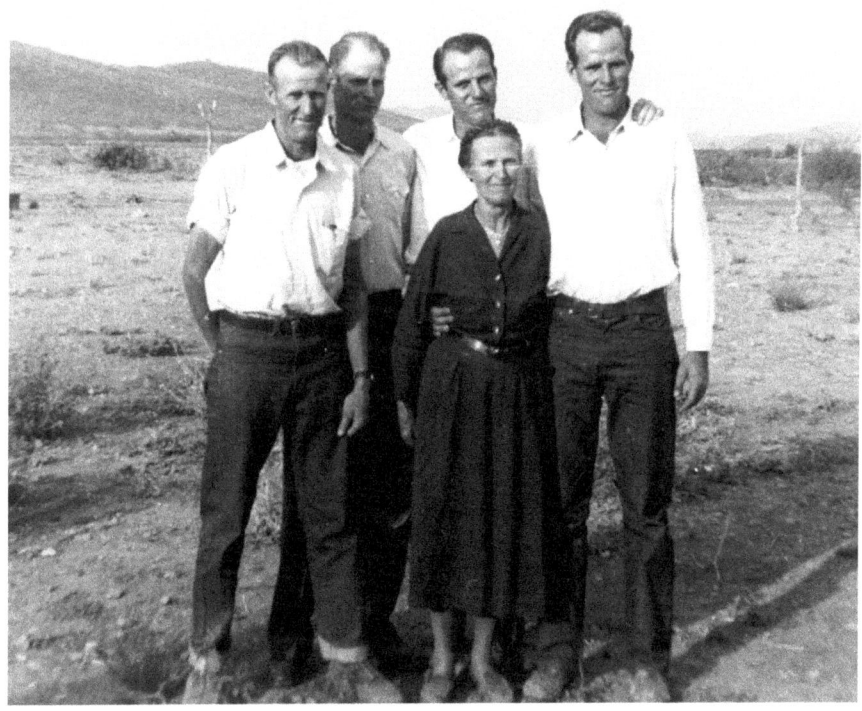

LeBaron brothers with their mother, 1950s. *Authors' collection.*

Almost immediately, within weeks, a rancorous rift began between Joel and Ross, each claiming the greater authority to preside. Floren sided with Joel. Seeing no possible reconciliation, Ross incorporated his own church, the Church of the Firstborn, on December 1, 1955. This act, among many more to come, permanently divided the LeBaron brothers.

One historian labeled the LeBaron family's disparate theologies as "LeBaronism," as distinct from other Fundamentalist Mormons who trace their authority through the Woolleys. This scholar showed that their innovated theologies were conspicuously different from Joseph Smith's restored gospel and that the family's various claims of evidence for priesthood authority from Joseph Smith to Benjamin F. Johnson could not be corroborated.

Two years later, the youngest brother, Verlan LeBaron, who had recently been excommunicated from the LDS Church after marrying two more wives, converted to Joel's church and joined his efforts in Colonia LeBaron, a new name they chose for the LeBaron ranch. The following year, several excommunicated LDS missionaries who had obtained Joel's proselyting pamphlets while serving in Belgium and France joined Joel's church.[244]

The French missionaries' infusion of enthusiasm began a new era in Joel's young church. Verlan's wife Charlotte observed that the French missionaries who joined them in Colonia LeBaron "brought much change to our community…and would leave a lasting mark upon it."[245]

During Joel's frequent proselyting absences, Ervil's harsh discipline in the community school, his reorganization of some church functions and "his infractions of both biblical, civil, and moral codes" brought distress and division among church members. Because of jealousy and "his personal actions and teaching contrary to [LeBaron] church doctrine over a period of time, Ervil was excommunicated," and Joel replaced him with Verlan as church patriarch.[246]

In response, Ervil and his followers, called "the Ervilites," began harassing Joel's people, sometimes violently. Ervil soon established his own church, the Church of the First Born of the Lamb of God, and "distributed writings stating that both Joel and Verlan deserved the death penalty!" Tensions finally culminated when Ervil ordered Joel's brutal murder in 1972 in Mexico. Verlan's horrified wife Charlotte wrote: "What greater shame could befall anyone than to have that crime committed within his family.…[E]ven the mention of our LeBaron name, would forever bring sentiments of horror, disgrace, and evil; all because of one vile and wicked man!"[247]

Ervil was soon arrested by Mexican authorities but served only a year before getting out on a technicality, or through bribery, as some suggested. Over the next five years, several murders were committed at Ervil's command. Most victims were members of his own family or church. He proclaimed himself "the true prophet" and demanded that all other Fundamentalist groups, not just the LeBarons, recognize him as the true leader and pay him tithes or die.

Rulon C. Allred was one among several Fundamentalist leaders, the LDS church president and the U.S. president, all threatened by LeBaron. But even before the latest series of threats, the LeBarons had been a pain in Rulon Allred's side for years. As early as 1962, Joel LeBaron had published a pamphlet denouncing Rulon and Owen Allred for "character assassination" for not acknowledging LeBaron's priesthood authority and paying tithes to him. The pamphlet stated that punishment for their sins was the same as in the Old Testament: death. In 1972, after Joel LeBaron's murder, Ervil LeBaron had made enough threats that FBI authorities warned the LDS Church, Rulon Allred and other religious leaders whom Ervil had promised to destroy if they "would not bow down" to his authority. Threats against Rulon continued in 1974, and in 1975, members of Ervil's Church of the Lamb of God distributed pamphlets on AUB car windshields titled "A Declaration of War," in which Allred, the LDS Church, Leroy S. Johnson of the Short Creek group, the Kingstons and others were ordered to repent and accept LeBaron as their head of the priesthood.[248]

Rulon Allred and the other religious leaders ignored LeBaron's threats, but it was Allred who was first on LeBaron's hit list. In May 1977, Ervil ordered one of his wives, Rena Chynoweth, and perhaps her brother, disguised as a woman, to murder Allred at his medical office in Murray, Utah. Rena did the actual shooting.[249]

Rulon Allred's murder shocked Utahans, his wide circle of friends and acquaintances from Canada to Mexico. His death once again brought negative publicity to Fundamentalist Mormons. Due to the violence caused by LeBaron and other extreme actions of some Fundamentalists, the LDS Church expressed concern that "because it had once practiced plural marriage it [would] become identified in the popular mind with the sects and their violence." The relationship between the LDS Church and the Fundamentalists was uncomfortable at best, and the actions of Ervil LeBaron and his followers exacerbated this relationship. Near the end of 1977, the LDS Church again issued a statement that any LDS member found practicing plural marriage would immediately be disciplined, "leading to excommunication."

Police eventually captured Ervil LeBaron in Mexico and extradited him to Utah, where he was tried and found guilty of having ordered

Rulon Allred's death. He began serving his sentence in 1980 but died in the Utah State Penitentiary in August 1981—but not before passing to his henchmen a hit list of disobedient church members. In the following years, LeBaron violence continued to shock the nation as it learned of more murders—some of Ervil's former wives, some of his children and others associated with him. Ultimately, between twenty-five and thirty people were killed by Ervil's followers, some of whom were caught and sent to prison, while others escaped and went into hiding.

Verlan LeBaron lived in fear, always on the watch for assassination attempts. Only two days after Ervil's death, Verlan and a companion were killed in an auto accident. Another brother, Ross LeBaron, had a following of religious devotees that for a time included Fred Collier and Tom Green. He spent his remaining years living in humble circumstances in the Salt Lake Valley and, later, on the west side of Utah Lake in Utah Valley.[250]

In the wake of Ervil's murderous legacy, Verlan wrote in his 1981 book *The LeBaron Story*, published after his death, "[S]uch a labyrinth of controversy and danger…[y]et behind the façade of publicity and notoriety surrounding my brother Ervil, lies another view—one of a family and people whose love, labors, and hopes have been marred by the evil doings of one man."[251]

THE PETERSON GROUP OR RIGHTEOUS BRANCH
OF THE CHURCH OF JESUS CHRIST
OF LATTER-DAY SAINTS

Gerald Wilbur Peterson Sr., a doctor, joined the Allred group in the early 1970s. Dr. Peterson was an enthusiastic convert, leading some meetings in his Cache Valley home and later moving to the Salt Lake Valley to be closer to the group's headquarters, where he joined Rulon Allred in his medical office.[252] According to a former wife of Dr. Peterson, although he was never ordained an apostle or member of the Priesthood Council, he claimed that Rulon, even before his death, wanted him (Peterson) to be the next leader of the Allred group when he was gone. Well before Allred's murder, Peterson expressed bewilderment and frustration to a friend that he had not yet been called to be a member of the Priesthood Council.[253] A later reminiscence by Rulon Allred's wife Melba, who worked in his medical office, however, portrayed Peterson as being "nothing more than a thorn in Brother Rulon's side."[254]

Shortly after Allred's murder, Dr. Peterson announced that Rulon Allred had "appeared to him and instructed him to preside over the keys of the

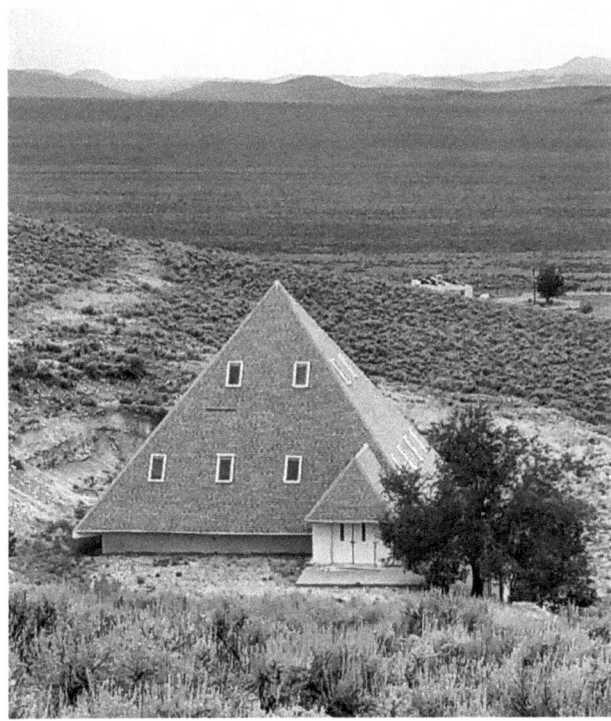

Peterson Group Paiquin Temple west of Cedar City, Utah. *Courtesy of Atrayu Pickering.*

priesthood," and be the new leader of the Allred group, something at complete odds with accepted priesthood protocol. According to Peterson, Allred appeared to him on at least two occasions, the first time shortly after Allred's murder. He said Allred first appeared wearing bloodied clothing and later appeared wearing white.[255] The vast majority of the Allred group, however, completely rejected Peterson's claims. Only a small number followed him. Gerald W. Peterson Sr. died in 1981, and Gerald W. "Jerry" Peterson Jr. became the president of the church, by then called the Righteous Branch. He moved church headquarters to St. George, Utah, and later to Tonopah, Nevada. Jerry Peterson died in May 2018, and his son Michael became the new church president.[256]

The Righteous Branch organization is similar in ways to the LDS Church. It has a First Presidency, Quorum of Twelve Apostles and Presiding Bishopric. It does not have seven Presidents of Seventy but plans to add that organization as the branch grows. The Righteous Branch has other priesthood quorums and auxiliary organizations, such as the female Relief Society.[257] It also actively proselytizes. The church has four full-time missionaries. Two are work missionaries residing in Nevada, while the

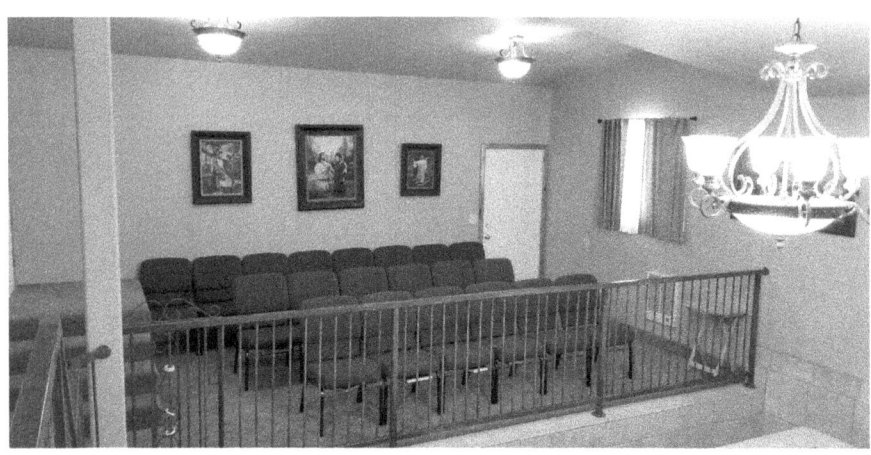

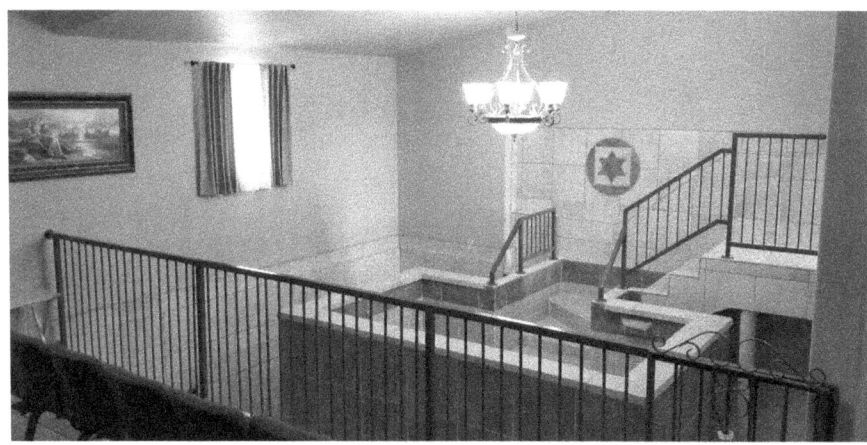

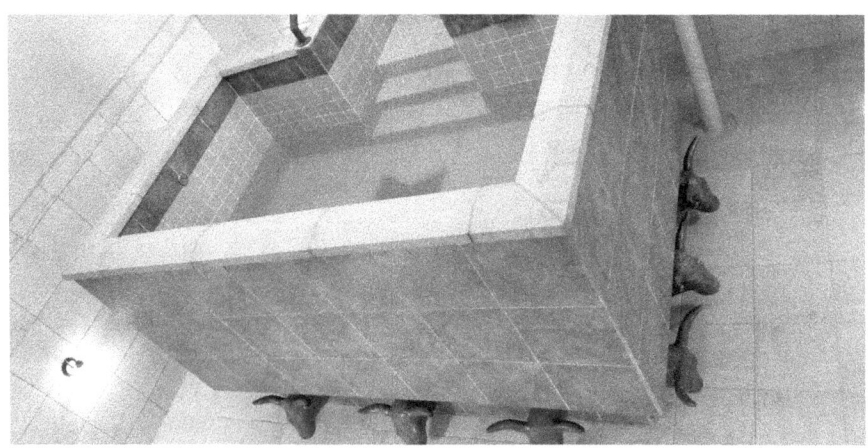

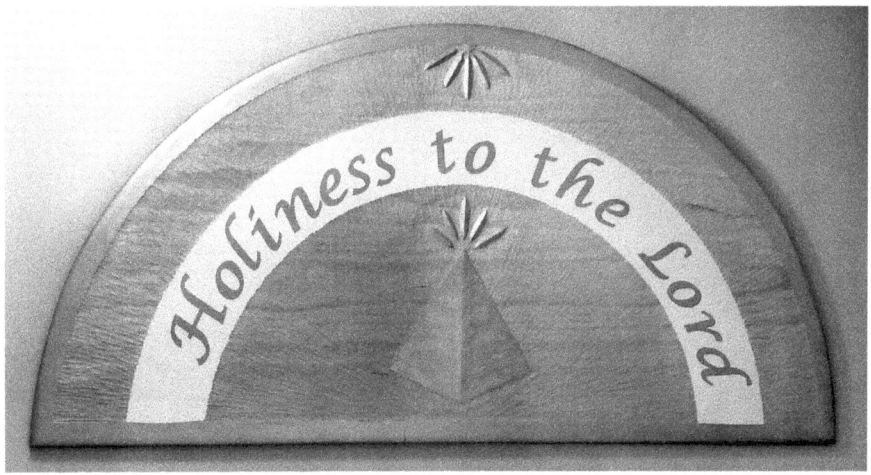

Above: Peterson Group Temple sign.

Opposite, top: Peterson Group Temple Baptistry seating.

Opposite, middle: Peterson Group Temple Baptismal font.

Opposite, bottom: Another view of Peterson Group Baptismal font. *Images courtesy of the Righteous Branch.*

other two are traveling missionaries. Missionary work has been conducted in ten states and Canada. There is talk that the leadership will soon send representatives to England. There are 286 members, most of whom live in Nevada and Utah. There also are members in Arizona, Texas, Missouri and Kansas.[258]

Some of the Righteous Branch's religious tenets are similar to those of both the LDS Church and the AUB. For example, adherents follow the Word of Wisdom, which forbids the consumption of alcohol, tobacco or even hot caffeinated drinks like coffee and tea. But the Righteous Branch goes one step further; it forbids eating pork or chocolate. The branch also believes in temple work and built a pyramid-shaped temple near Modena, approximately fifty miles west of Cedar City, Utah, as well as one in Tonopah. Their temples are plain on the outside as they "are a very reticent people, with good reason," and prefer not to attract attention, but the structures are more beautifully appointed on the inside.

THE 1980s: A TIME OF GROWTH
AND RELATIVE PEACE

Fundamentalist groups enjoyed relative peace and more openness about their plural marriages because of little threat of surveillance and prosecution. The fear of raids had dissipated a great deal, and while older generations remembered the difficult days of prosecution and persecution, the younger generation did not sense imminent threat, only caution.

In the 1980s, the AUB community in Ozumba, Mexico, prospered even though the country was suffering severe economic inflation. Some seventy miles southwest of Mexico City, Margarito Bautista founded Colonia Industrial in the town of Ozumba on a small parcel of land he and his sister inherited. There he gathered converts to the gospel who agreed to live the United Order and plural marriage. Bautista met Nathaniel Baldwin and Lorin Woolley in the 1920s and contacted the Priesthood Council in the 1940s. Joseph Musser called him as a member of the Priesthood Council in 1951. Bautista died in 1971. By the 1980s, the community had grown to a few hundred members and was prospering both economically and spiritually. They accounted this progress to being allowed to construct a temple in their community. At the same time, residents paved their streets, built a sewer

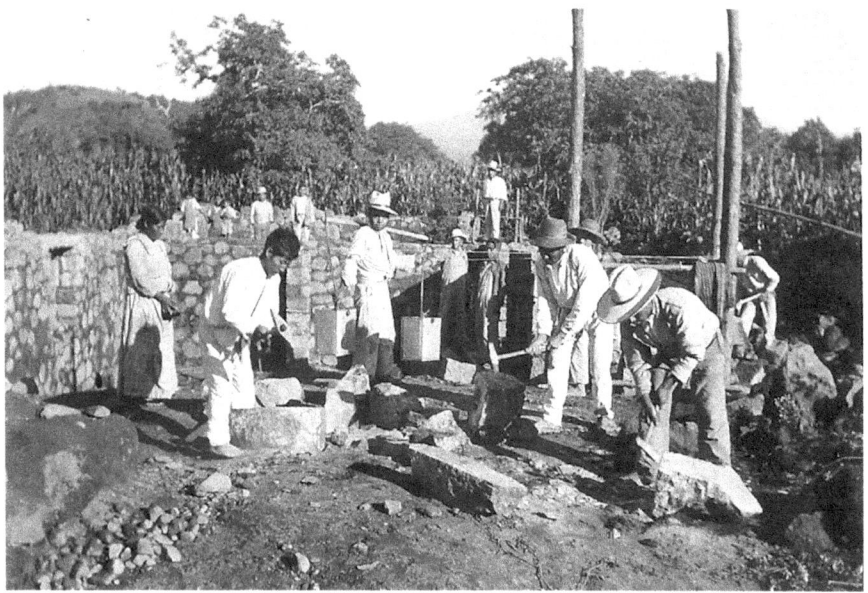

Residents of Colonia Industrial constructing first meetinghouse, circa 1940s. *Authors' collection.*

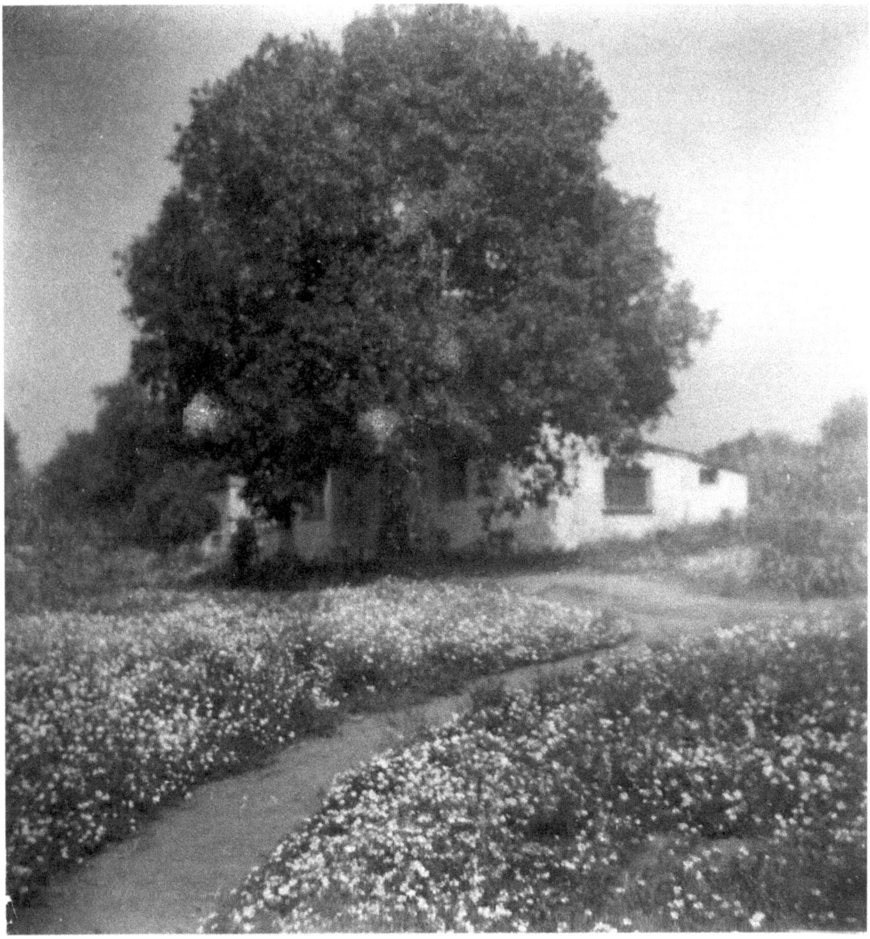

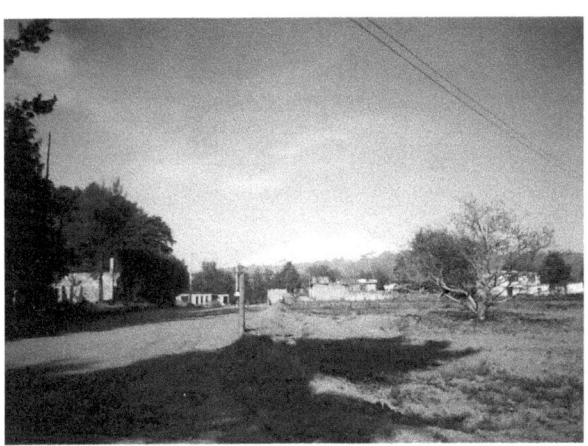

Above: Colonia Industrial early meetinghouse, circa 1940s. *Authors' collection.*

Left: Colonia Industrial street view, Popocatepetl volcano in background. *Authors' collection.*

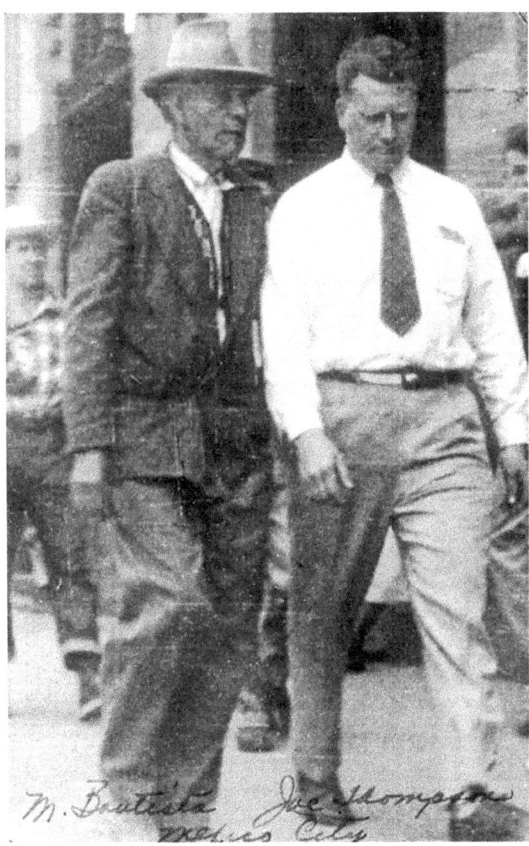

Left: Council members Margarito Bautista (*left*) and Joseph B. Thompson in Mexico City, circa 1961. *Authors' collection*.

Below: Colonia Industrial resident with wife and children, circa 1940s. *Authors' collection*.

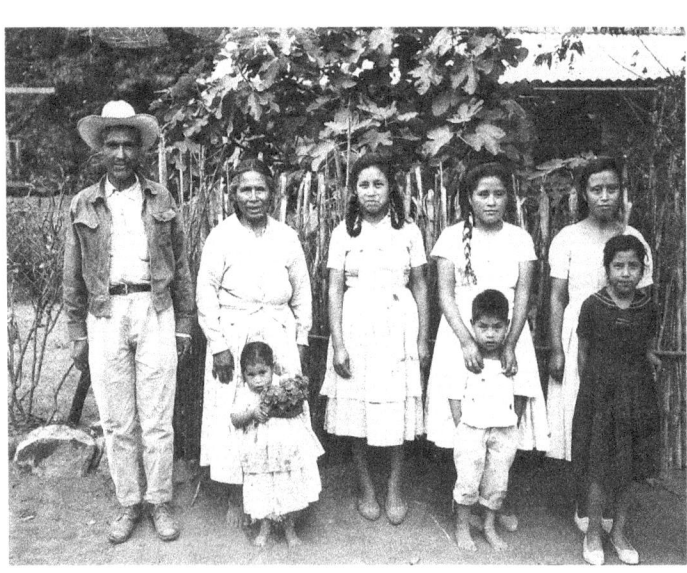

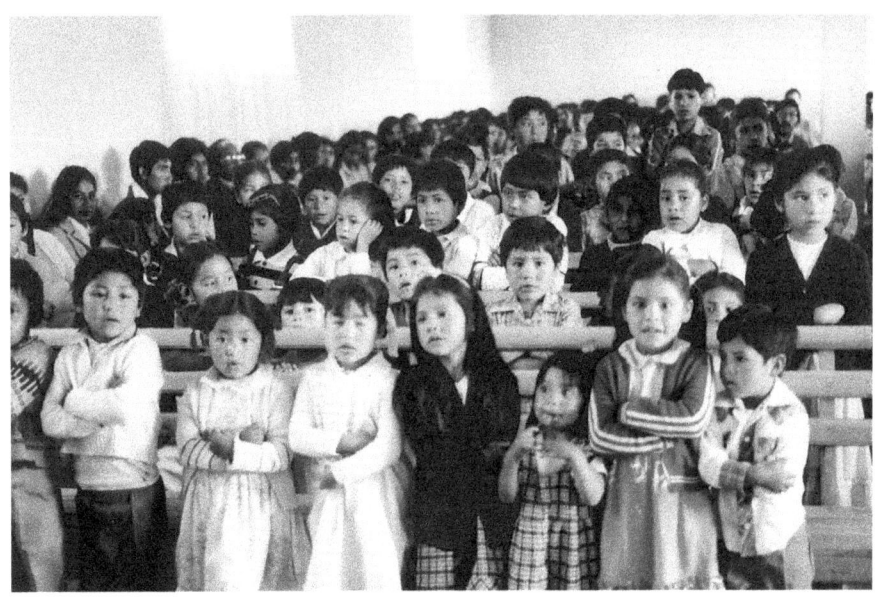

Primary children of Colonia Industrial, 1980s. *Authors' collection.*

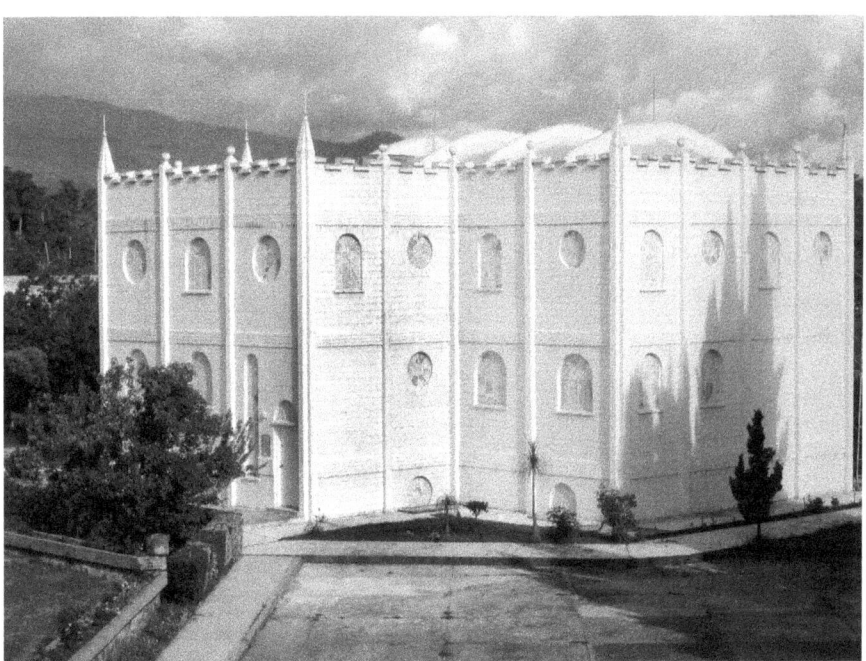

Colonia Industrial Temple, built in 1980s. *Authors' collection.*

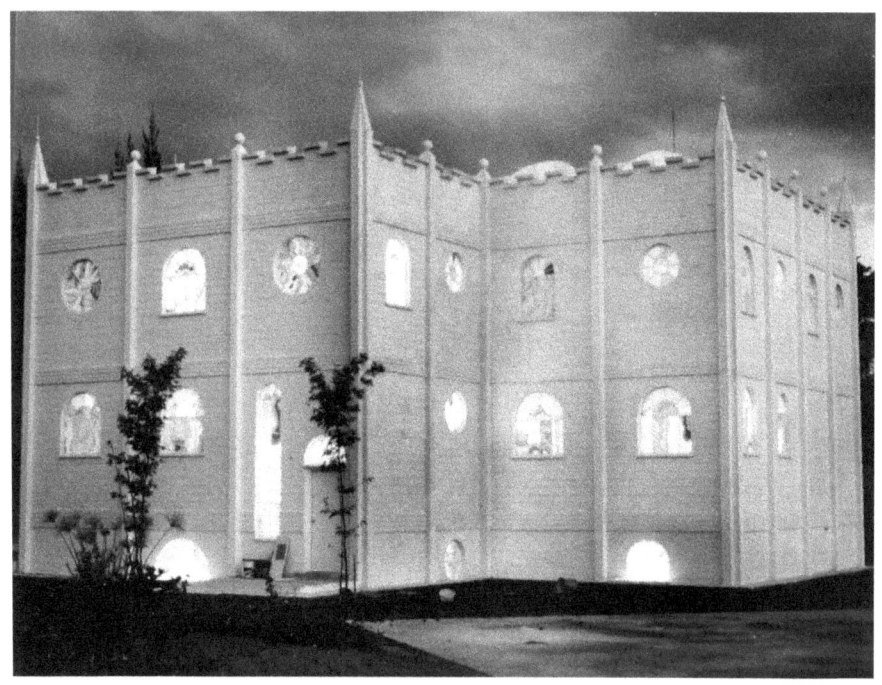

Colonia Industrial Temple at night. *Authors' collection.*

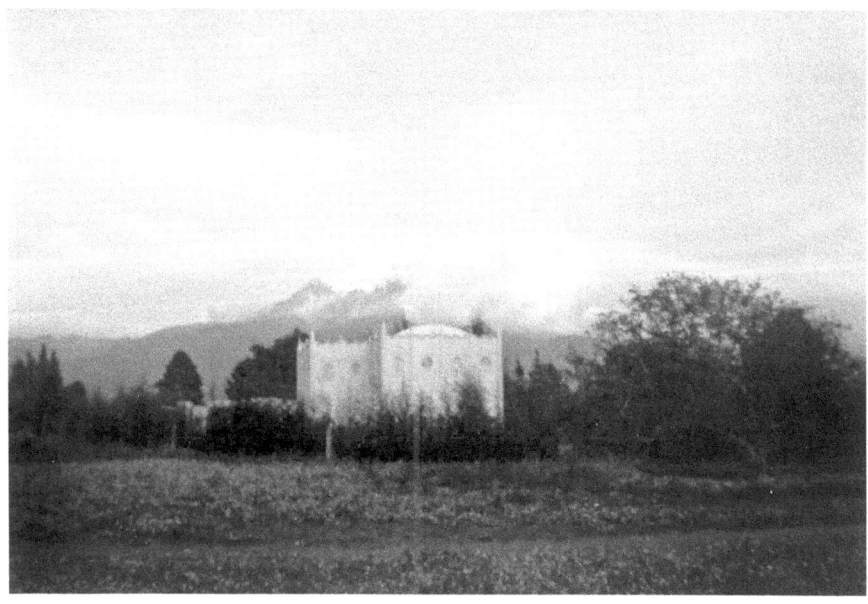

Colonia Industrial Temple, with Popocatepetl volcano in background. *Authors' collection.*

system, installed indoor plumbing in most of the homes and beautified their village. Most of the materials for the temple were manufactured in the colony by volunteer labor, and the temple was built under the direction of Priesthood Council. One of the temple's unique features is its Mexican onyx windows that have natural designs that light up at night. The temple was dedicated in 1985.

THE 1990s: UPS AND DOWNS

Despite the LeBarons' murderous rampage and other polygamy-related news articles, there was a perception of growing acceptance of polygamists by the general public. But perception didn't quite meet reality. A 1977 newspaper article told of one Utah man wearing a cowboy hat who complained, "Them pligs is comin' up like weeds." But most seemed to be more inclined to view polygamists like the Mormon who said, "Oh we have some [polygamists] who live just down the street from us. They are the nicest people. Very

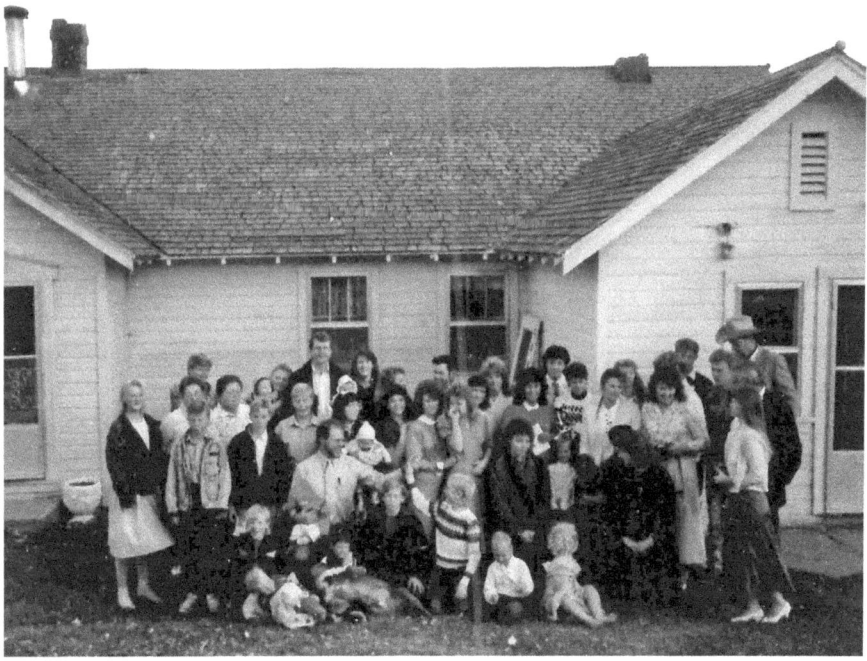

AUB Wyoming Congregation, circa 1991. *Authors' collection.*

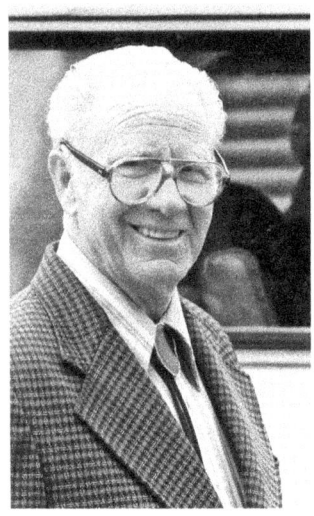

AUB leader Owen A. Allred
(1914–2005). *Authors' collection.*

clean and quiet and law-abiding." In this more relaxed atmosphere, some public authorities admitted that while polygamy was illegal, they seldom prosecuted because such actions had proven unpopular so they instead were taking a "live and let live" approach.[259]

Both the AUB and the groups in the Short Creek area experienced more growth and development. Converts to the AUB established a small community near Lovell, Wyoming. While most Fundamentalists preferred to keep their heads down and remain out of the glaring media spotlight, some were willing to reach out to non-Fundamentalist scholars interested in the history and doctrines of this diverse group of religionists. For example, in 1992, Martha Sonntag Bradley, on behalf of the Mormon History Association, arranged with Colorado City and Hildale leaders to visit their community. Over 140 conference participants were given a tour of the community and the newly built Leroy S. Johnson meetinghouse. Participants were provided refreshments and the opportunity to mingle freely with members of the community in what proved to be an extraordinary act of openness on the part of the FLDS. The next year, Martha Bradley published her sympathetic portrayal of the 1953 polygamy raid, *Kidnapped from that Land: The Government Raids on the Short Creek Polygamists.* The book was well received by those both on the inside and outside Fundamentalist Mormonism.

Thus, by the close of the twentieth century, Fundamentalist Mormonism had witnessed a number of ups and downs. It had experienced both triumph and tragedy as well as division among those identifying themselves as Fundamentalists. At the commencement of not only a new century but also a new millennium, some polygamist groups were faring better than others. In the following decade and a half, growth and success was accompanied by conflict and controversy, creating a mixed bag of success and failure for the Fundamentalists.

SHORT CREEK CHANGES

*Centennial Park and the Making
and Breaking of the FLDS*

I n 1980, Colorado City's steadily growing population tallied over
1,500. Hildale and other areas of the Arizona Strip evidenced similar
expansion. The entire area of these twin cities evidenced development
and economic progress. Yet a closer understanding of the polygamous
community dwelling in the area disclosed a growing controversy that had
begun tearing it asunder. An internal debate dividing the once unified group
centered on ruling power, separating those who supported the idea of a one-
man rule from those who wanted to continue, as in the past, with power
resting equilaterally among their leaders.

THE 1980S AND THE ONE-MAN RULE
CONTROVERSY

The one-man rule debate manifested in two doctrinal and social issues. First,
did the keys of the priesthood rest equally in the hands of all members of
the Short Creek Priesthood Council? Or did those keys reside solely in the
hands of the "One Man," the council member who presided? The second
question was an extension of the first, the question being over who had the
right to arrange and appoint marriages.

Evidence suggests that placement or arranged marriage, as it is sometimes
called, didn't even exist until the late 1940s and is perhaps a reflection and

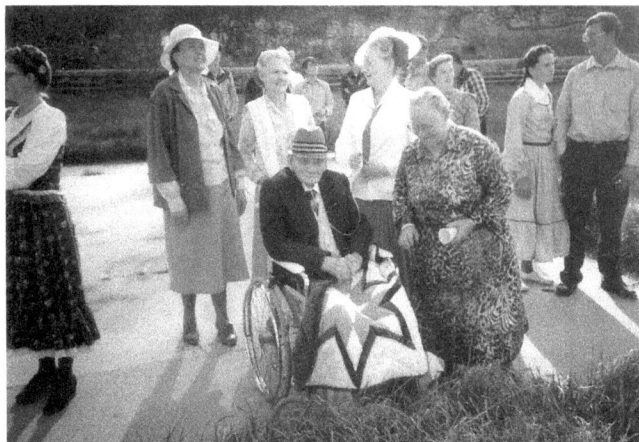

Left: Leroy S. Johnson with four of his wives. *Authors' collection.*

Below: View of Colorado City, Arizona. *Steven L. Mayfield Collection.*

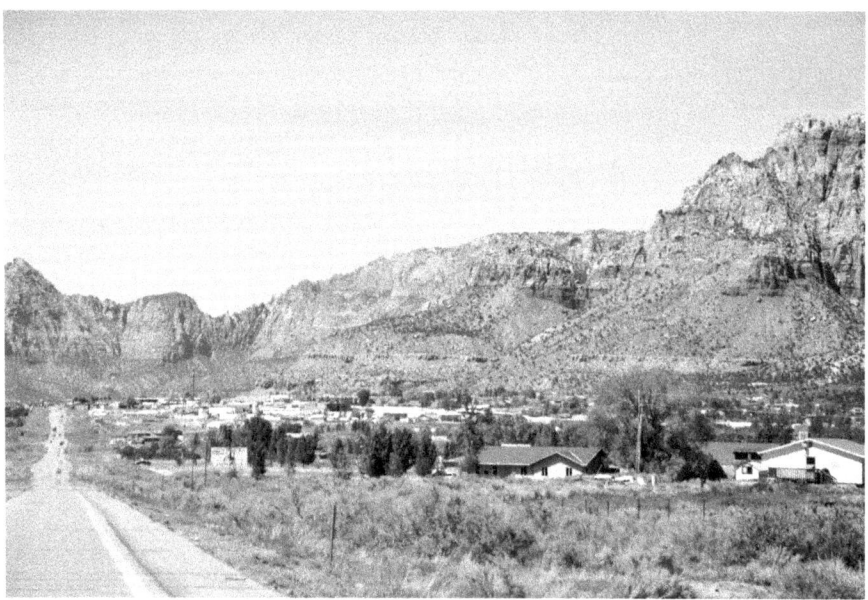

outgrowth of the strongly held belief among the Short Creek Fundamentalists in unquestioning obedience to priesthood leaders. The placement marriage system, universally followed by the FLDS, recognized that marriages were to be arranged by a priesthood leader or leaders receiving revelation on the bride and groom's behalf.[260]

Proponents of one-man rule argued that only the presiding council member held all priesthood keys and, therefore, held all authority. Furthermore, they argued that the presiding council member *alone* had the right to arrange marriages, particularly plural marriages. Dissenting

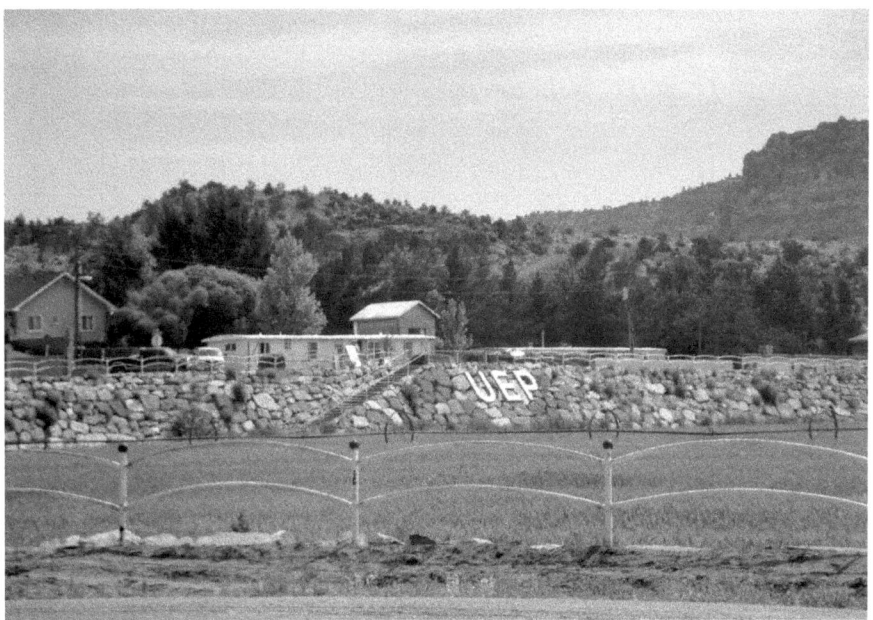

UEP Community Garden in Hildale, Utah. *Steven L. Mayfield Collection.*

council members countered that all members of the council held the same keys and authority in common and, therefore, could arrange and perform marriages as well as other priesthood ordinances.

Perhaps the most outspoken proponents of one-man rule were the sons of the late Fundamentalist leader John Y. Barlow. They had been "fathered" and mentored by then leader Leroy S. Johnson after their father died. These men became powerful and influential, as they held important positions within the Short Creek community. Dan Barlow served as mayor, while his brother Sam functioned as chief of police and another brother, Alvin, was the superintendent of schools. Louis Barlow worked as a teacher in the school and also taught young men in priesthood meetings. The Barlows were supported by council leaders Leroy Johnson and Rulon T. Jeffs, as well as by their uncle Fred Jessop, the Short Creek bishop.

On the other side were council members Marion Hammon, Alma Timpson and Guy Musser. Guy Musser died in 1983, leaving the council equally divided over this issue. The division seeped into the community and began to tear it apart, with supporters of the two factions arguing with one another. The conflict culminated in February 1984 when Leroy Johnson, who had been absent from community meetings due to suffering

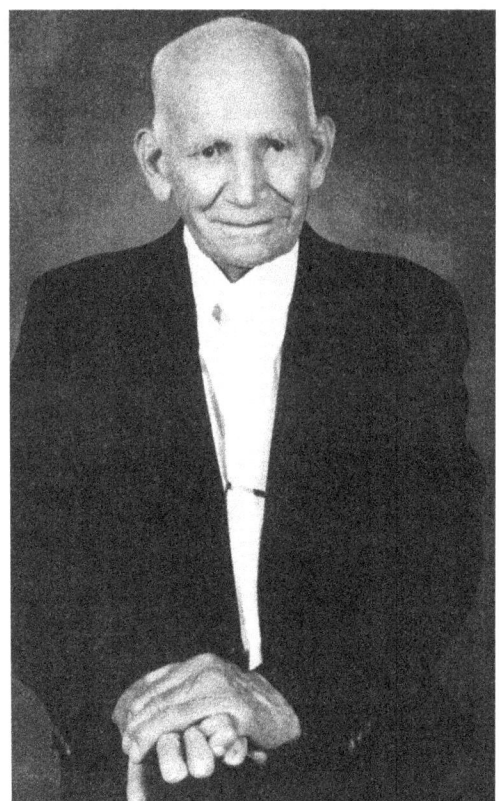

Left: Leroy S. Johnson (1888–1986). *Authors' collection.*

Below: FLDS Leroy S. Johnson Meeting House in Colorado City, Arizona. *Steven L. Mayfield Collection.*

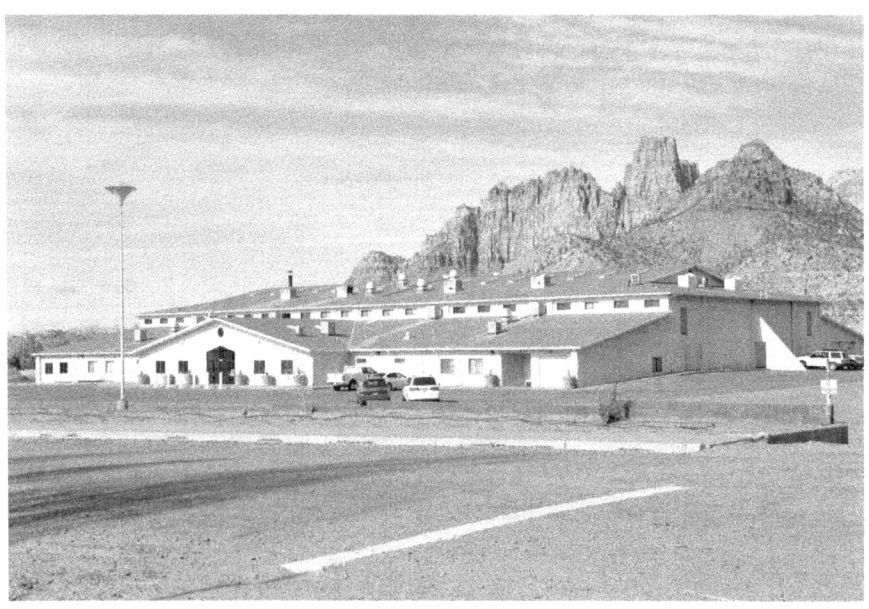

from shingles for six years, suddenly came to a church meeting. He publicly berated both Hammon and Timpson and then ordered them off of the speaker's stand. Johnson then pronounced both men removed from the priesthood council.[261]

CENTENNIAL PARK GROUP

Marion Hammon and Alma Timpson did not accept Leroy Johnson's pronouncement. Both men believed that Johnson, like they earlier viewed Joseph W. Musser during the 1952 split, was wrongfully influenced—in both cases by a man named Rulon. In Musser's case, they believed Rulon Allred took advantage of Musser's frailty from previous strokes for personal gain. With Johnson, they viewed Rulon Jeffs as having unduly influenced the aging and ill Johnson—again, for personal gain. Furthermore, both Hammon and Timpson insisted they had not sinned, and for that reason, they believed Johnson had neither the right nor the power to remove them from the council, and they began holding their own meetings, believing the Johnson-Jeffs faction to be out of order with proper priesthood protocol and therefore in apostasy.

Some outsiders in the area observing the turmoil began calling the disenfranchised group "Second Warders," in relationship to the larger body in Short Creek. The disassociated members do not appreciate the appellation because they don't see themselves as a second ward relative to a first ward in Short Creek. Rather, they believe they are carrying on the true priesthood and authority through Lorin Woolley. Furthermore, they do not feel they broke away from what became the FLDS. To the contrary, they believe they have remained true to the doctrines while the others wandered from the true principles.

One of the principles from which the FLDS had wandered was placement marriage, which Centennial Park members claim was created to control the marriage market, which they felt should not be put into the hands of one individual. The Centennial Park group's approach to marriage is still quite patriarchal in nature; but rather than one man deciding who would marry whom, the system places more power in the hands of the women, who are allowed to prayerfully decide when they are ready to marry. A woman initiates the process by first approaching her parents or father and then going with her father to Centennial Park's priesthood council and asking them to pray about who she should marry. Council members will ask a young woman if

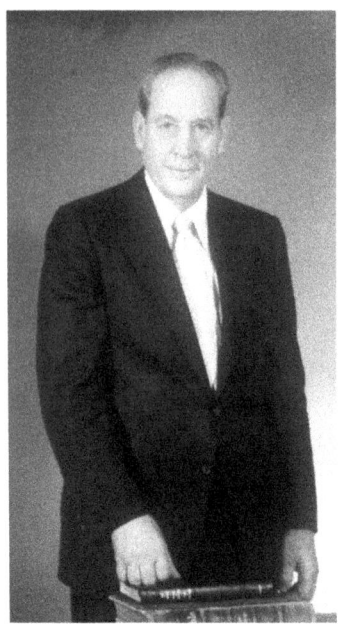

J. Marion Hammon, who led the Centennial Park Group until his death in 1988. *Findagrave.com*.

she has any man in mind, and she can state her thoughts and desires, but ultimately the council's preference is usually heeded. Council members do not allow marriages of underage girls.

There are two major differences between the Centennial Park and the FLDS marriage process. The first is that marriages continue to take place in Centennial Park, while sadly, Warren Jeffs ceased all FLDS marriages in 2006, which has ensured that practically a whole generation of faithful FLDS members remain unmarried and few births have taken place for more than a decade. The second difference is that for Centennial Park members, both the potential bride and groom have a right to agree or disagree to the council's proposed marriage match.[262]

The smaller but steady congregation following Hammon and Timpson sought a place where members could hold church and other meetings, as the Johnson-led group forbade the use of its buildings. Forced to separate themselves from a potentially volatile situation, the Hammon and Timpson followers purchased land from a non-Fundamentalist rancher named Hilda Perkins about three miles south of Colorado City on which they built a meetinghouse and homes for their members.[263] The community now includes a little over two square miles. On September 27, 1986, the group held its first services in the new meetinghouse. That year being the centennial anniversary of John Taylor's revelation regarding plural marriage, the group named the new town Centennial Park City, and from that time, the people there have been commonly known as the Centennial Park group.[264]

However, not every Centennial Park member could or even had the desire to move out of Colorado City–Hildale. Some families had lived in their homes for several generations and had put significant work into building comfortable homes. In 1993, Rulon Jeffs, then head of the FLDS after Johnson's death, sent letters to forty-five heads of household to legally disassociate them from the United Effort Plan (UEP) and evict them. This

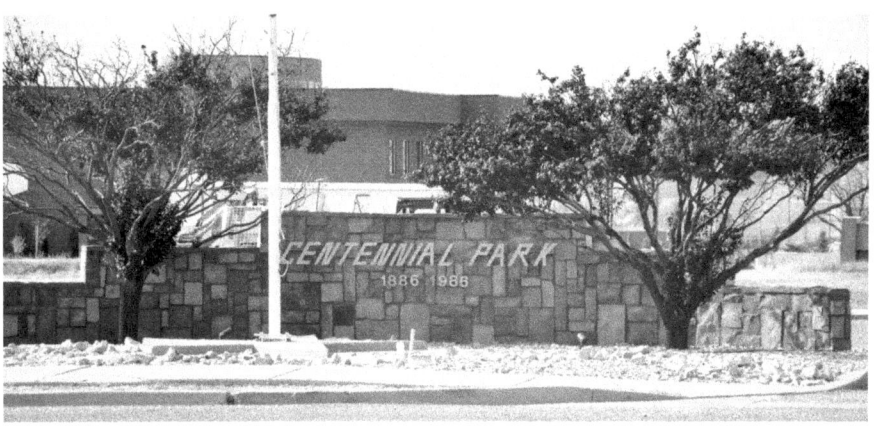

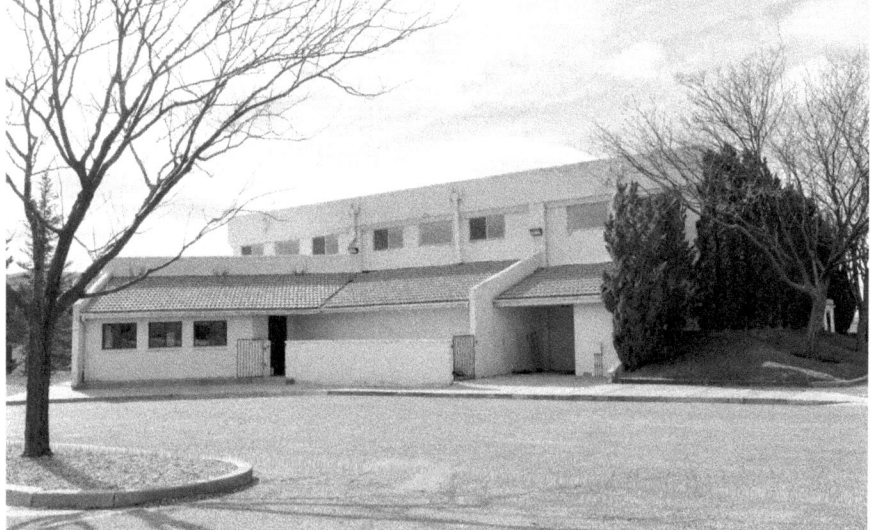

Top: Centennial Park Entrance, three miles from Colorado City.

Bottom: Centennial Park Group meetinghouse. *Images from the Steven L. Mayfield Collection.*

began a complex and prolonged legal battle that was ultimately ruled in favor of the Centennial Park members, granting them life estates for properties held.[265]

Since the breakup, members of the Centennial Park group have been considerably more open to the outside world than their FLDS neighbors. For example, in 2004, a group of Centennial Park women gave a presentation about their group at the annual Sunstone Symposium in Salt Lake City. These same women and others, including men, organized the Centennial

Park Action Committee and gave presentations at other forums to help dispel stereotypes and to promote better relations.[266]

Education plays an important role in the Centennial Park community, where members have a chartered elementary school, as well as a private middle and a high school. Many Centennial Park members have taken advantage of postsecondary education. A good portion of the student body of Mohave Community College located in Colorado City is from Centennial Park. Higher education has significantly strengthened the community. The Centennial Park Clinic, for example, is staffed by a physician, nurses and a midwife.[267]

Early on, the Centennial Park group leaders realized they needed home and community industry. They built a commercial complex at the entrance to their community and slowly expanded from there. The businesses in the small city attract customers from around the area. Indeed, during the FLDS's decade and a half of significant population loss and closing of businesses and support industries, members of Centennial Park stepped forward to provide services for many in the Short Creek–Cane Beds area of the Arizona Strip. The Centennial Park group continues to grow, mostly by birthrate, and has at least two thousand members.[268]

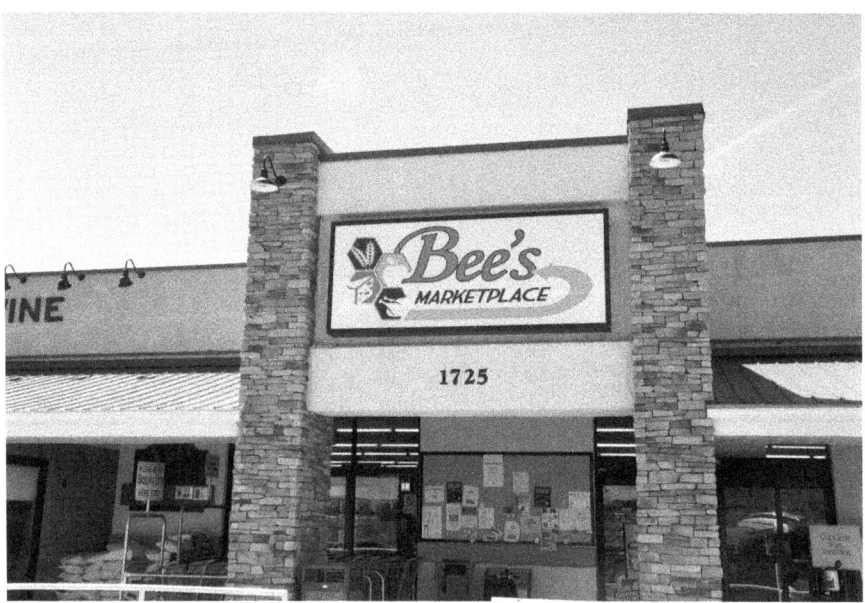

Grocery store in Centennial Park where local residents shop, including some FLDS and non-FLDS residents of Colorado City. *Steven L. Mayfield Collection.*

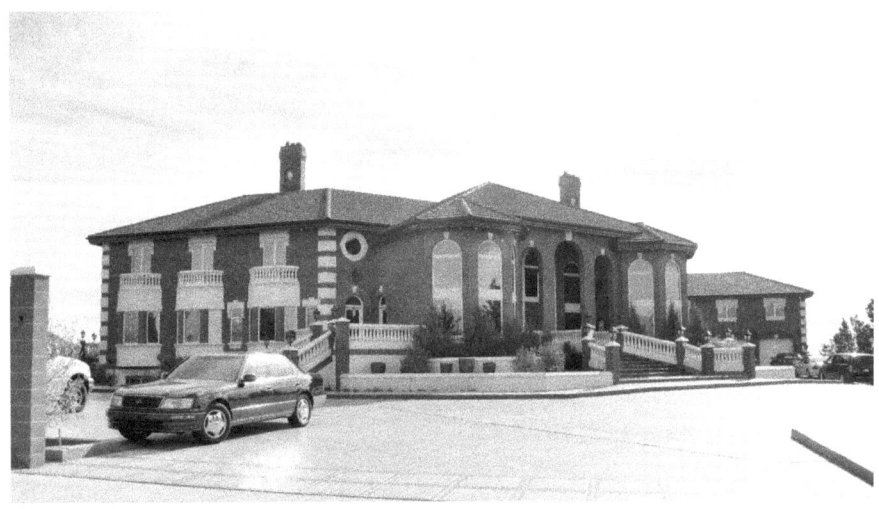

Home of John Timpson, son of Alma A. Timpson, current leader of Centennial Park group. *Steven L. Mayfield Collection.*

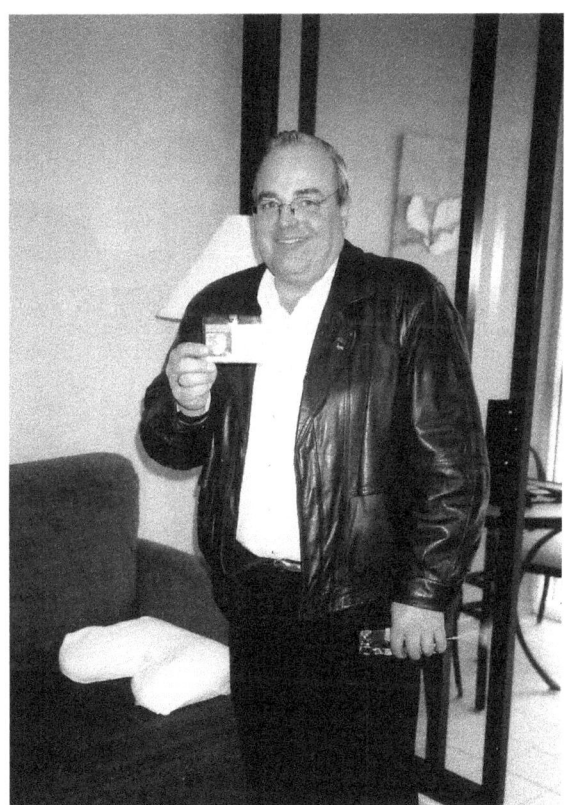

Former FLDS member Winston Blackmore now leading a fundamentalist group in Creston, British Columbia, Canada. *Authors' collection.*

After the death of Marion Hammon in 1988, Alma Timpson led the group. He was intimately involved in the building of the Centennial Park community until his death in 1997. His son John W. Timpson became the group's leader and organized a new council that included his adopted half brother Claude Cawley, Clayne Wayman, Jed Hammon (Marion Hammon's son), Joe Knudson and Lorin Zitting (Charles F. Zitting's son).

As with other Fundamentalist groups, there have also been divisions and departures from the Centennial Park group, such as the Nielsen-Naylor group. This group did not recognize John W. Timpson's authority as legitimate and therefore separated and moved to the Salt Lake Valley, where it has a few hundred active members. These later formally organized as the Church of Jesus Christ of Latter-day Saints and the Kingdom of God to legally protect important Fundamentalist records in their possession. Presently, the leader of the group is Ivan Nielsen. His two counselors are Frank Naylor and Alma Musser, a son of the late Guy Musser. There have been community interaction and marriages between their group and the Winston Blackmore group in Bountiful, Canada.[269]

RULON T. JEFFS AND THE RISE
OF WARREN S. JEFFS

Ironically, the antecedents to Warren Jeffs's odyssey as FLDS-leader-turned-fugitive and ultimately prisoner rests in religious decisions made by his father over the previous sixty-five years.

Rulon Timpson Jeffs was born in Salt Lake City on December 6, 1909, to David William Ward Jeffs and Nettie Lenora Timpson. He had polygamous heritage on both sides of his family. In fact, Rulon's mother was his father's plural wife in a 1909 post–Second Manifesto plural marriage. This sealing was performed by LDS Church patriarch Judson Tolman, who reportedly "received his authority from the President of the Church, and [through] John W. Woolley." Just one day later, Jeffs married another plural wife, Florence Tracy, in a ceremony also performed by Tolman.[270]

Previously, Rulon Jeffs served an LDS mission to Great Britain. After returning home in 1934, he married his first wife, Zola Grace Brown, the daughter of Hugh B. Brown, a prominent attorney and Latter-day Saint who eventually became an LDS Church leader.[271] Rulon and Zola had two sons, but by 1939, the marriage was in trouble because Rulon had become converted to the continued practice of plural marriage. He was influenced by his own father, David W. Jeffs, as well as by early Fundamentalist leaders like Joseph White Musser and John Y. Barlow.[272]

Rulon and Zola's marriage did not survive his embracing of old-fashioned Mormonism, but within a few years, he had married four other women. Nevertheless, Jeffs never stopped loving Zola, nor did he give up the belief that in the hereafter they would yet be together.

Jeffs entered his new religious life with marked enthusiasm, and Fundamentalist leaders recognized and appreciated his talents. He quickly rose in prominence within the tight-knit community and, by 1945, had reached the top ranks of Fundamentalist Mormonism when he was called to the Priesthood Council. In 1946, Jeffs, an accountant, started his own business, with offices in downtown Salt Lake City. In 1953, he branched out by helping found an insurance company with fellow Fundamentalists. These were the first of a handful of businesses owned in part or completely by Jeffs, the proceeds of which he used to take care of his large family.[273]

Rulon Jeffs, who supported the Short Creek Priesthood Council at the time of the 1952 priesthood split, felt the impact of the 1953 Short Creek raid and feared the same might happen to Fundamentalists in the Salt Lake Valley. Thus he secretly moved four of his wives to Sacramento, California. While living there, his fourth wife, Marilyn Steed Jeffs, gave birth to Warren Steed Jeffs, who was born prematurely on December 3, 1955, with Rulon, himself, delivering the baby.

Warren was the fourteenth of Rulon Jeffs's estimated sixty to sixty-five children. Warren's parents viewed his birth and survival as a miracle, especially given that Rulon had delivered him and both mother and child had almost died when he was born. Born two and a half months premature, he was so small he could fit comfortably in a shoe box. Compounding the precarious nature of the birth was the fact that they dared not take Warren to a hospital because he was born to a polygamous wife.[274]

Once his wives and children had returned to the Salt Lake Valley, Jeffs bought a four-acre parcel of land at the mouth of Little Cottonwood Canyon where eventually they built several large houses. The largest, a three-story building, they used as a residence, meetinghouse, school and even a birthing center where plural wives could labor and deliver without scrutiny. A large fence later installed around the property ensured the privacy of the Jeffs family and visitors but also garnered a suspicious perception from outsiders that it was a compound."[275]

Warren Jeffs spent his formative years in the Salt Lake Valley, first living in a fourplex as a small child and then in the Jeffs canyon property, where

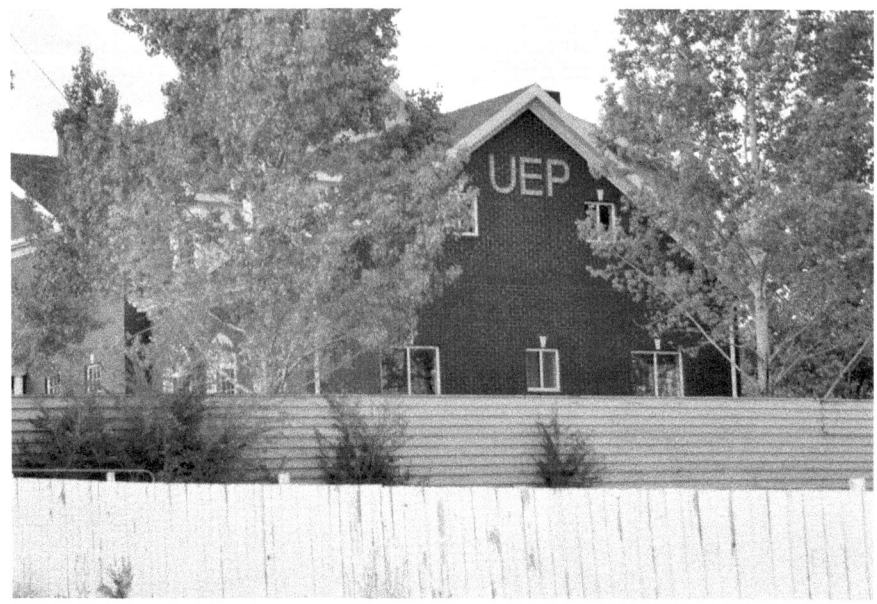

FLDS home in Hildale with UEP designation. *Steven L. Mayfield Collection.*

he was able to live with the numerous members of his large family. Such living conditions provided both positive and negative aspects, such as plenty of siblings to play with but also older brothers to pick on him. Frail, almost sickly looking, he grew very tall but continued to be thin and gaunt. While young, he was considered "a mama's boy" and felt intimidated by his older, more athletic brothers.[276] As a child and adolescent, he was terrified of girls. In fact, one time, when his older brothers tried to get him to talk to some girls, he broke down crying, ran away and hid.[277]

Warren stayed close to both of his parents, and his mother especially pushed him, telling him that "he was the most holy of Rulon's children."[278] Some older brothers complained that "Warren was raised like 'a little Lord Fauntleroy' riding through life on a pillow." To them, he presented himself as "pious, righteous and obedient."[279]

Behind Warren's public façade lurked a darker side to his personality. Though shy around the opposite sex, he had gained a reputation as a voyeur by the age of eight. A child of a Fundamentalist neighbor caught him peeking through the bathroom window when she was taking a bath. Her mother had to cover the bathroom window with black paper to keep Warren from looking in. She also recounted how Warren had talked her younger sister—near his age—into undressing for him. By the time Warren was in his teens, rumors spread that he had moved from voyeurism to molestation.[280] In fact, he was accused of molesting at least one of his sisters while still a youth and was sent away to live with a relative for a couple of years. These were not the only accusations of molestation and incest. In 2015, two of Warren's children accused him of sexual abuse. They were not alone. In 2017, Rachel Jeffs accused her father of years of sexual abuse, starting when she was eight years old and lasting until she was sixteen.[281]

These problems notwithstanding, Warren Jeffs had one thing going for him—he was extremely bright and did very well in school, especially in the subjects of math and science. One of his cousins claimed that both Warren and his father had photographic memories.[282]

In 1973, the same year after Warren graduated with honors from high school, his father gave him a teaching position in the newly organized and privately run Alta Academy, a school for the Jeffs family and children of fellow Fundamentalists in that group. He taught math, science and church history. Soon after, he became the principal of the academy and held that position for the next twenty-five years, during which time he played a decisive role, wielding tremendous influence in "molding the behavior of the church's rank and file members," most pointedly a whole generation of children."[283]

From the late 1960s through the 1990s, the large building on the Jeffs property that was used both for a school and a meeting place for religious services also served as a de facto headquarters and a spiritual center for the Short Creek group, including the estimated one thousand members of the Leroy Johnson faction of Fundamentalists living along Utah's Wasatch Front, especially in and around the Salt Lake valley.

Throughout this period, Rulon Jeffs continually reaffirmed his support of Leroy Johnson and supported a movement within the group that wanted to move the leadership away from the traditional priesthood council order to become a one-man rule. The debate between those who wanted one-man rule and those who wanted to continue as they had in the past came to a head in 1984 when Johnson removed two council members, Hammon and Timpson, as previously discussed. By default, Rulon Jeffs became the next in line for leadership, the *only* council member remaining other than Johnson himself.

When Leroy Johnson died in November 1986, Rulon Jeffs succeeded him. He introduced a new style of leadership that starkly contrasted with his predecessor's. Johnson had been described as "a man of the people" and "a man of the land." As one former member of the group noted, "When the people suffered, Uncle Roy suffered." She then went on to say, "The Jeffs [family] never suffered with the people." Another former member commented, "With Rulon, it was very much about him."[284]

Yet others admired Rulon Jeffs and his style of leadership, in which he consolidated power in a one-man rule and established tighter control over the economic arm of the organization, the United Effort Plan or UEP. In February 1991, he made one of the biggest changes when he officially incorporated a church, naming it the Fundamentalist Church of Jesus Christ of Latter Day Saints (FLDS). Prior to that, it had been a group following Lorin Woolley's counsel to maintain correct principles of the restored gospel of Jesus Christ but not an independently organized church. At the time of organizing, then in the middle of legal battles with Centennial Park members, FLDS leaders said the church creation was purely for tax, legal and business purposes. Experts at the time predicted that it would be only a matter of time before leaders would assign "spiritual credence" to the organization, rather than just viewing it as legal convenience. This began happening when FLDS leaders and members started proclaiming they were *the* true Church of Jesus Christ rather than the larger LDS Church, which they claimed had gone astray since the 1890 Manifesto. Predictions became fully accurate a little over a decade later after Jeffs died when Warren Jeffs proclaimed himself leader of the FLDS and he ordered documents and publications to be published leaving out the word *Fundamentalist* as part of their name. Instead, he identified the organizations as the Church of Jesus Christ of Latter Day Saints. Warren viewed himself as *the* true prophet of *the* true church.[285]

Until just a few years before his death, Rulon Jeffs had continued to reside in the Salt Lake Valley, where approximately a third of the group lived. During his administration, he made regular visits, usually traveling the three hundred miles south by private airplane, to Short Creek, which had been incorporated by then into the twin communities of Hildale, Utah, and Colorado City, Arizona.[286]

Early in Rulon Jeffs's administration, Warren established himself as his father's closest advisor, managing to push away other brothers, even older ones. Warren ingratiated himself with his father, offering to hear and then speak on his father's behalf. This was particularly the case after Rulon suffered a series of mini-strokes in 1997. After that, as one former member turned critic explained, Warren "hijacked" Rulon.[287]

Under Warren's influence, members were banned from accessing all types of media as well as watching movies and listening to music. He also banned celebrating traditional holidays and in 2000 ordered all FLDS members to remove their children from public schools. These measures further effectively isolated the FLDS from the outside world.[288]

FLDS members contracted a millenarian fervor after Rulon Jeffs prophesied imminent end-of-world destructions to begin in conjunction with the 2002 Salt Lake City Winter Olympics. He and most of his large family, including Warren's family, moved to Colorado City–Hildale. Despite the fact that several of Rulon's predictions had failed, Salt Lake area members followed his counsel and sold their homes, many of their possessions and moved to the twin cities. The Olympics came and went, the world was still here and the faithful FLDS were mostly all in Short Creek.[289]

After Rulon Jeffs died in September 2002, Warren, without precedent, strangely placed a large portrait photograph of his father next to the speaker's stand at his funeral and declared his father still presided. This meant he presided over his own funeral, something completely at odds with any Mormon doctrine. A little later, declaring it as the will of his father, Warren proclaimed himself leader and officially took charge of the FLDS

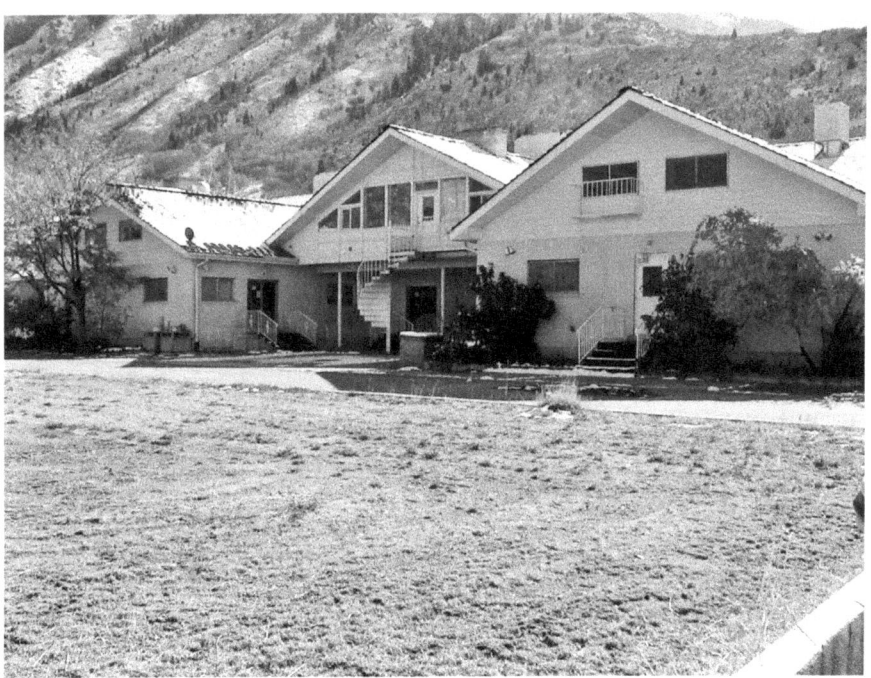

Rulon Jeffs's home at mouth of Little Cottonwood Canyon in the Salt Lake Valley. *Brian C. Hales Collection.*

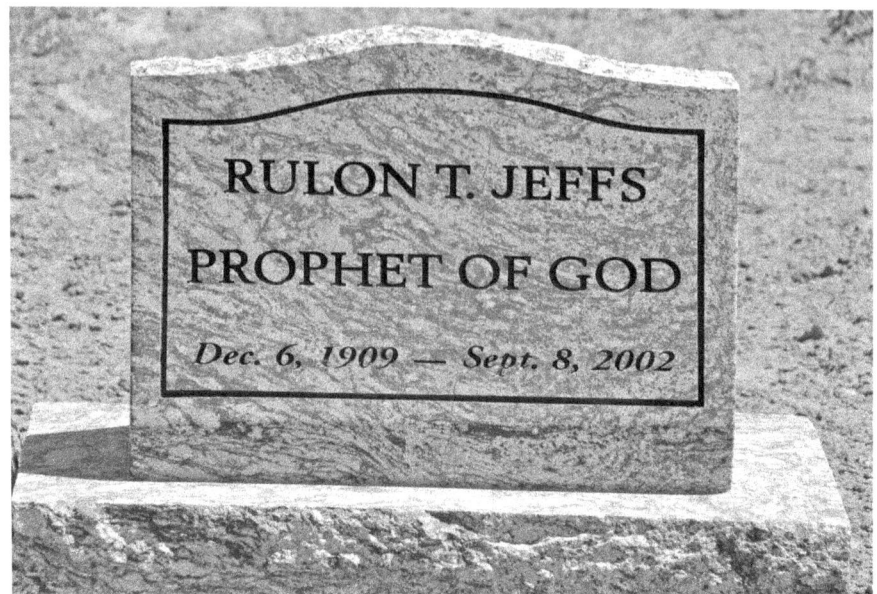

Rulon T. Jeffs headstone in Isaac Carling cemetery at Colorado City. *Steven L. Mayfield Collection.*

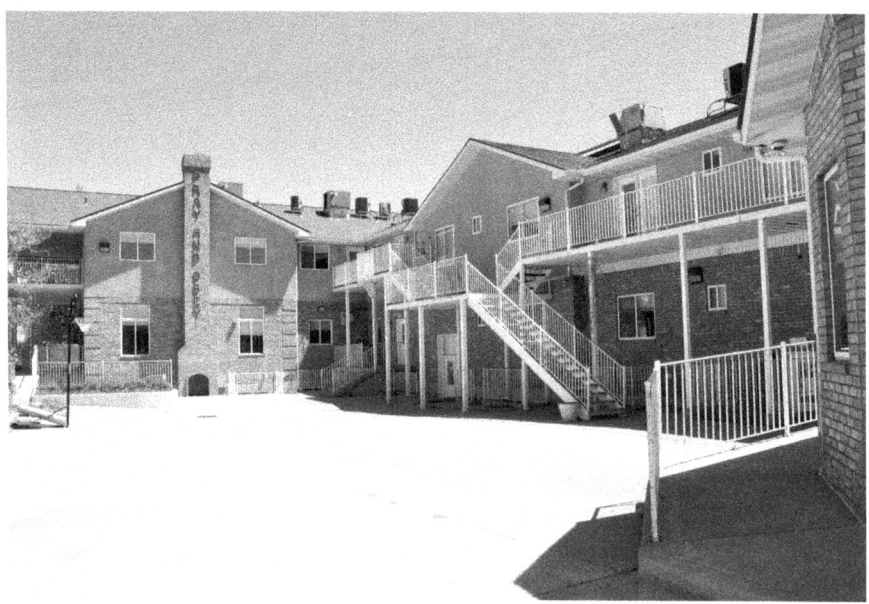

Rear view of Warren Jeffs's home in Colorado City. *Steven L. Mayfield Collection.*

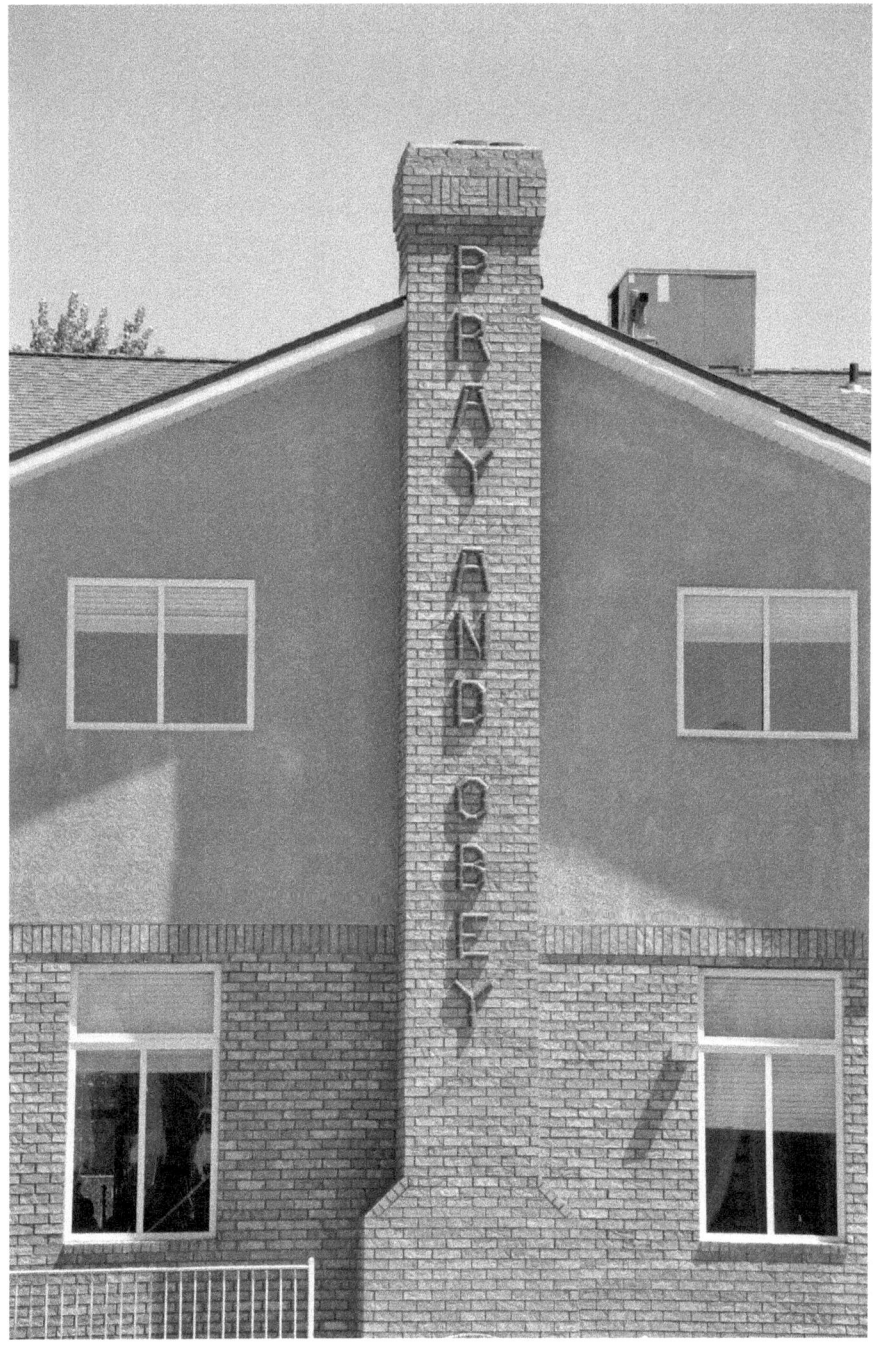

"Pray and Obey" chimney on Warren Jeff's home in Colorado City. *Steven L. Mayfield Collection.*

Church, suppressing any open questioning. Even openly doubting Warren was considered apostasy.

Some FLDS members as well as outside observers wondered how Warren Jeffs, without priesthood council apostleship, had any authority to assume leadership. Apparently, he sought to hide the facts of his priesthood records, which showed that his father only ordained him on February 14, 1998, as a seventy apostle and a first counselor to his father, but never as an apostle. That had not changed even after his father's death when a 2003 FLDS bishop's record still listed him in the same office.[290]

Critics of Jeffs believed that he was never ordained an apostle and patriarch for inclusion in his father's priesthood council or had received in any way the same authority and commission believed to have been given by John Taylor to and perpetuated through Lorin C. Woolley. They insisted that by all standards of priesthood order in Fundamentalist history, Warren did not qualify to preside, and his father, Rulon, failed to perpetuate the priesthood calling he had received, either as an individual or as one of a quorum; his apostolic priesthood authority died with him. Without the proper ordination and appointment, Warren could only assert himself legally as FLDS church president and then proclaim himself a prophet, which he did in two ways. First, he convinced one of Rulon's wives to announce to the people that it had been Rulon's direction for Warren to succeed him. Then, by excommunicating or sending away any who might oppose him, he silenced opposition. In this way, Warren avoided exposing the crux of the matter—that he acted without authority, all the while doing his public acts of ruin in the name of his father.

For almost a year, Jeffs autocratically ruled the FLDS Church with increasing rigidity as he reshaped the religion in his image. He claimed to receive revelations night after night (especially targeting the elite of the community) revealing what sins had been committed, naming members of the community, directing many to leave and repent from afar or casting them out completely. He took away men's wives and reassigned them to marry other men, shattering families as he reshuffled men, women and children from family to family and from home to home. As seen by Mormons and Fundamentalists alike as well as by other observers, this reprehensible dictatorial behavior was Warren's own dark invention and had nothing to do with Joseph Smith's restored gospel.

The FLDS had for years practiced placement marriage, wherein only the prophet could decide who would marry whom, thus arranging the marriages of all faithful. Under Rulon Jeffs, women had tended to marry around the age of twenty or so. When Warren seized control, he took arranged marriages to a new level and began ordering the marriages of men to increasingly younger brides. Warren himself married a number of underage girls and directed other men to do the same.

Because Utah state authorities and other law enforcement entities began investigating Jeffs for marriages to underage girls and other questionable and unlawful activities, he went into hiding in August 2003. Until his arrest in 2006, Jeffs traveled throughout the country visiting various cities and sites, including such places as Las Vegas and New Orleans during Mardi Gras. His purpose, as he explained, was to behold and condemn wickedness on behalf of God.

FBI'S MOST WANTED

One hot August evening in 2006, news flashed across television screens, announcing that another of the FBI's most wanted had been captured. The prisoner was none other than Warren S. Jeffs, the leader of the FLDS or Fundamentalist Church of Jesus Christ of Latter Day Saints.[291] This was significant to all Fundamentalist Mormons and Utahans.

Warren, accompanied by his wife Naomi, was caught near Las Vegas riding in a fully equipped 2006 red Cadillac Escalade driven by his brother Isaac. Something amazed most people who knew anything about Mormon Fundamentalists when they saw Warren on national TV that day. Ordinarily, when in public, Warren dressed conservatively, like most FLDS men when in public—in a suit and tie, or at least wearing a long-sleeved shirt with a collar. At the time of his arrest, Warren's attire was strikingly incongruous from his previous public appearances—he sported khaki knee-length shorts and a casual, white, short-sleeved "Mountain Outfitters" T-shirt. His very appearance would have shocked and distressed his faithful flock if they had seen him, because for any of them, especially married men, dressing in such clothes would have been reason alone for Warren's censure—surely ending in excommunication or at least being sent away to repent from afar.

Just as shocking, Naomi Jeffs wore blue jeans and a short-sleeved, low-cut, V-necked pink T-shirt. Traditionally, Fundamentalist women in Hildale–Colorado City dressed modestly, wearing mid-calf or long dresses and skirts of a wide variety of colors, prints and patterns. Warren Jeffs had tightened and modified that standard for all FLDS females. Under his rule, he allowed females from little girls to old women to wear only one certain pattern of long-sleeved, floor-length "prairie-style dresses" in approved fabrics and monotone colors. To understanding viewers, Warren and Naomi's clothing that day shouted loudly that something was terribly wrong. Warren clearly allowed a double standard for himself and Naomi when it suited him, while imposing strict conformity upon his followers

Troubling too were other contents found in the vehicle apart from a *Book of Mormon* and a photo of Warren with his late father, Rulon. The vehicle had a stash of bills—twenty-seven stacks of money each containing $2,500 for a total of $67,500; two female wigs, blond and brunette; fourteen cellphones; and two GPS navigation units.[292] These items alone alerted law authorities and may have caused concern to the faithful if they had been permitted to view such media. However, items found later ultimately put Warren Jeffs behind bars for life.

THE YFZ RANCH RAID AND WARREN IN PRISON FOR LIFE

After Warren Jeffs's arrest, he was placed in jail to await trials as an accessory to sexual conduct with a minor for marriages he had performed. While in jail waiting, he tried to commit suicide several times and early on announced through his brother, "I am not the prophet. I never was the prophet, and I have been deceived by the powers of evil….I ask for everyone's forgiveness." He admitted to another member that he had been immoral with a sister and a daughter.[293] Jailhouse cameras recorded these conversations, but his faithful followers refused to watch or listen, and he soon reneged and resumed his "Prophet" role.

In November 2007, Jeffs was sentenced to ten years to life in prison for being an accessory to rape and began serving time in the Utah State Penitentiary. While that verdict was eventually overturned on a technicality, there was even more trouble ahead for Jeffs and the FLDS. In April 2008, heavily armed local authorities and state troopers stormed the FLDS Yearning for Zion Ranch near Eldorado in the southwest part of Texas.

The raid of the Texas FLDS ranch was instigated by a phone call—charging forced marriage and sexual abuse—from a woman claiming to be an underage plural wife named Sarah Jessop Barlow. YFZ officials denied there was a woman by that name at the ranch. However, according to Nick Hanna, a Texas Ranger and one of the first law officials to the ranch, when the lawmen searched the membership files they immediately found

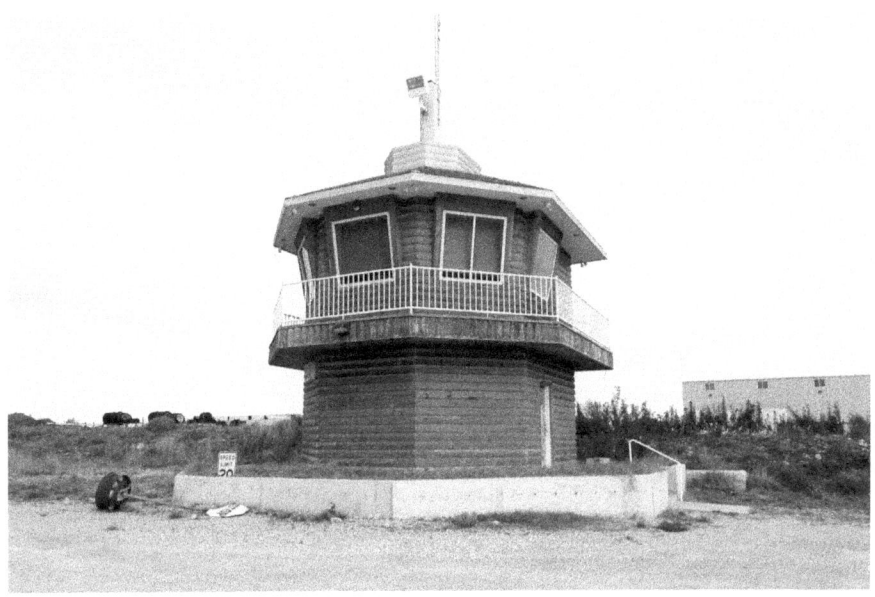

Watchtower at FLDS YFZ Ranch in Texas. *Authors' collection.*

the name of Sarah Jessop Barlow and were sure she was actually located at the ranch. This spurred their search for the underage wife. Adding to the surreal nature of the raid and fueling law officials' suspicions were the bizarre actions of ranch residents. Hanna explained how FLDS members tried moving girls from one building to another. They also caught members trying to shred documents and others stealing documents and taking them out and dropping them behind clumps of sagebrush.[294] Ultimately, the original complaining phone call was proved to be a hoax perpetrated by a mentally unstable woman who had no connection to the FLDS but who some say was put up to the trick by a former resident of Hildale with an axe to grind. Despite this fact, the results of the raid were significant.

Around 400 children and 129 mothers were removed from the ranch in what was called the "largest government seizure of children in the history of the United States."[295] The media coverage of the raid and its aftermath was extensive and ranged from the sensational to the sophisticated. While initially positive toward the government, like the news stories at the time of the 1953 Short Creek raid, many of the stories eventually turned critical of the authorities' handling of the raid and removal of so many children, especially treating the whole community as one family and one household. In contrast to 1953, the FLDS leadership quickly realized, rather than being secretive, benefits could be had from seeking out and using the media to their advantage by appearing on various national TV shows and in popular publications with their version of the raid and its impact.

Two days after the authorities entered the Texas ranch, they broke into the FLDS temple and nearby temple annex. In the vault of the temple annex, authorities found a treasure-trove of damning documents, including detailed records showing who married whom as well as audio tapes of Jeffs deflowering a girl barely twelve years old on a bed in the temple. Most FLDS members, even those in leadership positions, were not aware of Jeffs's sexual deviances with his underage wives, and the public did not become aware until his trial.

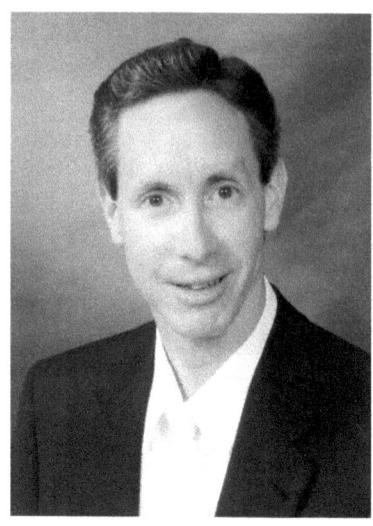

Warren S. Jeffs, 1980s. *Authors' collection.*

FLDS representatives worked overtime trying to legally protect Warren Jeffs and other church officials as well as address a number of lawsuits against the church and its leaders. They hired a bevvy of lawyers and fought Jeffs's extradition to Texas to stand trial on charges based on the evidence taken from the temple. From Short Creek, a constant stream of FLDS operatives came and went carrying messages and information regarding the various court cases and legal maneuvering. In an upstairs office of a nondescript construction company in Hildale, FLDS leadership coordinated in the "War Room" on white boards on three walls where they followed the status of all the different legal cases, as well as important dates. Also binders in the room held paperwork about the different cases as well as opposition research about former FLDS who were providing evidence to law officials.[296]

Despite FLDS efforts, Texas succeeded in extraditing Warren Jeffs to stand trial. He was found guilty in 2011 of sexual assault and aggravated sexual assault of underage girls. Jeffs received a life sentence plus twenty years, ensuring that he will spend the rest of his life in prison. The day he was sentenced, one of his brothers commented that justice was served and that he got what he deserved. He then stated that Warren Jeffs was a pervert driven by his sexual urges.[297]

Although Jeffs is serving a life sentence in Texas, he still exerts significant control over faithful FLDS members. A former member of the FLDS

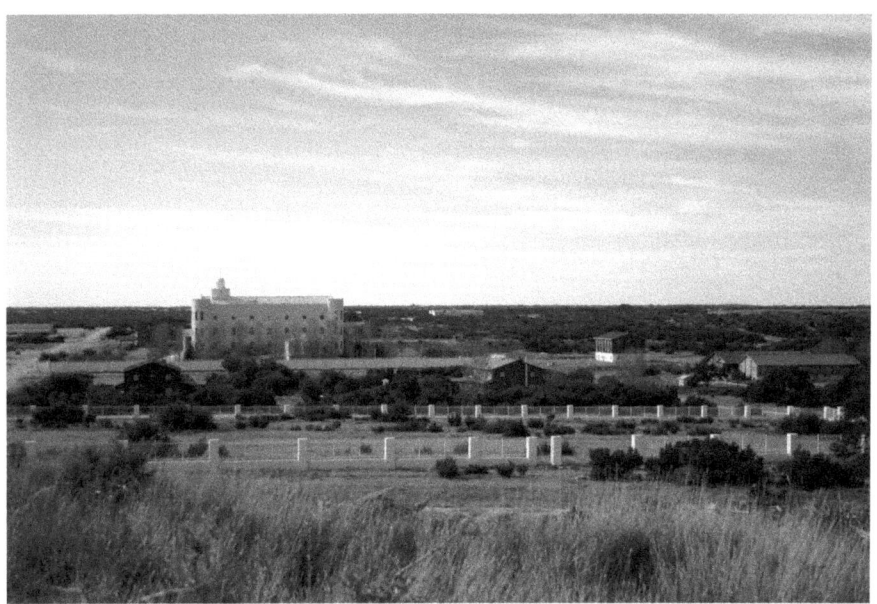

FLDS Texas temple. *Authors' collection.*

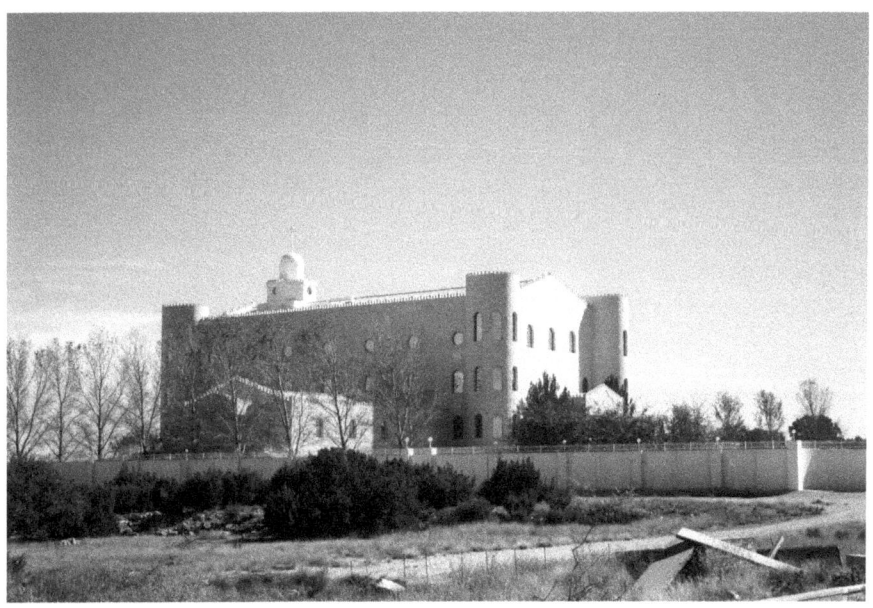

Another view of FLDS Texas temple. *Authors' collection.*

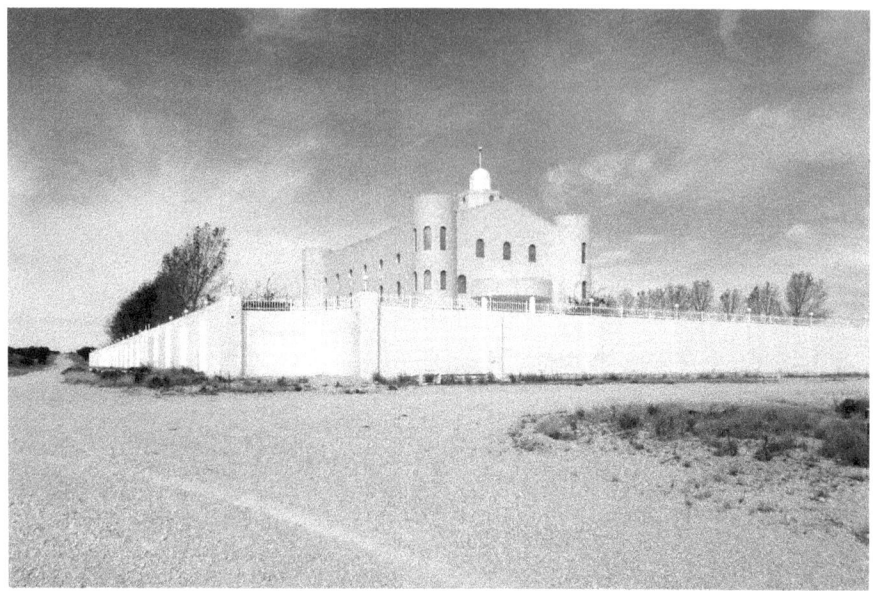

Third view of FLDS Texas temple. *Authors' collection.*

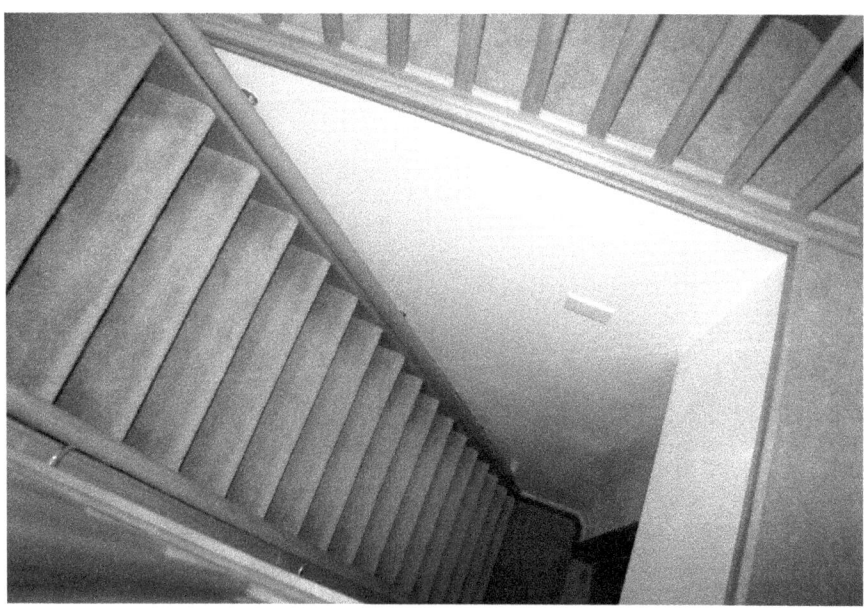

Secret stairs in Warren Jeff's FLDS R-17 Texas home. *Authors' collection.*

described Jeffs as "a control freak from hell."[298] Family members as well as other former church members described Jeffs as a person who not only liked to control but also liked to mess with other people's lives, and this is certainly demonstrated by his continued use of proclamations, prophecies and intimidation from his prison cell.

In order for Jeffs to continue to exert control over his flock, he and his most loyal followers, many of whom are family members, have portrayed him as an innocent man of God wrongfully accused and incarcerated by an evil government persecuting God's chosen prophet. A former member said they had been taught by the church's leaders that Warren Jeffs is in prison suffering for members to adequately prepare for the Second Coming of Jesus Christ.[299]

FLDS members have been repeatedly told that Jeffs's sufferings on their behalf could be lessened and that he would in fact be miraculously released from prison if they would only be more obedient and willing to sacrifice more. They have been continually told if they don't repent and show more

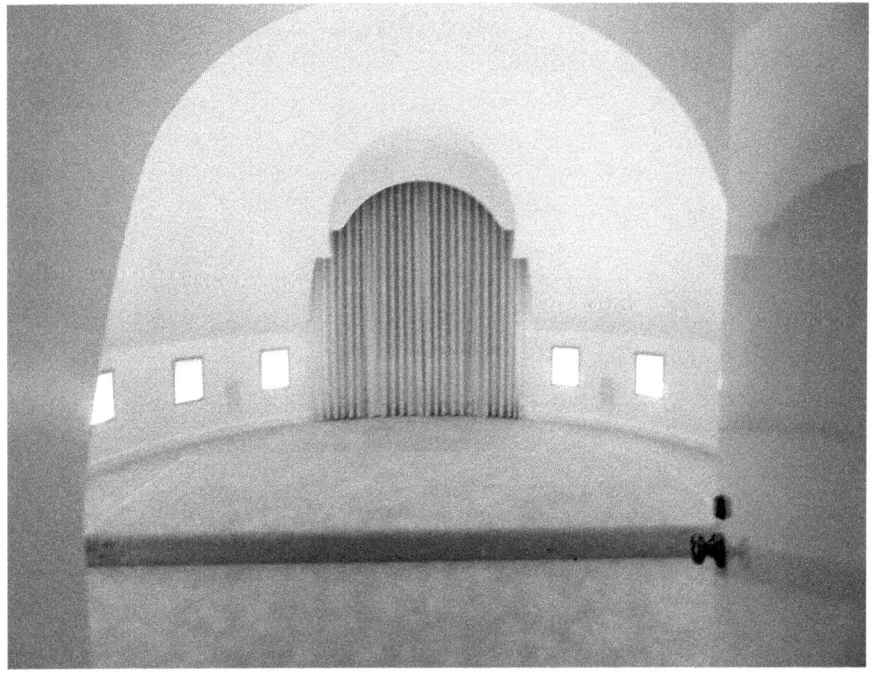

Warren Jeffs's secret sex room in his FLDS R-17 Texas home. *Authors' collection.*

183

faith and devotion leading to Jeffs's release, they will disqualify and God will raise up a new people.[300] With this admonition in mind, every day his faithful followers pray for his release. In fact, for quite a while, a prayer circle was held two to three times a day at the large meetinghouse in Colorado City, praying for him to miraculously be released from prison.[301]

There are many examples of Jeffs's continued control of the faithful FLDS. In the fall of 2011, members were interviewed to see if they were worthy enough to live the United Order. If found worthy, they were commanded to donate all their assets to the church, and the church would then provide for their needs by giving back a small portion on which to subsist. As part of this United Order movement, they were forbidden to shop at "Gentile" stores and had to obtain their groceries and other necessities from the bishop's storehouse—but more often than not there was little food or other goods available for the people.[302]

In a scenario reminiscent of George Orwell's *Animal Farm*, in which "all animals are equal, but some animals are more equal than others," some elite FLDS were able to eat what they wanted while others suffered from near starvation. Lyle Jeffs and Seth Jeffs, brothers of Warren, were the bishops of Hildale–Colorado City and the community in the Black Hills of South Dakota, respectively. Lyle was also recognized as the sect's leader and official representative of Warren. Because of his position, he and his family ate "feasts of lobster and shrimp," while others "subsisted on noodles, brown rice, tomato juice" and, for some, just toast. The food of necessity was rationed, and the quality was not good. As a part of rationing, most people were allowed one meal a day (two for those doing hard manual labor) and the allowed amount of food per person was actually weighed.[303]

Meanwhile, the FLDS elite purchased their food from nice stores and ate extremely well. The majority were starving in spite of the fact a number of the families were on food stamps and should have been able to eat fairly well. They were unable to do that because they were commanded to hand over their food stamps and other government assistance to leadership, who then used the welfare for themselves and church ventures. This process was called "bleeding the beast," with the "beast" being the federal government. In April 2015, "criminal charges were filed accusing eleven FLDS members—including Lyle and Seth Jeffs—of engaging in a food stamp swindle and money-laundering scheme that raked in some $12 million."[304]

All of the men were eventually released from jail on bail, including Lyle, who had been declared a flight risk. Less than two weeks after being released, Lyle Jeffs got his ankle bracelet off and disappeared. People wondered if he was hiding in the twin cities or at one of the numerous safe houses and secret compounds the FLDS is reputed to own. The FLDS has a 140-acre compound near Pringle, South Dakota, known among the FLDS as "R23" and is situated on "a gravel road, hidden by tall pine trees, a privacy fence and a guard tower. Authorities have said the small congregation is led by Seth Jeffs, brother of Lyle and Warren Jeffs." Lyle was arrested approximately four hundred miles east of Pringle, probably traveling between places of refuge or safe houses, almost a year after having gone on the lam. Late in 2017, Lyle Jeffs was sentenced to five years in a federal penitentiary for food stamp fraud and illegal flight.[305]

State and federal governments have also gone after the FLDS and its leaders with indictments and suits over corruption in the local government and law enforcement, housing and land issues and a number of cases dealing with child labor. A relative of Jeffs's recently confirmed that "[t]he mayor, city council, police, and others are still under the control" of Warren Jeffs, and action has been taken to wrest that control away from corrupt officials.[306] As for child labor, this has long been a problem among the FLDS. Private investigator and author Sam Brower has referred to the FLDS leadership as "a crime syndicate that specializes in child abuse."[307]

Within the last few years, there has been a significant exodus from Short Creek of the FLDS faithful. This is in response to the FLDS losing the legal struggle over control of the United Effort Plan. Members were told by leadership to not sign occupancy agreements or pay a $100-a-month-per-home fee to the trust.[308] The result was evictions and members being told to move to other places outside of the Colorado City–Hildale area and to await word to return.

The FLDS diaspora from Short Creek has been mostly within a day's drive; others have traveled much farther from their homes. Frederick Merril Jessop, the former bishop of the YFZ Ranch, bought eighty acres of land south of Cedar City, Utah, for the church where a number of members have settled. He also owns a large home and property north of Cedar City in the small community of Enoch, Utah, where he has moved some of his faithful family members, including his daughters married to Warren Jeffs. While his main home is now in Enoch, Merril still spends most of his time in Idaho on the direct orders of Jeffs.[309]

FLDS members settled along Utah's I-15 corridor running from St. George in the south as well as in New Harmony, Parowan, Beaver, Fillmore, Spanish Fork and Utah Valley, the Salt Lake Valley and Davis County. Members also live in Cache Valley, as well as in most western states, particularly Arizona,

Colorado, Idaho, Montana, Nevada and Wyoming. Those living farther afield reside in Nebraska, Oklahoma and South Dakota, even Pennsylvania and West Virginia. As for Warren Jeffs's most trusted followers, including his mother and other close family members, they live in "R23" near Pringle, South Dakota.[310]

Former FLDS followers feel this far-flung dispersion of the faithful will only lead to less blind faith on their part and less control by Warren Jeffs and his inner circle. While FLDS adherents are looked on with bemusement and suspicion by mainstream American society, wherever they go, they quickly earn a reputation for hard work and being quiet but good neighbors, which is slowly helping integrate them into the larger society.[311]

Of the numerous negative results of Warren Jeffs's warped influence on the FLDS, perhaps the most disturbing is the destruction of the families. Over the years, even from his Texas prison cell, Warren Jeffs has directed the breakup of countless FLDS families. And making things even worse, now that Jeffs is incarcerated, no faithful FLDS are allowed to have sexual relations with their spouse or spouses. There have not been any marriages performed since Jeffs was arrested in 2006, and in 2011, members were told their marriages were void and "they are not to live as husband and wife.... They can live in the same house, but they are not to have sexual relationships until Warren comes out and 'reseals' them."[312]

The rules became draconian. A member was told personally by Lyle Jeffs that he was "not to kiss, hug, touch or have sexual relations with his wife."[313] It was around this time that rumors spread that fifteen men whom Jeffs considered to be of good stock had been called by him to impregnate the women of the church. Some former members confirmed this was the case, but not much is known beyond that. What is known is that Jeffs "has so torn apart the meaning of families and marriage [that] many young men in the community no longer have a desire to be married."[314]

And for those who do want to be married, they cannot do so and remain faithful to Warren Jeffs and the FLDS Church. Many FLDS youth feel they have no future in the group, particularly as they are unable to marry and have children. For this and other reasons, the FLDS is experiencing unprecedented disaffection of the youth, estimated to be as high as 85 to 90 percent.[315]

The disintegration of the community and so many families has had a deleterious effect that is slowly, painfully destroying the FLDS. In order to keep control of the religious flock, Jeffs and other leaders have lied and misdirected, cajoled and condemned. And this because they know that

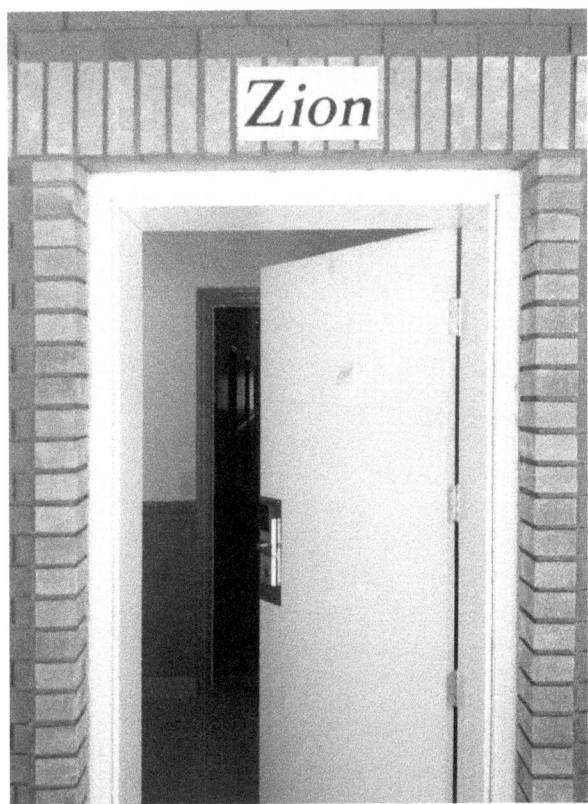

Left: Zion sign over door of home built for Warren Jeffs while in prison. Now America's Most Wanted Bed and Breakfast, owned by former FLDS member Willie Jessop. *Steven L. Mayfield Collection.*

Below: FLDS family working in Colorado City, circa 2017. *Steven L. Mayfield Collection.*

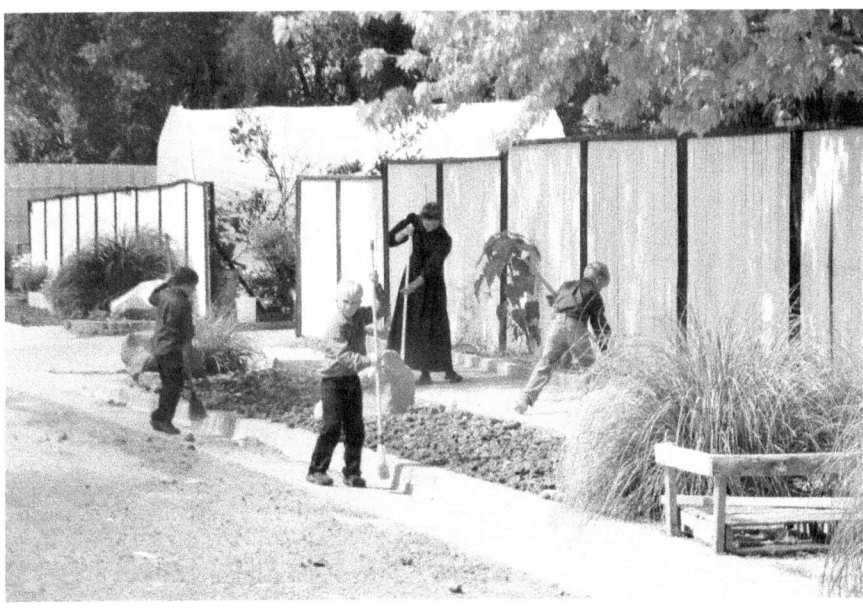

should the faithful members get the whole truth about Warren Jeffs and his ilk, it would, as one former member but still true believer in Fundamentalist Mormonism, explained, "be a catastrophic toll on the people." As it is, the FLDS Church has lost a good portion of its membership. For example, a couple of years ago, those attending sanctioned Sunday meetings only numbered about 250, as opposed to earlier days when Sunday attendance would be in the thousands.[316]

Ultimately, as one former FLDS member passionately explained, Warren Steed Jeffs destroyed the FLDS. He did so by pulling families apart, casting out numerous members and irrevocably damaging lives. But even more heartbreaking for this former member was Jeffs's destruction of the FLDS's faith and spirituality. In order to satisfy his own base desires, Jeffs went contrary to what the prophet Joseph Smith had taught. He vacated certain core principles of the gospel and carefully moved his members away from those core principles. Members, believing their prophet would never do wrong, shifted and moved their beliefs to accommodate Jeffs. Jeffs's revelations have no resemblance to the Restoration message of the prophet Joseph Smith or even to the 1886 events and the purpose of the continuation of the Principle. The FLDS religion shifted to a communal cult reverencing a man more than God. "Warren [Jeffs] led the FLDS into apostasy and corruption."[317]

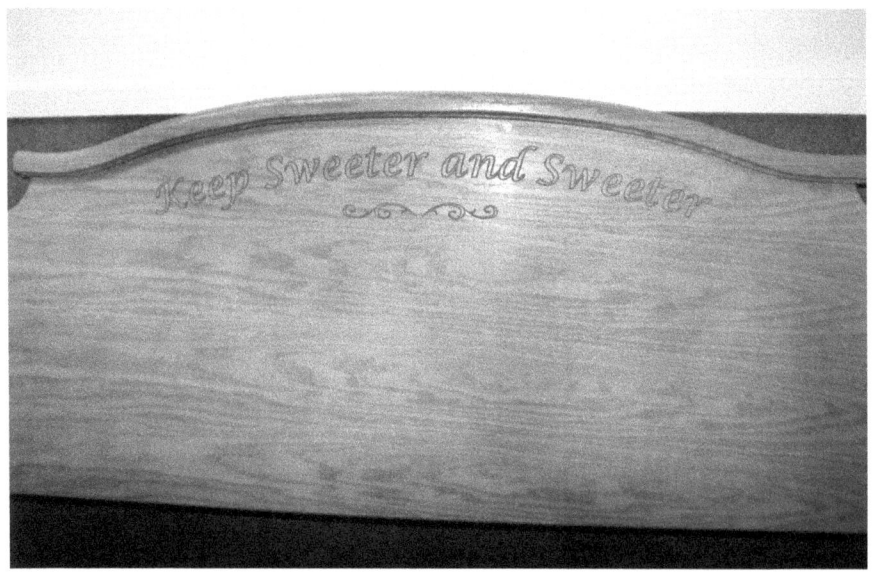

"Keep Sweeter and Sweeter" headboard abandoned in Warren Jeffs's Texas home. *Authors' collection.*

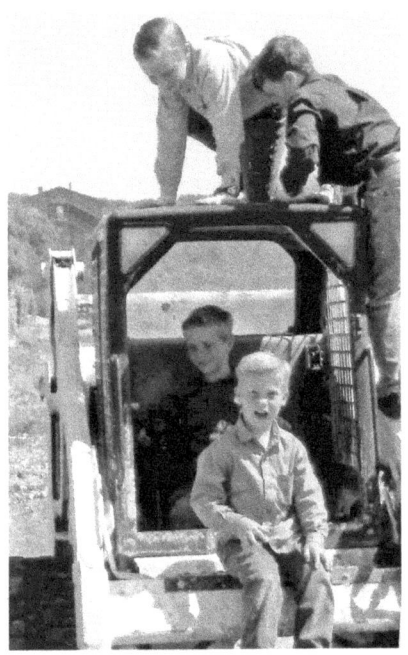 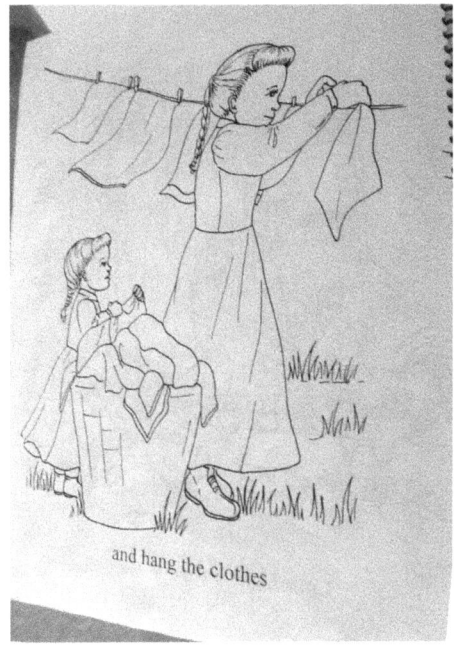

and hang the clothes

Left: FDLS boys at Texas ranch playing on equipment. *Authors' collection.*

Right: FLDS coloring book. *Authors' collection.*

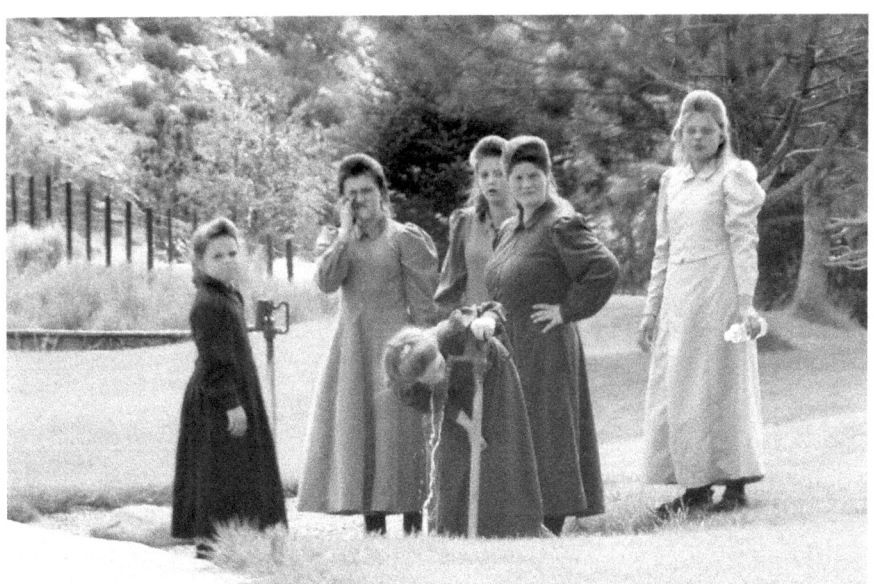

FLDS women filling water containers at a canyon park near Hildale, Utah. *Steven L. Mayfield Collection.*

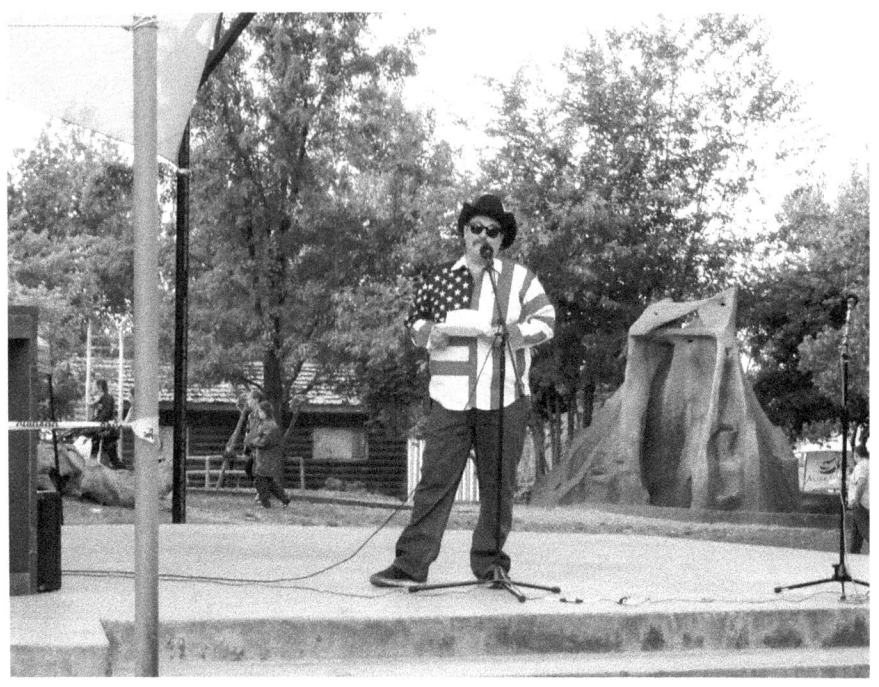

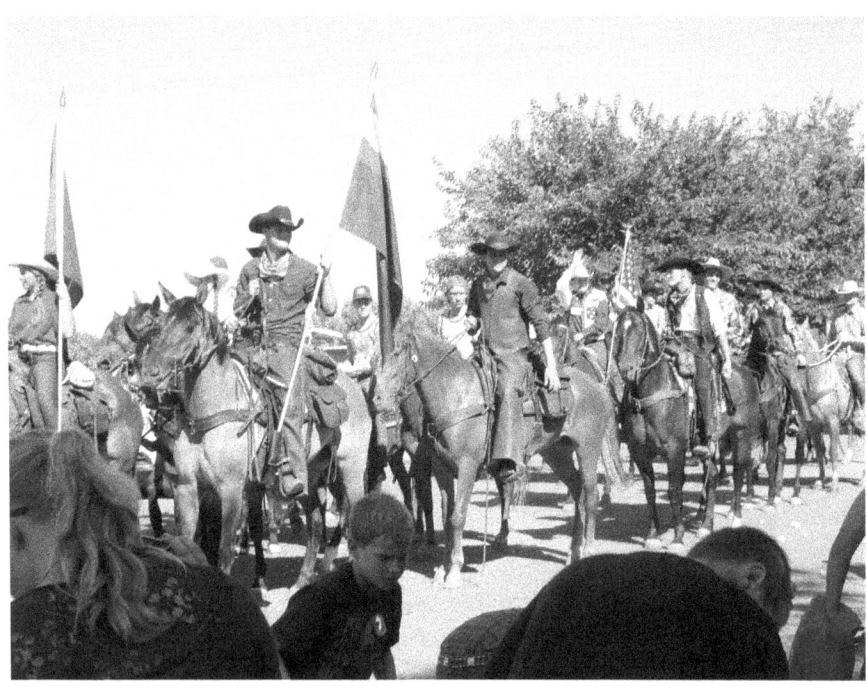

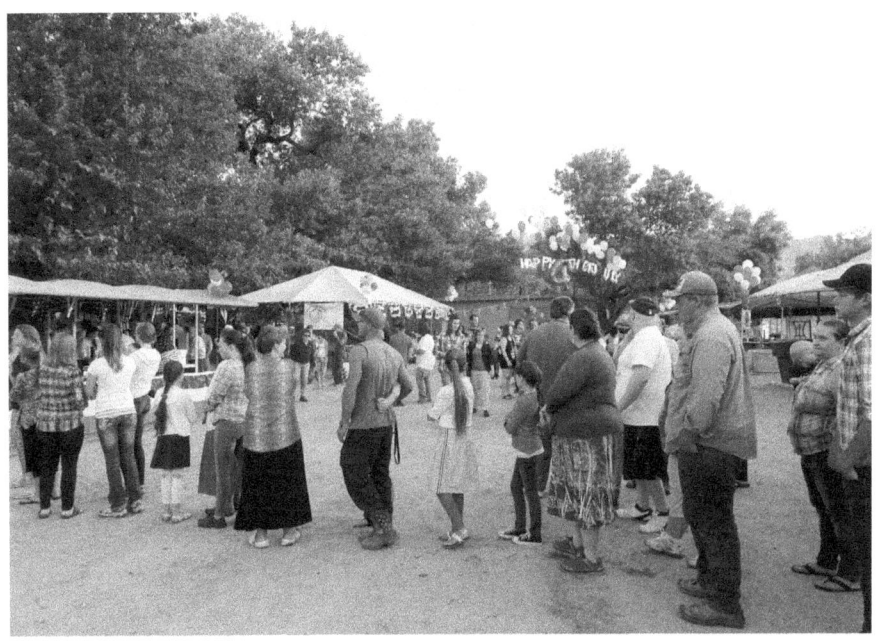

Above: Hildale–Colorado City Fourth of July Community Breakfast, 2017. *Steven L. Mayfield Collection.*

Opposite, top: Master of Ceremonies at Fourth of July celebration in Hildale–Colorado City, 2017. *Steven L. Mayfield Collection.*

Opposite, bottom: Hildale–Colorado City Fourth of July parade, 2017. *Steven L. Mayfield Collection.*

Despite Jeffs's attempts to destroy the Short Creek community, residents are moving on. In 2015, former FLDS and others gathered together to have "a good old Short Creek Fourth of July" like they used to celebrate before the Jeffses took control. The celebration in 2016 was even larger, with a flag-raising service, community breakfast, parade, games, music and even helicopter rides. People came from miles away to figuratively thumb their noses at Warren Jeffs and his cabal. The master of ceremonies for the event told the gathered crowd, "Today is about coming together and celebrating our home town." Ross Chatwin, who had previously publicly defied Jeffs and the FLDS leadership to save his home when they tried to evict him, stated, "This celebration is our openly fighting back, saying to Warren we're going to do what we want and are not going to listen to you anymore. We want to let the world know we are good people and we are no longer letting it be about Warren Jeffs."[318]

TWENTY-FIRST-CENTURY
FUNDAMENTALISM

Coming Out of the Shadows

During the last decades of twentieth-century Fundamentalist Mormonism, its adherents remained mostly in the shadowlands and on the fringes of American society. Most Fundamentalists readily acknowledge different forms of abuse are found among every people and community, theirs included, but they maintain that abuses are generally less pervasive as a whole in their communities, with the exception of Warren Jeffs and other rogue characters. At the dawn of a new century, Fundamentalists seemed to draw increasing negative publicity with one news story after another about scandals of various types. Three of the most publicized cases involving Fundamentalist Mormon communities other than the FLDS are discussed here. Also, one case is summarized about a former Mormon who used plural marriage as an excuse for kidnapping and rape but was not associated with any Fundamentalist Mormons; nevertheless, the case added considerably to the negative public perception of Fundamentalist Mormons.

THE DAWN OF A NEW CENTURY
AND BAD PRESS ABOUT POLYGAMY

In early 2001, as Warren Jeffs's power over the life of the FLDS Church began manifesting, the Utah State Legislature sought to further criminalize plural marriage, including proposed legislation that would punish Fundamentalist parents for teaching plural marriage to their

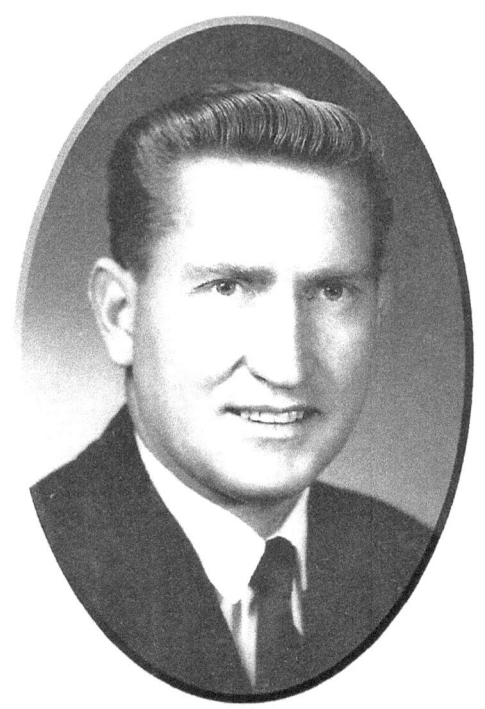

Left: J. LaMoine Jenson (1935–2014), AUB presiding council member 2005–2014. *Authors' collection.*

Below: AUB's meetinghouse and school in Bluffdale, Utah, about 2016. *Steven L. Mayfield collection.*

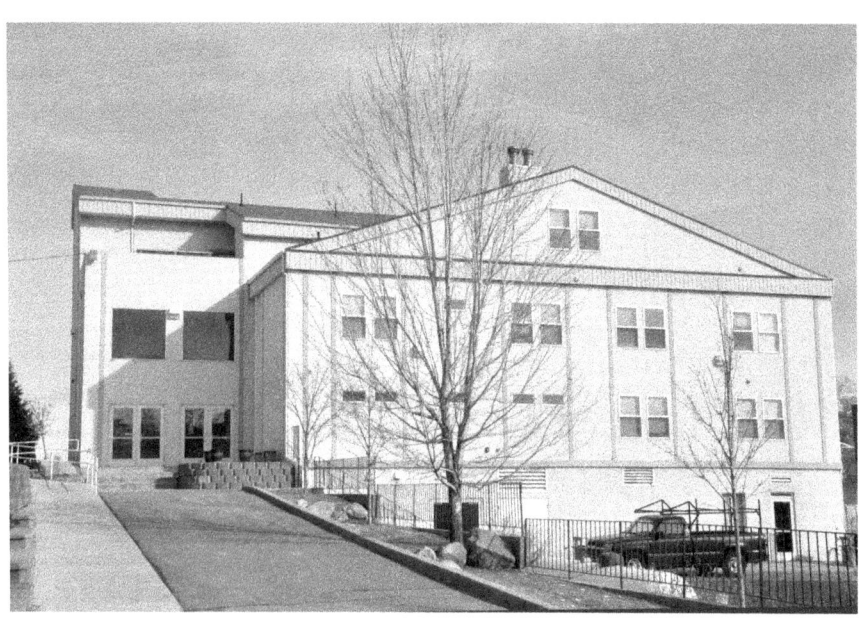

children, would make performing an illegal (plural) marriage a felony and would enhance penalties for relevant laws. Some Fundamentalist women reacted by organizing and lobbying at the state capitol against the bill. Even Owen Allred, leader of the Apostolic United Brethren (or AUB, more commonly known as the Allred group), appeared at legislative hearings, publicly voiced his opinion and published a lengthy commentary in the *Salt Lake Tribune* in which he defended Fundamentalist Mormons against allegations of widespread sexual abuse and misconduct that had arisen during the legislative hearings. He also strongly condemned polygamous marriages involving underage girls. Despite claims to the contrary, overwhelming evidence had surfaced that at least some Fundamentalists were marrying underage brides and perpetrating acts of sexual and other abuses.

TOM GREEN FAMILY

In May 2001, a trial began in Provo, Utah, for Tom Green, a mostly independent Fundamentalist who affiliated with various independents and groups over the years. Green had been one of a few Fundamentalists who not only refused to remain quiet in the shadows but also seemed to seek publicity and attention regarding his plural marriages. He and his wives appeared in several news articles and found their way onto *The Jerry Springer Show* and Sally Jessy Raphael's show *Sally*.

Green wanted to show his plural family's life as healthy and happy and fancied himself a good representative for educating the public about plural marriage and its potential advantages for families embracing it. However, Green unwittingly played into some of the most prevalent polygamy stereotypes. For example, in 1988, when Green and his family posed for photos and an interview for the French publication *Le Figaro*, the front page of the article showed Tom Green sitting on a large bed surrounded by his four wives. This scene reinforced a mistaken idea over a century old that Mormon polygamists and their wives all sleep in the same bed—incorrectly implying a sexual free-for-all.[319]

Also, Green felt he could exert his right to cohabit with his wives without a legal marriage to any of them because society in general had become more accepting of alternate lifestyles and Utah's "blue laws" against fornication and adultery were no longer being criminally prosecuted. By having no legal marriage, he believed he had not technically violated Utah's bigamy statute.

In flouting his plural family publicly, however, he challenged Utah law enforcement in a game he could not win. Green seemed oblivious to the fact that he had more than one skeleton in his closet that made him vulnerable and perhaps one of the worst examples for educating the public about plural marriage in order to generate increased tolerance and acceptance of plural families. But he had thrown down the gauntlet, and Utah law enforcement was happy to oblige.

In 2001, partially because of the media attention garnered by Green, Utah attorney general Mark Shurtleff told some Fundamentalists who visited his office that he intended going after Tom Green for "thumbing his nose" at the State of Utah. With Shurtleff's encouragement, Juab County prosecutor David Leavitt filed charges against Green.[320] By getting a judge to declare Green legally married to one of his wives, Linda Kunz (by utilizing a law that allows partners who live together for several years to petition for a retroactive "common-law" marriage), Green could then be charged with bigamy for his subsequent marriages. This was an unprecedented legal maneuver, because Linda and Tom did not petition for nor want this legal marriage that was forced upon them by the court. In trial, their attorney was not allowed to bring forth argument about the unasked-for court-ordered marriage. A judge eventually found Green guilty of four counts of bigamy and one count of criminal nonsupport. He bitterly complained, "It's lousy. It's wrong. I am amazed by the imbecilic hypocrisy of the leaders of this state. Leaders in Utah have turned their back on their heritage."[321]

But Green had other skeletons in his closet that made him even more vulnerable—he had married some underage brides who were between thirteen and sixteen years of age, with at least two of them also being stepdaughters. Most Fundamentalists considered Green's actions and subsequent self-promotion to the media extremely unwise, practically begging for trouble. In 2002, a Utah court found Green guilty of child rape for impregnating his wife Linda when she was thirteen years old.[322] Yet by comparison to Warren Jeffs, Green was a devoted religious and family man who foolishly took license with his own family, while Jeffs is clearly perverted almost beyond imagination and usurped his father's religious power to corrupt and disrupt an entire community of over ten thousand.

DAVIS COUNTY COOPERATIVE SOCIETY

Beginning in the 1990s, the Kingston group's legal troubles also added to the negative image of plural marriage. The Davis County Cooperative Society, or the Latter Day Church of Christ, is more commonly known by outsiders as the Kingston group and by insiders as "The Order" or "The Co-Op."[323] As already noted, the group has its origins with Charles William Kingston, his son Charles Elden Kingston, other family members and a small group of like-minded people.

In 1977, Davis County Cooperative Society (DCCS) members officially incorporated as the Latter Day Church of Christ (LDCC). While a total number of members is not known, most of its members live in Utah and Idaho. Two branches meet at the headquarters and main chapel, which seats 2,100, in West Valley City, Utah. Most recently, Bill Stoddard served as president of the church, assisted by two counselors and a council of twelve who helped direct the affairs of the church until spring 2018, when Stoddard passed away. As of this writing, a new church president has not been selected. Doctrinally, members of the Latter Day Church of Christ try to adhere to the teachings of the Bible, *The Book of Mormon*, *The Doctrine and Covenants* and *The Pearl of Great Price*, which are considered scriptural canon shared by mainstream Mormons as well as by most Fundamentalist groups. Like the mainstream LDS Church and other Fundamentalists, the LDCC performs baptisms, confirmations, ordinations to the priesthood and anointings for the sick with consecrated oil and laying on of hands.[324]

Also, like other Fundamentalists, some members of the LDCC practice plural marriage, but according to representatives, it is not a requirement for advancement or to maintain standing in the church. Even Bill Stoddard, the late church president, had only one wife for most of his life and during his whole tenure as church president.

Like some other Fundamentalist groups, dating is not allowed. Instead, members are encouraged to prayerfully seek guidance on the selection of their mates and then are permitted to pursue marriage through courtship, which they consider more appropriate and focused toward marriage than casual dating. They believe in "each individual's right to free agency as long as they don't force, suppress, restrain, deprive, jeopardize, or interfere with the rights of others." Members are free to choose their marriage partner or partners, as marriage is considered an individual's or family's personal choice. The LDCC hosts dances and social activities to allow members to meet and get to know one another and to provide suitable settings for courting. Once married, new couples find jobs and housing within the larger community, often with Co-Op assistance. Plural wives are no exception and typically manage their own homes without sharing space with their husband's other wives. The husband and families generally decide how often to have family get-togethers involving all wives and children.[325]

Paul Kingston, as the leader or trustee of the DCCS, takes the lead in the governance of the Co-Op.[326] Of the various Fundamentalist groups, the DCCS is probably the wealthiest and has the most diverse portfolio of businesses and investments. Member business interests include alarm and security, athletic facilities, casino, auto service and repair, bail bonds, dairies, energy and fuel, farms and ranches, human resource services, insurance, loan companies, mercantile, mining, pawn shops, property management, real estate, storage, vending companies and more.[327]

A reason for such diversification is that the group has a high percentage of high school and college graduates. According to representatives, the group's private schools save the State of Utah about "seven million dollars in tax expense annually" because they do not use taxpayer-funded educational facilities for their elementary-age schoolchildren. Members are encouraged to attend public colleges and universities for formal education and enter whatever field of labor interests them. Members are often given monetary and other assistance from within their group. Business and professional ventures are part of and dedicated to the DCCS but still maintain independence enough that they are not controlled by the

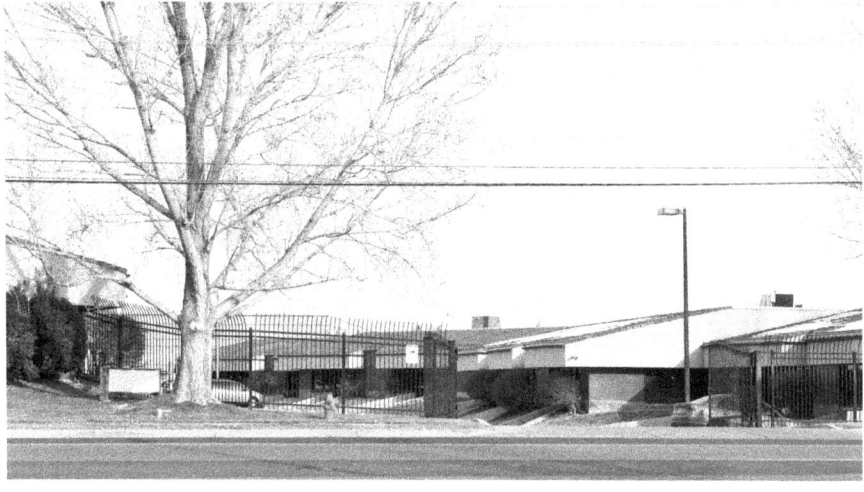

Kingston headquarters in West Valley City, Utah. *Steven L. Mayfield Collection.*

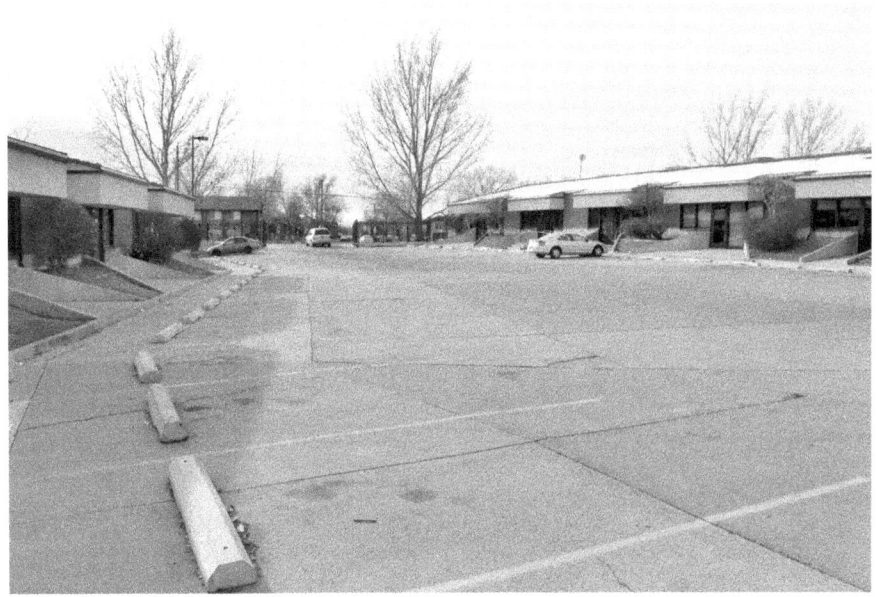

Kingston headquarters looking out. *Steven L. Mayfield Collection.*

Co-Op. Even with the success and high profits of the DCCS, members are "encouraged to be thrifty, frugal and self-sufficient," to give to the poor as able and save for the future.[328]

The economic success of the DCCS notwithstanding, negative media portrayal and public perception over the years, as well as legal problems of the group and its leaders, have caused members to build a bit of a fortress mentality and distrust for the outside. This reaction is not without reason. Some of the Co-Op companies have been boycotted over the years, and the press and other critics have portrayed them negatively. A scholarly study described the Kingstons as "a communal utopian society in which everything was shared—money, homes, and even marital relationships—for the expressed purpose of building the kingdom of God upon the earth."[329]

The Kingstons, at times, have been the target of investigations and have had an uneasy relationship with law officials. Group members recall "the grand jury days" of 1959 and 1960 when a Davis County Grand Jury investigated suspicion of polygamy against several members. During the investigation, Ardous Kingston Gustafson, a mother of four and a founding member of the DCCS, was jailed on Christmas Eve for contempt of court when she refused to produce records and membership rolls for the polygamy investigation.[330]

The head of the grand jury worried, "[P]olygamy is going to run all over the state in a generation unless we do something about it. Salt Lake City is infested with polygamy." During the days of the Raids in Territorial Utah when polygamists were actively hunted and arrested, polygamy was a very difficult charge to prove. Instead, early polygamists were charged with adultery and unlawful cohabitation. Like early polygamists, some DCCS members were charged with adultery or unlawful cohabitation, as well as perjury and contempt of court.[331]

In 1998, David Ortell Kingston drew legal scrutiny and media attention to the group with his arrest and later conviction with a ten-year sentence for marrying and having incestuous sexual relations with his then sixteen-year-old niece, Mary Ann Kingston. David served four years before being released in 2003. David's brother John Daniel Kingston served under six months for beating this same Mary Ann, his daughter, when she fled what she claimed to be a forced arranged marriage.[332]

During the trial of David Kingston, former member Connie Rugg spoke to members of the media, accusing the group of practicing incestuous marriages. She stated that David's father, John Ortell Kingston, had married a series of half sisters and nieces. Rugg stated, "My father experimented inbreeding with his cattle and then he turned to his children." She explained how the Kingstons believed their family was of a chosen lineage and therefore needed to keep their blood line pure through close family marriages.[333] However, Rugg's accusations were denied in an interview with a church representative who also denied any doctrine existed to justify marrying close relatives, but acknowledged that sometimes such marriages do "occur by personal choice…as is the case in many small religions and groups." He further added that the group has publicly spoken against marriages involving minors who are under the legal age of consent.[334]

Nevertheless, related cases from the 1998 problems continued to appear in the news in the first decade of the new century. In 2003, Jeremy Kingston pleaded guilty to incest for marrying his first cousin, Lu Ann Kingston—his mother and Lu Ann's mother being sisters. That same year, Mary Ann Kingston sued the Kingston group for $100 million in damages from her traumatic experience while living in the group. Her suit stated that "the powerful Kingston family maintains a life-style of incest, polygamy and sexual abuse of minors." While the case pended, another daughter of John Daniel Kingston countersued Mary Ann Kingston (by then Mary Ann Nichols) as well as Lu Ann Kingston and another relative who had left the Kingston group, accusing them of sexual abuse. The rancorous suits and counter suits continued in deliberation until 2009, when a global settlement was made in which all lawsuits were dropped and no money was paid out.[335]

Similar legal problems and harmful publicity still persist for various members of the Kingston group and associated families. In August 2018, a news article appeared in the *Salt Lake Tribune*, titled, "Girls in Polygamous Kingston Group Continue to Marry as Young as 15, Records Show, Sometimes Leaving Utah to Marry Cousins." The article stated that pressure to marry at a young age continues among DCCS members. "In a search of public records created since 1997, the *Salt Lake Tribune* found 65 marriages among members of the Kingston Group in which the bride was 15, 16 or 17. The two most recent of those marriages, according to wedding certificates, occurred in April [2018]." Those two marriages took place in Colorado, "where it's legal to marry your cousin." There also were three marriages in Missouri, where "15-year-olds can marry with a parent's permission." The article said some women who have left the group claimed they felt forced to marry at a young age. While this accusation was downplayed by group members, one member tacitly admitted that because of previous convictions and other charges of child abuse, sex with a minor and incest

girls who will be plural wives—meaning they have only a spiritual marriage to their husband—are left alone until they are 18 so laws about sex with a minor won't apply. Girls who agree to become plural wives tend to be more devout and usually live in homes without their husband, thus receiving less scrutiny.[336]

The article also stated that "more rebellious girls" are encouraged to marry as legal first wives because "it binds people together legally and financially" and keeps them in the group. In response, a Kingston group spokesman cited a statistic from a written statement that of "individuals who married under age 18 in the past 20 years, 95.1 percent remain married."[337] If accurate, this article implies that members of the DCCS are now strictly following the law but have also found loopholes to their advantage.

As is the case with other Fundamentalist families or groups, members of the DCCS have occasionally been the recipients of unwanted police and state child protective services investigations that have proven to be unsubstantiated. In 2016, state officials assisted the FBI and IRS in raids of some DCCS business offices and investigated for possible welfare fraud. It was announced two years later that they had found nothing. In June 2018, after receiving complaints about certain pawn shops fencing stolen merchandise, seven DCCS-owned pawn shops were raided in Salt Lake and Utah Counties for evidence of receiving stolen property and money laundering.[338] By the middle of September, although no charges had been filed against the pawn shop owners, the Utah Attorney General's Office, claiming right to asset forfeiture, asked a judge to allow it to keep $1 million in cash and merchandise.[339]

Of a more serious nature were the indictments in late August 2018 against two Kingstons—Jacob and Isaiah, CEO and CFO of Washakie Renewable Energy—charging them for tax fraud to the tune of $511 million. The indictments were based on a long investigation that included a 2016 raid of a home and offices. Authorities say the defendants heard of the raid before it happened and proceeded to destroy evidence, including files and computer hard drives. Furthermore, according to federal authorities, both men had tried to flee the country when they heard of the indictments. Jacob Kingston was arrested at the Salt Lake City International Airport trying to travel to Turkey with a wife and some children. Both men were considered flight risks and ordered to remain in jail.[340] Members claim these ongoing cases and many of the investigations are an overblown attempt to target polygamy and its proponents. Time will tell if the latest investigations are warranted or without merit and in reality veiled efforts against polygamists as DCCS members claim.

Despite problems with civil authorities and much adverse media attention, the overwhelming majority of DCCS members' interactions with mainstream society are positive. Since 2003, representatives of the group have joined forces and have been particularly active and outspoken with a coalition of various Fundamentalist groups and independents combining efforts to educate Fundamentalists about the law, assist government agencies and nongovernment organizations about how to work with and understand the unique challenges and needs of their families and communities and lobby to decriminalize polygamy. Many from the DCCS group, including teens, have participated in public rallies in support of these issues that affect them.

DIFFICULTIES IN THE AUB

For the AUB, the Virginia Hill case in the 1990s brought unwanted media attention for nearly two decades. The problem began in 1989, when two members of the group, John Putvin and Dennis Matthews, met Virginia Hill and learned that she had a significant amount of cash, more than $1 million, that she wanted to invest in real estate. Hill, a former Las Vegas stripper and mobster's girlfriend, had become connected through a family with a former AUB member, John Shugart, who had become an independent Fundamentalist and lived in southern Utah. Matthews associated with and pretended to join Shugart's small circle of believers, even accepting a calling of some importance from Shugart. Meanwhile, Matthews and Putvin conspired to defraud Hill of her money by involving AUB's aging leader, Owen Allred, telling him that she wanted to invest it and convincing him that her money could be used for the AUB group to pay for a ranch it had contracted to buy, also touching on Allred's desire to recuperate lost monies in past dealings with Shugart. The two men further persuaded Allred, by further playing on his sympathies, to keep the plan secret from the AUB Priesthood Council, which included both men's fathers-in-law. Tape recordings of the meeting showed Allred clearly approved of their plan, not seeming to recognize that Hill could not benefit by using her money to pay for an AUB ranch; further, the recordings reveal that his commitment to keep it secret was because he accepted their ruse of needing to prevent potential misunderstandings in family relationships. The scheme would not likely have been considered had it been presented to the AUB Priesthood Council collectively. Matthews and Putvin clearly manipulated the aging, trusting Allred, who gave his unwitting approval.

After taking Virginia's cash, the men did not invest it in any real estate for her, let alone enable the AUB to purchase a ranch. Instead they kept it for themselves, with most of it in Putvin's control. To launder some of the cash, Putvin paid $30,000 to one of Allred's co-council members, LaMoine Jenson, for materials he pretended to order from Jenson's lumber business; after Jenson deposited the cash, Putvin canceled the order, demanding the money be returned and getting a check for the same amount. Thus, he succeeded in using Jenson's company to launder the cash. Through Jenson, Putvin also requested a return of a cash payment of $30,000 tithing; for this Allred signed a check for that amount to John Galt, one of Putvin's aliases, thus laundering more of Hill's cash. Putvin and Matthews also gave Allred several thousand dollars, reportedly over $10,000 cash still stashed inside Hill's unopened metal cans carried in a banana box. By Allred's account, he put the box in a closet; then, feeling uncomfortable, he called Putvin or Matthews within a few days, insisting they come get it out of his house, which they did.

Putvin and Matthews involved other AUB members, Jim Sandmire and Jeff Norman, in laundering money through businesses. Sandmire got a significant amount of the money, or at least it passed through his hands. With some of the cash, he made a $9,000 payment to an AUB entity. This transaction eventually provided a paper money trail linked to Hill's cash.

Another of Allred's co-council members, Joseph B. Thompson, accidentally discovered the theft of Hill's money in the early 1990s after his daughter, a plural wife of Putvin's, left him and, with her brother, a private investigator, found evidence of Putvin's numerous illegal activities, including fraud and theft. The brother reported Putvin's activities to law enforcement, who revealed that Virginia Hill had filed a complaint against Allred, Putvin and Matthews. A Utah grand jury initiated an investigation on suspicion that Hill might be heavily involved in money laundering for organized crime and that the AUB organization might be involved as well. Putvin's estranged wife, her brother and her father, Joseph B. Thompson, drove to southern Utah to hear Hill's story directly. Upon their return, Thompson confronted Allred, who initially denied any involvement. Thompson told him, "You've got to make it right with that woman." Allred denied he ever kept any of the money or that the AUB had benefitted by it in any way, so he made no attempt to make it right with Hill, apparently believing Putvin and Matthews only were responsible. Allred's decision not to financially make it right with Hill was one he likely regretted to his grave. No criminal charges resulted from the grand jury investigation. Law enforcement wanted more proof.

Meanwhile, Putvin and Matthews found ways to launder, invest and spend Hill's money, including paying Putvin's attorneys in his child custody case. When Allred authorized the AUB to pay an attorney for Putvin's ex-wife, it angered Putvin. He enunciated to an AUB member his intention and determination to "take down" Allred and the AUB. Nevertheless, when Hill initiated her civil lawsuit to recover her money, Allred and Jenson were named as co-defendants along with Putvin and Matthews. Putvin found numerous ways to manipulate both Allred and Jenson. For example, during the lengthy process, he managed to persuade them to allow his personal attorney to represent them in the case, which did not prove beneficial, except for him.

In 2003, Virginia Hill won her civil suit against the defendants. The judge ruled that AUB members and leaders had "bilked [the] woman out of $1.54 million in a 1989 real estate deal." The judge further ruled "that Owen Allred, the 89-year-old leader of the Apostolic United Brethren, laundered thousands of dollars and conspired to steal more."[341] Putvin himself had provided the tape recording played in court of his and Matthews's original meeting with Allred, who had voiced his approval of the plan and later acknowledged in court the tape was accurate. Thus, the judge viewed Allred as using his position of ecclesiastical authority to encourage Matthews and Putvin in the fraud; Sandmire's money trail connected the AUB and provided proof to the judge of Allred's collusion in the fraud. While Hill had sued for millions in punitive damages, she was initially awarded only her original $1.54 million because of the questionable origin of her money. Allred and Jenson were found liable for $30,000 each. The judge ordered AUB to pay $250,000, Sandmire $500,000 and Putvin and Matthews the balance.

Allred and the AUB appealed, believing the ruling to be unjust because Sandmire's $9,000 payment was the only money they believed was actually received. Furthermore, they said they had received it without knowing its source. Post-hearing filings and counter filings kept the case going six more years. Meanwhile, Allred died in 2005, and Putvin died in 2006. A final settlement was agreed by the parties in 2009, with Jenson and the AUB required to pay Hill $7 million, which included mostly interest and some punitive damages. With Putvin dead and nothing left in his estate and Matthews broke, Sandmire provided evidence in exchange for being let out of the case, with no payment required at all. Jenson and the AUB alone were left holding the bag.[342] AUB representatives scrambled to prevent financial disaster, fearing the judge would attach AUB properties if the settlement was not immediately paid. But Hill did not want church properties, only money, so the court allowed her to receive payments over a short period of time. AUB leaders requested donations from members, who amazingly raised the funds within the specified time at great personal sacrifice. The Virginia Hill case cost the AUB organization and its members heavily. Furthermore, it besmirched the rather good public reputation of the group, acknowledged for its stance against underage marriage and its recent cooperation with the government in some cases of abuse.

THE ELIZABETH SMART KIDNAPPING

In 2003, fuel was added to the fire of the growing public negative perception of polygamy by association with a case of abuse with no connections to Fundamentalist Mormons. Brian David Mitchell, a former LDS Church member who had been excommunicated for his extreme religious views not in harmony with the teachings of the church, had kidnapped a fourteen-year-old girl, Elizabeth Smart, from her Salt Lake City home in the middle of the night. The kidnapping was highly publicized for the next nine months, until she was recognized walking down a street in a Salt Lake Valley town and rescued. After her rescue, it was revealed that her kidnapper, Mitchell, had immediately "married" her to himself as a plural wife, the first of his planned forty-nine plural wives, and then raped her almost daily until she was found. News media picked up on the polygamy storyline; one newspaper described it as "perceptions of fanaticism in Utah,"[343] thus linking Mitchell's bizarre interpretation of plural marriage with all Utah polygamists, tainting them, even though Mitchell had never contacted any Fundamentalist Mormons.

While stories of fraud, such as the Virginia Hill case, contributed to a poor public image of the Fundamentalists, the reports of underage marriages, sexual abuse and incest that continued from the 1990s through the first decade of the new century combined to produce an even greater unfavorable public perception. The unfavorable image of Fundamentalist polygamy grew as scandals constantly made headlines and became fodder for sensationalistic media stories—from Tom Green, the Kingstons and the Elizabeth Smart kidnapping to the repugnant escapades of Warren Jeffs, the government raid of the Yearning for Zion Ranch in Texas and the subsequent trials of FLDS men.

THE LDS REACTION TO FUNDAMENTALIST MORMON SCANDALS

The continued stream over many years of negative publicity regarding plural marriage affected the Church of Jesus Christ and some of its members and therefore became of special concern to church leaders and representatives. LDS Church officials reacted to the repeated scandals of their disavowed cousins by complaining that news media referred to the FLDS and other polygamist groups as "Mormons" or "Mormon sects." Then church president Gordon B. Hinckley emphatically stated to CNN's Larry King, "There are no Mormon fundamentalists," and LDS public relations officials accused Fundamentalists of trying to co-opt the nickname "Mormon" to their benefit.[344]

This LDS response to modern Fundamentalism generally was reflective of its uncomfortable relationship with its polygamous past. Most modern Latter-day Saints view the subject of contemporary plural marriage through a twenty-first-century lens that tends to distort their understanding of the history and morality of plural marriage in general. Many are uncomfortable and embarrassed at the idea of multiple wives and therefore react negatively not only to their church's own history but particularly to modern Fundamentalists who identify themselves as Mormon.[345]

Some LDS scholars and publications have gone to great lengths to downplay and even ignore the LDS Church's polygamous past. For the most part, these efforts have been unsuccessful, especially in the day and age of the internet and easily accessible digital media. Rather than helping, some of these efforts have made it more difficult for modern church members to understand Mormon polygamy. The reality is that "the Church and its members will never be able to divorce themselves from historical plural marriage. No matter how hard the LDS Church may try to cut ties to its polygamous past, the two are irrevocably and inseparably tied to each other."[346] Happily, the LDS Church has recently taken a more proactive approach to now teach its members about difficult subjects, including plural marriage, emphasizing that the church's founder, Joseph Smith, was commanded by God to live and teach the principle of plural marriage.

VOICES IN HARMONY AND PRINCIPLE VOICES

In response to some anti-polygamy activists publicly calling for all polygamist wives to be "de-programmed," three Fundamentalist women, Anne Wilde, Mary Batchelor and Marianne Watson (also coauthor of this volume), combined efforts to write a book from their perspectives as modern women who choose to live plural marriage. They wrote with the idea that knowledge and understanding helps break down barriers of bias and bigotry. They compiled their results in a book, *Voices in Harmony: Contemporary Women Celebrate Plural Marriage*, which they privately published in 2000. It contained a short history of fundamentalism, a doctrinal discussion about the practice of plural marriage and an explanation of why women would be willing to live "the Principle." Perhaps the most powerful and revealing part of the book is the section titled "Voices of Plural Wives," in which one hundred women share experiences living in polygamy. They describe love, joy, sorrow, heartache, personal progress and commitment to living such a difficult lifestyle. A few essays tell how some women chose plural marriage more than once, even after previous unions in monogamy or plurality failed.[347]

Voices in Harmony was generally well received. In November 2000, Utah representative David Zolman introduced the three authors to the Republican leadership caucus and gave a copy of their book to each of

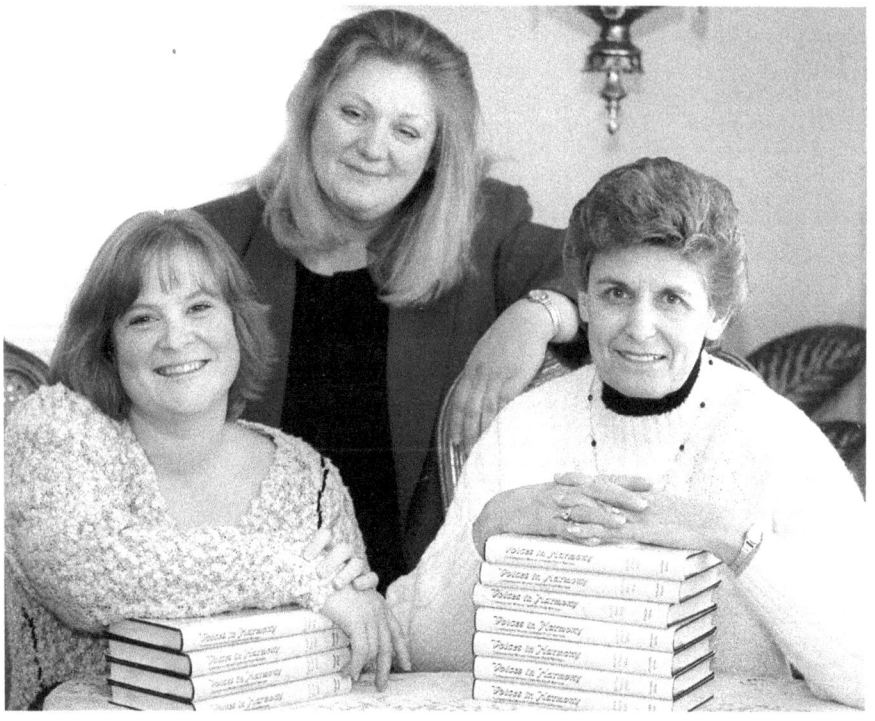

Authors of *Voices in Harmony* in 2000. Mary Batchelor (*left*), Marianne Watson (*center*) and Anne Wilde. *Authors' collection.*

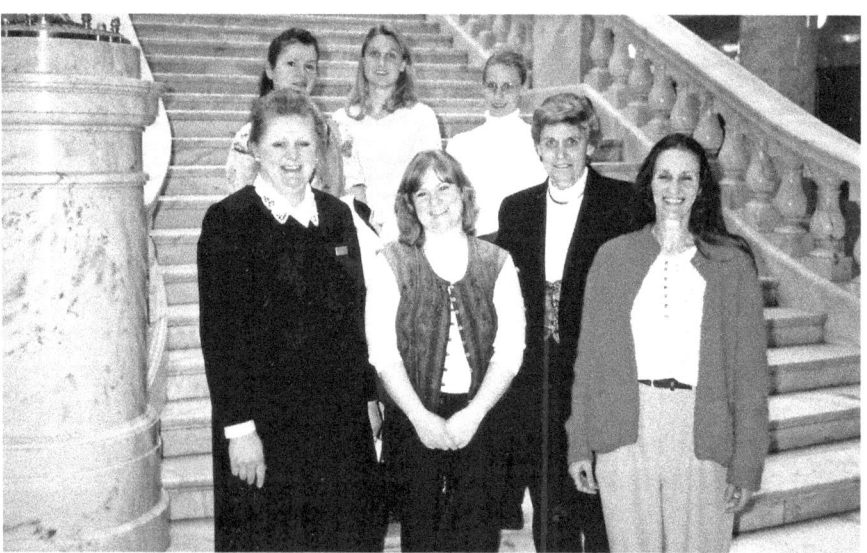

Fundamentalist women lobbying at Utah Capitol, 2001. *Authors' collection.*

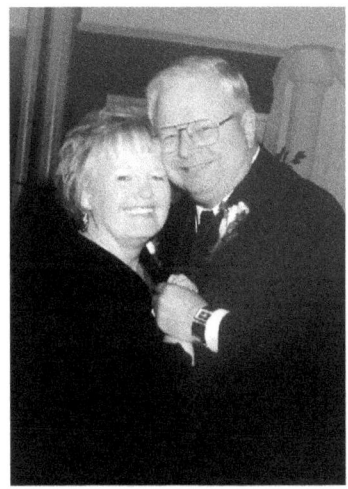

Former Utah legislator David Zolman and his wife, Sheila. *Courtesy of David Zolman.*

the seventy-five members of the Utah State Legislative House. The authors subsequently presented papers at several scholarly conferences. While the book was obviously an apologetic work, it was praised for its honesty in discussing difficult and potentially problematic aspects of plural marriage.

The authors did not stop at publishing *Voices in Harmony*. They initiated the formation of the Principle Voices Coalition to facilitate and encourage communication and cooperation among and between the various Fundamentalist groups and Independents in their common needs for education and training regarding abuse and interaction with government agencies and media. They coordinated with state service providers as well as the Domestic Violence Council to educate service providers and law enforcement about polygamist families and communities and made suggestions for improving communication. They also compiled information for Fundamentalist families and arranged educational training for Fundamentalists regarding the law, how to work with service providers, abuse prevention and so forth. They provided one- or two-day trainings to groups of Fundamentalists willing to learn how to interact with media and advocate for their rights. In 2006, they and other groups sponsored a "Youth and Family Rally" at the Utah State Capitol in which hundreds of youth from the Kingstons, AUB and Centennial Park groups, as well as numerous Independent Fundamentalist families, voluntarily participated in a public forum aimed at "unsealing the secrecy that normally envelopes their lives."[348] The goal of the rally was to break down stereotypes and show America they were just regular, normal people.

That same year, the Centennial Park group sponsored a town hall attended by numerous Fundamentalists, many sporting "Bigger Love" buttons. Joyce Steed of the Centennial Park group explained, "We hoped not to be in your faces about it, but we wanted to make a statement." Heidi Mattingly-Foster, a plural wife of John Daniel Kingston, was more outspoken: "The State of Utah won't let me get married. What makes them decide who I can and cannot love?" Besides acknowledging that abuse of all kinds exists in communities

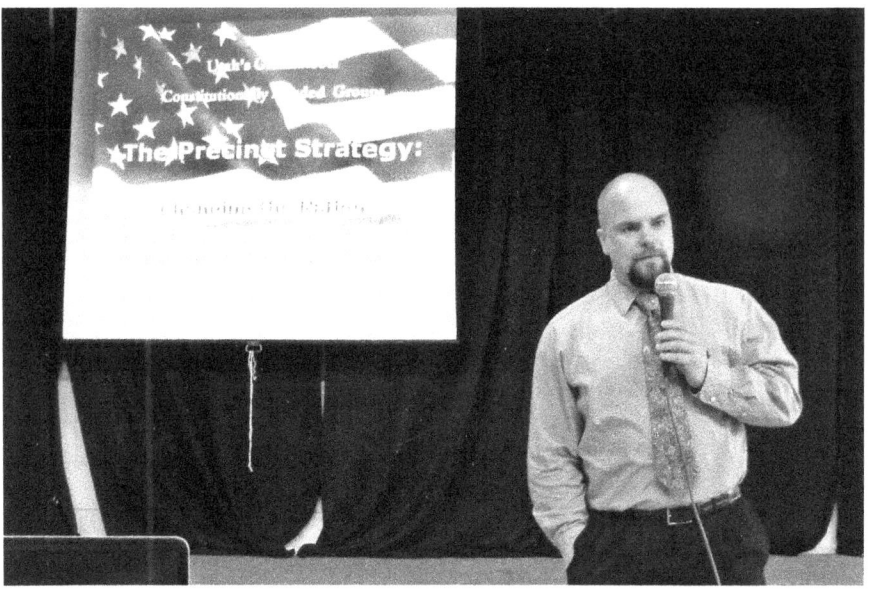

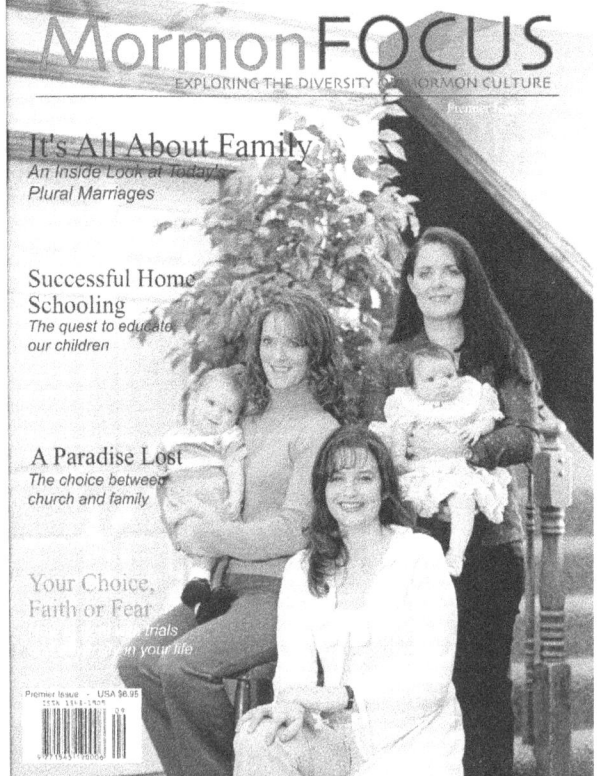

Above: Joe Darger conducting an educational session. *Anne Wilde Collection.*

Left: 2003 *Mormon Focus* magazine featuring three wives of Joe Darger. *Authors' collection.*

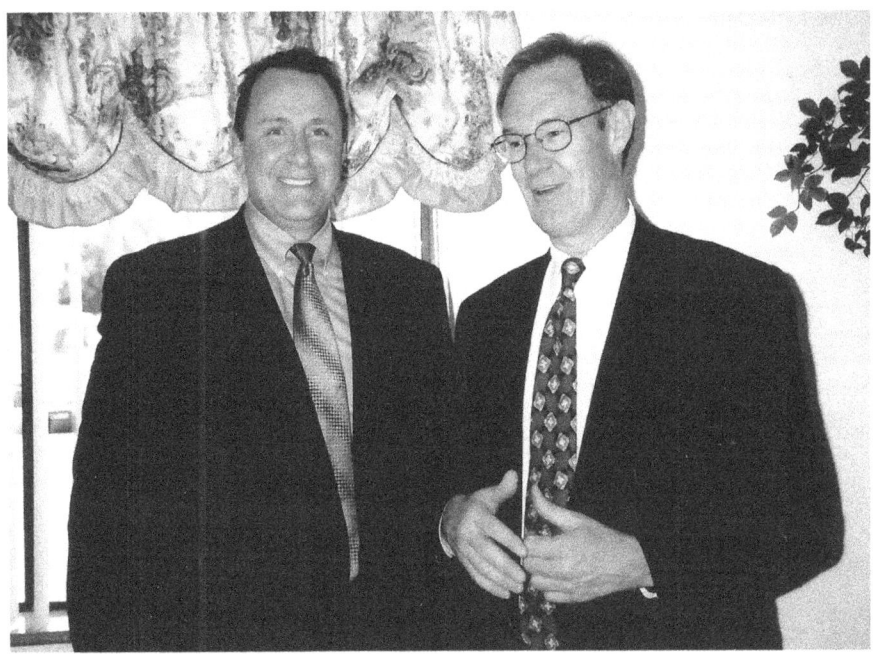

Utah attorney general Mark Shurtleff (*left*) and Arizona attorney general Terry Goddard at a 2003 conference in Centennial Park. *Anne Wilde Collection.*

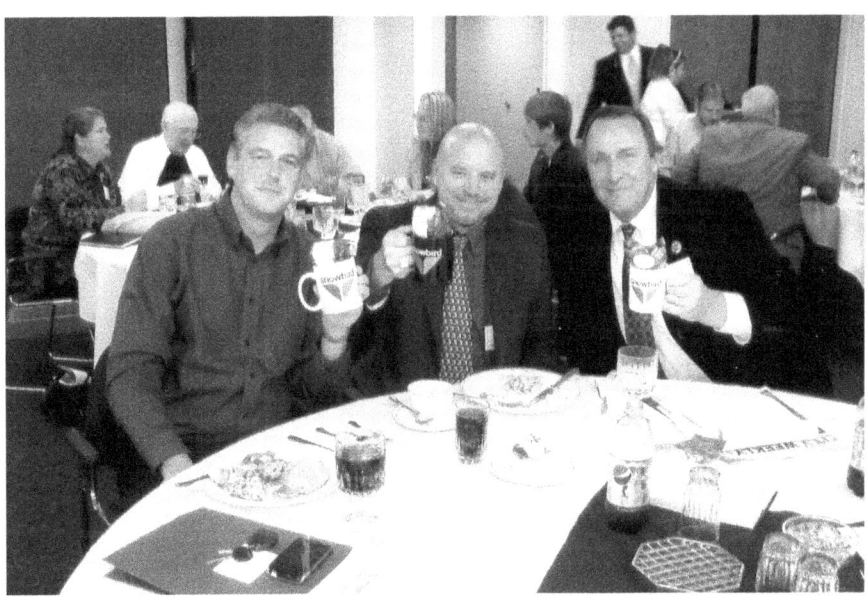

Utah attorney general Mark Shurtleff (*right*) and assistants Kirk Torgenson (*left*) and Paul Murphy at CLE training sponsored by a Fundamentalist coalition at Snowbird Lodge. *Anne Wilde Collection.*

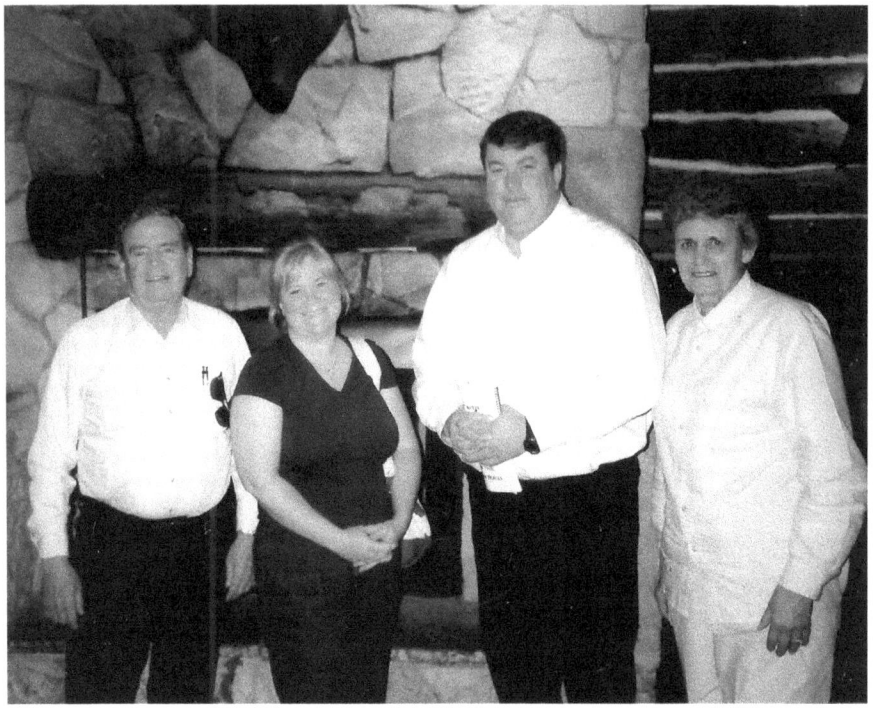

Fundamentalist coalition leaders Mary Batchelor (*center left*) and Anne Wilde meet with then FLDS representatives Willie Jessop and Merrill Jessop (*far left*). *Authors' collection.*

everywhere, including their own, Centennial Park representatives stated their intentions to prevent abuse as well as address abuse when it is found; they also expressed a commitment to not allow underage plural marriages in their group. At the same meeting, then attorney general Mark Shurtleff defended his policy not to prosecute bigamy among consenting adults in plural marriages, asking Utahans rhetorically, "Are you willing to pay for 10,000 new inmates?"[349]

SEEING IT TWO WAYS: MEDIA PORTRAYAL OF FUNDAMENTALIST POLYGAMY AND LEGAL MANEUVERING

Despite pro-polygamy efforts, negative articles and television shows about modern Fundamentalist polygamy continue to the present. Nevertheless, a marked shift began in attitude about polygamy among Americans across the nation. This started in part with the introduction of the popular HBO television series *Big Love*, which ran between 2006 and 2011. The show portrayed a Fundamentalist polygamist with multiple wives in suburban Salt Lake Valley. One news article explained at the start of the series, "[T]he debate about polygamy is about to change forever" and claimed the show "comes at a time when there is a growing clamor to decriminalize polygamy."[350]

Taking advantage of the popularity of *Big Love* and reality TV, *Sister Wives* premiered in 2010 with Kody Brown, his wives and children. They did the show to help break down stereotypes, remove some of the secrecy surrounding modern plural marriage and shed light on what life is really like for plural families. Kody realized that while people may not agree with their lifestyle, he wanted America to at least leave them alone so they and other modern polygamists could peacefully live their lives. He was "seeking acceptance and tolerance through transparency."[351]

The show became an immediate hit. *Sister Wives* and the Browns, however, were not popular with local Utah County law enforcement. According to Brown, Utah County attorney Jeffrey R. Buhman began investigating Brown

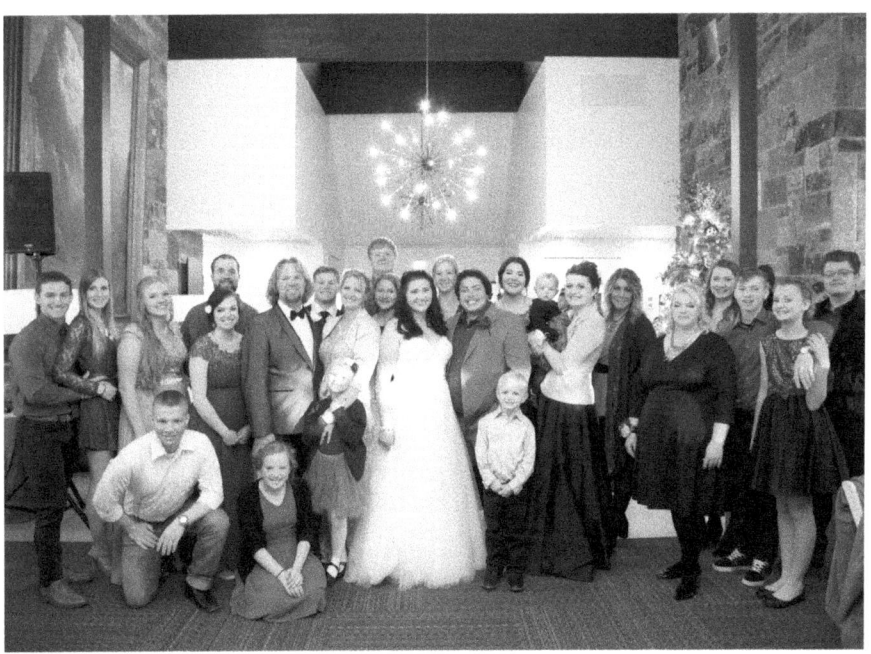

Kody Brown family at daughter Mykelti's wedding. *Courtesy of Kody Brown.*

and his family as soon as he heard they were going to have the TV series. The day after the show premiered, during a celebratory dinner with the show's producer and others, the Browns received word of the investigation and the threat of being arrested.[352]

The Browns moved to Las Vegas, Nevada, to avoid prosecution. As Kody explained, Las Vegas was the "fastest, safest, closest place" to move with the goal of moving back later. But Las Vegas wasn't far enough for the county attorney, who, according to Brown, threatened to pursue the investigation despite the Browns no longer living in Utah. In 2011, the Browns filed suit challenging Utah's bigamy law as unconstitutional.[353]

In December 2013, Judge Clark Waddoups ruled on what had come to be called the "Sister Wives case." He ruled that parts of Utah's anti-bigamy law were indeed unconstitutional because it violated freedom of religion. He went on to decriminalize cohabitation. While he did not specifically legalize polygamy, his decision effectively decriminalized it. The reaction to his ruling varied. Most polygamists were pleased, while Utah officials and most media outlets responded unfavorably.[354]

The reaction by Browns' spiritual leaders, AUB Council members, was decidedly more circumspect. After the announcement, one council member explained to an AUB congregation that Fundamentalists had practiced plural marriage in fear of prosecution but did so because God had commanded it. He then expressed concern the decision to decriminalize plural marriage was troubling because it came "on the coattails of *Lawrence v. Texas*" (a case that helped forward the cause of legalizing gay unions), noting the Browns' lawyer had used *Lawrence v. Texas* to argue their case. He went on to explain that they did not want polygamy legalized, just decriminalized. He also worried about the publicity of the ruling because "every time a Fundamentalist has stuck his head up, he's been whacked like whack-a-mole." He explained that despite the court ruling, "we need to be careful and keep our heads below the radar."[355]

Fundamentalists were wise in exercising caution; a little over two years later, the U.S. Court of Appeals for the Tenth Circuit overturned Waddoups's ruling on standing rather than merit, writing, "[T]he Browns' lawsuit should have been tossed out in 2012 after Utah County prosecutors [*sic*] office announced that it had adopted a policy only to target polygamists for bigamy when there is also evidence of other collateral crimes, such as fraud or abuse." Thus, the Browns were deemed to be in no danger of prosecution.[356] Naturally, the Browns and other Fundamentalists were disappointed with the ruling. They were also puzzled because one of the three justices who heard the case was Utah-born and raised, Scott M. Matheson Jr., son of a former Utah governor and a member of the Church of Jesus Christ of Latter-day Saints. Despite Matheson's pedigree being peppered with polygamists, Kody Brown wondered why the judge didn't recuse himself from a case that causes strong feelings among most Utah residents.[357]

The Browns appealed to the U.S. Supreme Court, which refused to hear the case in early 2017, allowing the lower court's decision to stand. Sean Reyes, Utah's new attorney general, and his office had argued the Supreme Court should not hear the case, in part because "Utah was forced to abandon the practice of polygamy as a condition of statehood." The Browns' attorney, Jonathan Turley, responded, "The refusal of the Supreme Court to hear their case will not make tens of thousands of families disappear or resolve the underlying claims of discrimination and harassment."[358]

Following on the heels of this disappointment came another blow to the polygamist community in Utah. The Utah State Legislature once again considered a bill from the previous legislative session that had been rewritten and resubmitted that stiffened the penalties for bigamy, particularly if committed with other crimes, including types of abuse, fraud and other loosely defined potential crimes. The bill stated, "A person is guilty of bigamy when, knowing the person has a husband or wife or knowing the other person has a husband or wife, the person purports to marry and cohabitates with the other person."[359]

The bill garnered both supporters and detractors. By the end of the legislative session, the process had produced a circus-like atmosphere of a grudge match with emotional and sensational oral and written testimonies for and against the bill and colorful protests on the steps of the Utah Capitol. At one protest, several hundred supporters of polygamy showed up to express their opposition to the proposed bill carrying signs that read, "I love ALL my moms," "Families not felons" and "If we were gay, we'd be OK." Well-known polygamists, including Kody Brown of *Sister Wives* and Joe Darger of *My Three Wives*, addressed the crowd.[360]

Obviously, Utah's Fundamentalist community stood against the bill, describing it as a witch hunt and religious bigotry because the bill specifically attacked their religious freedom but winked at nonreligious polyamorous relationships. They were not alone in opposing the bill. Several experts and service providers panned the bill as hurting rather than helping plural families. For example, Ken Driggs, a semiretired civil rights lawyer and expert on Fundamentalist Mormons, voiced his opposition to the bill, even writing a legal brief against it and a letter to Utah's governor.[361]

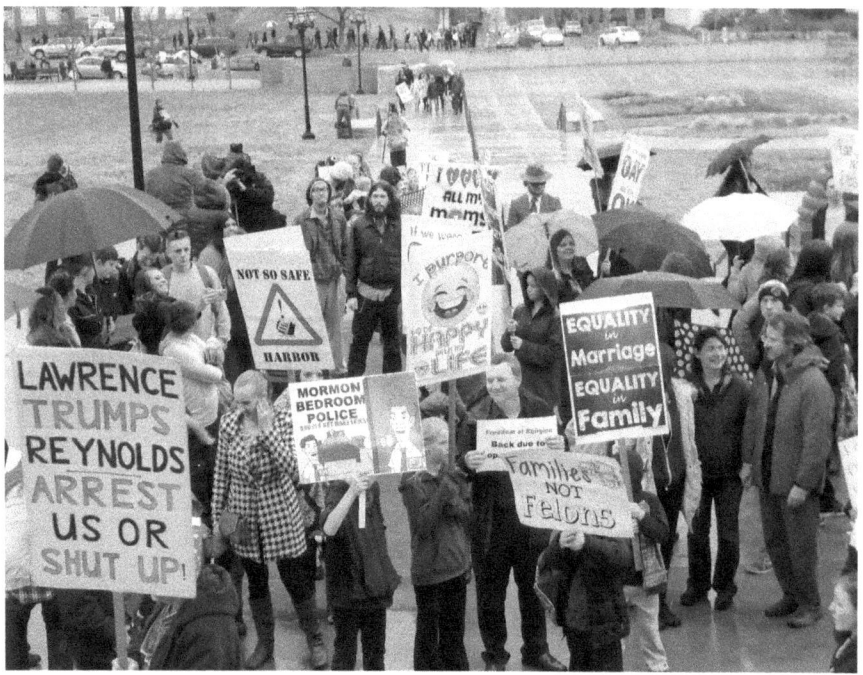

Polygamists protesting recriminalization of polygamy, February 2017. *Steven L. Mayfield Collection.*

Supporters of the bill attacked polygamy as harmful to women and children, a detriment to society and an embarrassment. The bill's author, Representative Mike Noel, explained that an ancestor of his who was a polygamist had served time in the penitentiary, and it had been awful for the family. Another time, he angrily commented, "It really bothers me that they [Fundamentalists] basically hijack my Church of Jesus Christ of Latter-day Saint's religion and say, 'We're Mormon.' But you're not, you're an apostate group and you need to recognize that."[362]

The bill passed the House and was finally voted on by the Senate on the last night of the legislative session. That last night took on a personal, almost bizarre twist when Senator Kevin Van Tassell, co-sponsor of the bill, began showing colleagues photos of bruises he claimed were his daughter's after suffering physical abuse at the hands of her husband, who has a second wife. His daughter sat next to him on the Senate floor during the floor debate. "Van Tassell's own grandchildren went to the Capitol to rebut the allegations against their father and to oppose the bill." One state senator described this move as a "kind of awkward situation."[363] Ultimately, the bill passed, and

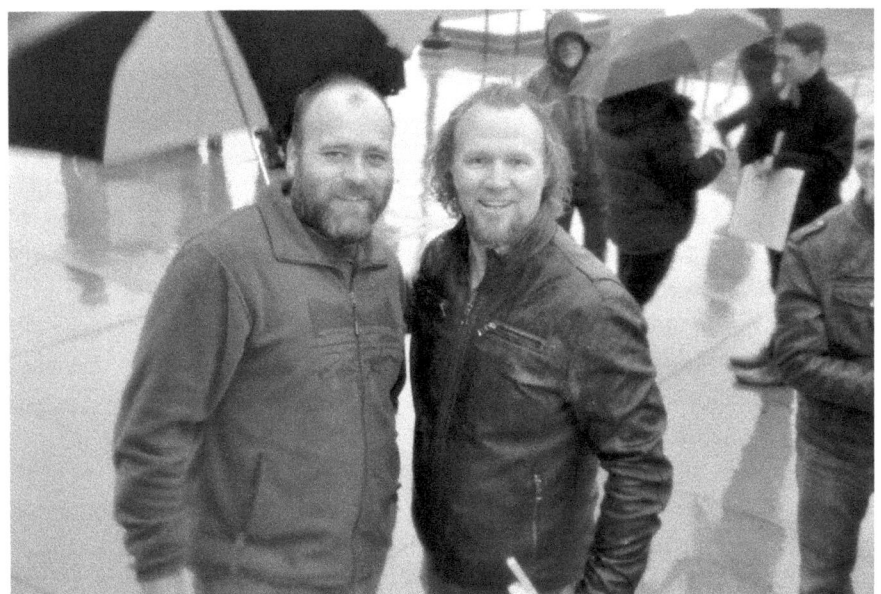

Above: TLC reality television polygamists Brady Williams (*left*) and Kody Brown participating in 2017 protests against recriminalizing plural marriage. *Steven L. Mayfield Collection.*

Right: Kody Brown holding protest sign, February 2017. *Anne Wilde Collection.*

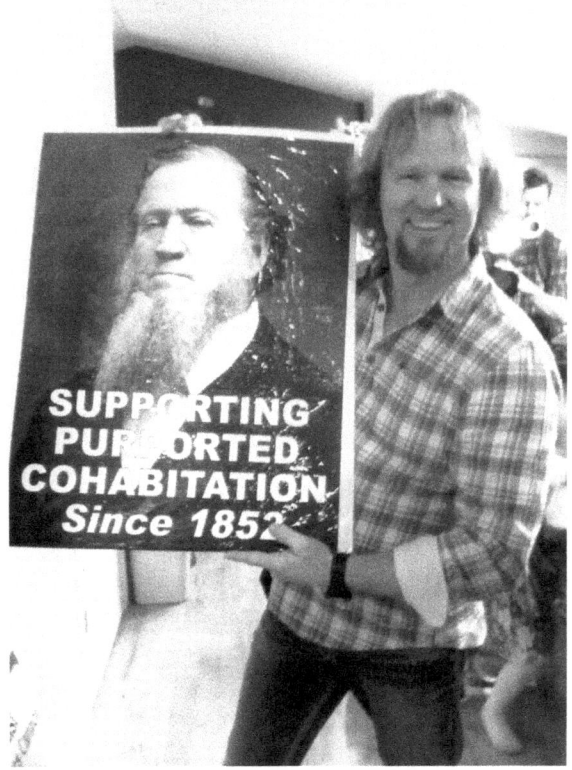

SUPPORTING PURPORTED COHABITATION Since 1852

even though hundreds made phone calls and wrote letters to Utah governor Gary Herbert, he signed it into law.

At the passage and signing of the bill, a ripple of unease spread through the various Utah Fundamentalist communities. Some began to ask if they should follow the Browns' lead and move out of the state. Others insisted the bill was meant to bully and intimidate them into silence, forcing them to stay in the shadows as a kind of "out of sight, out of mind" situation. As for Kody Brown, he felt at first depressed but has now moved on. Brown and his family have moved from Las Vegas to the Flagstaff, Arizona area. Kody explained that he had been forced to move into exile in Las Vegas and had seriously considered moving back to Utah to fight, perhaps even run for office as a way of fighting a law he still believes to be unconstitutional and unjust. His wives, however, talked him out of moving back, as they see it to be a quixotic quest on an unfair and unsafe field of competition. After much prayer and thought, they decided to move to Flagstaff and now "feel like [they're] living in heaven."[364]

Since then, Van Tassell's daughter lost her appeal for custody of the couple's minor children. With former Utah attorney general Mark Shurtleff as his attorney, her husband was acquitted by jury of his ex-wife's extortion and bribery charges and then settled an abuse case she brought.[365]

DISCORD AND GROWTH WITHIN THE AUB

J. LaMoine Jenson, the head of the AUB Priesthood Council, died in September 2014 and was replaced by Lynn A. Thompson. Two months later, one of Thompson's daughters, Rosemary Williams, one of the women in the reality TV show *My Five Wives*, published on social media accusations against her father, saying he touched her inappropriately when she was twelve years old. However, she never initiated civil or criminal charges against him. Rosemary's husband, Brady Williams, publicly stated that they wanted Lynn Thompson to "leave or be removed from his position of power." The accusations and recriminations reverberated through the AUB, with members quickly taking sides for or against Thompson.[366]

News of the accusations appeared in media as far away as England. AUB representatives immediately responded, stating the accusations would be investigated. Despite the quick reaction, some members expressed shock and quickly disassociated themselves from the main body. Most of those disassociating themselves from the AUB were from Pinesdale, and their

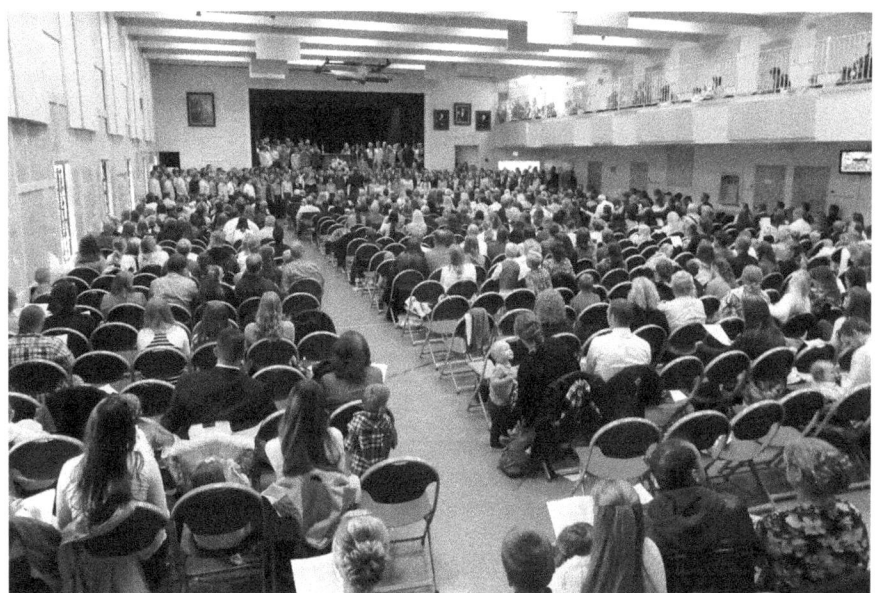

AUB congregation attending annual conference, 2017. *Authors' collection.*

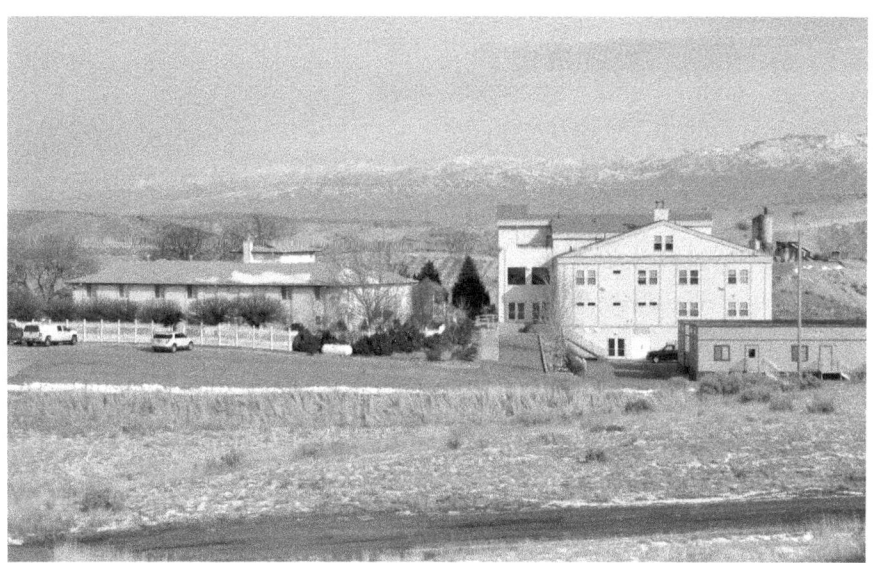

AUB headquarters in Bluffdale, Utah. *Authors' collection.*

dissatisfaction extended beyond the accusations against Thompson. Less than two weeks before Jenson died, he unexpectedly bypassed Marvin Jessop, who lives in Pinesdale, the presumed successor, and instead named Thompson to succeed as leader of the Priesthood Council, claiming revelation that changed his earlier statements and the precedent for the next in seniority to succeed. Even more surprising to members and totally without precedent, he reordered the quorum, placing junior council member Harry Bonnell next in seniority to Thompson, saying, "You will come to know sooner or later what I have done is the will of the Lord." This announcement was met with mixed reaction, with some being amazed and wholeheartedly accepting it, others guardedly going along, while yet others were stunned, disappointed and did not believe it was from God. Most of the Pinesdale community questioned Jenson's revelation, especially after Thompson had been accused. Such "Pineys" took Jenson's move almost as a personal affront and considered Thompson the legal head of the AUB organization but as not the legitimate priesthood head.[367]

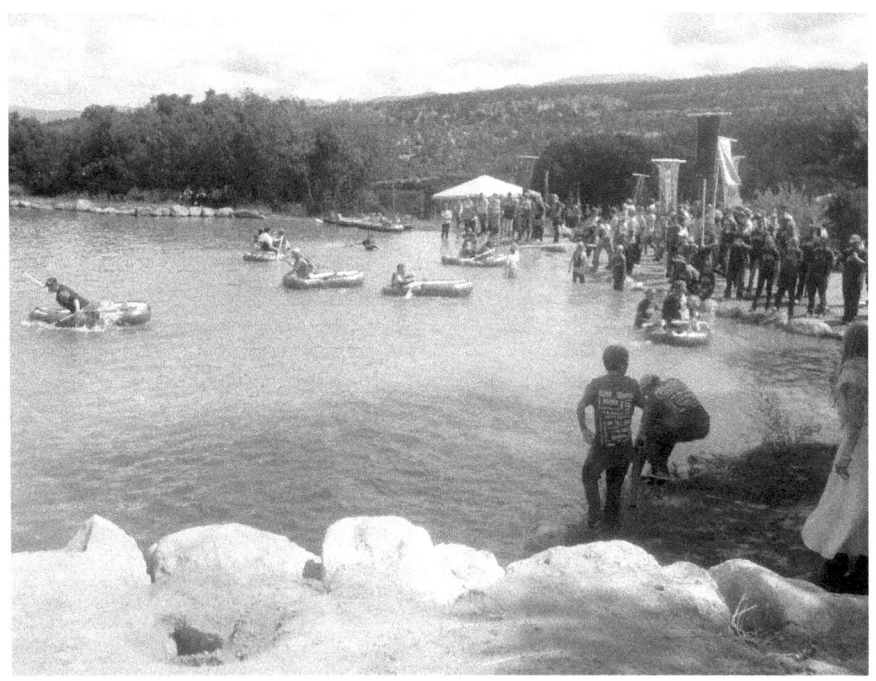

AUB Youth Camp, circa 2015. *Authors' collection.*

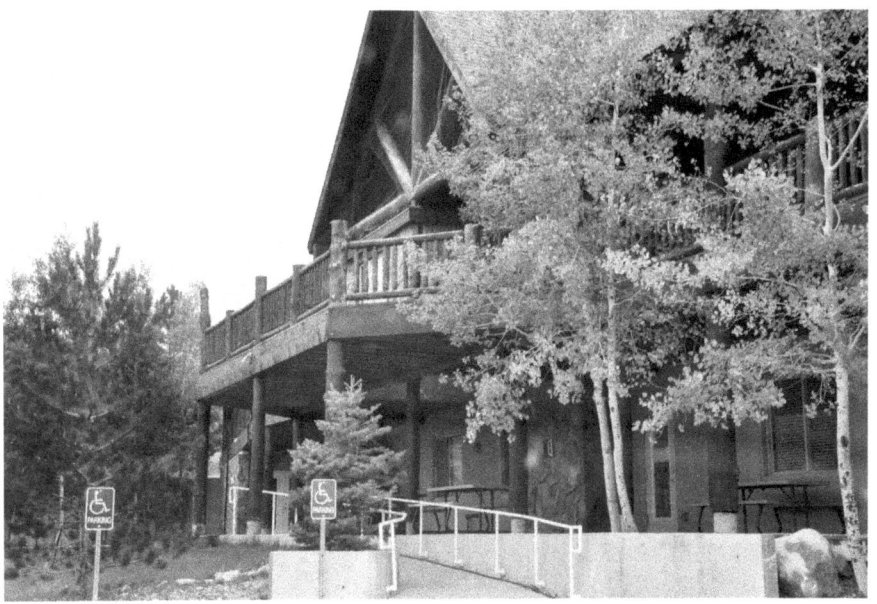

AUB meeting house in Mt. Pleasant, Utah. *Authors' collection.*

Ultimately, half or more of the Pinesdale community stopped attending AUB functions and started holding their own. The town fractured into four factions: 1) some remained faithful to the AUB Priesthood Council; 2) some began holding their own meetings; 3) some joined the LDS Church; and 4) some others gave up religion altogether. Gradually, several families have since returned to participation with the main body of the AUB.

Over many decades, the AUB has grown in membership. By far, the closest of the Fundamentalist groups in form and association to the LDS Church, the AUB has for years attracted a small but steady flow of Latter-day Saints into its ranks. The AUB has also had a more public presence. In 2008, the group purchased 877 acres in Mt. Pleasant in Utah's Sanpete Valley, where members have a meetinghouse, have built homes and have developed a public campground for youth and family activities. Because the arrival of AUB polygamists occurred shortly after the FLDS Texas raid, Mt. Pleasant residents initially responded by publicly opposing development of the purchased properties in town hearings, expressing fear of secretive enclaves and being overrun by polygamists, but the relationship between the two groups has developed respectfully.[368]

THE INDEPENDENTS

Independent Fundamentalists do not regularly affiliate with Fundamentalist groups, but most have relatives involved in one or more of the major groups. Independents mostly comprise large extended families that are descendants of "the Ianthius W. Barlow, Louis Kelsch, Arnold N. Boss, and Morris Kunz families, or are involved with smaller family units such as those of Fred Collier and the late Ogden Kraut, owner of Pioneer Press."[369]

The major Independent families separated when in 1944 Fundamentalists served time in prison. It became a matter of personal conscience when a "Declaration of Policy" was offered by the state for early release if they promised not to live plural marriage and to financially support *all* their wives and children. Most of the men signed the document but resumed their former lifestyles after (or even before) completing a one-year parole. Four men, Louis Kelsch, Morris Kunz, Albert Barlow and Arnold Boss, did not sign because they could not violate their consciences by signing a promise they knew they could not keep; they remained in prison for almost all of their five-year sentences. After being released from prison, these men disassociated themselves from the main body of Fundamentalists, became independent and over time became known and self-identified as "Independents." One man, Ianthius Barlow, became an Independent even though he had signed the document. Other families became Independents after the 1950–52 split.

Louis Alma Kelsch, by some, has been "considered the quintessential 'independent' fundamentalist." He was outspokenly adamant against making compromises or concessions. Between 1955 and 1959, he again served time in the penitentiary for living the Principle. Kelsch died in 1974 after a couple of decades remaining aloof from the polygamous groups.[370] Kelsch, Zitting, Kunz, Boss and Barlow left behind large families, many of whom continued as Independent Fundamentalists.

Ogden Kraut, a well-known Independent polygamist and prolific writer, published over sixty books on Fundamentalist topics. Excommunicated from the LDS Church in 1972, he became very public about being a Fundamentalist Mormon. He is said to have had five wives, including Anne Wilde, an author and well-known defender who calls herself a "Joseph Smith Mormon."[371]

Rockland Ranch or, "the Rock," as it is commonly called, was started as early as 1978 by a former LDS Seminary teacher turned polygamist, Robert "Bob" Foster, as a refuge for Fundamentalists or anyone in need. Located in the beautifully rugged red rock desert approximately halfway between Moab

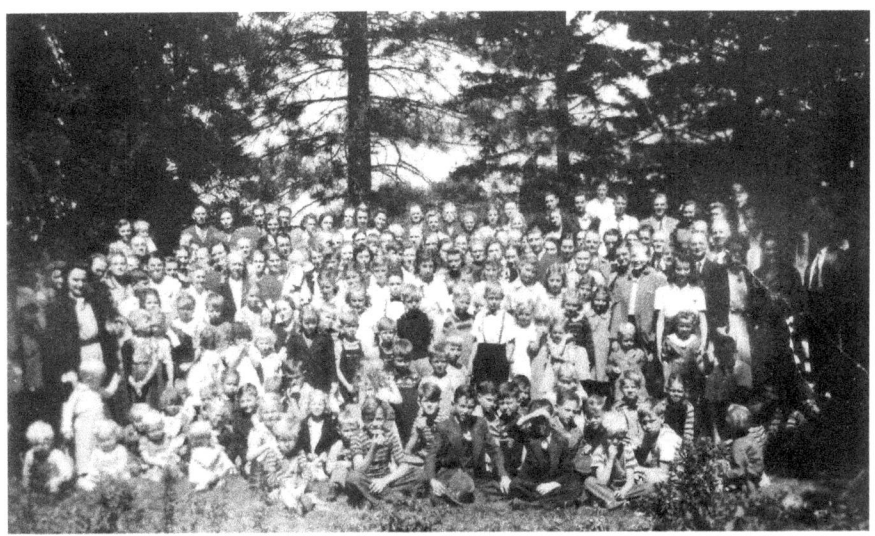

Independent Fundamentalist families meeting in a Utah canyon for Sunday school, about 1940s or 1950s. *Authors' collection.*

and Monticello, Utah, the eighty-three acres include a large, monolithic rock into which Foster blasted large caves to house his three wives and for many of his children to build homes.[372] He originally envisioned such a refuge after being convicted on a charge of bigamy and spending twenty days in a Nephi, Utah jail in 1972.

Enoch Foster, Bob's son, who took over management of the ranch after his father's death, explained that the community is completely off the grid, with its own solar panels, wells, gardens, orchards and livestock. Today, approximately sixteen families, making up about 140 people, live there, all with homes built in caves blasted from the rock. While not everyone there is Fundamentalist, they must agree to live certain standards for dress, music, avoiding alcohol in public, pornography, swearing and other social and personal ills. The majority are Independent Fundamentalists, but there are even a couple of LDS families. An absolute requirement for permanent residence at the Rock is having a belief in the prophetic mission of Joseph Smith.[373]

Enoch Foster, when questioned about interactions between his community with other citizens of San Juan County, answered that they got along very well with them, adding that the people living around them are "liberty-loving, conservative, many from a polygamous heritage, salt-of-the-earth people."[374] The Rock's community relationship of mutual

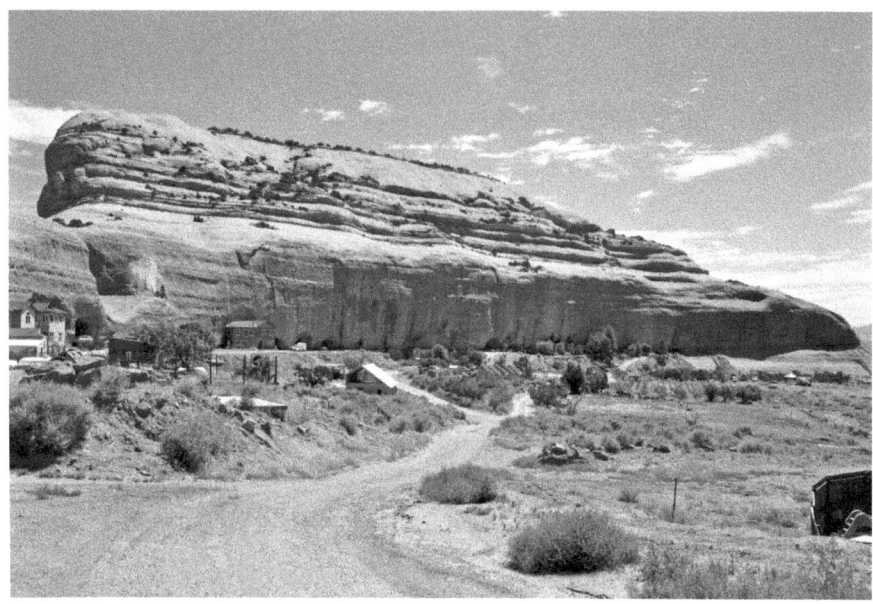

Rockland Ranch, "the Rock" Fundamentalist community. *Steven L. Mayfield Collection.*

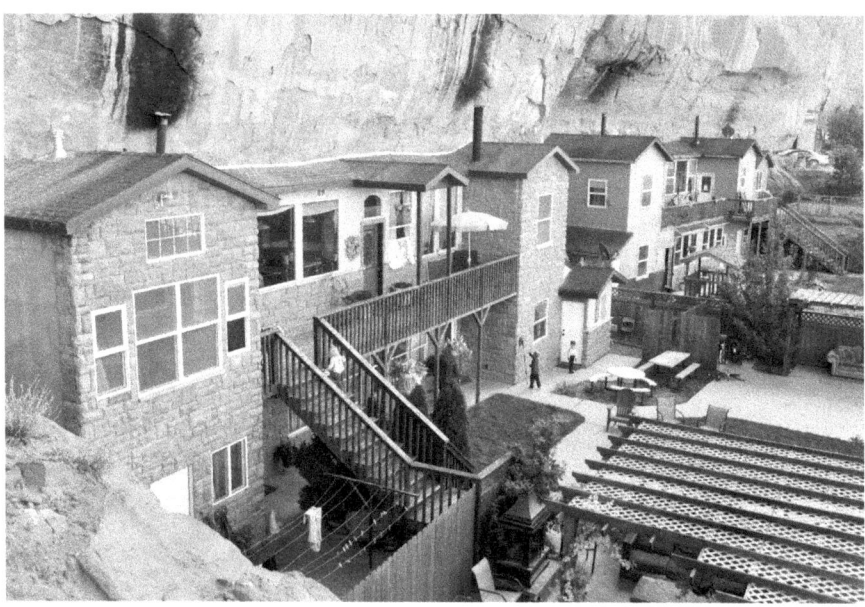

Enoch Foster's home (*at left*) and other homes built into blasted holes in the rock. *Steven L. Mayfield Collection.*

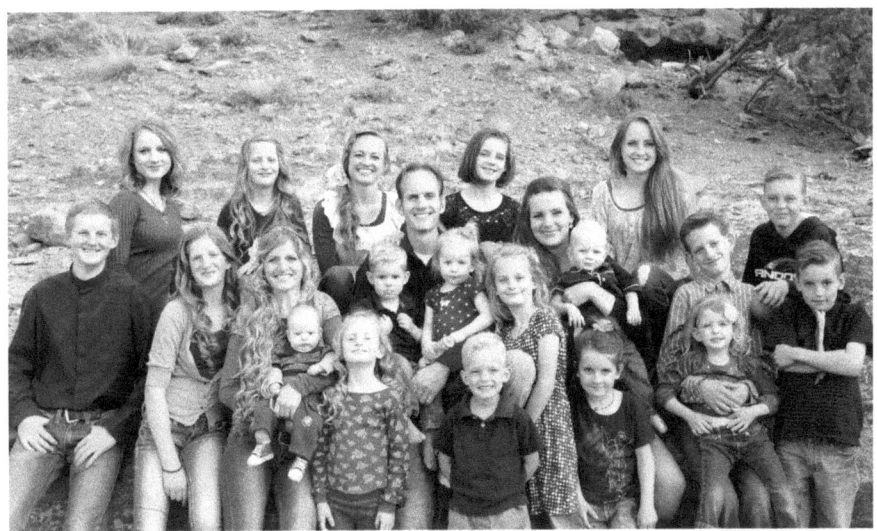

Enoch Foster's three wives and children, 2017. *Courtesy of Enoch Foster.*

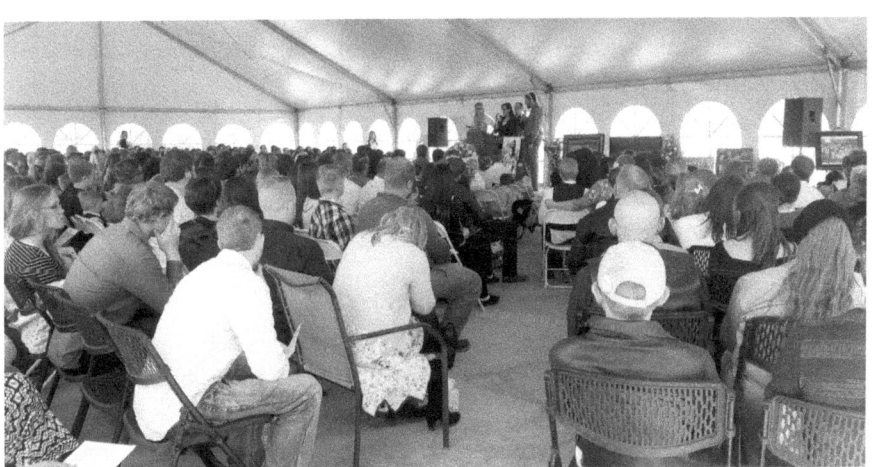

Funeral for Enoch Foster's son, April 2018, at Rockland Ranch. *Authors' collection.*

respect with county neighbors was strikingly demonstrated when tragedy struck the Foster family. In April 2018, their two-year-old son, Adonijah, died in an accidental house fire. His funeral was held a week later at the Rock. The Monticello LDS congregation provided food for the Fosters during that week and for people attending the very large funeral. Baptist church members from Moab, as well as other groups and neighbors, also stepped in to help. An AUB charity organization for families with

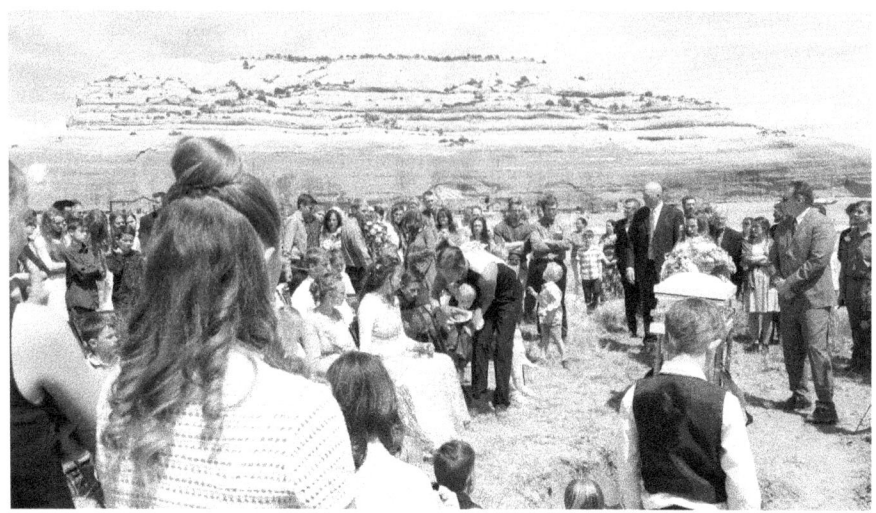

Burial of Enoch Foster's son at Rockland Ranch cemetery. *Authors' collection.*

children's hospitalizations or deaths provided for many funeral expenses. How these different communities came together to comfort and bless the Fosters at a time of tragedy and loss showed how Fundamentalists can be synergistically involved with others different from themselves.[375]

STILL A MATTER OF FAITH

n June 2018, three groups of youth converged in the same area on the high plains of Wyoming, part of the original Mormon Trail, to participate in and commemorate the Mormon handcart pioneer trek. Historically, between 1847 and 1869, approximately 70,000 Mormons traveled one thousand miles across America's western plains to Utah. While almost all came by wagon train, about 3,000 pushed and pulled handcarts all the way to the Salt Lake Valley. Handcarts were envisioned as a less-expensive way for poorer Saints to travel to Utah. Of the ten handcart companies that traveled between 1856 and 1860, eight were considered successful. The first year, however, the Martin and Willie companies left late in the season and were caught in Wyoming in early winter storms, and ultimately over 210 people died of the 1,164 pioneers in these two companies. Their suffering and sacrifices became legend among subsequent generations of the LDS Church members.

For the last few decades, Mormon youth reenactments of the handcart pioneers have become popular. Each summer, thousands spend a few days dressed in nineteenth-century garb retracing the pioneer "trek," cooking over fires and camping in tents at night, to better understand and appreciate their pioneer ancestors' travails for their faith and religious devotion. Most LDS pioneer trek groups number about one hundred, with some perhaps as many as four hundred.

Two of the mentioned youth groups in June 2018, about 100 to 200 in number, came from the Church of Jesus Christ. The third group was unusual for two reasons. First, its participants totaled over 650, with more than 500 youth and 150 adult chaperones. Second, they were not members of the LDS Church; all belonged to the AUB Fundamentalist group. Remarkably, given the history of a strained, often negative relationship between members of the LDS Church and its Fundamentalist "cousins," all three groups got along well. While generally staying apart, they treated one another with respect and affability. The trek proved to be a positive experience on several levels. For the church groups, the 650 Fundamentalist "pioneers" pushing and pulling dozens of handcarts made an incredible sight as their one- to two-mile-long procession wound over, around and across the desert hills for three days.[376]

If these youth follow the general trend of millennials and Generation Z in other religious denominations and groups, including the LDS Church, at least half of them will eventually choose to leave their religious upbringing, seeking another denomination or no religion at all. Jeffrey R. Holland, then Brigham Young University president and now an LDS Church Apostle, observed that "this Church is always only one generation away from extinction," meaning that if the youth are not converted, the church would eventually die away.[377] The same can certainly be said about Fundamentalist Mormons, and probably more so. Mormonism is a demanding religion, and LDS adherents dedicate time, energy and usually money to fully living its tenets. The same is true for Fundamentalists, as their beliefs encompass almost every aspect of their lives, plus commitment to a lifestyle that is difficult under the best of conditions. This, of course, begs the question of whether or not Mormon Fundamentalism will survive in the twenty-first century.

However, if the following example is representative of other Fundamentalist youth, then parents and leaders need be less concerned about the upcoming generation and continuation of the Principle. Some time ago, two sisters in their early- to mid-teens who reside in the small Utah Fundamentalist community of Rocky Ridge were questioned about growing up in a polygamous household and asked if they too wanted to become plural wives. The girls explained how they viewed both their father's wives as their mothers and how they felt having two mothers was a great experience. They expressed love for their family life and said there was no division between mothers and siblings. This family, as the parents explained, had been particularly drama-free and cohesive—one big, very close family.

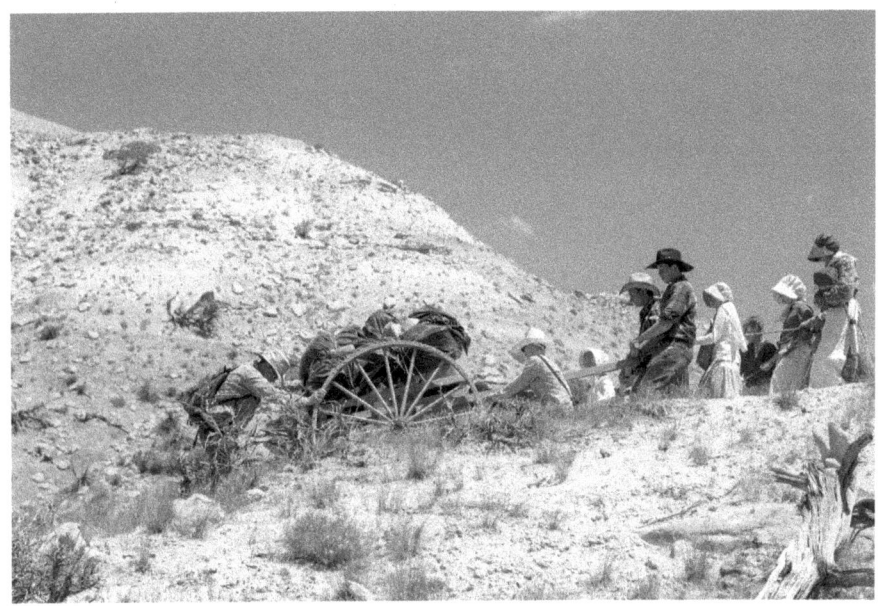

AUB youth reenactment of pioneer handcart trek, 2018. *Authors' collection.*

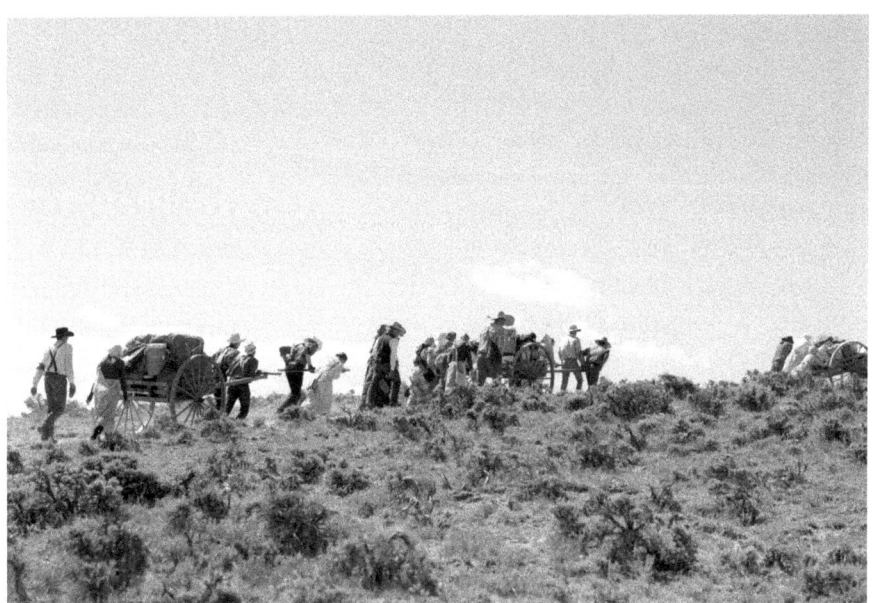

AUB youth push and pull handcarts up a hill. *Authors' collection.*

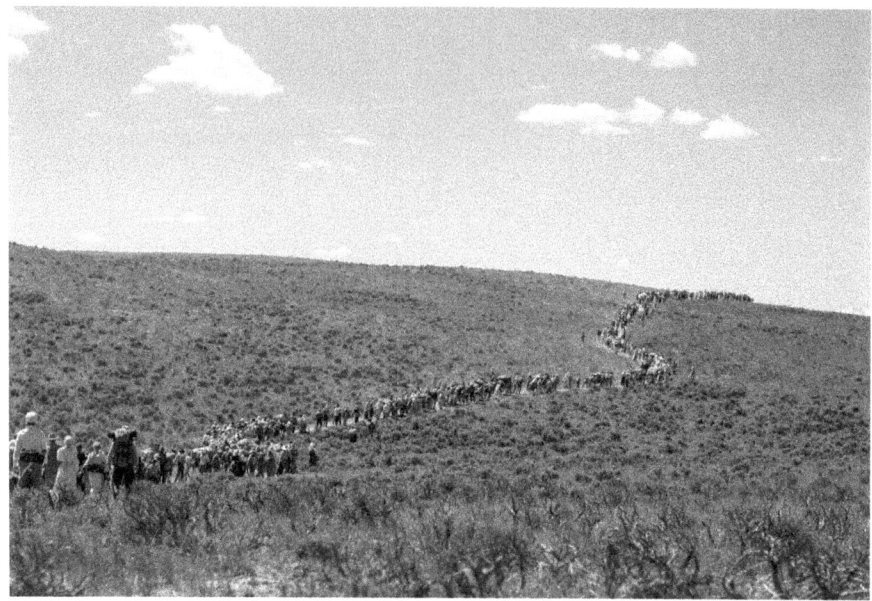

View of some 650 AUB members, about 500 youth and 150 chaperones, trailing across the Wyoming desert. *Authors' collection.*

It was, however, the girls' own marriage goals that seemed most profound. Both said they wouldn't mind living in plurality, either as a first wife or as a plural wife, "because it's the Celestial Law." Both also said they wouldn't mind marrying the same husband because they loved being with each other. Their expressions reflected sentiments of other women throughout the history of Mormon polygamy; many close friends or even sisters have later become sister wives. For the most part, being sisters or good friends helped make them more successful as sister wives because of their close bonds. Such ties between sister wives, being sisterly rather than conjugal love, can be almost as strong and godly as their respective marital relationships with their husband.

The older of the two sisters wondered out loud if she truly wanted to be a first wife—what if her husband decided *after* their marriage that he didn't want to live plural marriage? Marrying a single man might be risky, and she emphatically stated she wants to live the Principle.[378]

More recently, the sisters, by then ages seventeen and fifteen, were asked if they still want to live the Principle. Both firmly answered yes. They agreed that if any unmarried man showed interest in either of them, one of the first questions to be asked would be: does he want to live the Principle? The older sister had decided she doesn't care if the man is single or already married because she would pray to know the right decision about who to marry and only wants to do what God wishes.[379]

The desire of these girls to live the Principle is impressive because living plural marriage is not easy. It takes an incredible amount of faith, patience and sacrifice. In a recent book of personal stories and advice written by and for women living plural marriage today, page after page reflects plural wives' hopes and frustrations:[380]

> *I know you think you are failing at times, we all do.*
> *...it is extremely difficult to be happy in the Principle if a strong sisterwife relationship is not kept up*
> *Pray for love and friendship with your sisterwife.*
> *Pray for each other's everything.*
> *Remember that God didn't command us to live this way to see us suffer; he wants us to be happy and happiness is a choice.*

Among themselves, Fundamentalists readily admit the difficulties of living plural marriage, the trials being difficult for both men and women. In a recent annual AUB group conference, a priesthood council member acknowledged there were many problems in plural families and that "the council spends a lot of time trying to keep families together." Another council member recognized "the poor success rate of those trying to live celestial plural marriage." He explained that too many plural marriages "crash and burn right up front." Often, according to this leader, "it is the man's fault first," especially if he is "incapable of loving more than one woman." He explained privately that "too often young people marry plurally only because it is socially acceptable among us, but without study and prayer to obtain a solid testimony for themselves. Then they bail when they face problems."[381]

LIVING IN THE SHADOWLANDS
OF FUNDAMENTALISM

The expected trials and frustrations of plural family life are not the only problems Fundamentalist Mormons face. Thus, the devotion and willingness expressed by the two girls mentioned is particularly poignant when considering such a choice will place them in the shadowlands, on the fringes of accepted society for the remainder of their lives. It appears those who grow up in plural families have an array of experiences, depending upon whether they live in a Fundamentalist community among their own people or if they live among the wider population, trying to blend in with mainstream America. Naturally, there are varying degrees of success, and often Fundamentalists discover their uniqueness. As one wrote, "As I grew up, I became aware of how different our life was from the majority of the world."[382]

After the 1944 and 1953 raids, when polygamists were arrested and families were temporarily broken up, many Fundamentalist families began using pseudonymous surnames. Many still follow this practice for fear of legal or social repercussions, and some plural wives use either made-up names or their maiden names all their lives, while their children may or may not carry their father's surname. Meanwhile, society, the courts and other institutions have become more liberal in allowing people from nontraditional marriages, or from no marriage at all, to adopt different surnames. Yet with current laws, a plural wife cannot easily change her name to go by her husband's surname because she cannot get a legal marriage certificate.

Also, legal complexities make it almost impossible for a plural wife to obtain insurance for herself and her children under her husband's policy. This situation compels many plural wives to earn a living outside the home to pay for their own medical expenses or buy insurance. The fear of "being found out" keeps many plural wives and their children from asking for and receiving services when needed. To alleviate these tensions, along with pursuing decriminalization, Fundamentalist coalition groups that have formed since 2000 have focused on such issues and have worked to educate plural families about laws affecting them and to train and coordinate with government agencies and nongovernment service organizations about plural family fears and potential needs.

Unfortunately, Fundamentalists too often experienced instances of unpleasantness from mainstream American society. For example, one woman remembered that after the 1944 raid when her father had been arrested and sent to prison, other students would taunt her and her sisters, calling them "plygs" all the way to and from school, and boys sometimes chased them and put cockleburs in their hair. It was a painful ordeal when their mother had to comb them out, as bothersome as the unkind words. An older sister suffered so terribly from such ill treatment that her parents finally took her out of school and taught her at home.[383]

The next generation still had to be careful as they too experienced alienation and ostracism. One woman remembered that her mother and her father's other plural wives, to avoid trouble, all used fabricated surnames. Thankfully, she said, her dad insisted that all his children use his surname because he wanted them to feel wanted and loved and know their real identity. She and her siblings were taught not to discuss or share family dynamics when attending public school. As a second grader, she whispered to her best school friend her family secret that her father was a polygamist. She now laughs as she realizes the little girl probably didn't have the slightest idea what that meant. She later had a school friend who played with her and invited her to her birthday parties every year. After the girl's parents became aware of the family's plural status, the girl ignored her and they were no longer friends.[384]

For the next couple of generations, removed from the taint of the 1940s and 1950s raids, interactions with mainstream society have gotten easier. Nevertheless, stigma because of beliefs still exists. A woman in her thirties who grew up in Juab County, Utah, recalled when she was in middle school how some kids would throw scraps from a wood shop class at her and other Fundamentalist kids, calling them "Plygs" and other names.[385] Another woman in her thirties remembers growing up near Eagle Mountain, Utah, in a subdivision where several Fundamentalist families lived. Sometimes when she or her siblings played in the front yard, people driving by would slow down and yell "Plygs!" But how her relatives treated her, as a plural child, hurt her more. When her father left the LDS Church to become a Fundamentalist, his siblings became embarrassed about his religious decisions and lifestyle. They would invite him and his first wife and children to family events, but not the others. Her father's plural wives and children were treated with silence, as the family's dirty little secret.[386]

Notwithstanding the kind of negatives mentioned above, the two sisters discussed earlier are still willing to sacrifice in their solid dedication to live such a misunderstood lifestyle. They are not alone. Another devoted young woman, with a polygamous heritage going back generations, stated before ever seriously entertaining who she would marry, "I don't know what I would do if I could not live this way [in plural marriage]."[387]

Still another Fundamentalist woman wrote about people asking her if she thinks she is doing what is right by living the Principle. She responded:

> *What's the alternative? It's like questioning why I'm an American, or born in the 20th century, or female. That is what and who I am. These are my*

people. My life, my love, my commitments, my loyalties are all culturally, spiritually, emotionally here. What else, really, ought I to be or do? This is enough. And it is everything.[388]

Thus, the daunting possibility of living in the shadowlands on the fringes of society, and of ostracism and ridicule by mainstream society, has not dissuaded the young sisters spoken of, or numerous other young men and women like them, from their willingness to make life-changing sacrifices by participating in the principle of plural marriage. They faithfully do so because of their belief that it is commanded by God.

PUBLIC OPINION REGARDING POLYGAMY

So, what is the future of Fundamentalist Mormon polygamy? Will these young people like so many before them forever remain in the shadowlands of mainstream society? Or will polygamy, like other alternative forms of traditional marriage, eventually become acceptable or tolerable for at least a majority of society? And will its adherents be able to come in from the cold and participate as accepted members of American life?

Mormon polygamy has traditionally been despised and legislated against by American society. Indeed, history has painfully shown legal and social ramifications of practicing the principle of plural marriage. And even though traditional marriage has been redefined almost to the point of absurdity, legalized polygamy is still viewed by most Americans as "odious."[389] Acceptance of plural marriage is less tolerable than gay marriage for most Americans, as demonstrated throughout the oft-heated debate about same-sex marriage. Naysayers warning against homosexual rights made dire predictions that same-sex marriage is a slippery slope leading inevitably to legalized polygamy.[390]

At the same time, and despite the negative attitudes of most Americans, there have been some who have pushed for legalizing polygamy, especially after *Obergefell v. Hodges* and other pro-LGBT and gay marriage Supreme Court decisions. In one article, with nonreligious polygamy in mind, the writer announced that it is time to legalize polygamy, explaining "group marriage is the next horizon of social liberalism." The author wrote, "Polygamy today stands as a taboo just as strong as same-sex marriage was several decades ago—it's effectively only discussed as outdated jokes about Utah and Mormons, who banned the practice over 120 years ago." He then stated that "polyamory is a fact" and Americans need to recognize that and grant them the basic rights granted to other adults.[391]

Supporters of legalized polygamy, however, are still a small minority. One editorial warned, "Same-sex marriage may be an advance for human rights. Legalizing polygamy would undermine the stability of our society and deeply harm women and children." In an editorial condemning FLDS control of Colorado City–Hildale and polygamy in general, the *Arizona Republic* stated, "What's more, the problems are so anachronistic that it's hard to remember this is really going on in 2015. But it is happening, and it needs to be stopped." Pro–gay marriage author and activist Jonathan Rauch warned legalized polygamy would allow "high-status men to hoard wives at the expense of lower-status men."[392]

Such criticism has particularly been aimed at religious polygyny. Critics have portrayed this marriage system in negative terms, with the men as abusive and women as abused. Many members of mainstream society view polygamous women as submissive and without personal rights. Or, as one Fundamentalist sarcastically described outside perceptions of women's lot in Fundamentalist Mormonism—"in the kitchen, barefoot and pregnant." But Fundamentalist women scoff at such an image. Said one, "Most of the women in Fundamentalism are strong personalities who won't be bossed around."[393] A woman raised as a Fundamentalist but no longer practicing echoed those sentiments: "I realize that people look at this polygamous lifestyle as being a trap for women and children, but in most cases, it is a matter of choice. Most plural wives that I grew up with were the strongest that I have known."[394]

An aging husband of five wives, all in their sixties with longtime marriages, shared that he did "not want mamby-pamby, servile wives" and that "for marriages in a plural family to endure, it requires a real man to develop real relationships with real women as wives—who are adults, not little girls." He added:

> *I only want intelligent wives, each with her own testimony of Jesus Christ and the fullness of the Gospel, who can think, speak, and act for herself and is capable to participate in a synergistic, loving, caring relationship that provokes emotional, intellectual, and spiritual growth—first and foremost with me and then with other family members.*

He admitted, "Most men and women are unwilling to make the personal sacrifices that can produce such time-proven relationships."[395]

Historian Ken Driggs, who interviewed and made exceptional effort in the 1990s to get to know some families of Hildale–Colorado City and from the AUB in the Salt Lake area, said, "Many of the strongest, most assertive women I have ever met have been Fundamentalists. There are always people who fit the stereotypes, but you would be dead wrong if you view Fundamentalist women as intimidated victims."[396]

Still, skeptics are suspicious and ask how a polygamous wife can really have any power in a religion where one man can have multiple wives. Despite the much-publicized cases of underage wives being forced into polygamous marriages, most Fundamentalist women not only make their own decision to enter into plurality but also freely select their husband. Furthermore, the religious aspect of plural marriage is a compelling factor for both the females and males that allows them to remember the reason for plural marriage extends beyond more worldly reasons such as free love or sexual license. A close observer of the Fundamentalists wrote, "Many people, especially women, don't understand how several wives can live and work in harmony and at the same time share the affections of one man. The trouble is they don't understand the religion of the polygamists."[397]

The religious devotion of Fundamentalist Mormons cannot be overstated. And it is because of their religiosity that, ironically, many Fundamentalists don't want polygamy to be legalized. They fear if polygamy becomes secularized and legalized that people would be involved simply for their own selfish sexual gratification than for the more altruistic reason of following God's commandment. Thus, all they want is for polygamy to be decriminalized. In other words, for them to not live in constant fear of prosecution. As one practitioner explained, "We've been pushed into the shadows and that breeds problems." Being able to come into the light of accepted society would help alleviate the Fundamentalist community of cases of abuse and oppression. And to those on the outside, they plead, "Let us live our lives and practice our religion, as long as its among consenting adults."[398]

Will that happen? Legalizing polygamy does not appear to be probable in the near future, but interestingly enough, a Gallup poll conducted in the summer of 2017 shows a slight increase in Americans viewing polygamy as morally acceptable, moving from 14 percent in 2016 to 17 percent in 2017. While the number of those accepting polygamy is still a distinct minority, since 2003 the number accepting polygamy as morally acceptable has climbed ten points from a low of 7 percent.[399]

A Mormon blogger, discussing the rise in acceptance of polygamy, asked if this might be "the 'Sister Wives' effect." She concluded that while it might be, it was also a "clear generational difference," even among Mormons who were also part of the poll. Only 7 percent of the Boomer/Silent generation viewed polygamy as morally acceptable, while 13 percent of GenXers and a whopping 23 percent of millennials were okay with polygamy. This demonstrates the trend, even among mainstream Mormons, to have a "broader sexual ethic," which includes tolerance of polygamy.[400]

STILL A MATTER OF FAITH

Perhaps there is something to the so-called *Sister Wives* effect. What *Sister Wives* and other reality shows have done is to put a human face on plural marriage. This process of humanizing modern polygamists has changed popular perceptions and helped break down some of the clichéd stereotypes mainstream America harbors. Even the difficult, sometimes contentious, relationship mainstream LDS Church members have had with their Fundamentalist cousins has seen limited progress, although a wide cultural and theological gulf remains between the two.[401]

As previously discussed, the Church of Jesus Christ of Latter-day Saints reached a point where the church and most of its members went one direction and those who became Fundamentalists went another. Fundamentalists, according to historian Martha Sonntag Bradley, "chose a road often running parallel to the visible Mormon Church" in order, in their view, to "maintain the pure and unadulterated church, the 'invisible church,' the church of the original teachings of Joseph Smith." A Fundamentalist leader echoed this sentiment in a Sunday sermon, stating, "This is not a socially acceptable way of life. This is for ultra-Mormons willing to live the fulness of the gospel—moving parallel with the church."[402]

Modern members of the LDS Church are now generations and over one hundred years separated from when the church officially or even unofficially lived plural marriage. The Church of Jesus Christ, as an institution and its members particularly, have forgotten what it is like to live the Principle, and such a lifestyle is foreign and strange to them. Indeed, several Fundamentalists have recounted how they have been asked by LDS church members if all the wives sleep in the same bed with their husband. One woman remembered being asked that question when she was about sixteen. She was shocked that people, especially LDS church members, actually thought that was what polygamists did. Another woman, who was also asked the same question when in her teens, said she couldn't believe the lady, a faithful Latter-day Saint with pioneer ancestors, would think something like that. She wondered if the woman thought her own polygamous ancestors all slept in the same bed.[403]

Nevertheless, while many modern Latter-day Saints stumble over stereotypical misconceptions and shudder at the thought of being a plural wife or, for the men, being married to more than one woman, those with early ancestors in the LDS Church are probably products of polygamy. For their ancestors, they usually acknowledge, living the Principle was a matter of faith. There are many recorded accounts of early Mormon men and women seeking and receiving spiritual confirmation that a marriage practice, so contrary to their Victorian sensibilities, was actually heaven ordained, as they came to believe.

Fundamentalist Mormons have similar stories, old and new, of conversion and confirmation. For example, a young woman who prayed with all her heart about living plural marriage, "could feel the spirit of God—a joy and peace within that's almost indescribable"; another wrote that "celestial plural marriage" is "a true and pure law of God"; and yet another woman "entered plural marriage…by way of revelation," with a powerful witness of the Holy Spirit.[404]

Mary Viola Anderson Thompson Allred, an early Fundamentalist, explained:

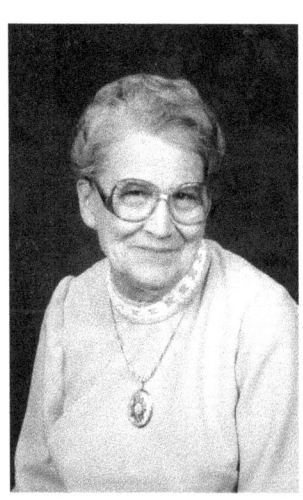

Mary Viola Anderson Thompson Allred (1900–1983). *Authors' collection.*

There's really no happiness more glorious than living the Principle. In order to be happy again, you have to purify your own soul, analyze yourself, look at yourself.…You cannot live Celestial Marriage perfectly unless you try your best to be perfect.…I would rather live…Plural Marriage than I would monogamy. I've lived both. I was happy in both, but I didn't know what true happiness was until I got into the Principle.[405]

More recent voices have echoed Mary Viola's sentiments. One woman wrote, "It takes a lot of courage, faith, perseverance and love to live this law." Another explained, "I wouldn't have it any other way. I am intellectually, spiritually, emotionally and physically fulfilled." Finally, "There is nothing on this earth that can make you more happy and full of true joy than to be doing God's will and knowing for yourself what He would have you do. What a feeling that fills the heart."[406]

So, for the sisters who as teens are already contemplating living the Principle, as well as for the majority of other Fundamentalists, their desires extend beyond the simple worldly considerations of most couples getting married. Naturally, there will be questions of physical attraction and compatibility. But, like their ancestors of old, either literally or spiritually, their marriage decisions also are a deep and powerful matter of faith involving a willingness to live the principle of plural marriage with the end goal of eternity and exaltation in the presence of God.

NOTES

Chapter 1

1. Bloom, *American Religion*, 81, 95–96, 98–99.
2. Eliza R. Snow Smith, *Biography and Family Record of Lorenzo Snow* (1884), 46, also cited in *Teachings of Presidents of the Church: Lorenzo Snow* (Salt Lake City: The Church of Jesus Christ of Latter-day Saints, 2011), 83.
3. Bloom, *American Religion*, 80–81, 95, 101.
4. Ibid., 104–6, 108.
5. Foster, "Joseph Smith's Plural Wives," 294–95; Bradley, "Mormon Polygamy," 14–58; Hales, "Joseph Smith," 99–151.
6. Foster, "Joseph Smith's Plural Wives," 294–95. For more detailed information on Joseph Smith and his plural marriages, see the other essays in Bringhurst and Foster, *Persistence of Polygamy*, vol. 1, and Hales, *Joseph Smith's Polygamy*.
7. Foster, "Wives of the Prophets," 127–133.
8. Ibid., 134–45.
9. For a discussion of women incarcerated for refusing to testify against their husbands, see Stromberg, "Prisoners for 'The Principle,'" 298–325.
10. Driggs, "Lorenzo Snow's Appellate Court Victory," 81–93.
11. *Salt Lake Tribune*, January 6, 1880.
12. Musser, *Four Hidden Revelations*, 15–18. See also Musser and Broadbent, *Supplement to the New and Everlasting* [hereafter *Supplement*], 62–63.
13. Briney, *Apostles on Trial*, 109.

14. Quinn, "LDS Church Authority," 29–30. See also Foster, "Wives of the Prophets," 134–36.
15. Hales, "John Taylor's 1886 Revelation," 59.
16. Fundamentalists point to three other revelations—in 1880, 1882 and 1899—that were never canonized. Musser and Broadbent, *Supplement*; Musser, *Four Hidden Revelations*.
17. Smoot and Sheriff, *City In-Between*, 361–62; Watson, "From Nineteenth-Century Mormon Polygamy," 151.
18. Parkinson, *Utah Woolley Family*, 213–14.
19. Musser and Broadbent, *Supplement*, 26.
20. Ibid.
21. Lorin C. Woolley statement recorded by Joseph W. Musser, Musser Book of Remembrance, September 27, 1932, 38.
22. Parkinson, *Utah Woolley Family*, 198.
23. Madsen, *Defender of the Faith*.
24. Rogers, *In the President's Office*, 211–12; Bitton, *George Q. Cannon*, 287–88.
25. *The Doctrine and Covenants*, Section 84:63. Fundamentalists believe Joseph Smith established this priesthood quorum of seven apostles *before* the Quorum of Twelve Apostles of the LDS Church and appointed them "to be stewards over the revelations and commandments" as recorded in *The Doctrine and Covenants*, Section 70:1–3; see also Section 84. Brigham Young may have continued this quorum as implied in an 1873 LDS Church conference in which Young discussed a quorum of seven, "one higher than the Twelve Apostles," as reported in an opposition news article, "A New Quorum of Priesthood," *Salt Lake Daily Tribune*, April 10, 1873. See also Musser and Broadbent, *Supplement*, 101–17, and Musser, *Priesthood Issue*.

Chapter 2

26. "The Manifesto and the End of Plural Marriage," Gospel Topics on LDS.org, accessed July 26, 2016, https://www.lds.org/topics/the-manifesto-and-the-end-of-plural-marriage?lang=eng.
27. Wilford Woodruff journal, September 25, 1890, as quoted in "Manifesto and the End of Plural Marriage."
28. Jorgenson and Hardy, "Taylor-Cowley Affair," 10.
29. Wright, "Origins and Development," 51.
30. Jorgenson and Hardy, "Taylor-Cowley Affair," 10, 20–21.

31. Clark, *Messages of the First Presidency*, 4:84–85.

32. Anonymous, "Loyal Opposition."

33. Ibid.

34. Quinn, "LDS Church Authority," 12. See also Quinn, "Plural Marriages."

35. Letter, First Presidency to Presidents of Stakes, October 5, 1910, in Clark, *Messages of the First Presidency*, 4:216–18.

36. For example, a short list of "new" polygamists was published that included the name of Joseph W. Musser, later a prominent Fundamentalist Mormon, in "Just So that People Know," *Salt Lake Tribune*, October 21, 1910.

37. Alexander, *Mormonism in Transition*, 65–66; Briney, *Apostles on Trial*, 54–55, 117–18.

38. Diary entry of August 1, 1915, in Nathaniel Baldwin Diaries, 1897–1961, University of Utah Marriott Library Special Collections, Manuscripts, Accession 1298. See also Baldwin, *Times of the Gentiles*.

39. Parkinson, *Utah Woolley Family*, 97.

40. "Edwin Dilworth Woolley," Family Tree, FamilySearch.org, accessed June 27, 2016.

41. Jenson, *Latter-day Saint Biographical Encyclopedia*, 3:285.

42. Smoot and Sheriff, *City In-Between*, 361–62. See also Watson, "From Nineteenth-Century Mormon Polygamy," 151.

43. Smoot and Sheriff, *City In-Between*.

44. [Allred], "Biographical Sketch," 302. Warren Longhurst married his third wife, Eva Allred, on November 17, 1909, and later married her legally on November 28, 1912, in El Paso, Texas, after the death of his first wife, Myra Irene Allred, in September 1912.

45. "A Life Sketch of Ann Reed Everington Roberts 1826–1910," Family Tree, FamilySearch.org, accessed October 6, 2018.

46. Ibid.; Madsen, *Defender of the Faith*, 11.

47. Richins, "Journal of Amy Irene Woolley."

48. Ibid. Also, Mary Jessop Lavery and Kathleen Thompson Lavery, "Notes of a Conversation with Sister Olive Coombs, Daughter of Lorin C. Woolley," circa spring 1966, copy in possession of authors; Olive Woolley Coombs, interview by Randy Witman and Jeff Norman, June 9, 1987, transcript, copy in possession of authors.

49. In early Utah, some others also received endowments at a young age. For example, Jonathan Golden Kimball, a son of early LDS Apostle Heber C. Kimball, recorded receiving his endowment at age fourteen along with two half-siblings near the same age on January 5, 1867. Taylor, *Sermons of J. Golden Kimball*, 269.

50. Parkinson, *Utah Woolley Family*, 213–14.

51. Allred, *Indian Territory Mission*, March 28, 1897. See also Andrew Kimball Diary, January 25, 1897, in MS 2694, Andrew Kimball Papers 1884–1923, Church History Library.

52. "Union State Bank of Bountiful Gets its Charter," *Davis County Clipper*, May 9, 1913, 8; "Building Association Organized Monday," *Davis County Clipper*, December 19, 1913, 1; "Underwriters Trust Company," *Salt Lake Tribune*, March 11, 1917, 41; Ancestry.com, U.S. City Directories, 1822–1995, accessed June 22, 2016, www.ancestry.com; "United Sugar Company," Bizstanding, accessed July 4, 2016, https://bizstanding.com/directory/UT/UN/192; "New Corporations," *Salt Lake Telegram*, October 5, 1921, 12.

53. Lavery and Lavery, "Notes of a Conversation."

54. Watson, "From Nineteenth-Century Mormon Polygamy," 154–55.

55. Foster, "Plural Wives," 499.

56. Lavery and Lavery, "Notes of a Conversation."

57. "Mormons of Kaysville Still Pondering Over Remarks of Speaker in Ward House," *Salt Lake Telegram*, February 28, 1911, 6.

58. Ibid.

59. Ibid.

60. "Mormons of Kaysville."

61. "The Trial of John W. Taylor," Reed C. Durham papers, University of Utah Libraries, Special Collections, J. Willard Marriott Library. See also Musser, *Four Hidden Revelations*; Watson, "Corroborative Evidence."

62. Hales, "John Taylor's 1886 Revelation," 79–80.

63. Affidavit of John W. Woolley, January 16, 1914, typed transcript in possession of authors.

64. "Excommunication of John W. Woolley," *Salt Lake Tribune*, April 1, 1914, 5.

65. Lavery and Lavery, "Notes of a Conversation."

66. Musser and Broadbent, *Supplement*, 26.

Chapter 3

67. James E. Talmage Journals, January 15, 1924, and James Talmage Correspondence File, January 18, 1924, as quoted in Hales, "'I Love to Hear Him.'"

68. Foster, "Like Sparks of a Wildfire." See also Watson, "Nathaniel Baldwin's Lasting Legacies."

69. *Journal of Discourses*, 21:9–13, as cited in Nathaniel Baldwin, "Some Personal Experiences," typescript manuscript, n.d., copy in author's possession.

70. Baldwin, "Some Personal Experiences."

71. Singer, "Utah Inventor and Patron," 42–53.

72. Baldwin, "Some Personal Experiences."

73. Ibid.

74. Baldwin Diaries, March 4, 5, 14 and 20, 1922.

75. Singer, "Utah Inventor and Patron," 49.

76. Baldwin Diaries, January 21, 1921.

77. Ibid., April 25, 1922.

78. Nathaniel Baldwin Inc. was incorporated on June 23, 1922. Salt Lake County, Record of Incorporations, Utah State Archives. Of the original incorporators, only Lorin C. Woolley *had not* been previously involved with Baldwin's radio manufacturing.

79. Omega Investment Company was incorporated on June 30, 1922. Salt Lake County Clerk, Incorporation Records, Utah State Archives. Three other signers of incorporation papers for Nathaniel Baldwin Inc.—Delbert Osguthorpe, Ebenezer Johnson and Harvey Melville—were never involved in continued plural marriage.

80. Boss, *Interview with Moroni Jessop*, 3.

81. Baldwin Radio International was incorporated on January 9, 1923. Salt Lake County Records of Incorporation, Utah State Archives.

82. Watson, "Nathaniel Baldwin's Lasting Legacies."

83. Foy, *City Bountiful*, 91; Syracuse Historical Commission, *Community of Syracuse*, 73; *East of Antelope Island*, 212, 247, 411; FamilySearch.org.

84. "In Davis County," *Washington County News*, September 17, 1898, 2; *East of Antelope Island*, 333, 411; Driggs, "Imprisonment, Defiance, and Division," 69; "Some New Polygamists," *Salt Lake Tribune*, May 30, 1910, 4; "The Tribune Thrice Sustained," *Salt Lake Tribune*, September 29, 1910, 6.

85. FamilySearch.org; Olson, *History of Millville*, 6; *Millville Memories*, 85, 89–90, 160, 162.

86. "Aunt Fawn Jessop Broadbent's Early Experiences," 3, 4, photocopy of typescript in authors' possession.

87. "Richard S. Jessop—Scenes of Early Days [Jessop's]," 5, photocopy of typescript in possession of author.

88. Ibid., 3.

89. 1930 United States Federal Census, population schedule, Millville, Utah, E.D. 3-22, sheet 3B.

90. Hales, "'I Have Been Fanatically Religious.'"

91. Joseph White Musser Journals, August 13, 1922, as quoted in Watson, "From Nineteenth-Century Mormon Polygamy," 171.

92. Joseph White Musser Journals, March 30, 1940, as quoted in Hales, "'I Have Been Fanatically Religious.'"

93. Jenson, *Latter-day Saint Biographical Encyclopedia*, 3:350–51.

94. Syracuse Historical Commission, *Community of Syracuse*, 124, 266–67.

95. FamilySearch.org.

96 "Ancestor O' the Month: Walter Steed," marthasteedhowletthistory, accessed May 16, 2016, https://marthasteedhowletthistory.wordpress.com/2013/10/26/ancestor-o-the-month-walter-steed. Lillie Sandberg's marriage was probably performed by Israel Barlow Jr. or perhaps by ex-Apostle Matthias F. Cowley.

97. Allred, *Indian Territory Mission*, March 28, 1897, 4.

98. B. Harvey Allred married Dorothea Elsabeth Von Qualen on August 14, 1935. Kunz, *Voices of Women*, 301. An account of Harvey's defense at his church trial appears in Kunz, *Second Leaf in Review*, 125–51.

99. Sylvia Allred married Isaac Carling Spencer on June 18, 1928. Mary Viola Anderson, widow of Joseph Orlando Thompson, married William John Worth Kilgrow on November 11, 1928. Both plural marriages were performed by John W. Woolley at his home in Centerville. R.L. Spencer, interview by Marianne T. Watson, September 23, 2018. Jessop, *Journal and Other Personal Papers*, 120, 163, 214.

100. Jessop, *Journal and Other Personal Papers*, 163.

101. *Diary of Joseph Lyman Jessop* [hereafter *Jessop Diary*], January 28, 1928.

102. Ibid., 7–8; Driggs, "This Will Someday Be," 207; Bradley, *Kidnapped from that Land*, 46.

103. Four sources mention this event: 1) Joseph W. Musser Journal, contained in Musser, *Autobiography of Saint Joseph White Musser*; 2) Joseph W. Musser Book of Remembrance; 3) Boss, *Interview with Moroni Jessop* (Privately published, circa 1942); 4) *Jessop Diary*.

104. Boss, *Interview with Moroni Jessop*.

105. Lavery and Lavery, "Notes of a Conversation." See also "Obsequies Held Dec 16 for John W. Woolley," *Davis County Clipper*, December 21, 1918, 5.

106. Anonymous, "John W. Woolley," typescript biography, circa 1970, copy in author's possession.

107. Watson, "From Nineteenth-Century Mormon Polygamy," 173–75.

Chapter 4

108. Early publications by Priesthood Council members and associates included: 1) B. Harvey Allred, *A Leaf in Review* (Caldwell, ID: Caxton Printers, 1933); 2) J.L. Broadbent, comp., *Celestial Marriage?* (Salt Lake City: n.p., n.d. [1933]); 3) Joseph W. Musser, *New and Everlasting Covenant of Marriage* (Salt Lake City, n.p, 1933); 4) Musser and Broadbent, *Supplement*; and (5) Joseph W. Musser, *The Ballard-Jenson Correspondence* (Salt Lake City: Truth Publishing Company, [1934]).

109. "Official Statement from the First Presidency of the Church of Jesus Christ of Latter-day Saints," *Deseret News*, June 17, 1933.

110. Bradley, *Kidnapped from that Land*, 16–17.

111. *Jessop Diary*, April 7 and 11, May 3, 1934, 17–19, 58; "Official Statement," *Deseret News*, June 17, 1933.

112. *Jessop Diary*, May 24, 1934.

113. Ibid., April 21, May 24 and June 25, 1934; 19, 21, 25.

114. Ibid., September 23, 1934.

115. Rulon C. Allred, "Lorin C. Woolley," unpublished paper, n.d.

116. *Truth* 2, no. 8 (January 1937): 122.

117. Utah department of Health, Office of Vital Records and Statistics, Death Certificates, series 81448, file no. 67; *Jessop Diary*, September 23, 1934.

118. Hyde, "Inside 'The Order.'" This was one of several sources that mentioned DCCS members calling the group "The Order."

119. A leader of the Latter Day Church of Christ, interview by Craig L. Foster, March 24, 2018, and typescript of the discussion, prepared by representatives of the Latter Day Church of Christ.

120. Ibid. See also "Articles of Incorporation of the Davis County Cooperative Society," State of Utah, Secretary of State's Office, August 23, 1941.

121. *Jessop Diary*, March 16, 1935.

122. Bradley, *Kidnapped from that Land*, 16–17.

123. *Jessop Diary*, March 23, March 25 and April 4, 1934.

124. Ibid., May 10, 1935.

125. Ibid., May 13–14, 17 and 23, 1935.

126. Ibid., May 17, 1935.

127. Driggs, "'There Must Be No Compromise," 210.

128. *Jessop Diary*, August 15, 1935.

129. Driggs, "'There Must Be No Compromise,'" 210; Bradley, *Kidnapped from that Land*, 52.

130. *Jessop Diary*, July 7 and 21, 1935.

131. Driggs, "'There Must Be No Compromise,'" 210; *Jessop Diary*, July 7 and 21, 1935. See also Watson, "Short Creek," 71–87.

132. *Jessop Diary*, July 26 and August 6, 1935.

133. Ibid., August 7 and 9, 1935; Driggs, "'There Must Be No Compromise,'" 213–14. *Truth*, January 1936; Bradley, *Kidnapped from that Land*, 54; Stegner, *Mormon Country*, 220. Jack Childress, a homesteader, signed the complaints.

134. Bradley, *Kidnapped from that Land*, 56; *Mohave County Miner*, September 6, 1935. See also Bradley, *Kidnapped from that Land*, 56–63, 224–25; Driggs, "'There Must Be No Compromise,'" 211.

135. Bradley, *Kidnapped from that Land*, 61.

136. Ibid., 54, 55, 62; Driggs, "'There Must Be No Compromise,'" 213, 214; "Short Creek Embroglio," *Truth* 1 (October 1935): 51.

137. Joseph W. Musser Diary, November 13, 1936. Today, "keys of priesthood," as it is commonly understood among Fundamentalists, refers to men who have been ordained apostles, set apart to seal marriages and keep the fulness of the gospel alive upon the earth.

138. Ibid.

139. Ibid.

140. Watson, "Short Creek," 80–81.

141. Ibid.

142. Ibid.

143. Quinn, *J. Reuben Clark*, 183.

144. Quinn, *Elder Statesman*, 237, 238, 244, 251. Quinn's biographies of Clark drew from Clark's correspondence, of which identical copies are included in Bishop Curtis's surveillance records in Utah State Archives' Polygamy Investigation Files, photocopies in authors' possession.

145. Letter, Hawthorne Ward Bishopric by Bishop to the First Presidency, Attention Pres. J. Reuben Clark Jr., October 4, 1939.

146. Ibid.

Chapter 5

147. *Jessop Diary*, March 7, 1945.

148. Ibid.

149. Ibid.

150. Ibid.

151. Ibid. See also Joseph W. Musser Journal, March 7, 1944, and Kelsch, *Louis Alma Kelsch*, 49.

152. "Utah Polygamy Probe Delayed," *Arizona Republic*, March 9, 1944, 4.

153. "LDS Leaders Uphold Action to Stamp Out Polygamy," *Salt Lake Tribune*, March 8, 1944, 1; "Church Makes Statement," *Arizona Republic*, March 8, 1944, 2.

154. *Time*, March 20, 1944, 55.

155. "20 Face Trial for Polygamy," *Detroit News*, March 8, 1944, 3; "Trial of Cult Leaders Set," *Milwaukee Journal*, March 8, 1944, 6; "Utah Cult Leaders Charged," *Arizona Republic*, March 11, 1944, 5; "Fundamental Polygamists," *Newsweek*, March 20, 1944, 86; "Fundamentalists," *Time*, March 20, 1944, 55; "Score Testify in Cult Trial," *Ogden Standard-Examiner*, October 1, 1944, 1.

156. *Jessop Diary*, March 7, 1945.

157. Ibid.

158. Musser, "Brief Biographical Sketch."

159. "Defense Calls Up Witnesses in Polygamy Trial," *Ogden Standard-Examiner*, October 3, 1944, 1.

160. "Excerpts from Sermon Given by President John Y. Barlow," February 6, 1944, *Johnson Sermons*, vol. 7. (Hildale, UT: Twin City Courier Press, 1990), 10.

161. Musser Journal, February 29, 1944.

162. Driggs, "John Boyden's 1944 Campaign."

163. Musser Journal, February 29, 1944.

164. *Truth*, December 1940.

165. Fred E. Curtis, Polygamy Investigations 1954–1960, Utah State Archives. See also Watson, "Fred E. Curtis Papers."

166. State charges were filed against thirty-two persons: Dr. Rulon C. Allred, Albert E. Barlow, Edmund F. Barlow, Ianthius W. Barlow, John Y. Barlow, Juanita Barlow, Ruth Barlow, Oswald Braininch, John G. Butchereit, Heber Kimball Cleveland, Marie Beth Barlow Cleveland, Zola Chatwin Cleveland, David Brigham Darger, Jean Barlow Darger, Mabel Finlayson, Melba Finlayson, J. Marion Hammon, Rulon Timpson Jeffs, Leona Jeffs, Joseph Lyman Jessop, George H. Kalmar, Louis Alma Kelsch, Morris Q. Kunz, Rhea Allred Kunz, Rose W. LeBaron, Myrtle Lloyd, Mary Mills, Guy Musser, Joseph W. Musser, Robert Leslie Shrewsbury, Alma A. Timpson and Charles F. Zitting. "Preliminaries Open in Prosecution of Polygamy Suspects," *Salt Lake Tribune*, March 9, 1944, 13. See also Utah Supreme Court file in case no. 6816, State of Utah v. Joseph White Musser, et al.

167. The twenty federal defendants were: Dr. Rulon C. Allred, John Y. Barlow, Arnold Boss, William Chatwin, Heber Kimball Cleveland, Edna

Christensen, David Brigham Darger, Theral Ray Dockstader, J. Marion Hammon, David W. Jeffs, Rulon T. Jeffs, Vergal T. Jessop, Leroy S. Johnson, Louis A. Kelsch, Guy H. Musser, Foillis Gardner Petty, L.R. Stubbs, Joseph W. Musser, Dr. LeGrand Woolley and Charles F. Zitting. "Jury Enters Total of 61 Indictments," *Salt Lake Tribune*, March 12, 1944, 1B.

168. "Cultists Appeal to High Court," *Salt Lake Tribune*, June 20, 1944, 11 (Part II).

169. United States v. Barlow et al, 56 F. Supp. 795, 796 (D. Utah 1944).

170. Driggs, "John Boyden's 1944 Campaign."

171. *Jessop Diary*, May 24, 1944. The photo essay was published by *Life* in its July 3, 1944 issue. Note also "UTAH POLYGAMY TRIALS," *Life*, April 3, 1944, 38–39, photographs of the Rulon Allred family.

172. Musser, *Celestial or Plural Marriage*.

173. Carter, *Heart Throbs*, 458–59. See also Musser, "Factions," 94–96.

174. "Polygamy Probe Names 46," *Salt Lake Tribune*, March 7, 1944; "Forty Arrested on Indictment in Polygamy Probe," *Deseret News*, March 7, 1944.

175. *Jessop Diary*, August 27 and 31, October 8 and December 2, 1945.

176. Bradley, *Kidnapped from that Land*, 86–87, 229; *Salt Lake Telegram*, November 10, 1944; *Salt Lake Tribune*, November 11, 1944; "The Conspiracy Cases," *TRUTH* 12, no. 9 (February 1947): 246.

177. Driggs, "Imprisonment, Defiance, and Division," 65–95.

178. Kelsch, *Louis Alma Kelsch*, 32–33; Driggs, "Imprisonment, Defiance, and Division"; Driggs, "Guide to Old Fashioned (Fundamentalist) Mormonism."

179. *Jessop Diary*, August 15, 1935.

180. Musser Journal, November 13, 1936.

181. Bronson, *Winnie*, 202

182. This ordination took place on September 18, 1950. Rulon C. Allred, Poulson, Montana, May 17, 1959, transcription, published in *History of the Priesthood Split*, 67–72. For an FLDS version of the Rulon Allred's "supposed ordination," see Jeffs, *History of Priesthood Succession*, 252–53.

183. Allred's calling was announced in a Fundamentalist meeting on October 29, 1950; Seventies Meeting Minutes, May 12, 1974, in *History of the Priesthood Split*, 80.

184. Ibid.

185. Vera Cook Allred recorded on May 2, 1952, that those opposing Musser were saying, "He is old and incapacitated and doesn't know what he's doing." Vera Allred, "A Personal Witness," in *History of the Priesthood Split*, 103. Robert Eaby recorded, "There are those going about telling that

Joseph has lost his mind because of his infirmaties [*sic*]....I told him that I believed he was not demented as some say." Robert Eaby, Diary, June 16, 1951, transcript of entry, photocopy in authors' possession.

186. *Jessop Diary*, July 2, 1952.

187. Seventies Meeting Minutes, May 12, 1974, in *History of the Priesthood Split*, 83.

188. Ibid., May 6, 1951; Seventies Meeting Minutes, May 12, 1974, in *History of the Priesthood Split*, 86–87.

189. *Jessop Diaries*, January 12, 1952; Marvin L. Allred, "Witness and Testimony by Marvin L. Allred," in *History of the Priesthood Split*, 13.

190. *Jessop Diaries*, November 15, 1952.

191. AUB Rulon C. Allred, Discourse, May 15, 1966, Murray, Utah in Fulton, *Gems*, 1:44; Briney, *Silencing Mormon Polygamy*, 28.

192. Charles F. Zitting died on July 14, 1954. Priesthood lineage charts changed sometime after 1978 when one of the authors visited homes of Short Creek (Colorado City) that included J. Leslie Broadbent, Joseph W. Musser and Charles F. Zitting. In 1991, new charts no longer included Zitting, Broadbent and Musser, consistent with Jeffs, *History of the Priesthood Succession*, 277.

193. Kelsch, *Louis Alma Kelsch*, 86.

194. *Jessop Diaries*, February 2, 1953.

195. Ibid., August 23–24, 1950.

196. Ibid., September 10, 1952.

197. Ibid., February 7, 1953.

Chapter 6

198. Bistline, *Polygamists*, 87, 91.

199. Ibid., 87.

200. Alvin Smith Barlow, interview by the authors, Colorado City, Arizona, July 2, 2016.

201. Bradley, *Kidnapped from that Land*, 131.

202. *Arizona Daily Star*, July 27, 1953, as quoted in Bradley, *Kidnapped from that Land*, 131.

203. Bradley, *Kidnapped from that Land*, 133.

204. Ibid.

205. Ibid., 134.

206. Ibid., 137.

207. Ibid., 138.

208. Ibid., 141.

209. "Patriarch of Polygamists Dies at 83," *Tucson Daily Citizen*, September 2, 1953.

210. Kelly and Cohn, "Arizona's 1953 Raid"; "Joseph Smith Jessop Arrested," *Tucson Daily Citizen*, July 27, 1953, accessed August 6, 2016, https://familysearch.org/photos/artifacts/9836481.

211. Bradley, *Kidnapped from that Land*, 196–206.

212. "Reprehensible Raid," *Iron County Record*, July 30, 1953, 2.

213. Kelly and Cohn, "Arizona's 1953 Raid."

214. Bistline, *Polygamists*, 94–95.

215. Judge Paul Anderson to Paul LaPrade, September 11, 1953, Utah State Archives, as quoted in Driggs, "Who Shall Raise the Children?," 34.

216. Driggs, "Who Shall Raise the Children?," 45.

217. Ibid.

Chapter 7

218. Bradley, *Kidnapped from that Land*, 163–64.

219. "Utahn Pleads Guilty of Cohabitation," *Salt Lake Tribune*, December 4, 1955, 10C; "Judge Orders Cohabitation Prison Term," *Salt Lake Tribune*, December 18, 1955, 8B. Special thanks to Ken Driggs for providing the authors with a copy of his unpublished 215-page manuscript "Chronology of Mormon Fundamentalism."

220. "Survey Totals Polygamy in Utah at 2,000," *Salt Lake Tribune*, February 29, 1956, 21.

221. Melba Allred, "Priesthood History," typescript, 28–29, photocopy in possession of authors. In 1961, Allred purchased the Pinesdale ranch, ten miles northwest of Hamilton possibly in response to public statements by Utah attorney general Walter Budge in 1960 urging "a stepped-up attack on polygamy" and tried to get a bill passed which would make it lawful to put in prison any woman who entered into polygyny and any legal wife who knew of and gave her consent to it. The bill did not pass. Budge died suddenly on December 10, 1961, and his successor, A. Pratt Kessler, "showed little interest in pursuing polygamy investigations." Also, "Walter Budge Urges Davis Attack on Polygamy," *Salt Lake Tribune*, February 26, 1960; "Attorney Notes Plan to Check on Polygamists," *Salt Lake Tribune*, April 6, 1960; Hilton, "Polygamy in Utah," 89.

222. Jessop and Baker, *Legacy of Love*, 250, 260.
223. Rogers and Roueche, "Rulon C. Allred," 266–68. Rogers and Roueche's essay is a fascinating account of the turmoil caused by numerous forced moves and the toll it took as the large Allred family avoided the law while seeking a place of refuge for Utah polygamists.
224. Former Pinesdale resident, interview by Craig L. Foster, November 8, 2018; Higgins, "Polygamy in Montana"; Jessop and Baker, *Legacy of Love*, 338.
225. "To Report on Polygamous Cult," *Logan Herald Journal*, October 12, 1962, 6.
226. Bistline, *Polygamists*, 139.
227. Ibid., 128.
228. Spafford, "Changing and Unchanging," 315–16.
229. Ibid., 322. From numerous visits to Colorado City and nearby Centennial Park between 2010 and 2016, it was apparent to the authors that jean skirts and other casual types of skirts are popular among Centennial Park women when working and running errands.
230. Ibid., 324–25. The last comment is attributed to Carolyn Jessop, who was raised in the group but later left it and is now a vocal critic.
231. Ibid., 316–19.
232. Ibid., 319–21. The men's and boys' clothing changed very little other than their shirts are plain and in a "pioneer"-type pattern and, of course, also in pastel (mostly yellows and blues) and white for church and indoor activities, with darker blue, green and brown for working outside.
233. Bronson, *History of Rocky Ridge*, 4–5, 11.
234. Ibid., 8–9, 11, 15; anonymous granddaughter of Marvin Allred, interview by Craig L. Foster, September 18, 2016.
235. Two anonymous granddaughters of Marvin Allred, interview by Craig L. Foster, September 18, 2016. Family Home Evening is a program started in the LDS Church where families gather together for spiritual lessons, games and activities. Many Fundamentalist Mormons also follow this program.
236. Anonymous granddaughters of Marvin Allred, interview; Bronson, *History of Rocky Ridge*, 79.
237. "Women Kill Utah Surgeon," *Visalia Times Delta*, May 11, 1977, 9A; "Murray Naturopath Slain," *Deseret News*, May 11, 1977, 12A; Jessop and Baker, *Legacy of Love*, 419–20.
238. [Youngest daughter of Rulon Allred], "Memories of When Daddy Died," and "From the Diary of [Anonymous] 1977," Diary transcripts,

May 10 and May 14, 1977; private collection of transcribed personal experiences concerning the death of Rulon C. Allred, copy in possession of authors.

239. "Doctor's Killers Elude Police," *Deseret News*, May 12, 1977, 6B.

240. "Murder Motive Still Unknown," *Deseret News*, May 13, 1977, 1B.

241. Jessop and Baker, *Legacy of Love*, 421.

242. Wright, "Origins and Development," 99–101.

243. Ibid. See also Hicks, "On the Trail," 39–40.

244. LeBaron, *Mark My Son*, 21.

245. Ibid., 42.

246. Ibid, 43–95.

247. Ibid., 96–98.

248. Jessop and Baker, *Legacy of Love*, 279, 345, 346, 382, 387, 388.

249. Ibid., 40–41; Harris, "LeBaron's Former Wife Admits to Murder."

250. Anonymous friend of Ross LeBaron, interview, August 24, 2018.

251. LeBaron, *LeBaron Story*, vii. See also Horiuchi, "Authorities Hope Convictions End LeBaron Saga," and "Ervil Morrell LeBaron," Murderpedia, accessed September 16, 2016, http://murderpedia.org/male.L/l/lebaron-ervil.htm.

252. A former friend of Gerald Peterson, interview by Craig L. Foster, August 24, 2018.

253. Ibid.

254. A former wife of Gerald W. Peterson Sr., interview by Marianne T. Watson, July 12, 2018. Notes in authors' possession. The former wife, who left Peterson, also claimed, "He said he would never die, but when it was time for him to leave, he would be taken up in a space ship. He said God lived in the center of the earth and sent angels in spacecraft to check on people. I got to where I didn't believe a thing he said." Righteous Branch representatives acknowledged the elder Peterson had a great interest in space, aliens and so on but were not aware of any claims of angels in spacecraft.

255. "Guy" and "Marie," representatives of the Righteous Branch, telephone interview by Craig L. Foster, September 1, 2018.

256. Marianne Watson phone interview with anonymous friend of the Peterson Group, July 8, 2018.

257. "Righteous Branch of the Church of Jesus Christ of Latter-day Saints," Revolvy, accessed August 6, 2018, https://www.revolvy.com/page/Righteous-Branch-of-the-Church-of-Jesus-Christ-of-Latter%252Dday-Saints.

258. "Guy" and "Marie," interview. Both Guy and Marie were converted by missionaries while living in Idaho. They eventually gathered to the church's headquarters outside of Tonopah.

259. Ivins, "Polygamy on Increase"; Briscoe, "Prosecution of Polygamists Waning."

Chapter 8

260. Watson, "1948 Secret Marriage," 84–85.

261. Bistline, *Colorado City Polygamists*, 106–8, 122–23.

262. Don Timpson, interview by Craig L. Foster and Newell G. Bringhurst, May 6, 2010.

263. Mark Timpson, interview by Craig L. Foster, August 9, 2011.

264. Ibid., 154–55. Also, Bringhurst and Foster, "1980s Schism within Fundamentalist Mormonism," 328–29. Among themselves, this group, like other Fundamentalists, call themselves and their endeavors "The Work," meaning the "Priesthood Work."

265. Bringhurst and Foster, "1980s Schism within Fundamentalist Mormonism," 333–34.

266. Ibid., 337.

267. M. Timpson, interview.

268. Bringhurst and Foster, "1980s Schism within Fundamentalist Mormonism," 328.

269. John Nielsen, interview by Craig L. Foster and Marianne T. Watson, October 27, 2018.

270. "Excerpts from the Journal of David William Ward Jeffs, Father of our Prophet" as reprinted in *Alta Academy Student Star* 16, no. 12 (April 1994): 287–90. According to "A Brief History of the Life of Judson Tolman," http://www.sedgewickresearch.com/tolman/jtolman.htm, accessed October 31, 2014. In October 1910, Tolman was excommunicated for "performing plural marriages, for marrying illegally himself, and for lying about it." He was re-baptized into the LDS Church in February 1912 and died in July 1916, just short of his ninetieth birthday. For a lengthier discussion of Rulon and Warren Jeffs, see Bringhurst and Foster, "Rulon and Warren Jeffs," 269–309.

271. "Rulon Timpson Jeffs," Family Tree of FamilySearch.org, accessed August 18, 2016, https://familysearch.org/tree/#view=ancestor&section=details&person=K2WT-131.

272. Jeffs, "Personal History," 20–21.

273. Bringhurst and Foster, "Rulon and Warren Jeffs," 281, 285.

274. Ibid., 287.

275. Ibid., 284–85.

276. Willie Jessop, interview by Newell G. Bringhurst and Craig L. Foster, March 29, 2013.

277. Brower, *Prophet's Prey*, 52–53.

278. W. Jessop, interview.

279. Jethro Barlow, interview by Newell G. Bringhurst and Craig L. Foster, April 8, 2012.

280. Bringhurst and Foster, "Rulon and Warren Jeffs," 291; "Anonymous," interview by Newell G. Bringhurst and Craig L. Foster, August 8, 2010. Note that "Anonymous" still has family who are FLDS and is concerned about repercussions against family members.

281. Escobedo, "Warren Jeffs' Son"; Collman, "Daughter of Polygamist Cult Leader."

282. Donald Timpson, interview by Newell G. Bringhurst and Craig L. Foster, May 6, 2012.

283. Bringhurst and Foster, "Rulon and Warren Jeffs, 292.

284. Rebecca Musser, telephone interview by Craig L. Foster on May 11, 2013; Jethro Barlow, interview by Craig L. Foster and Newell G. Bringhurst, August 9, 2011, as quoted in Bringhurst and Foster, "Rulon and Warren Jeffs," 302.

285. John Nielsen, email to Craig L. Foster, November 4, 2018. The email included attached "membership paper signed by Warren and his counselors in 2004, They [*sic*] church is listed as the Church of Jesus Christ of Latter Days Saints…Without the Fundamentalist.…BY [*sic*] this time Warren had the mindset that he was the true church and God wanted him to stop using the name FLDS."

286. Bringhurst and Foster, "Rulon and Warren Jeffs," 303.

287. W. Jessop, interview.

288. "Anonymous ex-FLDS," interview by Craig L. Foster, November 7, 2014.

289. Bringhurst and Foster, "Rulon and Warren Jeffs," 306–7.

290. Copies of Warren Steed Jeffs' Priesthood Ordination certificate and Bishop's Record provided courtesy of John Nielsen.

291. Perkins and Winslow, "Fugitive Polygamist Leader."

292. Ibid.

293. "Polygamist Jeffs Tried to Hang Himself in Jail, Documents Say," CNN, November 7, 2007, accessed August 29, 2016, http://www.cnn.

com/2007/US/law/11/07/jeffs/index.html?eref=yahoo. There were two suicide attempts: once by banging his head against the wall, second by attempting to hang himself.

294. Visit to the Yearning For Zion Ranch and interview with Nick Hanna of the Texas Rangers, October 28, 2017, interview notes in possession of authors.

295. Bennion, "Many Faces of Polygamy," 164.

296. This description is based on what one of the authors, Craig L. Foster, personally witnessed while visiting the office to conduct an interview on August 1, 2010.

297. David Jeffs, interview by Newell G. Bringhurst and Craig L. Foster, August 9, 2011.

298. Isaac Wyler, interview by Newell G. Bringhurst and Craig L. Foster, August 9, 2011.

299. James Zitting, interview by Newell G. Bringhurst and Craig L. Foster, July 26, 2013.

300. Anonymous uncle of Warren Jeffs, telephone interview by Craig L. Foster, September 16, 2015.

301. Lorin Holm, interview by Craig L. Foster, March 8, 2014.

302. O'Neill, "Witnesses." In the latter half of the 1800s, the LDS Church created the United Order movement in which members willingly worked together to produce goods, grow crops and raise animals and then shared with one another, ensuring there would be no poor in the community. The communities were allowed to choose to what extent they would live communally. Some communities like Brigham City, Utah, were patterned more like a collective, with selected community ventures such as a woolen mill; other communities went much further in communal living, such as eating all meals together as a community. Probably the most extreme was Orderville, Utah, where people had all in common, even dressing alike. Some united orders were more successful than others. Most had ceased functioning by the 1890s. The FLDS united order, called the United Effort Plan, while taking the name of the earlier LDS experiment, did not follow the same pattern.

303. O'Neill, "Witnesses"; anonymous uncle of Warren Jeffs, interview (2015).

304. O'Neill, "Witnesses."

305. Ferguson, "Tip Led to Lyle Jeffs' Capture"; Carlisle, "Lyle Jeffs."

306. Anonymous uncle of Warren Jeffs, interview (2015).

307. Benson, "About Utah."

308. Carlisle, "Why Polygamists Are Leaving."

309. Anonymous uncle of Warren Jeffs, telephone interview by Craig L. Foster, November 3, 2018. Warren Jeffs's former favorite wife, Naomi Jessop, now resides with other wives of Warren's in Merril Jessop's Cedar City home. A confidential source expressed surprise about Warren's exiling and punishing her this way inasmuch as she knows about his illicit activities. If she were to decide to talk, as a way of retaliation for her exile and punishment, she could reveal quite a lot.

310. Ibid.

311. Ibid.

312. Hollenhorst, "Sex Banned."

313. Phil Mackert Jr., interview by Newell G. Bringhurst & Craig L. Foster, July 26, 2013.

314. O'Neill, "Witnesses."

315. Anonymous uncle of Warren Jeffs, interview (2018).

316. Anonymous uncle of Warren Jeffs, interviews (2015, 2018).

317. Dowayne Barlow, interview by Craig L. Foster, July 3, 2017; text messaging between Dowayne Barlow and Craig L. Foster, November 9, 2018.

318. Notes taken by the authors at the July Fourth celebration, Colorado City, Arizona, July 2, 2016.

Chapter 9

319. Laforêt, "Ce Mormon," 106–7.

320. Rayburn, "Green Says Charges Bogus."

321. Cantera, "Green Bitter Over Verdict."

322. "Utah Polygamist Convicted of Child Rape for Sex with Young Bride." *Billings Gazette*, June 24, 2002, accessed August 26, 2017, http://billingsgazette.com/news/world/utah-polygamist-convicted-of-child-rape-for-sex-with-young/article_052c8320-341d-539e-aeaa-fd313407492c.html.

323. Hyde, "Inside 'The Order.'" This was one of a number of sources that mentioned DCCS members calling the group "The Order."

324. A leader of the Latter Day Church of Christ, interview by Craig L. Foster, March 24, 2018, and typescript prepared by representatives of the Latter Day Church of Christ.

325. Ibid.

326. Ibid.

327. "The Kingston Clan: The Largest Sex Crime Organization in the United States of America," www.thekingstonclan.com, accessed April 2, 2018. Please note that information about co-operative-owned businesses comes from a website critical of the Kingstons and that a DCCS representative said the list of businesses was inaccurate. As of July 2, 2018, the website no longer exists and is the property of a Bryan D. Nelson. However, the authors printed the list of businesses before they were taken down. Also, partial lists of the businesses may be found at "Escaping Polygamy: Support Young Girls and Boys," Facebook.com, accessed July 2, 2018; Adams, "Kingston Inc."

328. A leader of the Latter Day Church of Christ, interview by Craig L. Foster, March 24, 2018, and April 30, 2018, as well as typescript prepared by representatives of the Latter Day Church of Christ.

329. Ibid.; Carlisle, "New Website Targets Kingston"; Osmond, "Organizational Identification," 20.

330. "Polygamy Suspects Flee, Davis Grand Jury Reports," *Ogden Standard-Examiner*, September 23, 1959, 1B; "Judge Issues 30-Day Term to Davis Jury Witness," *Salt Lake Tribune*, December 24, 1959, 22; "Davis Jurors Meet Today to Prepare Final Report," *Salt Lake Tribune*, December 29, 1959, 20.

331. "Polygamy, Detention Homes Aired," *Sunday Herald*, March 13, 1960, 2.

332. "Polygamist Is Convicted of Incest," *New York Times*, June 4, 1999, accessed September 4, 2017, http://www.nytimes.com/1999/06/04/us/polygamist-is-convicted-of-incest.html.

333. "Incest Defines Kingstons: Ex-Member Speaks Out on the Multi-Million Dollar Empire," HJNews.com, April 26, 1999, accessed September 4, 2017, http://news.hjnews.com/incest-defines-kingstons-ex-member-speaks-out-on-the-multi/article_091108e7-6897-55c2-b804-ed3c54c4c5de.html.

334. Anonymous leader of the Latter Day Church of Christ, interview by Craig L. Foster.

335. "Mary Ann Kingston Files Lawsuit Against Family," CNN.com, August 29, 2003, http://transcripts.cnn.com/TRANSCRIPTS/0308/29/se.05.html; Winslow, "Kingston Daughter's Lawsuit"; Winslow, "Kingston Lawsuits Are Settled."

336. Carlisle, "Girls in Polygamous Kingston Group."

337. Ibid.

338. Carlisle, "Utah Investigated"; Carlisle, "Utah Attorney General."

339. Miller, "State Wants to Seize $1M."

340. Harkins, "Two Members of Polygamous Group"; Carlisle, "Suspects in Kingston Case"; Carlisle, "Brothers Accused."

341. "Polygamist Church Bilked Woman, Judge Rules." *Deseret News*, March 6, 2003, accessed September 4, 2017, http://www.deseretnews.com/article/968665/Polygamist-church-bilked-woman-judge-rules.html.

342. "Virginia HILL, Plaintiff, Appellant, and Cross-Appellee, v. ESTATE OF Owen A. ALLRED; Corporation of the Presiding Elder of the Apostolic United Brethren; J. LaMoine Jenson; Jenson Lumber Corporation, Inc.; and Estate of John C. Putvin, Defendants, Appellees, and Cross-Appellants, Dennis E. Matthews; Jeffrey J. Norman; James E. Sandmire; Diamond Auto Specialists, Inc.; Diamond Recreational Rentals, Inc.; Pacific Rim Mortgage and Loan Services, Inc.; Pacific Rim Mortgage Brokers, Inc.; Diamond Auto Body and Paint; Brisan Imports; and Last Resort Enterprises, Inc., Defendants and Appellee," FindLaw for Legal Professionals, May 1, 2009, accessed September 4, 2017, http://caselaw.findlaw.com/ut-supreme-court/1132717.html.

343. Cantera and Vigh, "Elizabeth a 'Plural Wife?'"; Dobner, "Manifesto Focuses on Plural Wives"; Bernick and Spangler, "Story Heightens Perceptions."

344. Adams, "LDS Church Criticizes Media."

345. Foster, "Separated but not Divorced," 54. The article can also be accessed electronically at http://www.mormoninterpreter.com/separated-but-not-divorced-the-lds-churchs-uncomfortable-relationship-with-its-polygamous-past.

346. Ibid., 74. Happily, in recent years, the Church of Jesus Christ has striven to help members and nonmembers alike understand its polygamous past by publishing gospel topics essays under the subject heading of "Plural Marriage in the Church of Jesus Christ of Latter-day Saints," found at https://www.lds.org/topics/plural-marriage-in-the-church-of-jesus-christ-of-latter-day-saints?lang=eng.

347. Batchelor, Watson and Wilde, *Voices in Harmony*.

348. Adams, "Polygamous Families Plan Rally."

349. Winslow, "State Urged to Scrap Its Law."

350. Adams, "Will the Polygamy Debate."

351. Kody Brown, telephone interview by Craig L. Foster, October 26, 2018.

352. Ibid.

353. Ibid.; Dobner, "'Sister Wives' Family."

354. Foster, "Modern Media Stereotyping," 555, 557, 559. For a detailed discussion of media reaction to the Waddoups decision, see the above article, 555–60.

355. Ibid. These comments were made on Sunday, December 15, 2013, at the weekly church meeting of the AUB in Bluffdale, Utah. Notes in authors' possession.

356. Dobner, "Appeals Court Strikes Down Ruling."

357. Brown, interview; "Family Tree," FamilySearch.org, accessed October 29, 2018. According to Family Tree, Matheson has at least three polygamous ancestors on his father's side of the family tree.

358. Winslow, "U.S. Supreme Court Won't Hear."

359. Utah State Legislature, "Bigamy Offense Amendments," by Representative Michael E. Noel, H.B. 99, 2017 General Session, Salt Lake City: Utah Legislature, 2017, accessed November 14, 2017, https://le.utah.gov/~2017/bills/static/HB0099.html.

360. Carlisle, "Utah Polygamists Unite"; Price, "Polygamous Families Protest Bigamy Law"; Lockhart, "We're Not Going Away.'"

361. Carlisle, "Lawyer Contends Bigamy Bill."

362. Mike Noel, interview by Craig L. Foster, February 10, 2017, notes in authors' possession; Ritchey, "Bigamy Bill Brings Dueling Protests."

363. Carlisle, "Utah Senator Pointed to His Daughter."

364. Brown, interview.

365. Kyler Henderson, adult son of Kyle and Nicole Henderson, said the prosecutor offered a plea in abeyance deal with only a one-year probation because he said his case was falling apart when even their own expert witness agreed that Nicole's bruising was inconsistent with abuse; Kyler Henderson, interview by Marianne T. Watson, February 10, 2019; Weeser, "Family of Spiritual Bigamist Defends"; Carlisle, "Jury Acquits Man."

366. McCombs, "Woman on 'My Five Wives' Accuses Father"; Carlisle, "Utah Polygamous Church Investigating Molestation."

367. "Star of 'My Five Wives' Claims She was Molested by Her Polygamist Father as a Child in Attempt to Take On "Cover-Ups' in Rural Utah Communities." *Daily Mail*, November 23, 2014, accessed November 24, 2014, https://www.dailymail.co.uk/news/article-2845810/Woman-reality-Five-Wives-claims-molested-group-leader-polygamist-father-12-years-old.html; Carlisle, "Sex Abuse Allegations."

368. Barrett, "Mt. Pleasant Subdivision Causes Controversy."

369. Driggs, "Imprisonment, Defiance, and Division," 72.

370. "Louis Alma Kelsch," MormonFundamentalism.com, accessed November 20, 2018, http://www.mormonfundamentalism.com/archive/ChartLinks/LouisAlmaKelsch.htm.

371. "Author Ogden Kraut, 75, Dies," *Deseret News*, July 21, 2002, accessed November 20, 2018, https://www.deseretnews.com/article/926667/Author-Ogden-Kraut-75-dies.html; "Ogden W. Kraut," Legacy.com, accessed November 20, 2018, http://www.legacy.com/obituaries/deseretnews/obituary.aspx?n=ogden-w-kraut&pid=408769.

372. Alan Taylor, "Polygamists in 'The Rock'"; Adams, "Fearing Doomsday."

373. Enoch Foster, interview by Craig L. Foster and Marianne Watson, July 21, 2017.

374. Ibid.

375. Carlisle, "Polygamists' Son."

Chapter 10

376. Many Fundamentalists have Mormon pioneer ancestors, including handcart pioneers, who crossed the plains to Utah. For a discussion about these early church members, particularly those who also lived polygamy, see Watson, "Polygamous Ancestry of Contemporary Fundamentalist Mormons," 434–71. According to several emails and telephone interviews with trek youth and leaders, the experience was positive. As they are accustomed to being misjudged and negatively treated by members of mainstream society, including many LDS Church members, a rumor spread among some AUB youth that the Mormon youth and their leaders didn't want any contact with the Fundamentalist group. However, AUB adults said the LDS leaders had been very friendly and accommodating. LDS youth leaders actually invited the AUB youth leaders to have their group join their camp one night to hear a program of historical narrations. The invitation was greatly appreciated but declined due to the logistics and safety of getting over five hundred youth to and from the other camp in the dark. Those aware of the friendly and generous invitation were genuinely touched by this demonstration of cooperation and respect.

377. Holland, "That Our Children May Know."

378. Anonymous Fundamentalist teen sisters, interview by Craig L. Foster, October 5, 2016.

379. Anonymous Fundamentalist teen sisters, interview by Craig L. Foster, September 9, 2018.

380. Word, *Letters to Sarah*, 52, 53, 64, and 71.

381. [Priesthood Council members], AUB Priesthood Conference, September 23, 2018. Notes in possession of authors.

382. Batchelor, Watson and Wilde, *Voices in Harmony*, 89.

383. Evelyn Jessop Thompson, telephone interview, September 7, 2018.

384. Personal knowledge of author, Marianne T. Watson, as related on September 7, 2018.

385. Anonymous Rocky Ridge woman, interview by Craig L. Foster, September 9, 2018.

386. Anonymous AUB woman, telephone interview by Craig L. Foster, September 15, 2018.

387. Watson, "Polygamous Ancestry of Contemporary Fundamentalist Mormons," 434–35.

388. Word, *Letters to Sarah*, 112.

389. Grossman and Friedman, "Is Three Still a Crowd?."

390. Berry, "Sister Wives and the Slippery Slope."

391. Deboer, "It's Time to Legalize Polygamy."

392. McDermott and Hudson, "Don't Legalize Polygamy"; "Hey, It's 2015. Polygamy Isn't OK Anymore, Anywhere," *Arizona Republic*, accessed May 12, 2015, https://www.azcentral.com/story/opinion/editorial/2015/05/12/polygamous-towns-remain-affront-justice/27199241; Rauch, "No, Polygamy Isn't."

393. "Marie," a member of the Righteous Branch, interview by Craig L. Foster, September 1, 2018.

394. Batchelor, Watson and Wilde, *Voices in Harmony*, 229.

395. Anonymous, interview by Marianne T. Watson, June 2008.

396. Driggs, "Guide to Old Fashioned (Fundamentalist) Mormonism."

397. Laurtizen, *Hidden Flowers*, 103.

398. Enoch Foster, interview by Craig L. Foster and Marianne Watson, July 21, 2017.

399. "Moral Acceptance of Polygamy at Record High—But Why?," Gallup News, July 28, 2017, accessed July 30, 2017, http://news.gallup.com/opinion/polling-matters/214601/moral-acceptance-polygamy-record-high-why.aspx.

400. Reiss, "Polygamy's Becoming More Acceptable."

401. For a discussion of the difficult relationship between the LDS Church and Fundamentalist Mormons, see Foster, "Separated but not Divorced."

402. Bradley, *Kidnapped from that Land*, 39; Sunday sermon by "AUB Priesthood Council member," November 11, 2018.

403. Anonymous AUB woman, interview by Craig L. Foster, September 15, 2018; sister-wife of first woman, interview, September 21, 2018.
404. Batchelor, Watson and Wilde, *Voices in Harmony*, 79, 82 and 97.
405. Jessop, *Journal and Other Personal Papers*, 170.
406. Batchelor, Watson and Wilde, *Voices in Harmony*, 79, 83, 219.

BIBLIOGRAPHY

Adams, Brooke. "Fearing Doomsday, Man Carves Homes into Rock." *Daily Herald*, January 26, 2008.

———. "Kingston Inc.: Polygamy's Entrepreneurial Empire; A Company, a Clan, a Corp. with a Plan." *Salt Lake Observer*, August 14–27, 1998, accessed July 2, 2018. https://user.xmission.com/~plporter/lds/kingston.htm.

———. "LDS Church Criticizes Media FLDS Stories." *Salt Lake Tribune*, May 13, 2006, B2.

———. "Polygamous Families Plan Rally." *Salt Lake Tribune*, August 10, 2006, B6.

———. "Will the Polygamy Debate Ever Be the Same?" *Salt Lake Tribune*, March 12, 2006, A1, A10.

Alexander, Thomas G. *Mormonism in Transition: A History of the Latter-day Saints, 1890–1930*. Urbana: University of Illinois Press, 1986.

Allred, B. Harvey. *Indian Territory Mission: The Missionary Journal of Byron Harvey Allred, Jr.* Hamilton, MT: Bitterroot Publishing, 1983.

———. *A Leaf in Review*. Caldwell, ID: Caxton Printers, 1933.

[Allred, Rulon C.]. "A Biographical Sketch of the Life of Mary Evelyn Clark Allred." *Star of Truth* 2, no. 11 (November 1954).

Anonymous. "The Loyal Opposition: John W. Woolley's Path to Mormon Fundamentalism." Unpublished paper, ca. 1995. Copy in possession of the authors.

Baldwin, Nathaniel. *Times of the Gentiles, Fulness of the Gentiles: A Discussion with Spiritual References*. Salt Lake City: Paragon Printing, 1917.

Barrett, Jessica. "Mt. Pleasant Subdivision Causes Controversy." *Daily Herald*, April 2, 2008.

Batchelor, Mary, Marianne Watson and Anne Wilde. *Voices in Harmony: Contemporary Women Celebrate Plural Marriage.* Salt Lake City: Principle Voices, 2000.

Bennion, Janet. "The Many Faces of Polygamy: An Analysis of the Variability in Modern Mormon Fundamentalism in the Intermountain West." In Jacobsen and Burton, *Modern Polygamy*, 163–84.

Benson, Lee. "About Utah: Exposing the Dictatorship in Our Backyard." *Deseret News*, June 11, 2015.

Bernick, Bob, Jr., and Jerry D. Spangler. "Story Heightens Perceptions of Fanaticism in Utah." *Deseret News*, March 16, 2003, A14.

Berry, Michael. "Sister Wives and the Slippery Slope: Utah, Polygamy, and Popular Opinion," CBMW.org: A Coalition for Biblical Sexuality, January 2, 2014, accessed November 27, 2017. https://cbmw.org/topics/culture/sister-wives-and-the-slippery-slope-utah-polygamy-and-popular-opinion.

Bistline, Benjamin G. *Colorado City Polygamists: An Inside Look for the Outsider.* N.p., B.G. Bistline, 2004.

———. *The Polygamists: A History of Colorado City, Arizona.* Scottsdale, AZ: Agreka, 2004.

Bitton, Davis. *George Q. Cannon, A Biography.* Salt Lake City: Deseret Book Company, 1999.

Bloom, Harold. *The American Religion: The Emergence of the Post-Christian Nation.* New York: Simon & Schuster, 1992.

Boss, Arnold. *An Interview with Moroni Jessop.* N.p.: privately published, ca. 1942.

Bradley, Don. "Mormon Polygamy before Nauvoo? The Relationship of Joseph Smith and Fanny Alger." In Bringhurst and Foster, *Persistence of Polygamy*, vol. 1, 14–58.

Bradley, Martha Sonntag. *Kidnapped from that Land: The Government Raids on the Short Creek Polygamists.* Salt Lake City: University of Utah Press, 1993.

Briney, Drew. *Apostles on Trial: Examining the Membership Trials of Apostles Taylor and Cowley.* Salt Lake City: Hindsight Publications, 2012.

———. *Silencing Mormon Polygamy: Failed Persecutions, Divided Saints, & the Rise of Mormon Fundamentalism.* Salt Lake City; Hindsight Publications, 2008.

Bringhurst, Newell G., and Craig L. Foster. "The 1980s Schism within Fundamentalist Mormonism: The Emergence of Centennial Park." In Bringhurst and Foster, *Persistence of Polygamy*, vol. 3, 328–39.

———. "Rulon and Warren Jeffs: The Making of Two FLDS Prophets and the Changing Face of Fundamentalist Mormonism." In Bringhurst and Foster, *Persistence of Polygamy*, vol. 3, 269–309.

Bringhurst, Newell G., and Craig L. Foster, eds. *The Persistence of Polygamy*. Vol. 1. *Joseph Smith and the Origins of Mormon Polygamy*. Independence, MO: John Whitmer Books, 2010.

———. *The Persistence of Polygamy*. Vol. 2. *From Joseph Smith's Martyrdom to the First Manifesto, 1844–1890*. Independence, MO: John Whitmer Books, 2013.

———. *The Persistence of Polygamy*. Vol. 3. *Fundamentalist Mormon Polygamy from 1890 to the Present*. Independence, MO: John Whitmer Books, 2015.

Briscoe, David. "Prosecution of Polygamists Waning; More Admitting Status in Public." *Appleton Post Crescent*, May 18, 1975, A-4.

Bronson, Lorraine A. *History of Rocky Ridge, 1972–1992*. N.p.: [1992].

———. *Winnie*. N.p., n.d.

Brower, Sam. *Prophet's Prey: My Seven Year Investigation into Warren Jeffs and the Fundamentalist Church of Latter-Day Saints*. New York: Bloomsbury, 2011.

Cantera, Kevin. "Green Bitter Over Verdict; Leavitt Did His 'Duty.'" *Salt Lake Tribune*, May 20, 2001, N5.

Cantera, Kevin, and Michael Vigh. "Elizabeth a 'Plural Wife?'" *Salt Lake Tribune*, March 15, 2003, A1, A7.

Carlisle, Nate. "Brothers Accused of $511M Fraud Scheme to Stay in Jail." *Salt Lake Tribune*, August 30, 2018, A12.

———. "Girls in Polygamous Kingston Group Continue to Marry as Young as 15, Records Show, Sometimes Leaving Utah to Marry Cousins." *Salt Lake Tribune*, August 4, 2018.

———. "Jury Acquits Man Accused of Extorting His Wife in a Case that Influenced Utah's Polygamy Law." *Salt Lake Tribune*, September 12, 2018.

———. "Lawyer Contends Bigamy Bill Is a Case of LDS Legislators Discriminating against Polygamists." *Salt Lake Tribune*, March 20, 2017.

———. "Lyle Jeffs, One-Time Leader of Utah Polygamous Sect, Sentenced to Prison for Food Stamp Fraud, Absconding." *Salt Lake Tribune*, December 13, 2017.

———. "New Website Targets Kingston Polygamous Group." *Salt Lake Tribune*, July 16, 2015.

———. "Polygamists' Son, Whose Birth Was Seen on Their TV Show, Dies in House Fire in Southeastern Utah." *Salt Lake Tribune*, April 18, 2018.

———. "Sex Abuse Allegations Have Rocked the Polygamous Church of 'Sister Wives,' Causing Rift from Utah to Montana." *Salt Lake Tribune*, October 21, 2017.

———. "Suspects in Kingston Case Tried to Flee, Feds Say." *Salt Lake Tribune*, August 29, 2018, A1, A4.

———. "Utah Attorney General, Police Raid Pawnshops Belonging to Members of Polygamous Kingston Group." *Salt Lake Tribune*, June 22, 2018.

———. "Utah Investigated the Polygamous Kingston Group for Welfare Fraud 2 Years Ago. It Didn't Find Any." *Salt Lake Tribune*, February 7, 2018, accessed February 8, 2018.

———. "Utah Polygamists Unite to Oppose Latest Bigamy Bill." *Salt Lake Tribune*, January 20, 2017.

———. "Utah Polygamous Church Investigating Molestation Accusation against Leader." *Salt Lake Tribune*, December 2, 2014.

———. "Utah Senator Pointed to His Daughter—A Plural Wife—To Push Passage of Polygamy Bill." *Salt Lake Tribune*, March 10, 2017.

———. "Why Polygamists Are Leaving Their Historic Hometowns along the Utah-Arizona Border." *Salt Lake Tribune*, May 24, 2017.

Carter, Kate B. *Heart Throbs of the West*. Vol. 4. Salt Lake City: Daughters of the Utah Pioneers, 1943.

Clark, James R. *Messages of the First Presidency*. Salt Lake City: Bookcraft, 1966.

Collman, Ashley. "Daughter of Polygamist Cult Leader Warren Jeffs Opens Up about Her Father Sexually Abusing for YEARS Starting When She Was Just Eight Years Old." *Daily Mail*, accessed November 10, 2017, http://www.dailymail.co.uk/news/article-5070237/Warren-Jeffs-molested-daughter-starting-8.html#ixzz4zeePnkxb.

Deboer, Fredrik. "It's Time to Legalize Polygamy." *Politico*, June 26, 2015, accessed June 27, 2015. https://www.politico.com/magazine/story/2015/06/gay-marriage-decision-polygamy-119469.

Diary of Joseph Lyman Jessop. [Midvale, UT?: privately published, 1995.] Copy in possession of authors.

Dobner, Jennifer. "Appeals Court Strikes Down Ruling that Decriminalized Polygamy in Utah." *Salt Lake Tribune*, April 11, 2016.

———. "Manifesto Focuses on Plural Wives." *Deseret News*, March 15, 2003, A1, A6.

———. "'Sister Wives' Family Challenges Utah Bigamy Law." SFGate, December 20, 2011, accessed September 4, 2017. http://www.sfgate.com/news/article/Sister-Wives-family-challenges-Utah-bigamy-law-2413172.php.

Driggs, Kenneth D. "A Guide to Old Fashioned (Fundamentalist) Mormonism." Paper presented at the Western History Association, October 14, 2015.

———. "Imprisonment, Defiance, and Division: A History of Mormon Fundamentalism in the 1940s and 1950s." *Dialogue: A Journal of Mormon Thought* 38, no.1 (1977): 65–95.

———. "John Boyden's 1944 Campaign to 'Halt the Practice of Polygamy.'" Unpublished paper, April 2015, copy in authors' possession.

———. "Lorenzo Snow's Appellate Court Victory." *Utah Historical Quarterly* 58, no. 1 (Winter 1990): 81–93.

———. "'There Must Be No Compromise with Evil': A History and Analysis of the Utah Supreme Court's 1955 Decision in *In Re Black*." Master's thesis, University of Wisconsin–Madison, 1991.

———. "'This Will Someday Be the Head and Not the Tail of the Church': A History of the Mormon Fundamentalists at Short Creek." *Journal of Church and State* 43 (Winter 2001): 207.

———. "Twentieth-Century Polygamy and Fundamentalist Mormons in Southern Utah." *Dialogue: A Journal of Mormon Thought* 24 no. 4 (1991): 44–58.

———. "Who Shall Raise the Children? Vera Black and the Rights of Polygamous Parents." *Utah Historical Quarterly* 60, no. 1 (Winter 1992): 27–46.

East of Antelope Island. 4th ed. N.p.: Daughter of the Utah Pioneers, South Davis County Company, 1971.

Escobedo, Tricia. "Warren Jeffs' Son, Daughter Allege Sexual Abuse." CNN, October 1, 2015, accessed November 26, 2017. http://www.cnn.com/2015/09/29/us/warren-jeffs-children-allegations/index.html.

Ferguson, Danielle. "Tip Led to Lyle Jeffs' Capture in Yankton, FBI Says." *Argus Leader*, June 15, 2017, accessed November 2, 2018. https://www.argusleader.com/story/news/crime/2017/06/15/fugitive-church-leader-arrested-south-dakota/399218001.

Foster, Craig L. "Idaho's Foundations to Fundamentalist Mormonism." Paper presented at the Mormon History Association Conference, Boise, Idaho, 2018.

———. "Joseph Smith's Plural Wives: Total Number, Reasons for, and Methods of Selection." In Bringhurst and Foster, *Persistence of Polygamy*, vol. 1, 290–98.

———. "Like Sparks of a Wildfire: The Spread of Pre-Fundamentalist Mormonism." Paper presented at the Mormon History Association Conference, Salt Lake City, Utah, 2016.

———. "Modern Media Stereotyping of Polygamy." In Bringhurst and Foster, *Persistence of Polygamy*, vol. 3, 538–73.

———. "Plural Wives of the Mormon Fundamentalist Leaders." In Bringhurst and Foster, *Persistence of Polygamy*, vol. 3, 472–502.

———. "Proclamations and Prophecies from a Prison Cell: How Warren Jeffs Continues to Control the FLDS." Utah State History Society Conference, West Valley City, Utah, 2015.

———. "Separated but not Divorced: The LDS Church's Uncomfortable Relationship with its Polygamous Past." *Interpreter: A Journal of Mormon Scripture* 10 (2014): 45–76.

———. "The Wives of the Prophets: The Plural Wives of Brigham Young to Heber J. Grant." In Bringhurst and Foster, *Persistence of Polygamy*, vol. 2, 113–47.

Foster, Craig L., David Keller and Gregory L. Smith. "The Age of Joseph Smith's Plural Wives in Social and Demographic Context." In Bringhurst and Foster, *Persistence of Polygamy*, vol. 1, 152–83.

Foster, Craig L., and Marianne T. Watson. "Mormon Fundamentalism: Foundations and First Families." Sunstone Short Creek Historical Conference, Colorado City, Arizona–Hildale, Utah, 2017.

Foy, Leslie T. *The City Bountiful: Utah's Second Settlement from Pioneers to Present.* Bountiful, UT: Horizon Publishers, 1975.

Fulton, Gilbert. *Gems.* 3 vols. Salt Lake City: Gems Publishing, 1967.

Grossman, Joanna L., and Lawrence M. Friedman. "Is Three Still a Crowd? Polygamy and the Law After Obergefell v. Hodges." *Verdict*, July 7, 2015, accessed July 8, 2015. https://verdict.justia.com/2015/07/07/is-three-still-a-crowd-polygamy-and-the-law-after-obergefell-v-hodges.

Hales, Brian C. "'I Have Been Fanatically Religious': Joseph White Musser, Father of the Fundamentalist Movement." Modern Polygamy and Mormon Fundamentalism, 1992, http://www.mormonfundamentalism.com/archive/JWM-Bio.html.

———. "'I Love to Hear Him Talk and Rehearse': The Life and Teachings of Lorin C. Woolley." Modern Polygamy and Mormon Fundamentalism, 1993. http://www.mormonfundamentalism.com/wp-content/uploads/2017/10/Lorin-Woolley-updated.pdf.

———. "John Taylor's 1886 Revelation." In Bringhurst and Foster, *Persistence of Polygamy*, vol. 3, 58–111.

———. "Joseph Smith and the Puzzlement of 'Polyandry.'" In Bringhurst and Foster, *Persistence of Polygamy*, vol. 1, 99–151.

———. *Joseph Smith's Polygamy.* 3 vols. Salt Lake City: Greg Kofford Books, 2013.

Harkins, Paighten. "Two Members of Polygamous Group Indicted in IRS Scheme." *Salt Lake Tribune*, August 25, 2018, A5.

Harris, Dan. "LeBaron's Former Wife Admits to Murder in Coming Book." *Salt Lake Tribune*, April 15, 1990, B1.

Hicks, Christopher. "On the Trail of Ervil LeBaron." *Mountain West* 4 (November, 1978): 38–42.

Higgins, Shaun. "Polygamy in Montana." *Independent Record*, October 23, 1977, 1, 5.

Hilton, Jerold A. "Polygamy in Utah and Surrounding Area Since the Manifesto of 1890." Master's thesis, Brigham Young University, May 1965.

History of the Priesthood Split and Additional Historical Items. [Bluffdale, UT?]: privately published, 2003. Copy in possession of authors.

Holland, Jeffrey R. "That Our Children May Know." BYU Speeches, accessed August 22, 2018. https://speeches.byu.edu/talks/jeffrey-r-holland_children-may-know.

Hollenhorst, John. "Sex Banned until Warren Jeffs' Prison Walls Crumble, FLDS Relatives Say." *Deseret News*, December 30, 2011.

Horiuchi, Vince. "Authorities Hope Convictions End LeBaron Saga." *Salt Lake Tribune*, January 24, 1993, B1, B3.

Hyde, Jesse. "Inside 'The Order,' One Mormon Cult's Secret Empire: America's Most Twisted Crime Family—And the Boys Who Dared to Defy It." *Rolling Stone*, June 15, 2011. Accessed July 2, 2018, https://www.rollingstone.com/culture/culture-news/inside-the-order-one-mormon-cults-secret-empire-244969.

Ivins, Molly. "Polygamy on Increase in Western States, including Montana." *Montana Standard*, October 12, 1977, 18.

Jacobsen, Cardell K., and Lara Burton, eds. *Modern Polygamy in the United States: Historical, Cultural and Legal Issues*. New York: Oxford University Press, 2011.

Jeffs, Rulon T. *History of the Priesthood Succession in the Dispensation of the Fullness of Times and Some Challenges to the One Man Rule: Also Includes Personal History of Rulon Jeffs*. Sandy, UT: President Rulon Jeffs for the Fundamentalist Church of Jesus Christ of Latter-day Saints, 1997.

———. "Personal History of Rulon Jeffs." *Alta Academy Student Star* 19, no. 7 (February 24, 1997).

Jenson, Andrew. *Latter-day Saint Biographical Encyclopedia*, 4 vols. Salt Lake City: Andrew Jenson History Company, 1920.

Jessop, Diane Allred, and Melanie Allred Baker. *Legacy of Love: The Life Story of Rulon Clark Allred*. N.p., n.d.

Jessop, Marla, comp. *The Journal and Other Personal Papers of Mary Viola Anderson Thompson*. N.p: privately published, 2001.

Johnson, Leroy S. *The Leroy S. Johnson Sermons.* 7 vols. Hildale, UT: Twin Cities Courier, 1983–1985, 1990.

Jorgenson, Victor W., and B. Carmon Hardy. "The Taylor-Cowley Affair and the Watershed of Mormon History." *Utah Historical Quarterly* 8, no. 1 (Winter 1980).

Kelly, David, and Gary Cohn. "Arizona's 1953 Raid on Polygamist Sect Backfired." *Los Angeles Times*, May 12, 2006, accessed August 6, 2016. http://articles.latimes.com/2006/may/12/news/la-polygamyside1-12may1206.

Kelsch, Barbara Owen. *Louis Alma Kelsch.* N.p.: privately published typescript, n.d. Copy in possession of authors.

Kunz, Rhea Allred, ed. *A Second Leaf in Review.* 2nd ed. N.p.: Latter Day Publications, 2011.

———. *Voices of Women Approbating Celestial or Plural Marriage.* Vol. 1, *My Sacred Heritage.* Draper, UT: Review and Preview Publishers, 1978.

Laforêt, Pierre. "Ce Mormon, Heureux, 'Règne' Sur Ses Quatre Femmes…." *Figaro Magazine* (April 16, 1988): 106–7.

Laurtizen, Elizabeth M., comp. *Hidden Flowers: The Life, Letters and Poetry of Jacob Marinus Lauritzen and His Wife Annie Pratt Gardner.* Brigham City, UT: Bradbury Print, 1982.

LeBaron, Charlotte K. *Mark My Son.* Deming, NM: Woodbine Books, 2017.

LeBaron, Verlan M. *The LeBaron Story.* Lubbock, TX: Keels & Company, 1981.

Lockhart, Ben. "'We're Not Going Away': Polygamous Groups March to Capitol to Protest Bill." *Deseret News*, February 10, 2017.

Mackert, Donna K. *Day of Infamy: Short Creek, Arizona, July 26, 1953.* Bluffdale, UT: Kolob Shadows Publishing, 2018.

Madsen, Truman G. *Defender of the Faith: The B.H. Roberts Story.* Salt Lake City: Bookcraft, 1980.

McCombs, Brady. "Woman on 'My Five Wives' Accuses Father of Sex Abuse." *Salt Lake Tribune*, November 22, 2014, accessed November 20, 2018. http://archive.sltrib.com/article.php?id=1859937&itype=CMSID.

McDermott, Rose, and Valerie M. Hudson. "Don't Legalize Polygamy." *Providence Journal*, August 23, 2015, accessed November 30, 2017, http://www.providencejournal.com/article/20150823/opinion/150829788.

Miller, Jessica. "State Wants to Seize $1M from Pawnshops with Polygamous Ties." *Salt Lake Tribune*, September 19, 2018, B5.

Millville Memories: A History of Millville, Utah from 1860 to 1990. Millville, UT: Cache County Historic and Preservation Commission, 1990.

Musser, Joseph W. *Autobiography of Saint Joseph White Musser—A Brief Sketch of the Life, Labors and Faith of Saint Joseph White Musser*. N.p., n.d., 1950.

———. "A Brief Biographical Sketch of the Life, Labors and Faith of St. Joseph White Musser." December 1946, Utah Historical Society Library, Mss 96 B, box 5, folder 11.

———. *Celestial or Plural Marriage: The Mormon Marriage System*. Salt Lake City: Truth Publishing Company, 1944.

———. "Factions." *Truth*, 9, no. 24 (September 1943): 94–96.

———. *Four Hidden Revelations*. Salt Lake City: Truth Publishing Company, [1948].

———. *New and Everlasting Covenant of Marriage*. Salt Lake City, 1933.

———. *A Priesthood Issue*. Salt Lake City, UT: Truth Publishing, [1948].

Musser, Joseph W., and J.L. Broadbent. *Supplement to the New and Everlasting Covenant of Marriage: An Interpretation of Celestial Marriage, Plural Marriage, Priesthood*. Salt Lake City: Truth Publishing Company, 1934.

Olson, Florence A. *History of Millville*. N.p., n.d., 1960.

O'Neill, Ann. "Witnesses: Scallops for the Bishop, Toast for the Kids." CNN, April 6, 2016, accessed September 2, 2016. http://www.cnn.com/2016/04/05/us/flds-secrets-warren-jeffs.

Osmond, Amy Kathlyn. "Organizational Identification: A Case Study of the Davis County Cooperative Society, the Latter Day Church of Christ, or Kingston Order." PhD diss. University of Utah, Salt Lake City, Utah, 2010.

Parkinson, Preston Woolley. *The Utah Woolley Family, Descendants of Thomas Woolley and Sarah Coppock of Pennsylvania*. Salt Lake City: Genealogical Society of Utah, 1957.

Perkins, Nancy, and Ben Winslow. "Fugitive Polygamist Leader Warren Jeffs Arrested near Las Vegas." *Deseret News*, August 29, 2006.

Price, Michelle L. "Polygamous Families Protest Bigamy Law in Utah: 'If We Were gay, We'd Be OK.'" LGBTQNation, February 12, 2017, accessed February 14, 2017. https://www.lgbtqnation.com/2017/02/polygamous-families-protest-bigamy-law-utah-gay-wed-ok.

Quinn, D. Michael. *Elder Statesman: A Biography of J. Reuben Clark*. Salt Lake City: Signature Books, 2002.

———. *J. Reuben Clark: The Church Years*. Provo, UT: Brigham Young University Press, 1983.

———. "LDS Church Authority and New Plural Marriages, 1890–1904," *Dialogue: A Journal of Mormon Thought* 18, no. 1 (Spring 1985): 9–105.

———. "Plural Marriages After the 1890 Manifesto." Paper presented at the Apostolic United Brethren, Bluffdale, Utah, August 11, 1991.

Rauch, Jonathan. "No, Polygamy Isn't the Next Gay Marriage." *Politico*, November 27, 2017.

Rayburn, Jim. "Green Says Charges Bogus: Polygamist Is Accused of Rape of a Child, Bigamy," *Deseret News*, May 2, 2000.

Reiss, Jana. "Polygamy's Becoming More Acceptable. Is This the 'Sister Wives' Effect?" Religion News Service, August 1, 2017, accessed August 2, 2017. http://religionnews.com/2017/08/01/polygamys-becoming-more-acceptable-is-this-the-sister-wives-effect.

Religious Sects, and Cults that Sprang from Mormonism. Salt Lake City: Daughters of Utah Pioneers Central Company, 1942.

Richins, Philip N. "Journal of Amy Irene Woolley." Digital manuscript, 2009. Family Tree, FamilySearch.org, accessed September 15, 2018.

Ritchey, Julia. "Bigamy Bill Brings Dueling Protests to Capitol." KUER.org, accessed February 10, 2017. http://kuer.org/post/bigamy-bill-brings-dueling-protests-capitol#stream/0.

Rogers, Eric Paul, and Kari Roueche. "Rulon C. Allred and the Search for Refuge." In Bringhurst and Foster, *Persistence of Polygamy*, vol. 3, 266–68.

Rogers, Jedediah S. *In the President's Office: The Diaries of L. John Nuttall, 1879–1892*. Salt Lake City: Signature Books, 2007.

Singer, Merrill. "Utah Inventor and Patron of the Fundamentalist Movement." *Utah Historical Quarterly* 47, no. 1 (Winter 1979): 42–53.

Smith, Eliza R. Snow. *Biography and Family Record of Lorenzo Snow, One of the Twelve Apostles of the Church of Jesus Christ of Latter-day Saints*. Salt Lake City: Deseret News Company, 1884.

Smoot, Mary Ellen, and Marilyn Sheriff. *The City In-Between: History of Centerville, Utah, including Biographies and Autobiographies of Some of Its Original Settlers*. Salt Lake City: M.E. Smoot and M. Sheriff, 1975.

Spafford, Shannon E. "The Changing and Unchanging Nature of Fundamentalist Clothing Styles." In Bringhurst and Foster, *Persistence of Polygamy*, vol. 3, 310–27.

Stegner, Wallace. *Mormon Country*. Lincoln: University of Nebraska Press, 1942.

Stromberg, Lorie Winder. "Prisoners for 'The Principle': The Incarceration of Mormon Plural Wives, 1882–1890," In Bringhurst and Foster, *Persistence of Polygamy*, vol. 2, 298–325.

Syracuse Historical Commission. *The Community of Syracuse, 1820–1995: Our Heritage*. Syracuse, UT: Syracuse Historical Commission, 1994.

Taylor, Alan. "Polygamists in 'The Rock.'" *The Atlantic*, November 15, 2012. https://www.theatlantic.com/photo/2012/11/polygamists-in-the-rock/100406/

Taylor, Bonnie, ed. *The Sermons of J. Golden Kimball, December 1891–April 1938.* Salt Lake City: Latter-Day Publishing, 2007.

Teachings of Presidents of the Church: Lorenzo Snow. Salt Lake City: The Church of Jesus Christ of Latter-day Saints, 2011.

Watson, Marianne T. "B. Harvey Allred, Jr.: Observing a Covenant of Sacrifice." Paper presented at the Mormon History Association Conference, Boise, Idaho, 2018.

———. "Corroborative Evidence Linking Joseph F. Smith and John W. Taylor with John W. and Lorin C. Woolley and with John Taylor's 1886 Revelation." Unpublished paper, 2017.

———. "The Fred E. Curtis Papers: L.D.S. Church Surveillance of Fundamentalist Mormons 1937 to 1954." Unpublished paper, 2002.

———. "From Nineteenth-Century Mormon Polygamy to Twentieth-Century Mormon Fundamentalism: Three Contemporary Perspectives on John W. and Lorin C. Woolley." In Bringhurst and Foster, *Persistence of Polygamy*, vol. 3, 144–80.

———. "Nathaniel Baldwin's Lasting Legacies." Paper presented at the Mormon History Association Conference, Salt Lake City, Utah, 2016.

———. "The 1948 Secret Marriage of Louis J. Barlow: Origins of FLDS Placement Marriage." *Dialogue: A Journal of Mormon Thought* 40, no.1 (1997): 83–136.

———. "Polygamous Ancestry of Contemporary Fundamentalist Mormons." In Bringhurst and Foster, *Persistence of Polygamy*, vol. 3, 434–71.

———. "Short Creek, 'A Refuge for the Saints.'" *Dialogue: A Journal of Mormon Thought* 36, no.1 (Spring 2003): 71–87.

Weeser, Andrew. "Family of Spiritual Bigamist Defends Against Abuse Allegations." ABC4 News. Accessed January 9, 2019. https://www.abc4.com/news/local-news/family-of-spiritual-bigamist-defends-against-abuse-allegations/1809497868.

Winslow, Ben. "Kingston Daughter's Lawsuit Accuses 3 of Sex Abuse." *Deseret News*, June 2, 2006.

———. "Kingston Lawsuits Are Settled." *Deseret News*, April 18, 2009.

———. "State Urged to Scrap Its Law against Polygamy." *Deseret Morning News*, March 2, 2006, B1, B2.

————. "U.S. Supreme Court Won't Hear 'Sister Wives' Polygamy Case." Fox 13 TV, January 23, 2017, accessed January 23, 2017. http://fox13now.com/2017/01/23/u-s-supreme-court-wont-hear-sister-wives-polygamy-case.

Word, Ehven [pseud.]. *Letters to Sarah*. N.p., n.d., 2013. Copy in possession of authors.

Wright, Lyle O. "Origins and Development of the Church of the Firstborn of the Fullness of Times." Master's thesis. Brigham Young University, 1963.

INDEX

Z

ABOUT THE AUTHORS

CRAIG L. FOSTER is a sixth-generation member of the Church of Jesus Christ of Latter-day Saints and great-grandson of Mormon polygamists. He has presented and published extensively on a wide variety of Mormon history topics, including plural marriage. He is the author/coauthor of three books and is the coeditor of the three-volume *The Persistence of Polygamy* series. He has been with the Family History Library in Salt Lake City, Utah, for almost thirty years, where he has worked in Library Public Affairs and preparing VIP genealogies. He is presently a research specialist in British Isles research.

MARIANNE T. WATSON of Lehi, Utah, has a degree in history from the University of Utah. She was born and raised in a plural family as a Fundamentalist Mormon in the group known commonly as the Allred group, or more recently as the AUB (Apostolic United Brethren). She feels a connection with many other Fundamentalist Mormons through family relationships and shared commonalities in culture, history and religion. She also identifies historically and doctrinally as well as through ancestry with members of the Church of Jesus Christ of Latter-day Saints. She is a seventh-generation descendant of early Mormon pioneers and has a total of twenty-five polygamous ancestors. Marianne has thirty years' experience in genealogical research and family history and has authored several family history books. Since 1994, she has presented research papers about Fundamentalist Mormonism in several forums and conferences throughout the western United States and one in Brazil. In 2000, she coauthored the book *Voices in Harmony: Contemporary Women Celebrate Plural Marriage*.

Visit us at
www.historypress.com
··